Arthur Miller Plays 1

Arthur Miller Plays 1

All My Sons
Death of a Salesman
The Crucible
A Memory of Two Mondays
A View from the Bridge

ARTHUR MILLER

methuen | drama
LONDON • NEW YORK • OXFORD • NEW DELHI • SYDNEY

METHUEN DRAMA
Bloomsbury Publishing Plc
50 Bedford Square, London, WC1B 3DP, UK
1385 Broadway, New York, NY 10018, USA
29 Earlsfort Terrace, Dublin 2, Ireland

BLOOMSBURY, METHUEN DRAMA and the Methuen Drama logo are trademarks of
Bloomsbury Publishing Plc

Originally published in Great Britain in 1958 by the Cresset Press as *Collected Plays* and
subsequently by Martin Secker & Warburg in 1967
First published in Great Britain in paperback in 1988 by Methuen London Ltd
Reissued with a new cover design 1993, 2000, 2009
Reprinted by Bloomsbury Methuen Drama 2010, 2011, 2012, 2013, 2014
Reissued with a new cover design in 2022

Cover design: Ben Anslow

A catalogue record for this book is available from the British Library.

A catalog record for this book is available from the Library of Congress.

ISBN: PB: 978-1-3502-7751-9
        ePDF: 978-1-3502-7753-3
        eBook: 978-1-3502-7752-6

Series: World Classics

Typeset by RefineCatch Limited, Bungay, Suffolk
Printed and bound in India

To find out more about our authors and books visit www.bloomsbury.com
and sign up for our newsletters.

Contents

Arthur Miller: Chronology of Professionally Produced Plays

	First US production	First UK production
The Man Who Had All the Luck	23.1.44	28.4.60
All My Sons	29.1.47	11.5.48
Death of a Salesman	10.2.49	28.7.49
An Enemy of the People (adapted from Ibsen)	28.12.50	
The Crucible	22.1.53	9.11.54
A Memory of Two Mondays	29.9.55	29.9.58
A View from the Bridge		
(one-act version)	29.9.55	
(two-act version)	28.1.65	11.10.56
After the Fall	23.1.64	31.10.67
Incident at Vichy	3.12.64	10.1.66
The Price	7.2.68	4.3.69
The Creation of the World and Other Business	30.11.72	17.8.74
Up from Paradise (musical)	23.4.74	
The Archbishop's Ceiling	30.4.77	1.4.85
The American Clock	24.5.80	18.4.83
Two-Way Mirror	26.10.82	1.89
Playing for Time (adapted from his screenplay)	22.9.85	10.11.05
Danger: Memory!	8.2.87	6.4.88
The Golden Years	(world première)	6.11.87
The Ride Down Mount Morgan	17.7.97	11.10.91
The Last Yankee	5.1.91	21.1.93
Broken Glass	9.3.94	4.8.94
Mr. Peters' Connections	17.5.98	20.7.00
Resurrection Blues	3.8.02	11.2.06
Finishing the Picture	21.9.04	

Introduction
Ivo van Hove

Alarm Bells

I can still hear myself say it, on the most important Belgian cultural television programme, in the 1980s: that I have no interest whatsoever in the modern American theatre of Tennessee Williams, Eugene O'Neill or Arthur Miller. Since then, almost forty years later, I have directed seven plays by all these authors (some in several different versions) and I am deeply ashamed of my reckless, provocative statement.

What has changed over the years? Not the work written by these authors. What has changed is my love for America, and a deeper knowledge of how these authors, through their plays, portrayed and dissected America in a very personal way; and made their insights accessible to a large audience around the world.

Arthur Miller was my last passionate love of the three American grandmasters. I only directed his *A View from the Bridge* in 2014, and even then after a lot of resistance. That resistance quickly dissipated when, during my preparations, I could feel that every sentence was there for a reason. That the drama gradually, but crystal clearly, develops into a tragedy of Greek proportions. That his characters are real people, with all their frustrated dreams, their traditionalism and their shortcomings. That, in effect, he is a master in the art of writing for the stage.

Miller's special quality is that he writes stories that are social and deal with important moral issues. He takes us into the past, to people who are removed from us, to help us understand the present and ourselves better. Miller gives us the safety of the distance of time in order to strike hard, to make us look in the mirror at our own stained souls. Just as Shakespeare did and as the Greeks did. His work is overwhelming and frightening because it is never politically correct. Ambivalence and subversion are his deadly weapons.

Let me talk more about the plays I know best.

The Crucible, which I directed in 2016, is set in Salem 400 years ago. You could easily defuse it as a memory of what America once was like, a relic of a distant past. A community founded on the principle that nobody deviates from the accepted rules, norms and values. John Proctor is a righteous farmer who has made a fatal mistake before the play begins; he has cheated on his wife with young Abigail. He is not the most obvious hero of a tragedy. But he is a hero who is aware of and wants to put an end to his sexual misstep right away. And that is Miller's unique strength. John Proctor becomes, scene after scene, the man you love to hate and you hate to love. He struggles to survive as he is made, by the whole community, the scapegoat for all the sins and sinners of Salem. Proctor is accused of illicit sexual behaviour and condemned. It is the underage Abigail that's the source of the public accusation. And so Miller's plays confront us with complex moral and social problems. Because the ruthless Abigail is herself a traumatised girl who has witnessed her parents being killed in front of her eyes. She found respect in her relationship with Proctor, who made her feel important. Miller shows us each character battling their own demons. Everyone wants to be good but everyone has the bad in them.

This is the power of Miller's ambivalence. The vulnerable are treated ruthlessly in Salem and want to be free. Think of Mary's feminist outcry: 'I am 18. And a woman!' – she breaks the rules by demanding to be heard, by refusing to be excluded due to her age and gender. Or think of Tituba – treated differently not only because of her gender but also the colour of her skin. All these events and crises give the people of Salem an opportunity to utter old grudges. John Proctor and his wife Elizabeth must pay. They are tortured mentally and physically until the guillotine falls. Miller's heroes are people like us. And that's scary. Because I also want to be good, everywhere and always. And I also know that I am not. Arthur Miller holds up that dark mirror to me.

Arthur Miller is also a great structuralist who takes the time to build up his plays, letting you descend into pitch-black mines that lead you to the darkest, loneliest points of human beings. In *A View from the Bridge*, we meet Eddie Carbone, an Italian immigrant who outwardly conforms to the laws, rules and customs of American society, but dominantly enforces within his own family that the old customs and laws of his country of origin are maintained. They nurture social togetherness so that the small community of Italian immigrants in Brooklyn forms a solid front against the large and threatening America. At home, Eddie is the king. But Eddie, like John Proctor, has an Achilles heel, a fatal flaw; his suffocating, unreasonable and far-reaching inclination to protect his cousin Catherine from the threatening outside world of young men. When she falls in love with Rodolpho, a young Italian immigrant, all normal thinking is derailed and lost. What begins as the drama of an immigrant family striving for a better life in America focuses more and more, scene after scene, on Eddie's catastrophe: his betrayal and eventual death. At the end he exclaims: 'I want my name!' And just before his execution, John Proctor also says 'How may I live without my name? I have given you my soul; leave me my name!' Doesn't every human being, anywhere on earth, want to be respected for who he or she is, to be part of a community? Eddie's jealousy and fixation on Rodolpho, Catherine's lover, becomes self-destructive. Just as Agamemnon sacrifices his daughter to appease the gods and gain wind so that the Greek fleet can set sail for a war against the Trojans, Eddie Carbone betrays his own family from an obsessive protective instinct that leads to sheer jealousy. 'His eyes were like tunnels,' Alfieri concludes. A more complex piece on identity politics will be hard to find.

Like the great playwrights throughout history, Arthur Miller is able to connect major themes to recognisable people and situations. His characters have the same poetic power as those in the Greek tragedies. They are people who intend to do good and, often in spite of themselves, but just as often premeditated, do the bad. In Miller, people who are good in themselves fall off their pedestal. With him there are no gods anymore; in his work man is responsible for his actions, no matter how good the intentions. The characters Miller has created are timeless and tragic.

And, as always in Miller's world, the private and public spaces merge into each other. How to be an individual and at the same time be part of society? His plays are always situated in a specific moment in history, but with his masterly research and rich imagination Miller succeeds in connecting the Salem of 1692 with the McCarthy era of the 1950s. 'I sought a metaphor', he said, and he found it. A metaphor for a framed society that creates their own extreme rules of justice and narrow religious beliefs in order to keep the community together. A metaphor for a venom that has spread all over America. Of a divided society, which has become the elephant in the room in the USA, but also many other countries around the world. A society that doesn't accept people who think, feel or behave differently. You are with us, or against us. The sickness of Salem reflects the sickness of our society today.

Miller's theatre confronts us with our darkest impulses. His theatre is pitch black. It is human.

His plays are alarms, waking us up to who we are, what we are becoming and the havoc we are wreaking.

Introduction
Arthur Miller

As a writer of plays I share with all specialists a suspicion of generalities about the art and technique of my craft, and I lack both the scholarly patience and the zeal to define terms in such a way as to satisfy everyone. The only other course, therefore, is to stop along the way to say what *I* mean by the terms I use, quite certain as I do so that I will be taken to task by no small number of people, but hopeful at the same time that something useful may be said about this art, a form of writing which generates more opinions and fewer instructive critical statements than any other. To be useful it seems impossible not to risk the obvious by returning always to the fundamental nature of theater, its historic human function, so to speak. For it seems odd, when one thinks of it, that an art which has always been so expensive to produce and so difficult to do well should have survived in much the same general form that it possessed when it began. This is especially striking now, when almost alone among the arts the theater has managed to live despite the devouring mechanization of the age, and, in some places and instances, even to thrive and grow. Under these circumstances of a very long if frequently interrupted history, one may make the assumption that the drama and its production must represent a well-defined expression of profound social needs, needs which transcend any particular form of society or any particular historic moment. It is therefore possible to speak of fundamentals of the form too when its only tools of importance never change, there being no possibility of a drama without mimicry, conflict, tale, or speech.

My approach to playwriting and the drama itself is organic; and to make this glaringly evident at once it is necessary to separate drama from what we think of today as literature. A drama ought not be looked at first and foremost from literary perspectives merely because it uses words, verbal rhythm, and poetic image. These can be its most memorable parts, it is true, but they are not its inevitable accompaniments. Nor is it only convention which from Aristotle onward decreed that the play must be dramatic rather than narrative in concept and execution. A Greek's seat was harder than an American's and even he had to call a halt to a dramatic presentation after a couple of hours. The physiological limits of attention in a seated position enforce upon this art an interconnected group of laws, in turn expressed by aesthetic criteria, which no other writing art requires. But it is not my intention here to vivisect dramatic form or the techniques of playwriting. I only want to take advantage of this rare opportunity—a collected edition—to speak for myself as to my own aims; not to give my estimates of what can portentously be called the dramatic problem in this time, but simply to talk in workaday language about the problem of how to write so that one's changing vision of people in the world is more accurately represented in each succeeding work.

A few of the inevitable materials of the art dictate to me certain aesthetic commitments which may as well be mentioned at the outset, for they move silently but nevertheless with potent influence through the plays in this book as well as in my thoughts about them. These plays were written on the assumption that they would be acted before audiences. The "actor" is a person, and he no sooner appears than certain elementary questions are broached. Who is he? What is he doing here? How does he live or make his living? Who is he related to? Is he rich or poor? What does he think of himself? What do other people think of him, and why? What are his hopes and fears; and what does he say they are? What does he claim to want, and what does he really want?

The actor brings questions onto the stage just as any person does when we first meet him in our ordinary lives. Which of them a play chooses to answer, and how they are answered, are the ruling and highly consequential imperatives which create the style of the play, and control what are later called the stylistic levels of its writing. If, for instance, the actor is masked as he appears and his body movements are constricted and highly ordered, we instantly expect that the common surfaces of life will also be breached by the kinds of questions he or the play will respond to. He will very probably speak about the theme or essential preoccupation of the play directly and without getting to it by circuitous routes of naturalistic detail. If he appears in the costume of his trade, class, or profession, however, we expect that he or the play will give us the answers to his common identity, and if they do not they risk our dissatisfaction and frustration. In a word, the actor's appearance on the stage in normal human guise leads us to expect a realistic treatment. The play will either be intent upon rounding out the characters by virtue of its complete answers to the common questions, or will substitute answers to a more limited group of questions which, instead of being "human," are thematic and are designed to form a symbol of meaning rather than an apparency of the "real" It is the nature of the questions asked and answered, rather than the language used— whether verse, ordinary slang, or colorless prose—that determines whether the style is realistic or non-realistic. When I speak of style, therefore, this is one of the relationships I intend to convey. In this sense the tragedies of Shakespeare are species of realism, and those of Aeschylus and Sophocles are not. We know a great deal more about Macbeth and Hamlet, apart from their functions as characters in their particular given dramas, than we can ever surmise about Oedipus the king, or the heroes and heroines of Strindberg's plays. To put it another way, when the career of a person rather than the detail of his motives stands at the forefront of the play, we move closer to non-realistic styles, and vice versa. I regard this as the one immovable and irremediable quality which goes to create one style or another. And there is always an organic connection rather than a temperamental choice involved in the style in which a play is written and must be performed. The first two plays in this book were written and performed with the intention of answering as many of the common questions as was possible. *The Crucible, A Memory of Two Mondays*, and *A View from the Bridge* were not so designed and to this extent they are a departure from realism.

Another decisive influence upon style is the conception and manipulation of time in a play. Broadly speaking, where it is conceived and used so as to convey a natural passage of hours, days, or months, the style it enforces is pressed toward realism. Where action is quite openly freed so that things mature in a moment, for instance, which would take a year in life, a true license for non-realistic styles is thereby won. As is obvious, the destruction of temporal necessity occurs in every play if only to a rudimentary degree; it is impossible that in life people should behave and speak in reference to a single thematic point for so continuous a time. Events, therefore, are always collapsed and drawn together in any drama. But as the collapsing process becomes more self-evident, and as the selection of events becomes less and less dominated by the question of their natural maturation, the style of the play moves further and further away from realism. *All My Sons* attempts to account for time in terms of months, days, and hours. *Death of a Salesman* explodes the watch and the calendar. *The Crucible* is bound by natural time—or strives to appear so.

The compacting of time destroys the realistic style not only because it violates our sense of reality, but because collapsing time inevitably emphasizes an element of existence which in life is not visible or ordinarily felt with equivalent power, and this is its symbolic meaning. When a criminal is arraigned, for instance, it is the prosecutor's job to symbolize his behavior for the jury so that the man's entire life can be characterized in one way and not in another. The prosecutor does not mention the accused as a dog lover, a good husband and father, a sufferer from eczema, or a man with the habit of chewing tobacco on the left and not the right side of his mouth. Nor does he strive to account for the long intervals of time when the accused was behaving in a way quite contrary to that symbolic characterization. The prosecutor is collapsing time—and destroying realism—by fastening only on those actions germane to the construction of his symbol. To one degree or another every play must do this or we should have to sit in a theater for years in order to appreciate a character and his story. But where the play does pretend to give us details of hours, months, and years which are not clearly and avowedly germane to the symbolic meaning, we come closer and closer to what is called a realistic style. In passing, I should say that the Greek "unity" of time imposed on the drama was not arbitrary but a concomitant of the preponderant Greek interest in the fate and career of the hero rather than his private characteristics, or, to put it another way, his social and symbolic side rather than his family role.

Another material, so to speak, of drama is not describable in a word, and has a less direct influence on style. I mention it, however, because it is probably the single most powerful influence on my way of writing and enforces on me a kind of taste and approach to the art which marks these plays. It is necessary, if one is to reflect reality, not only to depict why a man does what he does, or why he nearly didn't do it, but why he cannot simply walk away and say to hell with it. To ask this last question of a play is a cruel thing, for evasion is probably the most developed technique most men have, and in truth there is an extrordinarily small number of conflicts which we must, at any cost, live out to their conclusions. To ask this question is immediately to impose on oneself not, perhaps, a style of writing but at least a kind of dramatic construction. For I understand the symbolic meaning of a character and his career to consist of the kind of commitment he makes to life or refuses to make, the kind of challenge he accepts and the kind he can pass by. I take it that if one could know enough about a human being one could discover some conflict, some value, some challenge, however minor or major, which he cannot find it in himself to walk away from or turn his back on. The structure of these plays, in this respect, is to the end that such a conflict be discovered and clarified. Idea, in these plays, is the generalized meaning of that discovery applied to men other than the hero. Time, characterizations, and other elements are treated differently from play to play, but all to the end that that moment of commitment be brought forth, that moment when, in my eyes, a man differentiates himself from every other man, that moment when out of a sky full of stars he fixes on one star. I take it, as well, that the less capable a man is of walking away from the central conflict of the play, the closer he approaches a tragic existence. In turn, this implies that the closer a man approaches tragedy the more intense is his concentration of emotion upon the fixed point of his commitment, which is to say the closer he approaches what in life we call fanaticism. From this flows the necessity for scenes of high and open emotion, and plays constructed toward climax rather than the evocation of a mood alone or of bizarre spectacle. (The one exception among these plays is *A Memory of Two Mondays*—as will be seen later.) From such considerations it ought to be clear that the common tokens of realism and non-realism are in themselves not acceptable as criteria. That a play is written prosaically does not make it a realistic play, and that the speech is heightened and intensified by imagery does not set it to one side of realism necessarily. The underlying poem of a play I take to be the organic necessity of its parts. I find in the arbitrary not poetry but indulgence. (The novel is another matter entirely.) A very great play can be mimed and still issue forth its essential actions and their rudiments of symbolic meaning; the word, in drama, is the transformation into speech of what is *happening*, and the fiat for intense language is intensity of happening. We have had more than one extraordinary dramatist who was a cripple as a writer, and this is lamentable but not ruinous. Which is to say that I prize the poetic above else in the theater, and because I do I insist that the poem truly be there.

II

The assumption—or presumption—behind these plays is that life has meaning. I would now add, as their momentary commentator, that what they meant to me at the time of writing is not in each instance the same as what they mean to me now in the light of further experience. Plato, by banning artists from citizenship in his ideal republic, expressed at least a partial truth; the intention behind a work of art and its effects upon the public are not always the same. Worse yet, in his conscious intention the artist often conceals from himself an aim which can be quite opposed to his fondest beliefs and ideas. Those more tempted by an evil, for instance, are more likely to feel deeply about it than those who have only known the good. From this, two ironic propositions logically flow. The first is that a play's "idea" may be useful as a unifying force empowering the artist to evoke a cogent emotional life on the stage, but that in itself it has no aesthetic value, since, after all, it is only a means to an end. The second is that since every play means something—even the play which denies all meaning to existence—the "idea" of a play is its measure of value and importance and beauty, and that a play which appears merely to exist to one side of "ideas" is an aesthetic nullity.

Idea is very important to me as a dramatist, but I think it is time someone said that playwrights, including the greatest, have not been noted for the new ideas they have broached in their plays. By new I mean an original idea invented by the playwright, quite as such things are created, if infrequently, by scientists, and occasionally by philosophers. Surely there is no known philosophy which was first announced through a play, nor any ethical idea. No social concept in Shaw's plays could have been much of a surprise to the Webbs and thousands of other Socialists of the time; nor can Ibsen, Chekhov, Strindberg, or O'Neill be credited with inventing any new thoughts. As a matter of fact, it is highly unlikely that a new idea could be successfully launched through a play at all, and this for several good reasons.

A genuine invention in the realm of ideas must first emerge as an abstruse and even partial concept. Be it Christianity, Darwinism, Marxism, or any other that can with reason be called original it has always been the product of proofs which, before they go to form a complete and new concept, require years and often generations of testing, research, and polemic. At first blush a new idea appears to be very close to insanity because to be new it must reverse important basic beliefs and assumptions which, in turn, have been institutionalized and are administered by one or another kind of priesthood with a vested interest in the old idea. Nor would the old idea be an idea at all, strictly speaking, if some goodly section of the population did not believe in it. If only because no dramatic structure can bear the brunt of the incredulity with which any really new idea is greeted, the play form would collapse under the burdens of having to deliver up the mountain of proof required for a new idea to be believed. And this would be true even if the audience were all philosophers— perhaps even truer, for the philosopher requires proofs even more exact than the layman does.

The dramatic form is a dynamic thing. It is not possible to dally in it for reflection. The polemical method, as well as the scientific exposition, the parable, or the ethical teaching, all depend upon a process which, in effect, says, "What you believe is wrong for these reasons; what the truth is is as follows." Tremendous energy must go into destroying the validity of the ancient proposition, and destroying it from an absolutely opposite viewpoint. An idea, if it is really new, is a genuine humiliation for the majority of the people; it is an affront not only to their sensibilities but to their deepest convictions. It offends against the things they worship, whether God or science or money.

The conflict between a new idea and the very notion of drama is remorseless and not resolvable because, among other things, plays are always performed before people sitting en masse and not alone. To a very large degree, much greater than is generally realized, we react *with* a surrounding crowd rather than against it; our individual criteria of truth are set to one side and we are no longer at the mercy of a performance alone, but of the surrounding reaction to it. A man walking down a deserted street sees another man beating a horse; he does not like this, he is possibly revolted by it, even angered. Perhaps he walks on, or perhaps he stops to remonstrate with the horsewhipper, who then perhaps threatens *him* with the same whip. Depending on the character of the man, he either fights or decides it is none of his business, really, and goes on about his life. The same man on the same street, but this time a busy street with many people; sees the same scene of cruelty. He is now behaving in public; he cries out and hears his cries echoed; he is encouraged; he moves in to stop the cruelty and when he himself is threatened the conflict in him over whether to back off or to fight is much higher and more intense, for now he is surrounded by the administrators of shame or the bestowers of honor—his fellow men. He is no longer looking at the same scene in the same way; the very significance of the experience is changed and more likely than not his own actions. So it is in the theater. Inevitably, to one degree or another, we see what we see on the stage not only with our own eyes but with the eyes of others. Our standards of right and wrong, good taste and bad, must in some way come into either conflict or agreement with social standards, and a truth, however true, is no longer merely itself, but itself plus the conventional reaction to it; and in the case of a genuinely new idea the conventional reaction, by definition, will come down on it like a ton of bricks, and it is finished, however beautifully written.

If plays have not broached new ideas, they have enunciated not-yet-popular ideas which are already in the air, ideas for which there has already been a preparation by non-dramatic media. Which is to say that once an idea is "in the air" it is no longer an idea but a feeling, a sensation, an emotion, and with these the drama can deal. For one thing, where no doubt exists in the hearts of the people, a play cannot create doubt; where no desire to believe exists, a play cannot create a belief. And again, this springs from the nature of dramatic form and its inevitable dynamism; it must communicate as it proceeds and it literally has no existence if it must wait until the audience goes home to think before it can be appreciated. It is the art of the present tense par excellence.

Thus it is that the forms, the accents, the intentions of the plays in this book are not the same from play to play. I could say that my awareness of life was not the same and leave it at that, but the truth is wider, for good or for ill. It is also that the society to which I responded in the past decade was constantly changing, as it is changing while I write this sentence. These plays, in one sense, are my response to what was "in the air," they are one man's way of saying to his fellow men, "This is what you see every day, or think or feel; now I will show you what you really know but have not had the time, or the disinterestedness, or the insight, or the information to understand consciously." Each of these plays, in varying degrees, was begun in the belief that it was unveiling a truth already known but unrecognized as such. My concept of the audience is of a public each member of which is carrying about with him what he thinks is an anxiety, or a hope, or a preoccupation which is his alone and isolates him from mankind; and in this respect at least the function of a play is to reveal him to himself so that he may touch others by virtue of the revelation of his mutuality with them. If only for this reason I regard the theater as a serious business, one that makes or should make man more human, which is to say, less alone.

III

When *All My Sons* opened on Broadway it was called an "Ibsenesque" play. Some people liked it for this reason and others did not. Ibsen is relevant to this play but what he means to me is not always what he means to others, either his advocates or his detractors. More often than not, these days, he is thought of as a stage carpenter with a flair for ideas of importance. The whole aim of shaping a dramatic work on strict lines which will elicit a distinct meaning reducible to a sentence is now suspect. "Life" is now more complicated than such a mechanical contrasting of forces can hope to reflect. Instead, the aim is a "poetic" drama, preferably one whose ultimate thought or meaning is elusive, a drama which appears not to have been composed or constructed, but which somehow comes to life on a stage and then flickers away. To come quickly to the point, our theater inclines toward the forms of adolescence rather than analytical adulthood. It is not my place to deal in praise or blame but it seems to me that a fair judge would be compelled to conclude, as a minimum, that the run of serious works of the past decade have been written and played under an intellectually—as well as electrically—diffused light. It is believed that any attempt to "prove" something in a play is somehow unfair and certainly inartistic, if not gauche, more particularly if what is being proved happens to be in any overt way of social moment. Indeed, one American critic believes that the narrowness of the theater audience —as compared with that for movies and television—is the result of the masses" having been driven away from the theater by plays that preached.

This is not, of course, a new attitude in the world. Every major playwright has had to make his way against it, for there is and always will be a certain amount of resentfulness toward the presumption of any playwright to teach. And there will never be a satisfactory way of explaining that no playwright can be praised for his high seriousness and at the same time be praised for not trying to teach; the very conception of a dramatic theme inevitably means that certain aspects of life are selected and others left out, and to imagine that a play can be written distinterestedly is to believe that one can make love disinterestedly.

The debatable question is never whether a play ought to teach but whether it is art, and in this connection the basic criterion—purely technical considerations to one side—is the passion with which the teaching is made. I hasten to add the obvious—that a work cannot be judged by the validity of its teaching. But it is entirely misleading to state that there is some profound conflict between art and the philosophically or socially meaningful theme. I say this not out of a preference for plays that teach but in deference to the nature of the creative act. A work of art is not handed down from Olympus from a creature with a vision as wide as the world. If that could be done a play would never end, just as history has no end. A play must end, and end with a climax, and to forge a climax the forces in life, which are of infinite complexity, must be made finite and capable of a more or less succinct culmination. Thus, all dramas are to that extent arbitrary—in comparison with life itself—and embody a viewpoint if not an obsession on the author's part. So that when I am told that a play is beautiful and (or because) it does not try to teach anything, I can only wonder which of two things is true about it: either what it teaches is so obvious, so inconsiderable as to appear to the critic to be "natural," or its teaching has been embedded and articulated so thoroughly in the action itself as not to appear as an objective but only a subjective fact.

All My Sons was not my first play but the eighth or ninth I had written up to the mid-forties. But for the one immediately preceding it, none of the others were produced in the professional theater, and since the reader can have little knowledge of this one—which lasted less than a week on Broadway—and no knowledge at all of the others, a word is in order about these desk-drawer plays, particularly the failure called *The Man Who Had All the Luck.*

This play was an investigation to discover what exact part a man played in his own fate. It deals with a young man in a small town who, by the time he is in his mid-twenties, owns several growing businesses, has married the girl he loves, is the father of a child he has always wanted, and is daily becoming convinced that as his desires are gratified he is causing to accumulate around his own head an invisible but nearly palpable fund, so to speak, of retribution. The law of life, as he observes life around him, is that people are always frustrated in some important regard; and he conceives that he must be too, and the play is built around his conviction of impending disaster. The disaster never comes, even when, in effect, he tries to bring it on in order to survive it and find peace. Instead, he comes to believe in his own superiority, and in his remarkable ability to succeed.

Now, more than a decade later, it is possible for me to see that far from being a waste and a failure this play was a preparation, and possibly a necessary one, for those that followed, especially *All My Sons* and *Death of a Salesman*, and this for many reasons. In the more than half-dozen plays before it I had picked themes at random—which is to say that I had had no awareness of any inner continuity running from one of these plays to the next, and I did not perceive myself in what I had written. I had begun with a play about a family, then a play about two brothers caught on either side of radicalism in a university, then a play about a psychologist's dilemma in a prison where the sane were inexorably moving over to join the mad, a play about a bizarre ship's officer whose desire for death led him to piracy on the seas, a tragedy on the Cortes–Montezuma conflict, and others. Once again, as I worked on *The Man Who Had All the Luck* I was writing, I would have said, about what lay outside me. I had heard the story of a young man in a Midwestern town who had earned the respect and love of his town and great personal prosperity as well, and who, suddenly and for no known reason, took to suspecting everyone of wanting to rob him, and within a year of his obsession's onset had taken his own life.

In the past I had rarely spent more than three months on a play. Now the months went by with the end never in sight. After nearly ten years of writing I had struck upon what seemed a bottomless pit of mutually canceling meanings and implications. In the past I had had less difficulty with forming a "story" and more with the exploration of its meanings. Now, in contrast, I was working with an overwhelming sense of meaning, but however I tried I could not make the drama continuous and of a piece; it persisted, with the beginning of each scene, in starting afresh as though each scene were the beginning of a new play. Then one day, while I was lying on a beach, a simple shift of relationships came to mind, a shift which did not and could not solve the problem of writing *The Man Who Had All the Luck*, but, I think now, made at least two of the plays that followed possible, and a great deal else besides.

What I saw, without laboring the details, was that two of the characters, who had been friends in the previous drafts, were logically brothers and had the same father. Had I known then what I know now I could have saved myself a lot of trouble. The play was impossible to fix because the overt story was only tangential to the secret drama its author was quite unconsciously trying to write. But in writing of the father–son relationship and of the son's search for his relatedness there was a fullness of feeling I had never known before; a crescendo was struck with a force I could almost touch. The crux of *All My Sons*, which would not be written until nearly three years later, was formed; and the roots of *Death of a Salesman* were sprouted.

The form of *All My Sons* is a reflection and an expression of several forces, of only some of which I was conscious. I desired above all to write rationally, to write so that I could tell the story of the play to even an unlettered person and spark a look of recognition on his face. The accusation I harbored against the earlier play was that it could not make sense to common-sense people. I have always been in love with wonder, the wonder of how things and people got to be what they are, and in *The Man Who Had All the Luck* I had tried to grasp wonder, I had tried to make it on the stage, by writing wonder. But wonder had betrayed me and the only other course I had was the one I took—to seek cause and effect, hard actions, facts, the geometry of relationships, and to hold back any tendency to express an idea in itself unless it was literally forced out of a character's mouth; in other words, to let wonder rise up like a mist, a gas, a vapor from the gradual and remorseless crush of factual and psychological conflict. I went back to the great book of wonder, *The Brothers Karamazov*, and I found what suddenly I felt must be true of it: that if one reads its most colorful, breathtaking, wonderful pages, one finds the thickest concentration of hard facts. Facts about the biographies of the characters, about the kind of bark on the moonlit trees, the way a window is hinged, the exact position of Dmitri as he peers through the window at his father, the precise description of his father's dress. Above all, the precise collision of inner themes during, not before or after, the high dramatic scenes. And quite as suddenly I noticed in Beethoven the holding back of climax until it was ready, the grasp of the rising line and the unwillingness to divert to an easy climax until the true one was ready. If there is one word to name the mood I felt it was *Forego*. Let nothing interfere with the shape, the direction, the intention. I believed that I had felt too much in the previous play and understood too little.

I was turning thirty then, the author of perhaps a dozen plays, none of which I could truly believe were finished. I had written many scenes, but not a play. A play, I saw then, was an organism of which I had fashioned only certain parts. The decision formed to write one more, and if again it turned out to be unrealizable, I would go into another line of work. I have never loved the brick and mortar of the theater, and only once in my life had I been truly engrossed in a production—when Ruth Gordon played in the Jed Harris production of *A Doll's House*. The sole sense of connection with theater came when I saw the productions of the Group Theatre. It was not only the brilliance of ensemble acting, which in my opinion has never been equaled since in America, but the air of union created between actors and the audience. Here was the promise of prophetic theater which suggested to my mind the Greek situation when religion and belief were the heart of drama. I watched the Group Theatre from fifty-five-cent seats in the balcony, and at intermission time it was possible to feel the heat and the passion of people moved not only in their bellies but in their thoughts. If I say that my own writer's ego found fault with the plays it does not detract from the fact that the performances were almost all inspiring to me, and when I heard that the Group was falling apart it seemed incredible that a society of saints—which they were to me, artistically, even as I had never met one of them—should be made up of people with less than absolute dedication to their cause.

All My Sons was begun several years after the Group had ceased to be, but it was what I can only call now a play written for a prophetic theater. I am aware of the vagueness of the term but I cannot do very well at defining what I mean. Perhaps it signifies a theater, a play, which is meant to become part of the lives of its audience—a play seriously meant for people of common sense, and relevant to both their domestic lives and their daily work, but an experience which widens their awareness of connection—the filaments to the past and the future which lie concealed in "life."

My intention in this play was to be as untheatrical as possible. To that end any metaphor, any image, any figure of speech, however creditable to me, was removed if it even slightly brought to consciousness the hand of a writer. So far as was possible nothing was to be permitted to interfere with its artlessness.

It seems to me now that I had the attitude of one laying siege to a fortress in this form. The sapping operation was to take place without a sound beneath a clear landscape in the broad light of a peaceful day. Nor was this approach arbitrary. It grew out of a determination to reverse my past playwriting errors, and from the kind of story I happened to have discovered.

During an idle chat in my living room, a pious lady from the Middle West told of a family in her neighborhood which had been destroyed when the daughter turned the father in to the authorities on discovering that he had been selling faulty machinery to the Army. The war was then in full blast. By the time she had finished the tale I had transformed the daughter into a son and the climax of the second act was full and clear in my mind.

I knew my informant's neighborhood, I knew its middle-class ordinariness, and I knew how rarely the great issues penetrate such environments. But the fact that a girl had not only wanted to, but had actually moved against an erring father transformed into fact and common reality what in my previous play I had only begun to hint at. I had no awareness of the slightest connection between the two plays. All I knew was that somehow a hard thing had entered into me, a crux toward which it seemed possible to move in strong and straight lines. Something was crystal clear to me for the first time since I had begun to write plays, and it was the crisis of the second act, the revelation of the full loathesomeness of an anti-social action.

With this sense of dealing with an existing objective fact, I began to feel a difference in my role as a writer. It occurred to me that I must write this play so that even the actual criminal, on reading it, would have to say that it was true and sensible and as real as his life. It began to seem to me that what I had written until then, as well as almost all the plays I had ever seen, had been written for a theatrical performance, when they should have been written as a kind of testimony whose relevance far surpassed theatrics.

For these reasons the play begins in an atmosphere of undisturbed normality. Its first act was later called slow, but it was designed to be slow. It was made so that even boredom might threaten, so that when the first intimation of the crime is dropped a genuine horror might begin to move into the heart of the audience, a horror born of the contrast between the placidity of the civilization on view and the threat to it that a rage of conscience could create.

It took some two years to fashion this play, chiefly, I think now, because of a difficulty not unconnected with a similar one in the previous play. It was the question of relatedness. The crime in *All My Sons* is not one that is about to be committed but one that has long since been committed. There is no question of its consequences' being ameliorated by anything Chris Keller or his father can do; the damage has been done irreparably. The stakes remaining are purely the conscience of Joe Keller and its awakening to the evil he has done, and the conscience of his son in the face of what he has discovered about his father. One could say that the problem was to make a fact of morality, but it is more precise, I think, to say that the structure of the play is designed to bring a man into the direct path of the consequences he has wrought. In one sense, it was the same problem of writing about David Beeves in the earlier play, for he too could not relate himself to what he had done. In both plays the dramatic obsession, so to speak, was with the twofold nature of the individual—his own concept of his deeds, and what turns out to be the "real" description of them. *All My Sons* has often been called a moral play, and it is that, but the concept of morality is not quite as purely ethical as it has been made to appear, nor is it so in the plays that follow. That the deed of Joe Keller at issue in *All My Sons* is his having been the cause of the death of pilots in war obscures the other kind of morality in which the play is primarily interested. Morality is probably a faulty word to use in the connection, but what I was after was the wonder in the fact that consequences of actions are as real as the actions themselves, yet we rarely take them into consideration as we perform actions, and we cannot hope to do so fully when we must always act with only partial knowledge of consequences. Joe Keller's trouble, in a word, is not that he cannot tell right from wrong but that his cast of mind cannot admit that he, personally, has any viable connection with his world, his universe, or his society. He is not a partner in society, but an incorporated member, so to speak, and you cannot sue personally the officers of a corporation. I hasten to make clear here that I am not merely speaking of a literal corporation but the concept of a man's becoming a function of production or distribution to the point where his personality becomes divorced from the actions it propels.

The fortress which *All My Sons* lays siege to is the fortress of unrelatedness. It is an assertion not so much of a morality in terms of right and wrong, but of a moral world's being such because men cannot walk away from certain of their deeds. In this sense Joe Keller is a threat to society and in this sense the play is a social play. Its "socialness." does not reside in its having dealt with the crime of selling defective materials to a nation at war—the same crime could easily be the basis of a thriller which would have no place in social dramaturgy. It is that the crime is seen as having roots in a certain relationship of the individual to society, and to a certain indoctrination he embodies, which, if dominant, can mean a jungle existence for all of us no matter how high our buildings soar. And it is in this sense that loneliness is socially meaningful in these plays.

To return to Ibsen's influence upon this play, I should have to split the question in order to make sense of it. First, there was the real impact of his work upon me at the time: this consisted mainly in what I then saw as his ability to forge a play upon a factual bedrock. A situation in his plays is never stated but revealed in terms of hard actions, irrevocable deeds; and sentiment is never confused with the action it conceals. Having for so long written in terms of what people felt rather than what they did, I turned to his works at the time with a sense of homecoming. As I have said, I wanted then to write so that people of common sense would mistake my play for life itself and not be required to lend it some poetic license before it could be believed. I wanted to make the moral world as real and evident as the immoral one so splendidly is.

But my own belief is that the shadow of Ibsen was seen on this play for another reason, and it is that *All My Sons* begins very late in its story. Thus, as in Ibsen's best-known work, a great amount of time is taken up with bringing the past into the present. In passing, I ought to add that this view of action is presently antipathetic to our commonly held feeling about the drama. More than any other quality of realism, or, to be more exact, of Ibsenism as a technique, this creates a sense of artificiality which we now tend to reject, for in other respects realism is still our reigning style. But it is no longer acceptable that characters should sit about discussing events of a year ago, or ten years ago, when in "life" they would be busy with the present. In truth, the effort to eliminate antecedent material has threatened to eliminate the past entirely from many plays. We are impatient to get on with it—so much so that anyone making a study of some highly creditable plays of the moment would be hard put to imagine what their characters were like a month before their actions and stories begin. *All My Sons* takes its time with the past, not in deference to Ibsen's method as I saw it then, but because its theme is the question of actions and consequences, and a way had to be found to throw a long line into the past in order to make that kind of connection viable.

That the idea of connection was central to me is indicated again in the kind of revision the play underwent. In its earlier versions the mother, Kate Keller, was in a dominating position; more precisely, her astrological beliefs were given great prominence. (The play's original title was *The Sign of the Archer*.) And this, because I sought in every sphere to give body and life to connection. But as the play progressed the conflict between Joe and his son Chris pressed astrology to the wall until its mysticism gave way to psychology. There was also the impulse to regard the mystical with suspicion, since it had, in the past, given me only turgid works that could never develop a true climax based upon revealed psychological truths. In short, where in previous plays I might well have been satisfied to create only an astrologically obsessed woman, the obsession now had to be opened up to reveal its core of self-interest and intention on the character's part. Wonder must have feet with which to walk the earth.

But before I leave this play it seems wise to say a few more words about the kind of dramatic impulse it represents, and one aspect of "Ibsenism" as a technique is the quickest path into that discussion. I have no vested interest in any one form—as the variety of forms I have used attests—but there is one element in Ibsen's method which I do not think ought to be overlooked, let alone dismissed as it so often is nowadays. If his plays, and his method, do nothing else they reveal the evolutionary quality of life. One is constantly aware, in watching his plays, of process, change, development. I think too many modern plays assume, so to speak, that their duty is merely to show the present countenance rather than to account for what happens. It is therefore wrong to imagine that because his first and sometimes his second acts devote so much time to a studied revelation of antecedent material, his view is static compared to our own. In truth, it is profoundly dynamic, for that enormous past was always heavily documented to the end that the present be comprehended with wholeness, as a moment in a flow of time, and not—as with so many modern plays—as a situation without roots. Indeed, even though I can myself reject other aspects of his work, it nevertheless presents barely and unadorned what I believe is the biggest single dramatic problem, namely, how to dramatize what has gone before. I say this not merely out of technical interest, but because dramatic characters, and the drama itself, can never hope to attain a maximum degree of consciousness unless they contain a viable unveiling of the contrast between past and present, and an awareness of the process by which the present has become what it is. And I say this, finally, because I take it as a truth that the end of drama is the creation of a higher consciousness and not merely a subjective attack upon the audience's nerves and feelings. What is precious in the Ibsen method is its insistence upon valid causation, and this cannot be dismissed as a wooden notion.

This is the "real" in Ibsen's realism for me, for he was, after all, as much a mystic as a realist. Which is simply to say that while there are mysteries in life which no amount of analyzing will reduce to reason, it is perfectly realistic to admit and even to proclaim that hiatus as a truth. But the problem is not to make complex what is essentially explainable; it is to make understandable what is complex without distorting and oversimplifying what cannot be explained. I think many of his devices are, in fact, quite arbitrary; that he betrays a Germanic ponderousness at times and a tendency to over-prove what is quite clear in the first place. But we could do with more of his basic intention, which was to assert nothing he had not proved, and to cling always to the marvelous spectacle of life forcing one event out of the jaws of the preceding one and to reveal its elemental consistencies with surprise. In other words, I contrast his realism not with the lyrical, which I prize, but with sentimentality, which is always a leak in the dramatic dike. He sought to make a play as weighty and living a fact as the discovery of the steam engine or algebra. This can be scoffed away only at a price, and the price is a living drama.

IV

I think now that the straightforwardness of the *All My Sons* form was in some part due to the relatively sharp definition of the social aspects of the problem it dealt with. It was conceived in wartime and begun in wartime; the spectacle of human sacrifice in contrast with aggrandizement is a sharp and heartbreaking one. At a time when all public voices were announcing the arrival of that great day when industry and labor were one, my personal experience was daily demonstrating that beneath the slogans very little had changed. In this sense the play was a response to what I felt "in the air." It was an unveiling of what I believed everybody knew and nobody publicly said. At the same time, however, I believed I was bringing news, and it was news which I half expected would be denied as truth.

When, in effect, it was accepted, I was gratified, but a little surprised. The success of a play, especially one's first success, is somewhat like pushing against a door which is suddenly opened from the other side. One may fall on one's face or not, but certainly a new room is opened that was always securely shut until then. For myself, the experience was invigorating. It suddenly seemed that the audience was a mass of blood relations and I sensed a warmth in the world that had not been there before. It made it possible to dream of daring more and risking more. The Wonderful was no longer something that would inevitably trap me into disastrously confusing works, for the audience sat in silence before the unwinding of *All My Sons* and gasped when they should have, and I tasted that power which is reserved, I imagine, for playwrights, which is to know that by one's invention a mass of strangers has been publicly transfixed.

As well, the production of the play was an introduction to the acting art and its awesome potentials. I wanted to use more of what lay in actors to be used. To me, the most incredible spectacle of this first successful production was the silence it enforced. It seemed then that the stage was as wide and free and towering and laughingly inventive as the human mind itself, and I wanted to press closer toward its distant edges. A success places one among friends. The world is friendly, the audience is friendly, and that is good. It also reveals, even more starkly than a failure—for a failure is always ill-defined—what remains undone.

The wonder in *All My Sons* lay in its revelation of process, and it was made a stitch at a time, so to speak, in order to weave a tapestry before our eyes. What it wanted, however, was a kind of moment-to-moment wildness in addition to its organic wholeness. The form of the play, I felt, was not sensuous enough in itself. Which means that its conception of time came to appear at odds with my own experience.

The first image that occurred to me which was to result in *Death of a Salesman* was of an enormous face the height of the proscenium arch which would appear and then open up, and we would see the inside of a man's head. In fact, *The Inside of His Head* was the first title. It was conceived half in laughter, for the inside of his head was a mass of contradictions. The image was in direct opposition to the method of *All My Sons*—a method one might call linear or eventual in that one fact or incident creates the necessity for the next. The *Salesman* image was from the beginning absorbed with the concept that nothing in life comes "next" but that everything exists together and at the same time within us; that there is no past to be "brought forward" in a human being, but that he is his past at every moment and that the present is merely that which his past is capable of noticing and smelling and reacting to.

I wished to create a form which, in itself as a form, would literally be the process of Willy Loman's way of mind. But to say "wished" is not accurate. Any dramatic form is an artifice, a way of transforming a subjective feeling into something that can be comprehended through public symbols. Its efficiency as a form is to be judged—at least by the writer—by how much of the original vision and feeling is lost or distorted by this transformation. I wished to speak of the salesman most precisely as I felt about him, to give no part of that feeling away for the sake of any effect or any dramatic necessity. What was wanted now was not a mounting line of tension, nor a gradually narrowing cone of intensifying suspense, but a bloc, a single chord presented as such at the outset, within which all the strains and melodies would already be contained. The strategy, as with *All My Sons,* was to appear entirely unstrategic but with a difference. This time, if I could, I would have told the whole story and set forth all the characters in one unbroken speech or even one sentence or a single flash of light. As I look at the play now its form seems the form of a confession, for that is how it is told, now speaking of what happened yesterday, then suddenly following some connection to a time twenty years ago, then leaping even further back and then returning to the present and even speculating about the future.

Where in *All My Sons* it had seemed necessary to prove the connections between the present and the past, between events and moral consequences, between the manifest and the hidden, in this play all was assumed as proven to begin with. All I was doing was bringing things to mind. The assumption, also, was that everyone knew Willy Loman. I can realize this only now, it is true, but it is equally apparent to me that I took it somehow for granted then. There was still the attitude of the unveiler, but no bringing together of hitherto unrelated things; only pre-existing images, events, confrontations, moods, and pieces of knowledge. So there was a kind of confidence underlying this play which the form itself expresses, even a naïveté, a self-disarming quality that was in part born of my belief in the audience as being essentially the same as myself. If I had wanted, then, to put the audience reaction into words, it would not have been "What happens next and why?" so much as "Oh, God, of course!"

In one sense a play is a species of jurisprudence, and some part of it must take the advocate's role, something else must act in defense, and the entirety must engage the Law. Against my will, *All My Sons* states, and even proclaims, that it is a form and that a writer wrote it and organized it. In *Death of a Salesman* the original impulse was to make that same proclamation in an immeasurably more violent, abrupt, and openly conscious way. Willy Loman does not merely suggest or hint that he is at the end of his strength and of his justifications, he is hardly on the stage for five minutes when he says so; he does not gradually imply a deadly conflict with his son, an implication dropped into the midst of serenity and surface calm, he is avowedly grappling with that conflict at the outset. The ultimate matter with which the play will close is announced at the outset and is the matter of its every moment from the first. There is enough revealed in the first scene of *Death of a Salesman* to fill another kind of play which, in service to another dramatic form, would hold back and only gradually release it. I wanted to proclaim that an artist had made this play, but the nature of the proclamation was to be entirely "inartistic" and avowedly unstrategic; it was to hold back nothing, at any moment, which life would have revealed, even at the cost of suspense and climax. It was to forego the usual preparations for scenes and to permit—and even seek—whatever in each character contradicted his position in the advocate-defense scheme of its jurisprudence. The play was begun with only one firm piece of knowledge and this was that Loman was to destroy himself. How it would wander before it got to that point I did not know and resolved not to care. I was convinced only that if I could make him remember enough he would kill himself, and the structure of the play was determined by what was needed to draw up his memories like a mass of tangled roots without end or beginning.

As I have said, the structure of events and the nature of its form are also the direct reflection of Willy Loman's way of thinking at this moment of his life. He was the kind of man you see muttering to himself on a subway, decently dressed, on his way home or to the office, perfectly integrated with his surroundings excepting that unlike other people he can no longer restrain the power of his experience from disrupting the superficial sociality of his behavior. Consequently he is working on two logics which often collide. For instance, if he meets his son Happy while in the midst of some memory in which Happy disappointed him, he is instantly furious at Happy, despite the fact that Happy at this particular moment deeply desires to be of use to him. He is literally at that terrible moment when the voice of the past is no longer distant but quite as loud as the voice of the present. In dramatic terms the form, therefore, *is* this process, instead of being a once-removed summation or indication of it.

The way of telling the tale, in this sense, is as mad as Willy and as abrupt and as suddenly lyrical. And it is difficult not to add that the subsequent imitations of the form had to collapse for this particular reason. It is not possible, in my opinion, to graft it onto a character whose psychology it does not reflect, and I have not used it since because it would be false to a more integrated—or less disintegrating—personality to pretend that the past and the present are so openly and vocally intertwined in his mind. The ability of people to down their past is normal, and without it we could have no comprehensible communication among men. In the hands of writers who see it as an easy way to elicit anterior information in a play it becomes merely a flashback. There are no flashbacks in this play but only a mobile concurrency of past and present, and this, again, because in his desperation to justify his life Willy Loman has destroyed the boundaries between now and then, just as anyone would do who, on picking up his telephone, discovered that this perfectly harmless act had somehow set off an explosion in his basement. The previously assumed and believed-in results of ordinary and accepted actions, and their abrupt and unforeseen—but apparently logical—effects, form the basic collision in this play, and, I suppose, its ultimate irony.

It may be in place to remark, in this connection, that while the play was sometimes called cinematographic in its structure, it failed as a motion picture. I believe that the basic reason—aside from the gross insensitivity permeating its film production—was that the dramatic tension of Willy's memories was destroyed by transferring him, literally, to the locales he had only imagined in the play. There is an inevitable horror in the spectacle of a man losing consciousness of his immediate surroundings to the point where he engages in conversations with unseen persons. The horror is lost—and drama becomes narrative—when the context actually becomes his imagined world. And the drama evaporates because psychological truth has been amended, a truth which depends not only on what images we recall but in what connections and contexts we recall them. The setting on the stage was never shifted, despite the many changes in locale, for the precise reason that, quite simply, the mere fact that a man forgets where he is does not mean that he has really moved. Indeed, his terror springs from his never-lost awareness of time and place. It did not need this play to teach me that the screen is time-bound and earth-bound compared to the stage, if only because its preponderant emphasis is on the visual image, which, however rapidly it may be changed before our eyes, still displaces its predecessor, while scene-changing with words is instantaneous; and because of the flexibility of language, especially of English, a preceding image can be kept alive through the image that succeeds it. The movie's tendency is always to wipe out what has gone before, and it is thus in constant danger of transforming the dramatic into narrative. There is no swifter method of telling a "story" but neither is there a more difficult medium in which to keep a pattern of relationships constantly in being. Even in those sequences which retained the real backgrounds for Willy's imaginary confrontations the tension between now and then was lost. I suspect this loss was due to the necessity of shooting the actors close-up

—effectively eliminating awareness of their surroundings. The basic failure of the picture was a formal one. It did not solve, nor really attempt to find, a resolution for the problem of keeping the past constantly alive, and that friction, collision, and tension between past and present was the heart of the play's particular construction.

A great deal has been said and written about what *Death of a Salesman* is supposed to signify, both psychologically and from the socio-political viewpoints. For instance, in one periodical of the far Right it was called a "time bomb expertly placed under the edifice of Americanism," while the *Daily Worker* reviewer thought it entirely decadent. In Catholic Spain it ran longer than any modern play and it has been refused production in Russia but not, from time to time, in certain satellite countries, depending on the direction and velocity of the wind. The Spanish press, thoroughly controlled by Catholic orthodoxy, regarded the play as commendable proof of the spirit's death where there is no God. In America, even as it was being cannonaded as a piece of Communist propaganda, two of the largest manufacturing corporations in the country invited me to address their sales organizations in conventions assembled, while the road company was here and there picketed by the Catholic War Veterans and the American Legion. It made only a fair impression in London, but in the area of the Norwegian Arctic Circle fishermen whose only contact with civilization was the radio and the occasional visit of the government boat insisted on seeing it night after night—the same few people—believing it to be some kind of religious rite. One organization of salesmen raised me up nearly to patron-sainthood, and another, a national sales managers' group, complained that the difficulty of recruiting salesmen was directly traceable to the play. When the movie was made, the producing company got so frightened it produced a sort of trailer to be shown before the picture, a documentary short film which demonstrated how exceptional Willy Loman was; how necessary selling is to the economy; how secure the salesman's life really is; how idiotic, in short, was the feature film they had just spent more than a million dollars to produce. Fright does odd things to people.

On the psychological front the play spawned a small hill of doctoral theses explaining its Freudian symbolism, and there were innumerable letters asking if I was aware that the fountain pen which Biff steals is a phallic symbol. Some, on the other hand, felt it was merely a fountain pen and dismissed the whole play. I received visits from men over sixty from as far away as California who had come across the country to have me write the stories of their lives, because the story of Willy Loman was exactly like theirs. The letters from women made it clear that the central character of the play was Linda; sons saw the entire action revolving around Biff or Happy, and fathers wanted advice, in effect, on how to avoid parricide. Probably the most succinct reaction to the play was voiced by a man who, on leaving the theater, said, "I always said that New England territory was no damned good." This, at least, was a fact.

That I have and had not the slightest interest in the selling profession is probably unbelievable to most people, and I very early gave up trying even to say so. And when asked what Willy was selling, what was in his bags, I could only reply, "Himself." I was trying neither to condemn a profession nor particularly to improve it, and, I will admit, I was little better than ignorant of Freud's teachings when I wrote it. There was no attempt to bring down the American edifice nor to raise it higher, to show up family relations or to cure the ills afflicting that inevitable institution. The truth, at least of my aim—which is all I can speak of authoritatively —is much simpler and more complex.

The play grew from simple images. From a little frame house on a street of little frame houses, which had once been loud with the noise of growing boys, and then was empty and silent and finally occupied by strangers. Strangers who could not know with what conquistadorial joy Willy and his boys had once re-shingled the roof. Now it was quiet in the house, and the wrong people in the beds.

It grew from images of futility—the cavernous Sunday afternoons polishing the car. Where is that car now? And the chamois cloths carefully washed and put up to dry, where are the chamois cloths?

And the endless, convoluted discussions, wonderments, arguments, belittlements, encouragements, fiery resolutions, abdications, returns, partings, voyages out and voyages back, tremendous opportunities and small, squeaking denouements—and all in the kitchen now occupied by strangers who cannot hear what the walls are saying.

The image of aging and so many of your friends already gone and strangers in the seats of the mighty who do not know you or your triumphs or your incredible value.

The image of the son's hard, public eye upon you, no longer swept by your myth, no longer rousable from his separateness, no longer knowing you have lived for him and have wept for him.

The image of ferocity when love has turned to something else and yet is there, is somewhere in the room if one could only find it.

The image of people turning into strangers who only evaluate one another.

Above all, perhaps, the image of a need greater than hunger or sex or thirst, a need to leave a thumbprint somewhere on the world. A need for immortality, and by admitting it, the knowing that one has carefully inscribed one's name on a cake of ice on a hot July day.

I sought the relatedness of all things by isolating their unrelatedness, a man superbly alone with his sense of not having touched, and finally knowing in his last extremity that the love which had always been in the room unlocated was now found.

The image of a suicide so mixed in motive as to be unfathomable and yet demanding statement. Revenge was in it and a power of love, a victory in that it would bequeath a fortune to the living and a flight from emptiness. With it an image of peace at the final curtain, the peace that is between wars, the peace leaving the issues above ground and viable yet.

And always, throughout, the image of private man in a world full of strangers, a world that is not home nor even an open battle-ground but only galaxies of high promise over a fear of falling.

And the image of a man making something with his hands being a rock to touch and return to. "He was always so wonderful with his hands," says his wife over his grave, and I laughed when the line came, laughed with the artist-devil's laugh, for it had all come together in this line, she having been made by him though he did not know it or believe in it or receive it into himself. Only rank, height of power, the sense of having won he believed was real—the galaxy thrust up into the sky by projectors on the rooftops of the city he believed were real stars.

It came from structural images. The play's eye was to revolve from within Willy's head, sweeping endlessly in all directions like a light on the sea, and nothing that formed in the distant mist was to be left uninvestigated. It was thought of as having the density of the novel form in its interchange of viewpoints, so that while all roads led to Willy the other characters were to feel it was their play, a story about them and not him.

There were two undulating lines in mind, one above the other, the past webbed to the present moving on together in him and sometimes openly joined and once, finally, colliding in the show-down which defined him in his eyes at least—and so to sleep.

Above all, in the structural sense, I aimed to make a play with the veritable countenance of life. To make one the many, as in life, so that "society" is a power and a mystery of custom and inside the man and surrounding him, as the fish is in the sea and the sea inside the fish, his birthplace and burial ground, promise and threat. To speak commonsensically of social facts which every businessman knows and talks about but which are too prosaic to mention or are usually fancied up on the stage as philosophical problems. When a man gets old you fire him, you have to, he can't do the work. To speak and even to celebrate the common sense of businessmen, who love the personality that wins the day but know that you've got to have the right goods at the right price, handsome and well-spoken as you are. (To some, these were scandalous and infamous arraignments of society when uttered in the context of art. But not to the businessmen themselves; they knew it was all true and I cherished their clear-eyed talk.)

The image of a play without transitional scenes was there in the beginning. There was too much to say to waste precious stage time with feints and preparations, in themselves agonizing "structural" bridges for a writer to work out since they are not why he is writing. There was a resolution, as in *All My Sons*, not to waste motion or moments, but in this case to shear through everything up to the meat of a scene; a resolution not to write an unmeant word for the sake of the form but to make the form give and stretch and contract for the sake of the thing to be said. To cling to the process of Willy's mind as the form the story would take.

The play was always heroic to me, and in later years the academy's charge that Willy lacked the "stature" for the tragic hero seemed incredible to me. I had not understood that these matters are measured by Greco-Elizabethan paragraphs which hold no mention of insurance payments, front porches, refrigerator fan belts, steering knuckles, Chevrolets, and visions seen not through the portals of Delphi but in the blue flame of the hot-water heater. How could "Tragedy" make people weep, of all things?

I set out not to "write a tragedy" in this play, but to show the truth as I saw it. However, some of the attacks upon it as a pseudo-tragedy contain ideas so misleading, and in some cases so laughable, that it might be in place here to deal with a few of them.

Aristotle having spoken of a fall from the heights, it goes without saying that someone of the common mold cannot be a fit tragic hero. It is now many centuries since Aristotle lived. There is no more reason for falling down in a faint before his *Poetics* than before Euclid's geometry, which has been amended numerous times by men with new insights; nor, for that matter, would I choose to have my illnesses diagnosed by Hippocrates rather than the most ordinary graduate of an American medical school, despite the Greek's genius. Things do change, and even a genius is limited by his time and the nature of his society.

I would deny, on grounds of simple logic, this one of Aristotle's contentions if only because he lived in a slave society. When a vast number of people are divested of alternatives, as slaves are, it is rather inevitable that one will not be able to imagine drama, let alone tragedy, as being possible for any but the higher ranks of society. There is a legitimate question of stature here, but none of rank, which is so often confused with it. So long as the hero may be said to have had alternatives of a magnitude to have materially changed the course of his life, it seems to me that in this respect at least, he cannot be debarred from the heroic role.

The question of rank is significant to me only as it reflects the question of the social application of the hero's career. There is no doubt that if a character is shown on the stage who goes through the most ordinary actions, and is suddenly revealed to be the President of the United States, his actions immediately assume a much greater magnitude, and pose the possibilities of much greater meaning, than if he is the corner grocer. But at the same time, his stature as a hero is not so utterly dependent upon his rank that the corner grocer cannot outdistance him as a tragic figure—providing, of course, that the grocer's career engages the issues of, for instance, the survival of the race, the relationships of man to God—the questions, in short, whose answers define humanity and the right way to live so that the world is a home, instead of a battle-ground or a fog in which disembodied spirits pass each other in an endless twilight.

In this respect *Death of a Salesman* is a slippery play to categorize because nobody in it stops to make a speech objectively stating the great issues which I believe it embodies. If it were a worse play, less closely articulating its meanings with its actions, I think it would have more quickly satisfied a certain kind of criticism. But it was meant to be less a play than a fact; it refused admission to its author's opinions and opened itself to a revelation of process and the operations of an ethic, of social laws of action no less powerful in their effects upon individuals than any tribal law administered by gods with names. I need not claim that this play is a genuine solid gold tragedy for my opinions on tragedy to be held valid. My purpose here is simply to point out a historical fact which must be taken into account in any consideration of tragedy, and it is the sharp alteration in the meaning of rank in society between the present time and the distant past. More important to me is the fact that this particular kind of argument obscures much more relevant considerations.

One of these is the question of intensity. It matters not at all whether a modern play concerns itself with a grocer or a president if the intensity of the hero's commitment to his course is less than the maximum possible. It matters not at all whether the hero falls from a great height or a small one, whether he is highly conscious or only dimly aware of what is happening, whether his pride brings the fall or an unseen pattern written behind clouds; if the intensity, the human passion to surpass his given bounds, the fanatic insistence upon his self-conceived role—if these are not present there can only be an outline of tragedy but no living thing. I believe, for myself, that the lasting appeal of tragedy is due to our need to face the fact of death in order to strengthen ourselves for life, and that over and above this function of the tragic viewpoint there are and will be a great number of formal variations which no single definition will ever embrace.

Another issue worth considering is the so-called tragic victory, a question closely related to the consciousness of the hero. One makes nonsense of this if a "victory" means that the hero makes us feel some certain joy when, for instance, he sacrifices himself for a "cause," and unhappy and morose because he dies without one. To begin at the bottom, a man's death is and ought to be an essentially terrifying thing and ought to make nobody happy. But in a great variety of ways even death, the ultimate negative, can be, and appear to be, an assertion of bravery, and can serve to separate the death of man from the death of animals; and I think it is this distinction which underlies any conception of a victory in death. For a society of faith, the nature of the death can prove the existence of the spirit, and posit its immortality. For a secular society it is perhaps more difficult for such a victory to document itself and to make itself felt, but, conversely, the need to offer greater proofs of the humanity of man can make that victory more real. It goes without saying that in a society where there is basic disagreement as to the right way to live, there can hardly be agreement as to the right way to die, and both life and death must be heavily weighted with meaningness futility.

It was not out of any deference to a tragic definition that Willy Loman is filled with a joy, however broken-hearted, as he approaches his end, but simply that my sense of his character dictated his joy, and even what I felt was an exultation. In terms of his character, he has achieved a very powerful piece of knowledge, which is that he is loved by his son and has been embraced by him and forgiven. In this he is given his existence, so to speak—his fatherhood, for which he has always striven and which until now he could not achieve. That he is unable to take this victory thoroughly to his heart, that it closes the circle for him and propels him to his death, is the wage of his sin, which was to have committed himself so completely to the counterfeits of dignity and the false coinage embodied in his idea of success that he can prove his existence only by bestowing "power" on his posterity, a power deriving from the sale of his last asset, himself, for the price of his insurance policy.

I must confess here to a miscalculation, however. I did not realize while writing the play that so many people in the world do not see as clearly, or would not admit, as I thought they must, how futile most lives are; so there could be no hope of consoling the audience for the death of this man. I did not realize either how few would be impressed by the fact that this man is actually a very brave spirit who cannot settle for half but must pursue his dream of himself to the end. Finally, I thought it must be clear, even obvious, that this was no dumb brute heading mindlessly to his catastrophe.

I have no need to be Willy's advocate before the jury which decides who is and who is not a tragic hero. I am merely noting that the lingering ponderousness of so many ancient definitions has blinded students and critics to the facts before them, and not only in regard to this play. Had Willy been unaware of his separation from values that endure he would have died contentedly while polishing his car, probably on a Sunday afternoon with the ball game coming over the radio. But he was agonized by his awareness of being in a false position, so constantly haunted by the hollowness of all he had placed his faith in, so aware, in short, that he must somehow be filled in his spirit or fly apart, that he staked his very life on the ultimate assertion. That he had not the intellectual fluency to verbalize his situation is not the same thing as saying that he lacked awareness, even an overly intensified consciousness that the life he had made was without form and inner meaning.

To be sure, had he been able to know that he was as much the victim of his beliefs as their defeated exemplar, had he known how much of guilt he ought to bear and how much to shed from his soul, he would be more conscious. But it seems to me that there is of necessity a severe limitation of self-awareness in any character, even the most knowing, which serves to define him as a character, and more, that this very limit serves to complete the tragedy and, indeed, to make it at all possible. Complete consciousness is possible only in a play about forces, like *Prometheus*, but not in a play about people. I think that the point is whether there is a sufficient awareness in the hero's career to make the audience supply the rest. Had Oedipus, for instance, been more conscious and more aware of the forces at work upon him he must surely have said that he was not really to blame for having cohabited with his mother since neither he nor anyone else knew she was his mother. He must surely decide to divorce her, provide for their children, firmly resolve to investigate the family background of his next wife, and thus deprive us of a very fine play and the name for a famous neurosis. But he is conscious only up to a point, the point at which guilt begins. Now he is inconsolable and must tear out his eyes. What is tragic about this? Why is it not even ridiculous? How can we respect a man who goes to such extremities over something he could in no way help or prevent? The answer, I think, is not that we respect the man, but that we respect the Law he has so completely broken, wittingly or not, for it is that Law which, we believe, defines us as men. The confusion of some critics viewing *Death of a Salesman* in this regard is that they do not see that Willy Loman has broken a law without whose protection life is insupportable if not incomprehensible to him and to many others; it is the law which says that a failure in society and in business has no right to live. Unlike the law against incest, the law of success is not administered by statute or church, but it is very nearly as powerful in its grip upon men. The confusion increases because, while it is a law, it is by no means a wholly agreeable one even as it is slavishly obeyed, for to fail is no longer to belong to society, in his estimate. Therefore, the path is opened for those who wish to call Willy merely a foolish man even as they themselves are living in obedience to the same law that killed him. Equally, the fact that Willy's law—the belief, in other words, which administers guilt to him—is not a civilizing statute whose destruction menaces us all; it is, rather, a deeply believed and deeply suspect "good" which, when questioned as to its value, as it is in this play, serves more to raise our anxieties than to reassure us of the existence of an unseen but humane metaphysical system in the world. My attempt in the play was to counter this anxiety with an opposing system which, so to speak, is in a race for Willy's faith, and it is the system of love which is the opposite of the law of success. It is embodied in Biff Loman, but by the time Willy can perceive his love it can serve only as an ironic comment upon the life he sacrificed for power and for success and its tokens.

V

A play cannot be equated with a political philosophy, at least not in the way a smaller number, by simple multiplication, can be assimilated into a larger. I do not believe that any work of art can help but be diminished by its adherence at any cost to a political program, including its author's, and not for any other reason than that there is no political program—any more than there is a theory of tragedy—which can encompass the complexities of real life. Doubtless an author's politics must be one element, and even an important one, in the germination of his art, but if it is art he has created it must by definition bend itself to his observation rather than to his opinions or even his hopes. If I have shown a preference for plays which seek causation not only in psychology but in society, I may also believe in the autonomy of art, and I believe this because my experience with *All My Sons* and *Death of a Salesman* forces the belief upon me. If the earlier play was Marxist, it was a Marxism of a strange hue. Joe Keller is arraigned by his son for a willfully unethical use of his economic position; and this, as the Russians said when they removed the play from their stages, be-speaks an assumption that the norm of capitalist behavior is ethical or at least can be, an assumption no Marxist can hold. Nor does Chris propose to liquidate the business built in part on soldiers' blood; he will run it himself, but cleanly.

The most decent man in *Death of a Salesman* is a capitalist (Charley) whose aims are not different from Willy Loman's. The great difference between them is that Charley is not a fanatic. Equally, however, he has learned how to live without that frenzy, that ecstasy of spirit which Willy chases to his end. And even as Willy's sons are unhappy men, Charley's boy, Bernard, works hard, attends to his studies, and attains a worthwhile objective. These people are all of the same class, the same background, the same neighborhood. What theory lies behind this double view? None whatever. It is simply that I knew and know that I feel better when my work is reflecting a balance of the truth as it exists. A muffled debate arose with the success of *Death of a Salesman* in which attempts were made to justify or dismiss the play as a Left-Wing piece, or as a Right-Wing manifestation of decadence. The presumption underlying both views is that a work of art is the sum of its author's political outlook, real or alleged, and more, that its political implications are valid elements in its aesthetic evaluation. I do not believe this, either for my own or other writers' works.

The most radical play I ever saw was not *Waiting for Lefty* but *The Madwoman of Chaillot*. I know nothing of Giradoux's political alignment, and it is of no moment to me; I am able to read this play, which is the most open indictment of private exploitation of the earth I know about. By the evidence of his plays, Shaw, the socialist, was in love not with the working class, whose characters he could only caricature, but with the middle of the economic aristocracy, those men who, in his estimate, lived without social and economic illusions. There is a strain of mystic fatalism in Ibsen so powerful as to throw all his scientific tenets into doubt, and a good measure besides of contempt—in this radical—for the men who are usually called the public. The list is long and the contradictions are embarrassing until one concedes a perfectly simple proposition. It is merely that a writter of any worth creates out of his total perception, the vaster part of which is subjective and not within his intellectual control. For myself, it has never been possible to generate the energy to write and complete a play if I know in advance everything it signifies and all it will contain. The very impulse to write, I think, springs from an inner chaos crying for order, for meaning, and that meaning must be discovered in the process of writing or the work lies dead as it is finished. To speak, therefore, of a play as though it were the objective work of a propagandist is an almost biological kind of nonsense, provided, of course, that it is a play, which is to say a work of art.

VI

In the writing of *Death of a Salesman* I tried, of course, to achieve a maximum power of effect. But when I saw the devastating force with which it struck its audiences, something within me was shocked and put off. I had thought of myself as rather an optimistic man. I looked at what I had wrought and was forced to wonder whether I knew myself at all if this play, which I had written half in laughter and joy, was as morose and as utterly sad as its audiences found it. Either I was much tougher than they, and could stare at calamity with fewer terrors, or I was harboring with myself another man who was only tangentially connected with what I would have called my rather bright viewpoint about mankind. As I watched and saw tears in the eyes of the audience I felt a certain embarrassment at having, as I thought then, convinced so many people that life was not worth living—for so the play was widely interpreted. I hasten to add now that I ought not have been embarrassed, and that I am convinced the play is not a document of pessimism, a philosophy in which I do not believe.

Nevertheless, the emotionalism with which the play was received helped to generate an opposite impulse and an altered dramatic aim. This ultimately took shape in *The Crucible,* but before it became quite so definite and formed into idea, it was taking hold of my thoughts in a purely dramatic and theatrical context. Perhaps I can indicate its basic elements by saying that *Salesman* moves with its arms open wide, sweeping into itself by means of a subjective process of thought-connection a multitude of observations, feelings, suggestions, and shadings much as the mind does in its ordinary daily functionings. Its author chose its path, of course, but, once chosen, that path could meander as it pleased through a world that was well recognized by the audience. From the theatrical viewpoint that play desired the audience to forget it was in a theater even as it broke the bounds, I believe, of a long convention of realism. Its expressionistic elements were consciously used as such, but since the approach to Willy Loman's characterization was consistently and rigorously subjective, the audience would not ever be aware—if I could help it—that they were witnessing the use of a technique which had until then created only coldness, objectivity, and a highly styled sort of play. I had willingly employed expressionism but always to create a subjective truth, and this play, which was so manifestly "written," seemed as though nobody had written it at all but that it had simply "happened." I had always been attracted and repelled by the brilliance of German expressionism after World War I, and one aim in *Salesman* was to employ its quite marvelous shorthand for humane, "felt" characterizations rather than for purposes of demonstration for which the Germans had used it.

These and other technical and theatrical considerations were a preparation for what turned out to be *The Crucible*, but "what was in the air" provided the actual locus of the tale. If the reception of *All My Sons* and *Death of a Salesman* had made the world a friendly place for me, events of the early fifties quickly turned that warmth into an illusion. It was not only the rise of "McCarthyism" that moved me, but something which seemed much more weird and mysterious. It was the fact that a political, objective, knowledgeable campaign from the far Right was capable of creating not only a terror, but a new subjective reality, a veritable mystique which was gradually assuming even a holy resonance. The wonder of it all struck me that so practical and picayune a cause, carried forward by such manifestly ridiculous men, should be capable of paralyzing thought itself, and worse, causing to billow up such persuasive clouds of "mysterious" feelings within people. It was as though the whole country had been born anew, without a memory even of certain elemental decencies which a year or two earlier no one would have imagined could be altered, let alone forgotten. Astounded, I watched men pass me by without a nod whom I had known rather well for years; and again, the astonishment was produced by my knowledge, which I could not give up, that the terror in these people was being knowingly planned and consciously engineered, and yet that all they knew was terror. That so interior and subjective an emotion could have been so manifestly created from without was a marvel to me. It underlies every word in *The Crucible*.

I wondered, at first, whether it must be that self-preservation and the need to hold on to opportunity, the thought of being exiled and "put out," was what the fear was feeding on, for there were people who had had only the remotest connections with the Left who were quite as terrified as those who had been closer. I knew of one man who had been summoned to the office of a network executive and, on explaining that he had had no Left connections at all, despite the then current attacks upon him, was told that this was precisely the trouble; "You have nothing to give them," he was told, meaning he had no confession to make, and so he was fired from his job and for more than a year could not recover the will to leave his house.

It seemed to me after a time that this, as well as other kinds of social compliance, is the result of the sense of guilt which individuals strive to conceal by complying. Generally it was a guilt, in this historic instance, resulting from their awareness that they were not as Rightist as people were supposed to be; that the tenor of public pronouncements was alien to them and that they must be somehow discoverable as enemies of the power overhead. There was a new religiosity in the air, not merely the kind expressed by the spurt in church construction and church attendance, but an official piety which my reading of American history could not reconcile with the free-wheeling iconoclasm of the country's past. I saw forming a kind of interior mechanism of confession and forgiveness of sins which until now had not been rightly categorized as sins. New sins were being created monthly. It was very odd how quickly these were accepted into the new orthodoxy, quite as though they had been there since the beginning of time. Above all, above all horrors, I saw accepted the notion that conscience was no longer a private matter but one of state administration. I saw men handing conscience to other men and thanking other men for the opportunity of doing so.

I wished for a way to write a play that would be sharp, that would lift out of the morass of subjectivism the squirming, single, defined process which would show that the sin of public terror is that it divests man of conscience, of himself. It was a theme not unrelated to those that had invested the previous plays. In *The Crucible*, however, there was an attempt to move beyond the discovery and unveiling of the hero's guilt, a guilt that kills the personality. I had grown increasingly conscious of this theme in my past work, and aware too that it was no longer enough for me to build a play, as it were, upon the revelation of guilt, and to rely solely upon a fate which exacts payment from the culpable man. Now guilt appeared to me no longer the bedrock beneath which the probe could not penetrate. I saw it now as a betrayer, as possibly the most real of our illusions, but nevertheless a quality of mind capable of being overthrown.

I had known of the Salem witch hunt for many years before "McCarthyism" had arrived, and it had always remained an inexplicable darkness to me. When I looked into it now, however, it was with the contemporary situation at my back, particularly the mystery of the handing over of conscience which seemed to me the central and informing fact of the time. One finds, I suppose, what one seeks. I doubt I should ever have tempted agony by actually writing a play on the subject had I not come upon a single fact. It was that Abigail Williams, the prime mover of the Salem hysteria, so far as the hysterical children were concerned, had a short time earlier been the house servant of the Proctors and now was crying out Elizabeth Proctor as a witch; but more—it was clear from the record that with entirely uncharacteristic fastidiousness she was refusing to include John Proctor, Elizabeth's husband, in her accusations despite the urgings of the prosecutors. Why? I searched the records of the trials in the courthouse at Salem but in no other instance could I find such a careful avoidance of the implicating stutter, the murderous, ambivalent answer to the sharp questions of the prosecutors. Only here, in Proctor's case, was there so clear an attempt to differentiate between a wife's culpability and a husband's.

The testimony of Proctor himself is one of the least elaborate in the records, and Elizabeth is not one of the major cases either. There could have been numerous reasons for his having been ultimately apprehended and hanged which are nowhere to be found. After the play opened, several of his descendants wrote to me; and one of them believes that Proctor fell under suspicion because, according to family tradition, he had for years been an amateur inventor whose machines appeared to some people as devilish in their ingenuity, and—again according to tradition—he had had to conceal them and work on them privately long before the witch hunt had started, for fear of censure if not worse. The explanation does not account for everything, but it does fall in with his evidently liberated cast of mind as revealed in the record; he was one of the few who not only refused to admit consorting with evil spirits, but who persisted in calling the entire business a ruse and a fake. Most, if not all, of the other victims were of their time in conceding the existence of the immemorial plot by the Devil to take over the visible world, their only reservation being that they happened not to have taken part in it themselves.

It was the fact that Abigail, their former servant, was their accuser, and her apparent desire to convict Elizabeth and save John, that made the play conceivable for me.

As in any such mass phenomenon, the number of characters of vital, if not decisive, importance is so great as to make the dramatic problem excessively difficult. For a time it seemed best to approach the town impressionistically, and, by a mosaic of seemingly disconnected scenes, gradually to form a context of cause and effect. This I believe I might well have done had it not been that the central impulse for writing at all was not the social but the interior psychological question, which was the question of that guilt residing in Salem which the hysteria merely unleashed, but did not create. Consequently, the structure reflects that understanding, and it centers in John, Elizabeth, and Abigail.

In reading the record, which was taken down verbatim at the trial, I found one recurring note which had a growing effect upon my concept, not only of the phenomenon itself, but of our modern way of thinking about people, and especially of the treatment of evil in contemporary drama. Some critics have taken exception, for instance, to the unrelieved badness of the prosecution in my play. I understand how this is possible, and I plead no mitigation, but I was up against historical facts which were immutable. I do not think that either the record itself or the numerous commentaries upon it reveal any mitigation of the unrelieved, straight-forward, and absolute dedication to evil displayed by the judges of these trials and the prosecutors. After days of study it became quite incredible how perfect they were in this respect. I recall, almost as in a dream, how Rebecca Nurse, a pious and universally respected woman of great age, was literally taken by force from her sickbed and ferociously cross-examined. No human weakness could be displayed without the prosecution's stabbing into it with greater fury. The most patent contradictions, almost laughable even in that day, were overridden with warnings not to repeat their mention. There was a sadism here that was breathtaking.

So much so, that I sought but could not at the time take hold of a concept of man which might really begin to account for such evil. For instance, it seems beyond doubt that members of the Putnam family consciously, coldly, and with malice aforethought conferred in private with some of the girls, and told them whom it was desirable to cry out upon next. There is and will always be in my mind the spectacle of the great minister, and ideological authority behind the prosecution, Cotton Mather, galloping up to the scaffold to beat back a crowd of villagers so moved by the towering dignity of the victims as to want to free them.

It was not difficult to foresee the objections to such absolute evil in men; we are committed, after all, to the belief that it does not and cannot exist. Had I this play to write now, however, I might proceed on an altered concept. I should say that my own—and the critics'—unbelief in this depth of evil is concomitant with our unbelief in good, too. I should now examine this fact of evil as such. Instead, I sought to make Danforth, for instance, perceptible as a human being by showing him somewhat put off by Mary Warren's turnabout at the height of the trials, which caused no little confusion. In my play, Danforth seems about to conceive of the truth, and surely there is a disposition in him at least to listen to arguments that go counter to the line of the prosecution. There is no such swerving in the record, and I think now, almost four years after the writing of it, that I was wrong in mitigating the evil of this man and the judges he represents. Instead, I would perfect his evil to its utmost and make an open issue, a thematic consideration of it in the play. I believe now, as I did not conceive then, that there are people dedicated to evil in the world; that without their perverse example we should not know the good. Evil is not a mistake but a fact in itself. I have never proceeded psychoanalytically in my thought, but neither have I been separated from that humane if not humanistic conception of man as being essentially innocent while the evil in him represents but a perversion of his frustrated love. I posit no metaphysical force of evil which totally possesses certain individuals, nor do I even deny that given infinite wisdom and patience and knowledge any human being can be saved from himself. I believe merely that, from whatever cause, a dedication to evil, not mistaking it for good, but knowing it as evil and loving it as evil, is possible in human beings who appear agreeable and normal. I think now that one of the hidden weaknesses of our whole approach to dramatic psychology is our inability to face this fact—to conceive, in effect, of Iago.

The Crucible is a "tough" play. My criticism of it now would be that it is not tough enough. I say this not merely out of deference to the record of these trials, but out of a consideration for drama. We are so intent upon getting sympathy for our characters that the consequences of evil are being muddied by sentimentality under the guise of a temperate weighing of causes. The tranquility of the bad man lies at the heart of not only moral philosophy but dramaturgy as well. But my central intention in this play was to one side of this idea, which was realized only as the play was in production. All I sought here was to take a step not only beyond the realization of guilt, but beyond the helpless victimization of the hero.

The society of Salem was "morally" vocal. People then avowed principles, sought to live by them and die by them. Issues of faith, conduct, society, pervaded their private lives in a conscious way. They needed but to disapprove to act. I was drawn to this subject because the historical moment seemed to give me the poetic right to create people of higher self-awareness than the contemporary scene affords. I had explored the subjective world in *Salesman* and I wanted now to move closer to a conscious hero.

The decidedly mixed reception to the play was not easily traceable, but I believe there are causes for it which are of moment to more than this play alone. I believe that the very moral awareness of the play and its characters—which are historically correct—was repulsive to the audience. For a variety of reasons I think that the Anglo-Saxon audience cannot believe the reality of characters who live by principles and know very much about their own characters and situations, and who say what they know. Our drama, for this among other reasons, is condemned, so to speak, to the emotions of subjectivism, which, as they approach knowledge and self-awareness, become less and less actual and real to us. In retrospect I think that my course in *The Crucible* should have been toward greater self-awareness and not, as my critics have implied, toward an enlarged and more pervasive subjectivism. The realistic form and style of the play would then have had to give way. What new form might have evolved I cannot now say, but certainly the passion of knowing is as powerful as the passion of feeling alone, and the writing of the play broached the question of that new form for me.

The work of Bertolt Brecht inevitably rises up in any such quest. It seems to me that, while I cannot agree with his concept of the human situation, his solution of the problem of consciousness is admirably honest and theatrically powerful. One cannot watch his productions without knowing that he is at work not on the periphery of the contemporary dramatic problem, but directly upon its center—which is again the problem of consciousness.

VII

The Crucible, then, opened up a new prospect, and, like every work when completed, it left behind it unfinished business. It made a new freedom possible, and it also threw a certain light upon the difference between the modern playwriting problem of meaning and that of the age preceding the secularization of society. It is impossible to study the trial record without feeling the immanence of a veritable pantheon of life values in whose name both prosecution and defense could speak. The testimony is thick with reference to biblical examples, and even as religious belief did nothing to temper cruelty—and in fact might be shown to have made the cruel crueler—it often served to raise this swirling and ludicrous mysticism to a level of high moral debate; and it did this despite the fact that most of the participants were unlettered, simple folk. They lived and would die more in the shadow of the other world than in the light of this one (and it is no mean irony that the theocratic prosecution should seek out the most religious people for its victims).

The longer I dwelt on the whole spectacle, the more clear became the failure of the present age to find a universal moral sanction, and the power of realism's hold on our theater was an aspect of this vacuum. For it began to appear that our inability to break more than the surfaces of realism reflected our inability—playwrights and audiences—to agree upon the pantheon of forces and values which must lie behind the realistic surfaces of life. In this light, realism, as a style, could seem to be a defense against the assertion of meaning. How strange a conclusion this is when one realizes that the same style seventy years ago was the prime instrument of those who sought to illuminate meaning in the theater, who divested their plays of fancy talk and improbable locales and bizarre characters in order to bring "life" onto the stage. And I wondered then what was true. Was it that we had come to fear the hard glare of life on the stage and under the guise of an aesthetic surfeited with realism were merely expressing our flight from reality? Or was our condemned realism only the counterfeit of the original, whose most powerful single impetus was to deal with man as a social animal? Any form can be drained of its informing purpose, can be used to convey, like the Tudor façades of college dormitories, the now vanished dignity and necessity of a former age in order to lend specious justification for a present hollowness. Was it realism that stood in the way of meaning or was it the counterfeit of realism?

Increasingly over the past five years and more the poetic plays, so-called, some of them much admired by all sorts of critics, were surprisingly full of what in the university years ago was called "fine" writing. If one heard less of the creak of plot machinery there was more of the squeak of self-pity, the humming of the poetic poseur, the new romance of the arbitrary and the uncompleted. For one, I had seen enough of the "borrowings" of the set, the plot, the time-shifting methods, and the lighting of *Death of a Salesman* to have an intimate understanding of how a vessel could be emplied and still purveyed to the public as new wine. Was realism called futile now because it needed to illuminate an exact meaning behind it, a conviction that was no more with us? Confusion, the inability to describe one's sense of a thing, often issues in a genuine poetry of feeling, and feeling was now raised up as the highest good and the ultimate attainment in drama. I had known that kind of victory myself with *Salesman*; but was there not another realm even higher, where feeling took awareness more openly by the hand and both equally ruled and were illuminated? I had found a kind of self-awareness in the bloody book of Salem and had thought that since the natural, realistic surface of that society was one already immersed in the questions of meaning and the relations of men to God, to write a realistic play of that world was already to write in a style beyond contemporary realism. That more than one critic had found the play "cold" when I had never written more passionately was by this time an acceptable and inevitable detail of my fate, for, while it will never confess to it, our theater is trained—actors, directors, audience, and critics—to take to its heart anything that does not prick the mind and to suspect everything that does not supinely reassure.

If *Salesman* was written in a mood of friendly partnership with the audience, *The Crucible* reminded me that we had not yet come to terms. The latter play has been produced more often than any of the others, and more successfully the more time elapses from the headline "McCarthyism" which it was supposed to be "about." I believe that on the night of its opening, a time when the gale from the Right was blowing at its fullest fury, it inspired a part of its audience with an unsettling fear and partisanship which deflected the sight of the real and inner theme, which, again, was the handing over of conscience to another, be it woman, the state, or a terror, and the realization that with conscience goes the person, the soul immortal, and the "name." That there was not one mention of this process in any review, favorable or not, was the measure of my sense of defeat, and the impulse to separate, openly and without concealment, the action of the next play, *A View from the Bridge*, from its generalized significance. The engaged narrator, in short, appeared.

I had heard its story years before, quite as it appears in the play, and quite as complete, and from time to time there were efforts to break up its arc, to reshuffle its action so that I might be able to find what there was in it which drew me back to it again and again—until it became like a fact in my mind, an unbreakable series of actions that went to create a closed circle impervious to all interpretation. It was written experimentally not only as a form, but as an exercise in interpretation. I found in myself a passionate detachment toward its story as one does toward a spectacle in which one is not engaged but which holds a fascination deriving from its monolithic perfection. If this had happened, and if I could not forget it after so many years, there must be some meaning in it for me, and I could write what had happened, why it had happened, and to one side, as it were, express as much as I knew of my sense of its meaning for me. Yet I wished to leave the action intact so that the onlooker could seize the right to interpret it entirely for himself and to accept or reject my reading of its significance.

That reading was the awesomeness of a passion which, despite its contradicting the self-interest of the individual it inhabits, despite every kind of warning, despite even its destruction of the moral beliefs of the individual, proceeds to magnify its power over him until it destroys him.

I have not dealt with the business of production until now because it is a subject large enough for separate treatment, but at this point it is unavoidable. *A View from the Bridge* was relatively a failure in New York when it was first produced; a revised version, published in this volume, became a great success in London not long afterward. The present version is a better play, I think, but not that much better; and the sharp difference between the impressions each of the productions created has a bearing on many themes that have been treated here.

Certain objective factors ought to be mentioned first. In New York, the play was preceded by *A Memory of Two Mondays.* That one of its leading performers on opening night completely lost his bearings and played in a state bordering on terror destroyed at the outset any hope that something human might be communicated by this evening in the theater. *A Memory of Two Mondays* was dismissed so thoroughly that in one of the reviews, and one of the most important, it was not even mentioned as having been played. By the time *A View from the Bridge* came on, I suppose the critics were certain that they were witnessing an aberration, for there had been no suggestion of any theatrical authority in the first play's performance. It was too much to hope that the second play could retrieve what had been so completely dissipated by the first.

A Memory of Two Mondays is a pathetic comedy; a boy works among people for a couple of years, shares their troubles, their victories, their hopes, and when it is time for him to be on his way he expects some memorable moment, some sign from them that he has been among them, that he has touched them and been touched by them. In the sea of routine that swells around them they barely note his departure. It is a kind of letter to that sub-culture where the sinews of the economy are rooted, that darkest Africa of our society from whose interior only the sketchiest messages ever reach our literature or our stage. I wrote it, I suppose, in part out of a desire to relive a sort of reality where necessity was open and bare; I hoped to define for myself the value of hope, why it must arise, as well as the heroism of those who know, at least, how to endure its absence. Nothing in this book was written with greater love, and for myself I love nothing printed here better than this play.

Nevertheless, the fact that it was seen as something utterly sad and hopeless as a comment on life quite astonishes me still. After all, from this endless, timeless, will-less environment, a boy emerges who will not accept its defeat or its mood as final, and literally takes himself off on a quest for a higher gratification. I suppose we simply do not want to see how empty the lives of so many of us are even when the depiction is made hopefully and not at all in despair. The play speaks not of obsession but of rent and hunger and the need for a little poetry in life and is entirely out of date in those respects—so much so that many took it for granted it had been written a long time ago and exhumed.

It shares with *A View from the Bridge* the impulse to present rather than to represent an interpretation of reality. Incident and character are set forth with the barest naïveté, and action is stopped abruptly while commentary takes its place. The organic impulse behind *Salesman*, for instance, and *All My Sons* is avowedly split apart; for a moment I was striving not to make people forget they were in a theater, not to obliterate an awareness of form, not to forge a pretense of life, but to be abrupt, clear, and explicit in setting forth fact as fact and art as art so that the sea of theatrical sentiment, which is so easily let in to drown all shape, meaning, and perspective, might be held back and some hard outline of a human dilemma be allowed to rise and stand. *A Memory of Two Mondays* has a story but not a plot, because the life it reflects appears to me to strip people of alternatives and will beyond a close and tight periphery in which they may exercise a meager choice.

The contradiction in my attitude toward these two plays and what was hoped for them is indicated by the experience of the two productions of *A View from the Bridge*, the one a failure and "cold," the other quite the opposite. In writing this play originally I obeyed the impulse to indicate, to telegraph, so to speak, rather than to explore and exploit what at first had seemed to me the inevitable and therefore unnecessary emotional implications of the conflict. The Broadway production's setting followed the same impulse, as it should have, and revealed nothing more than a platform to contain the living room, the sea behind the house, and a Grecian-style pediment overhanging the abstract doorway to the house. The austerity of the production, in a word, expressed the reticence of the writing.

This version was in one act because it had seemed to me that the essentials of the dilemma were all that was required, for I wished it to be kept distant from the empathic flood which a realistic portrayal of the same tale and characters might unloose.

On seeing the production played several times I came to understand that, like the plays written previously, this one was expressing a very personal preoccupation and that it was not at all apart from my own psychological life. I discovered my own relationships to what quite suddenly appeared as, in some part, an analogy to situations in my life, a distant analogy but a heartening proof that under the reticence of its original method my own spirit was attempting to speak. So that when a new production was planned for London it was not possible to let the original go on as it was. Now there were additional things to be said which it became necessary to say because I had come to the awareness that this play had not, as I had almost believed before, been "given" to me from without, but that my life had created it.

Therefore, many decisive alterations, small in themselves but nonetheless great in their overall consequences, began to flow into the conception of the play. Perhaps the two most important were an altered attitude toward Eddie Carbone, the hero, and toward the two women in his life. I had originally conceived Eddie as a phenomenon, a rather awesome fact of existence, and I had kept a certain distance from involvement in his self-justifications. Consequently, he had appeared as a kind of biological sport, and to a degree a repelling figure not quite admissible into the human family. In revising the play it became possible to accept for myself the implication I had sought to make clear in the original version, which was that however one might dislike this man, who does all sorts of frightful things, he possesses or exemplifies the wondrous and humane fact that he too can be driven to what in the last analysis is a sacrifice of himself for his conception, however misguided, of right, dignity, and justice. In revising it I found it possible to move beyond contemplation of the man as a phenomenon into an acceptance for dramatic purposes of his aims themselves. Once this occurred the autonomous viewpoints of his wife and niece could be expressed more fully and, instead of remaining muted counterpoints to the march of Eddie's career, became involved forces pressing him forward or holding him back and eventually forming, in part, the nature of his disaster. The discovery of my own involvement in what I had written modified its original friezelike character and the play moved closer toward realism and called up the emphatic response of its audience.

The conception of the new production was in accordance with this new perspective. Peter Brook, the London director, designed a set which was more realistically detailed than the rather bare, if beautiful, New York background, and at the same time emphasized the environment of the neighborhood. Its central idea was to bring the people of the neighborhood into the foreground of the action. Two high wings closed to form the face of the house where Eddie lived, a brick tenement, and when opened revealed a basement living room. Overhead and at the sides and across the back were stairways, fire escapes, passages, quite like a whole neighborhood constructed vertically. The easier economics of the London theater made it possible to use many more neighbors than the three or four extras we could hire in New York, and there was a temperate but nevertheless full flow of strangers across the stage and up and down its stairways and passages. The maturing of Eddie's need to destroy Rodolpho was consequently seen in the context which could make it of real moment, for the betrayal achieves its true proportions as it flies in the face of the mores administered by Eddie's conscience—which is also the conscience of his friends, co-workers, and neighbors and not just his own autonomous creation. Thus his "oddness" came to disappear as he was seen in context, as a creature of his environment as well as an exception to it; and where originally there had been only a removed sense of terror at the oncoming catastrophe, now there was pity and, I think, the kind of wonder which it had been my aim to create in the first place. It was finally possible to mourn this man.

Perhaps more than any other production experience, this helped to resolve for me one important question of form and meaning. I warn, however, that like everything else said here this is highly personal, and even as I avow it I know that there are other paths and other standards which can issue in a worthwhile kind of dramatic experience. For myself, the theater is above all else an instrument of passion. However important considerations of style and form have been to me, they are only means, tools to pry up the well-worn, "inevitable" surfaces of experience behind which swarm the living thoughts and feelings whose expression is the essential purpose of art. I have stood squarely in conventional realism; I have tried to expand it with an imposition of various forms in order to speak more directly, even more abruptly and nakedly of what has moved me behind the visible façades of life. Critics have given me more praise than a writer can reasonably hope for, and more condemnation than one dares believe one has the power to survive. There are certain distillations which remain after the dross rises to the top and boils away, certain old and new commitments which, despite the heat applied to them and the turmoil that has threatened to sweep them away, nevertheless remain, some of them purified.

A play, I think, ought to make sense to common-sense people. I know what it is to have been rejected by them, even unfairly so, but the only challenge worth the effort is the widest one and the tallest one, which is the people themselves. It is their innate conservatism which, I think, is and ought to be the barrier to excess in experiment and the exploitation of the bizarre, even as it is the proper aim of drama to break down the limits of conventional unawareness and acceptance of outmoded and banal forms.

By whatever means it is accomplished, the prime business of a play is to arouse the passions of its audience so that by the route of passion may be opened up new relationships between a man and men, and between men and Man. Drama is akin to the other inventions of man in that it ought to help us to know more, and not merely to spend our feelings.

The ultimate justification for a genuine new form is the new and heightened consciousness it creates and makes possible—a consciousness of causation in the light of known but hitherto inexplicable effects.

Not only in the drama, but in sociology, psychology, psychiatry, and religion, the past half century has created an almost overwhelming documentation of man as a nearly passive creation of environment and family-created psychological drives. If only from the dramatic point of view, this dictum cannot be accepted as final and "realistic" any more than man's ultimate position can be accepted as his efficient use by state or corporate apparatus. It is no more "real," however, for drama to "liberate" itself from this vise by the route of romance and the spectacle of free will and a new heroic formula than it is "real" now to represent man's defeat as the ultimate implication of an overwhelming determinism.

Realism, heightened or conventional, is neither more nor less an artifice, a species of poetic symbolization, than any other form. It is merely more familiar in this age. If it is used as a covering of safety against the evaluation of life it must be overthrown, and for that reason above all the rest. But neither poetry nor liberation can come merely from a rearrangement of the lights or from leaving the skeletons of the flats exposed instead of covered by painted cloths; nor can it come merely from the masking of the human face or the transformation of speech into rhythmic verse, or from the expunging of common details of life's apparencies. A new poem on the stage is a new concept of relationships between the one and the many and the many and history, and to create it requires greater attention, not less, to the inexorable, common, pervasive conditions of existence in this time and this hour. Otherwise only a new self-indulgence is created, and it will be left behind, however poetic its surface.

A drama worthy of its time must first, knowingly or by instinctive means, recognize its major and most valuable traditions and where it has departed from them. Determinism, whether it is based on the iron necessities of economics or on psychoanalytic theory seen as a closed circle, is a contradiction of the idea of drama itself as drama has come down to us in its fullest developments. The idea of the hero, let alone the mere protagonist, is incompatible with a drama whose bounds are set in advance by the concept of an unbreakable trap. Nor is it merely that one wants arbitrarily to find a hero and a victory. The history of man is a ceaseless process of overthrowing one determinism to make way for another more faithful to life's changing relationships. And it is a process inconceivable without the existence of the will of man. His will is as much a fact as his defeat. Any determinism, even the most scientific, is only that stasis, that seemingly endless pause, before the application of man's will administering a new insight into causation.

The analogy to physics may not be out of place. The once-irreducible elements of matter, whose behavior was seen as fixed and remorseless, disintegrated under the controlled bombardment of atomic particles until so fine a perception as the scale of atomic weights appears as a relatively gross concept on the road to man's manipulation of the material world. More to the point: even as the paths, the powers, and the behavior of smaller and smaller elements and forces in nature are brought into the fields of measurement, we are faced with the dialectical irony that the act of measurement itself changes the particle being measured, so that we can know only what it is at the moment when it receives the impact of our rays, not what it was before it was struck. The idea of realism has become wedded to the idea that man is at best the sum of forces working upon him and of given psychological forces within him. Yet an innate value, an innate will, does in fact posit itself as real not alone because it is devoutly to be wished, but because, however closely he is measured and systematically accounted for, he is more than the sum of his stimuli and is unpredictable beyond a certain point. A drama, like a history, which stops at this point, the point of conditioning, is not reflecting reality. What is wanted, therefore, is not a poetry of escape from process and determinism, like that mood play which stops where feeling ends or that inverted romanticism which would mirror all the world in the sado-masochistic relationship. Nor will the heightening of the intensity of language alone yield the prize. A new poem will appear because a new balance has been struck which embraces both determinism and the paradox of will. If there is one unseen goal toward which every play in this book strives, it is that very discovery and its proof—that we are made and yet are more than what made us.

All My Sons

A Play in Three Acts

The Characters

Joe Keller   Doctor Jim Bayliss
Kate Keller   Sue Bayliss
Chris Keller   Frank Lubey
Ann Deever   Lydia Lubey
George Deever   Bert

Act One

*The back yard of the **Keller** home in the outskirts of an American town. August of our era.*

The stage is hedged on right and left by tall, closely planted poplars which lend the yard a secluded atmosphere. Upstage is filled with the back of the house and its open, unroofed porch which extends into the yard some six feet. The house is two stories high and has seven rooms. It would have cost perhaps fifteen thousand in the early twenties when it was built. Now it is nicely painted, looks tight and comfortable, and the yard is green with sod, here and there plants whose season is gone. At the right, beside the house, the entrance of the driveway can be seen, but the poplars cut off view of its continuation downstage. In the left corner, downstage, stands the four-foot-high stump of a slender apple tree whose upper trunk and branches lie toppled beside it, fruit still clinging to its branches.

Downstage right is a small, trellised arbor, shaped like a sea shell, with a decorative bulb hanging from its forward-curving roof. Garden chairs and a table are scattered about. A garbage pail on the ground next to the porch steps, a wire leaf-burner near it.

*On the rise: It is early Sunday morning. **Joe Keller** is sitting in the sun reading the want ads of the Sunday paper, the other sections of which lie neatly on the ground beside him. Behind his back, inside the arbor, **Doctor Jim Bayliss** is reading part of the paper at the table.*

***Keller** is nearing sixty. A heavy man of stolid mind and build, a business man these many years, but with the imprint of the machine-shop worker and boss still upon him. When he reads, when he speaks, when he listens, it is with the terrible comentration of the uneducated man for whom there is still wonder in many commonly known things, a man whose judgments must be dredged out of experience and a peasant-like common sense. A man among men.*

***Doctor Bayliss** is nearly forty. A wry self-controlled man, an easy talker, but with a wisp of sadness that clings even to his self-effacing humor.*

*At curtain, **Jim** is standing at left, staring at the broken tree. He taps a pipe on it, blows through the pipe, feels in his pockets for tobacco, then speaks.*

Jim   Where's your tobacco?

Keller   I think I left it on the table. (**Jim** *goes slowly to table on the arbor, finds a pouch, and sits there on the bench, filling his pipe.*) Gonna rain tonight.

Jim   Paper says so?

Keller   Yeah, right here.

Jim   Then it can't rain.

Frank Lubey *enters, through a small space between the poplars.* **Frank** *is thirty-two but balding. A pleasant, opinionated man, uncertain of himself, with a tendency toward peevishness when crossed, but always wanting it pleasant and neighborly. He rather saunters in, leisurely, nothing to do. He does not notice* **Jim** *in the arbor. On his greeting,* **Jim** *does not bother looking up.*

Frank   Hya.

Keller   Hello, Frank. What's doin'?

Frank   Nothin'. Walking off my breakfast. (*Looks up at the sky.*) That beautiful? Not a cloud.

Keller (*looking up*)   Yeah, nice.

Frank   Every Sunday ought to be like this.

Keller (*indicating the sections beside him*)   Want the paper?

Frank   What's the difference, it's all bad news. What's today's calamity?

Keller   I don't know, I don't read the news part any more. It's more interesting in the want ads.

Frank   Why, you trying to buy something?

Keller   No, I'm just interested. To see what people want, y'know?

For instance, here's a guy is lookin' for two Newfoundland dogs. Now what's he want with two Newfoundland dogs?

Frank   That is funny.

Keller   Here's another one. Wanted—old dictionaries. High prices paid. Now what's a man going to do with an old dictionary?

Frank   Why not? Probably a book collector.

Keller   You mean he'll make a living out of that?

Frank   Sure, there's a lot of them.

Keller (*shaking his head*)   All the kind of business goin' on. In my day, either you were a lawyer, or a doctor, or you worked in a shop. Now—

Frank   Well, I was going to be a forester once.

Keller   Well, that shows you; in my day, there was no such thing. (*Scanning the page, sweeping it with his hand:*) You look at a page like this you realize how ignorant you are. (*Softly, with wonder, as he scans page:*) Psss!

Frank (*noticing tree*)   Hey, what happened to your tree?

Keller   Ain't that awful? The wind must've got it last night. You heard the wind, didn't you?

Frank   Yeah, I got a mess in my yard, too. (*Goes to tree.*) What a pity. (*Turning to* **Keller***:*) What'd Kate say?

Keller   They're all asleep yet. I'm just waiting for her to see it.

Frank (*struck*)   You know?—it's funny.

Keller   What?

Frank   Larry was born in August. He'd been twenty-seven this month. And his tree blows down.

Keller (*touched*)   I'm surprised you remember his birthday, Frank. That's nice.

Frank   Well, I'm working on his horoscope.

Keller   How can you make him a horoscope? That's for the future, ain't it?

Frank   Well, what I'm doing is this, see. Larry was reported missing on November twenty-fifth, right?

Keller   Yeah?

Frank   Well, then, we assume that if he was killed it was on November twenty-fifth. Now, what Kate wants—

Keller   Oh, Kate asked you to make a horoscope?

Frank   Yeah, what she wants to find out is whether November twenty-fifth was a favorable day for Larry.

Keller   What is that, favorable day?

Frank   Well, a favorable day for a person is a fortunate day, according to his stars. In other words it would be practically impossible for him to have died on his favorable day.

Keller   Well, was that his favorable day?—November twenty-fifth?

Frank   That's what I'm working on to find out. It takes time! See, the point is, if November twenty-fifth was his favorable day, then it's completely possible he's alive somewhere, because—I mean it's possible. (*He notices* **Jim** *now.* **Jim** *is looking at him as though at an idiot. To* **Jim**—*with an uncertain laugh:*) I didn't even see you.

Keller (*to* **Jim**)   Is he talkin' sense?

Jim   Him? He's all right. He's just completely out of his mind, that's all.

Frank (*peeved*)   The trouble with you is, you don't *believe* in anything.

Jim   And your trouble is that you believe in *anything*. *You* didn't see my kid this morning, did you?

Frank   No.

Keller   Imagine? He walked off with his thermometer. Right out of his bag.

Jim (*getting up*)   What a problem. One look at a girl and he takes her temperature. (*Goes to driveway, looks upstage toward street.*)

Frank   That boy's going to be a real doctor; he's smart.

Jim   Over my dead body he'll be a doctor. A good beginning, too.

Frank   Why? It's an honorable profession.

Jim (*looking at him tiredly*)   Frank, will you stop talking like a civics book? (**Keller** *laughs.*)

Frank   Why, I saw a movie a couple of weeks ago, reminded me of you. There was a doctor in that picture—

Keller   Don Ameche!

Frank   I think it was, yeah. And he worked in his basement discovering things. That's what you ought to do; you could help humanity, instead of—

Jim   I would love to help humanity on a Warner Brothers salary.

Keller (*pointing at him, laughing*)   That's very good, Jim.

Jim (*looking toward house*)   Well, where's the beautiful girl was supposed to be here?

Frank (*excited*)   Annie came?

Keller   Sure, sleepin' upstairs. We picked her up on the one o'clock train last night. Wonderful thing. Girl leaves here, a scrawny kid. Couple of years go by, she's a regular woman. Hardly recognized her, and she was running in and out of this yard all her life. That was a very happy family used to live in your house, Jim.

Jim   Like to meet her. The block can use a pretty girl. In the whole neighborhood there's not a damned thing to look at. (**Sue**, **Jim**'s *wife, enters. She is rounding forty, an overweight woman who fears it. On seeing her* **Jim** *wryly adds:*) Except my wife, of course.

Sue (*in same spirit*)   Mrs. Adams is on the phone, you dog.

Jim (*to* **Keller**)   Such is the condition which prevails—(*Going to his wife:*) my love, my light.

Sue   Don't sniff around me. (*Pointing to their house:*) And give her a nasty answer. I can smell her perfume over the phone.

Jim   What's the matter with her now?

Sue   I don't know, dear. She sounds like she's in terrible pain—unless her mouth is full of candy.

Jim   Why don't you just tell her to lay down?

Sue   She enjoys it more when you tell her to lay down. And when are you going to see Mr. Hubbard?

Jim   My dear; Mr. Hubbard is not sick, and I have better things to do than to sit there and hold his hand.

Sue   It seems to me that for ten dollars you could hold his hand.

Jim (*to* **Keller**)   If your son wants to play golf tell him I'm ready. Or if he'd like to take a trip around the world for about thirty years. (*He exits.*)

Keller   Why do you needle him? He's a doctor, women are supposed to call him up.

Sue   All I said was Mrs. Adams is on the phone. Can I have some of your parsley?

Keller   Yeah, sure. (*She goes to parsley box and pulls some parsley.*) You were a nurse too long, Susie. You're too . . . too . . . realistic.

Sue (*laughing, pointing at him*)   Now you said it!

Lydia Lubey *enters. She is a robust, laughing girl of twenty-seven.*

Lydia   Frank, the toaster—(*Sees the others.*) Hya.

Keller   Hello!

Lydia (*to* **Frank**)   The toaster is off again.

Frank   Well, plug it in, I just fixed it.

Lydia (*kindly, but insistently*)   Please, dear, fix it back like it was before.

Frank   I don't know why you can't learn to turn on a simple thing like a toaster! (*He exits.*)

Sue (*laughing*)   Thomas Edison.

Lydia (*apologetically*)   He's really very handy. (*She sees broken tree.*) Oh, did the wind get your tree?

Keller   Yeah, last night.

Lydia   Oh, what a pity. Annie get in?

Keller   She'll be down soon. Wait'll you meet her, Sue, she's a knockout.

Sue   I should've been a man. People are always introducing me to beautiful women. (*To* **Joe***:*) Tell her to come over later: I imagine she'd like to see what we did with her house. And thanks. (*She exits.*)

Lydia   Is she still unhappy, Joe?

Keller   Annie? I don't suppose she goes around dancing on her toes, but she seems to be over it.

Lydia   She going to get married? Is there anybody—?

Keller   I suppose—say, it's a couple years already. She can't mourn a boy forever.

Lydia   It's so strange—Annie's here and not even married. And I've got three babies. I always thought it'd be the other way around.

Keller   Well, that's what a war does. I had two sons, now I got one. It changed all the tallies. In my day when you had sons it was an honor. Today a doctor could make a million dollars if he could figure out a way to bring a boy into the world without a trigger finger.

Lydia   You know, I was just reading—

Enter **Chris Keller** *from house, stands in doorway.*

Lydia   Hya, Chris.

Frank *shouts from offstage.*

Frank   Lydia, come in here! If you want the toaster to work don't plug in the malted mixer.

Lydia (*embarrassed, laughing*)   Did I?

Frank   And the next time I fix something don't tell me I'm crazy! Now come in here!

Lydia (*to* **Keller**)   I'll never hear the end of this one.

Keller (*calling to* **Frank**)   So what's the difference? Instead of toast have a malted!

Lydia   Sh! sh! (*She exits, laughing.*)

Chris *watches her off. He is thirty-two; like his father, solidly built, a listener. A man capable of immense affection and loyalty. He has a cup of coffee in one hand, part of a doughnut in the other.*

Keller   You want the paper?

Chris   That's all right, just the book section. (*He bends down and pulls out part of paper on porch floor.*)

Keller   You're always reading the book section and you never buy a book.

Chris (*coming down to settee*)   I like to keep abreast of my ignorance. (*He sits on settee.*)

Keller   What is that, every week a new book comes out?

Chris   Lot of new books.

Keller   All different.

Chris   All different.

Keller *shakes his head, puts knife down on bench, takes oil-stone up to the cabinet.*

Keller   Psss! Annie up yet?

Chris   Mother's giving her breakfast in the dining room.

Keller (*looking at broken tree*)   See what happened to the tree?

Chris (*without looking up*)   Yeah.

Keller   What's Mother going to say?

Bert *runs on from driveway. He is about eight. He jumps on stool, then on* **Keller***'s back.*

Bert   You're finally up.

Keller (*swinging him around and putting him down*)   Ha! Bert's here! Where's Tommy? He's got his father's thermometer again.

Bert   He's taking a reading.

Chris   What!

Bert   But it's only oral.

Keller   Oh, well, there's no harm in oral. So what's new this morning, Bert?

Bert   Nothin'. (*He goes to broken tree, walks around it.*)

Keller   Then you couldn't've made a complete inspection of the block. In the beginning, when I first made you a policeman you used to come in every morning with something new. Now, nothin's ever new.

Bert   Except some kids from Thirtieth Street. They started kicking a can down the block, and I made them go away because you were sleeping.

Keller   Now you're talkin', Bert. Now you're on the ball. First thing you know I'm liable to make you a detective.

Bert (*pulling him down by the lapel and whispering in his ear*)   Can I see the jail now?

Keller   Seein' the jail ain't allowed, Bert. You know that.

Bert   Aw, I betcha there isn't even a jail. I don't see any bars on the cellar windows.

Keller   Bert, on my word of honor there's a jail in the basement. I showed you my gun, didn't I?

Bert   But that's a hunting gun.

Keller   That's an arresting gun!

Bert   Then why don't you ever arrest anybody? Tommy said another dirty word to Doris yesterday, and you didn't even demote him.

Keller *chuckles and winks at* **Chris**, *who is enjoying all this.*

Keller   Yeah, that's a dangerous character, that Tommy. (*Beckons him closer.*) What word does he say?

Bert (*backing away quickly in great embarrassment*)   Oh, I can't say that.

Keller (*grabbing him by the shirt and pulling him back*)   Well, gimme an idea.

Bert   I can't. It's not a nice word.

Keller   Just whisper it in my ear. I'll close my eyes. Maybe I won't even hear it.

Bert, *on tiptoe, puts his lips to* **Keller**'s *ear, then in unbearable embarrassment steps back.*

Bert   I can't, Mr. Keller.

Chris (*laughing*)   Don't make him do that.

Keller   Okay, Bert. I take your word. Now go out, and keep both eyes peeled.

Bert (*interested*)   For what?

Keller   For what! Bert, the whole neighborhood is depending on you. A policeman don't ask questions. Now peel them eyes!

Bert (*mystified, but willing*)   Okay. (*He runs off stage back of arbor.*)

Keller (*calling after him*)   And mum's the word, Bert.

Bert *stops and sticks his head through the arbor.*

Bert   About what?

Keller   Just in general. Be v-e-r-y careful.

Bert (*nodding in bewilderment*)   Okay. (*He exits.*)

Keller (*laughing*)   I got all the kids crazy!

Chris   One of these days, they'll all come in here and beat your brains out.

Keller   What's she going to say? Maybe we ought to tell her before she sees it.

Chris   She saw it.

Keller   How could she see it? I was the first one up. She was still in bed.

Chris   She was out here when it broke.

Keller   When?

Chris   About four this morning. (*Indicating window above them:*) I heard it cracking and I woke up and looked out. She was standing right here when it cracked.

Keller   What was she doing out here four in the morning?

Chris   I don't know. When it cracked she ran back into the house and cried in the kitchen.

Keller   Did you talk to her?

Chris   No, I—I figured the best thing was to leave her alone.

Pause.

Keller (*deeply touched*)   She cried hard?

Chris   I could hear her right through the floor of my room.

Keller (*after slight pause*)   What was she doing out here at that hour? (**Chris** *silent. With an undertone of anger showing:*) She's dreaming about him again. She's walking around at night.

Chris   I guess she is.

Keller   She's getting just like after he died. (*Slight pause.*) What's the meaning of that?

Chris   I don't know the meaning of it. (*Slight pause.*) But I know one thing, Dad. We've made a terrible mistake with Mother.

Keller   What?

Chris   Being dishonest with her. That kind of thing always pays off, and now it's paying off.

Keller   What do you mean, dishonest?

Chris   You know Larry's not coming back and I know it. Why do we allow her to go on thinking that we believe with her?

Keller   What do you want to do, argue with her?

Chris   I don't want to argue with her, but it's time she realized that nobody believes Larry is alive any more. (**Keller** *simply moves away,* *thinking, looking at the ground.*) Why shouldn't she dream of him, walk the nights waiting for him? Do we contradict her? Do we say straight out that we have no hope any more? That we haven't had any hope for years now?

Keller (*frightened at the thought*)   You can't say that to her.

Chris   We've got to say it to her.

Keller   How're you going to prove it? Can you prove it?

Chris   For God's sake, three years! Nobody comes back after three years. It's insane.

Keller   To you it is, and to me. But not to her. You can talk yourself blue in the face, but there's no body and there's no grave, so where are you?

Chris   Sit down, Dad. I want to talk to you.

Keller *looks at him searchingly a moment.*

Keller   The trouble is the goddam newspapers. Every month some boy turns up from nowhere, so the next one is going to be Larry, so—

Chris   All right, all right, listen to me. (*Slight pause.* **Keller** *sits on settee.*) You know why I asked Annie here, don't you?

Keller (*he knows, but—*)   Why?

Chris   You know.

Keller   Well, I got an idea, but—What's the story?

Chris   I'm going to ask her to marry me. (*Slight pause.*)

Keller *nods.*

Keller   Well, that's only your business, Chris.

Chris   You know it's not only my business.

Keller   What do you want me to do? You're old enough to know your own mind.

Chris (*asking, annoyed*)   Then it's all right, I'll go ahead with it?

Keller   Well, you want to be sure Mother isn't going to—

Chris   Then it isn't just my business.

Keller   I'm just sayin'—

Chris   Sometimes you infuriate me, you know that? Isn't it your business, too, if I tell this to Mother and she throws a fit about it? You have such a talent for ignoring things.

Keller   I ignore what I gotta ignore. The girl is Larry's girl.

Chris   She's not Larry's girl.

Keller   From Mother's point of view he is not dead and you have no right to take his girl. (*Slight pause.*) Now you can go on from there if you know where to go, but I'm tellin' you I don't know where to go. See? I don't know. Now what can I do for you?

Chris   I don't know why it is, but every time I reach out for something I want, I have to pull back because other people will suffer. My whole bloody life, time after time after time.

Keller   You're a considerate fella, there's nothing wrong in that.

Chris   To hell with that.

Keller   Did you ask Annie yet?

Chris   I wanted to get this settled first.

Keller   How do you know she'll marry you? Maybe she feels the same way Mother does?

Chris   Well, if she does, then that's the end of it. From her letters I think she's forgotten him. I'll find out. And then we'll thrash it out with Mother? Right? Dad, don't avoid me.

Keller   The trouble is, you don't see enough women. You never did.

Chris   So what? I'm not fast with women.

Keller   I don't see why it has to be Annie.

Chris   Because it is.

Keller   That's a good answer, but it don't answer anything. You haven't seen her since you went to war. It's five years.

Chris   I can't help it. I know her best. I was brought up next door to her. These years when I think of someone for my wife, I think of Annie. What do you want, a diagram?

Keller   I don't want a diagram . . . I—I'm—She thinks he's coming back, Chris. You marry that girl and you're pronouncing him dead. Now what's going to happen to Mother? Do you know? I don't! (*Pause.*)

Chris   All right, then, Dad.

Keller (*thinking* **Chris** *has retreated*)   Give it some more thought.

Chris   I've given it three years of thought. I'd hoped that if I waited, Mother would forget Larry and then we'd have a regular wedding and everything happy. But if that can't happen here, then I'll have to get out.

Keller   What the hell is *this*?

Chris   I'll get out. I'll get married and live some place else. Maybe in New York.

Keller   Are you crazy?

Chris   I've been a good son too long, a good sucker. I'm through with it.

Keller   You've got a business here, what the hell is this?

Chris   The business! The business doesn't inspire me.

Keller   Must you be inspired?

Chris   Yes. I like it an hour a day. If I have to grub for money all day long at least at evening I want it beautiful. I want a family, I want some kids, I want to build something I can give myself to. Annie is in the middle of that. Now . . . where do I find it?

Keller   You mean—(*Goes to him.*) Tell me something, you mean you'd leave the business?

Chris   Yes. On this I would.

Keller (*after a pause*)   Well . . . you don't want to think like that.

Chris   Then help me stay here.

Keller   All right, but—but don't think like that. Because what the hell did I work for? That's only for you, Chris, the whole shootin' match is for you!

Chris   I know that, Dad. Just you help me stay here.

Keller (*putting a fist up to* **Chris**'s *jaw*)   But don't think that way, you hear me?

Chris   I am thinking that way.

Keller (*lowering his hand*)   I don't understand you, do I?

Chris   No, you don't. I'm a pretty tough guy.

Keller   Yeah. I can see that.

Mother *appears on porch. She is in her early fifties, a woman of uncontrolled inspirations and an overwhelming capacity for love.*

Mother   Joe?

Chris (*going toward porch*)   Hello, Mom.

Mother (*indicating house behind her; to* **Keller**)   Did you take a bag from under the sink?

Keller   Yeah, I put it in the pail.

Mother   Well, get it out of the pail. That's my potatoes.

Chris *bursts out laughing—goes up into alley.*

Keller (*laughing*)   I thought it was garbage.

Mother   Will you do me a favor, Joe? Don't be helpful.

Keller   I can afford another bag of potatoes.

Mother   Minnie scoured that pail in boiling water last night. It's cleaner than your teeth.

Keller   And I don't understand why, after I worked forty years and I got a maid, why I have to take out the garbage.

Mother   If you would make up your mind that every bag in the kitchen isn't full of garbage you wouldn't be throwing out my vegetables. Last time it was the onions.

Chris *comes on, hands her bag.*

Keller   I don't like garbage in the house.

Mother   Then don't eat. (*She goes into the kitchen with bag.*)

Chris   That settles you for today.

Keller   Yeah, I'm in last place again. I don't know, once upon a time I used to think that when I got money again I would have a maid and my wife would take it easy. Now I got money, and I got a maid, and my wife is workin' for the maid. (*He sits in one of the chairs.*)

Mother *comes out on last line. She carries a pot of string beans.*

Mother   It's her day off, what are you crabbing about?

Chris (*to* **Mother**)   Isn't Annie finished eating?

Mother (*looking around preoccupiedly at yard*)   She'll be right out. (*Moves.*) That wind did some job on this place. (*Of the tree:*) So much for that, thank God.

Keller (*indicating chair beside him*)   Sit down, take it easy.

Mother (*pressing her hand to top of her head*)   I've got such a funny pain on the top of my head.

Chris   Can I get you an aspirin?

Mother *picks a few petals off ground, stands there smelling them in her hand, then sprinkles them over plants.*

Mother   No more roses. It's so funny . . . everything decides to happen at the same time. This month is his birthday; his tree blows down, Annie comes. Everything that happened seems to be coming back. I was just down the cellar, and what do I stumble over? His baseball glove. I haven't seen it in a century.

Chris   Don't you think Annie looks well?

Mother   Fine. There's no question about it. She's a beauty . . . I still don't know what brought her here. Not that I'm not glad to see her, but—

Chris   I just thought we'd all like to see each other again. (**Mother** *just looks at him, nodding ever so slightly—almost as though admitting something.*) And I wanted to see her myself.

Mother (*as her nods halt, to* **Keller**)   The only thing is I think her nose got longer. But I'll always love that girl. She's one that didn't jump into bed with somebody else as soon as it happened with her fella.

Keller (*as though that were impossible for* **Annie**)   Oh, what're you—?

Mother   Never mind. Most of them didn't wait till the telegrams were opened. I'm just glad she came, so you can see I'm not (*completely*) out of my mind. (*Sits, and rapidly breaks string beans in the pot.*)

Chris   Just because she isn't married doesn't mean she's been mourning Larry.

Mother (*with an undercurrent of observation*)   Why then isn't she?

Chris (*a little flustered*)   Well . . . it could've been any number of things.

Mother (*directly at him*)   Like what, for instance?

Chris (*embarrassed, but standing his ground*)   I don't know. Whatever it is. Can I get you an aspirin?

Mother *puts her hand to her head. She gets up and goes aimlessly toward the trees on rising.*

Mother   It's not like a headache.

Keller   You don't sleep, that's why. She's wearing out more bedroom slippers than shoes.

Mother   I had a terrible night. (*She stops moving.*) I never had a night like that.

Chris (*looking at* **Keller**)   What was it, Mom? Did you dream?

Mother   More, more than a dream.

Chris (*hesitantly*)   About Larry?

Mother   I was fast asleep, and—(*Raising her arm over the audience:*) Remember the way he used to fly low past the house when he was in training? When we used to see his face in the cockpit going by? That's the way I saw him. Only high up. Way, way up, where the clouds are. He was so real I could reach out and touch him. And suddenly he started to fall. And crying, crying to me . . . Mom, Mom! I could hear him like he was in the room. Mom! . . . it was his voice! If I could touch him I knew I could stop him, if I could only—(*Breaks off, allowing her outstretched hand to fall.*) I woke up and it was so funny—The wind . . . it was like the roaring of his engine. I came out here . . . I must've still been half asleep. I could hear that roaring like he was going by. The tree snapped right in front of me—and I like—came awake. (*She is looking at tree. She suddenly realizes something, turns with a reprimanding finger shaking slightly at* **Keller**.) See? We should never have planted that tree. I said so in the first place; it was too soon to plant a tree for him.

Chris (*alarmed*)   Too soon!

Mother (*angering*)   We rushed into it. Everybody was in such a hurry to bury him. I *said* not to plant it yet. (*To* **Keller***:*) I *told* you to—!

Chris   Mother, Mother! (*She looks into his face.*) The wind blew it down. What significance has that got? What are you talking about? Mother, please . . . Don't go through it all again, will you? It's no good, it doesn't accomplish anything. I've been thinking, y'know?—maybe we ought to put our minds to forgetting him?

Mother   That's the third time you've said that this week.

Chris   Because it's not right; we never took up our lives again. We're like at a railroad station waiting for a train that never comes in.

Mother (*pressing top of her head*)   Get me an aspirin, heh?

Chris   Sure, and let's break out of this, heh, Mom? I thought the four of us might go out to dinner a couple of nights, maybe go dancing out at the shore.

Mother   Fine. (*To* **Keller**:) We can do it tonight.

Keller   Swell with me!

Chris   Sure, let's have some fun. (*To* **Mother**:) You'll start with this aspirin. (*He goes up and into house with new spirit. Her smile vanishes.*)

Mother (*with an accusing undertone*)   Why did he invite her here?

Keller   Why does that bother you?

Mother   She's been in New York three and a half years, why all of a sudden—?

Keller   Well, maybe—maybe he just wanted to see her.

Mother   Nobody comes seven hundred miles "just to see."

Keller   What do you mean? He lived next door to the girl all his life, why shouldn't he want to see her again? (**Mother** *looks at him critically.*) Don't look at me like that, he didn't tell me any more than he told you.

Mother (*a warning and a question*)   He's not going to marry her.

Keller   How do you know he's even thinking of it?

Mother   It's got that about it.

Keller (*sharply watching her reaction*)   Well? So what?

Mother (*alarmed*)   What's going on here, Joe?

Keller   Now listen, kid—

Mother (*avoiding contact with him*)   She's not his girl, Joe; she knows she's not.

Keller   You can't read her mind.

Mother   Then why is she still single? New York is full of men, why isn't she married? (*Pause.*) Probably a hundred people told her she's foolish, but she's waited.

Keller   How do you know why she waited?

Mother   She knows what I know, that's why. She's faithful as a rock. In my worst moments, I think of her waiting, and I know again that I'm right.

Keller   Look, it's a nice day. What are we arguing for?

Mother (*warningly*)   Nobody in this house dast take her faith away, Joe. Strangers might. But not his father, not his brother.

Keller (*exasperated*)   What do you want me to do? What do you want?

Mother   I want you to act like he's coming back. Both of you. Don't think I haven't noticed you since Chris invited her. I won't stand for any nonsense.

Keller   But, Kate—

Mother   Because if he's not coming back, then I'll kill myself! Laugh. Laugh at me. (*She points to tree.*) But why did that happen the very night she came back? Laugh, but there are meanings in such things. She goes to sleep in his room and his memorial breaks in pieces. Look at it; look. (*She sits on bench.*) Joe—

Keller   Calm yourself.

Mother   Believe with me, Joe. I can't stand all alone.

Keller   Calm yourself.

Mother   Only last week a man turned up in Detroit, missing longer than Larry. You read it yourself.

Keller   All right, all right, calm yourself.

Mother   You above all have got to believe, you—

Keller (*rising*)   Why me above all?

Mother   Just don't stop believing.

Keller   What does that mean, me above all?

Bert *comes rushing on.*

Bert   Mr. Keller! Say, Mr. Keller . . . (*Pointing up driveway:*) Tommy just said it again!

Keller (*not remembering any of it*)   Said what? Who?

Bert   The dirty word.

Keller   Oh. Well—

Bert   Gee, aren't you going to arrest him? I warned him.

Mother (*with suddenness*)   Stop that, Bert. Go home. (**Bert** *backs up, as she advances.*) There's no jail here.

Keller (*as though to say, "Oh-what-the-hell-let-him-believe-there-is"*)   Kate—

Mother (*turning on **Keller** furiously*)   There's no jail here! I want you to stop that jail business! (*He turns, shamed, but peeved.*)

Bert (*past her to **Keller***)   He's right across the street.

Mother   Go home, Bert. (**Bert** *turns around and goes up drive-way. She is shaken. Her speech is bitten off, extremely urgent.*) I want you to stop that, Joe. That whole jail business!

Keller (*alarmed, therefore angered*)   Look at you, look at you shaking.

Mother (*trying to control herself, moving about clasping her hands*)   I can't help it.

Keller   What have I got to hide? What the hell is the matter with you, Kate?

Mother   I didn't say you had anything to hide, I'm just telling you to stop it! Now stop it! (*As **Ann** and **Chris** appear on porch. **Ann** is twenty-six, gentle but despite herself capable of holding fast to what she knows. **Chris** opens door for her.*)

Ann   Hya, Joe! (*She leads off a general laugh that is not self-conscious because they know one another too well.*)

Chris (*bringing **Ann** down, with an outstretched, chivalric arm*)   Take a breath of that air, kid. You never get air like that in New York.

Mother (*genuinely overcome with it*)   Annie, where did you get that dress!

Ann   I couldn't resist. I'm taking it right off before I ruin it. (*Swings around.*) How's that for three weeks' salary?

Mother (*to **Keller***)   Isn't she the most—? (*To **Ann**:*) It's gorgeous, simply gar—

Chris (*to **Mother***)   No kidding, now, isn't she the prettiest gal you ever saw?

Mother (*caught short by his obvious admiration, she finds herself reaching out for a glass of water and aspirin in his hand, and—*)   You gained a little weight, didn't you, darling? (*She gulps pill and drinks.*)

Ann   It comes and goes.

Keller   Look how nice her legs turned out!

Ann (*as she runs to fence*)   Boy, the poplars got thick, didn't they?

Keller *moves to settee and sits.*

Keller   Well, it's three years, Annie. We're gettin' old, kid.

Mother   How does Mom like New York? (**Ann** *keeps looking through trees.*)

Ann (*a little hurt*)   Why'd they take our hammock away?

Keller   Oh, no, it broke. Couple of years ago.

Mother   What broke? He had one of his light lunches and flopped into it.

Ann (*laughs and turns back toward* **Jim***'s yard*)   Oh, excuse me!

Jim *has come to fence and is looking over it. He is smoking a cigar. As she cries out, he comes on around on stage.*

Jim   How do you do. (*To* **Chris***:*) She looks very intelligent!

Chris   Ann, this is Jim—Doctor Bayliss.

Ann (*shaking* **Jim***'s hand*)   Oh, sure, he writes a lot about you.

Jim   Don't you believe it. He likes everybody. In the battalion he was known as Mother McKeller.

Ann   I can believe it. You know—? (*To* **Mother***:*) It's so strange seeing him come out of that yard. (*To* **Chris***:*) I guess I never grew up. It almost seems that Mom and Pop are in there now. And you and my brother doing algebra, and Larry trying to copy my homework. Gosh, those dear dead days beyond recall.

Jim   Well, I hope that doesn't mean you want me to move out?

Sue (*calling from offstage*)   Jim, come in here! Mr. Hubbard is on the phone!

Jim   I told you I don't want—

Sue (*commandingly sweet*)   Please, dear! Please!

Jim (*resigned*)   All right, Susie. (*Trailing off:*) All right, all right . . . (*To* **Ann***:*) I've only met you, Ann, but if I may offer you a piece of advice—When you marry, never—even in your mind—never count your husband's money.

Sue (*from offstage*)   Jim?

Jim   At once! (*Turns and goes off.*) At once. (*He exits.*)

Mother (**Ann** *is looking at her. She speaks meaningfully*)   I told her to take up the guitar. It'd be a common interest for them. (*They laugh.*) Well, he loves the guitar!

Ann, *as though to overcome* **Mother**, *becomes suddenly lively, crosses to* **Keller** *on settee, sits on his lap.*

Ann   Let's eat at the shore tonight! Raise some hell around here, like we used to before Larry went!

Mother (*emotionally*)   You think of him! You see? (*Triumphantly.*) She thinks of him!

Ann (*with an uncomprehending smile*)   What do you mean, Kate?

Mother   Nothing. Just that you—remember him, he's in your thoughts.

Ann   That's a funny thing to say; how could I help remembering him?

Mother (*it is drawing to a head the wrong way for her; she starts anew. She rises and comes to* **Ann**)   Did you hang up your things?

Ann   Yeah . . . (*To* **Chris***:*) Say, you've sure gone in for clothes. I could hardly find room in the closet.

Mother   No, don't you remember? That's Larry's room.

Ann   You mean . . . they're Larry's?

Mother   Didn't you recognize them?

Ann (*slowly rising, a little embarrassed*)   Well, it never occurred to me that you'd—I mean the shoes are all shined.

Mother   Yes, dear. (*Slight pause.* **Ann** *can't stop staring at her.* **Mother** *breaks it by speaking with the relish of gossip, putting her arm around* **Ann** *and walking with her.*) For so long I've been aching for a nice conversation with you, Annie. Tell me something.

Ann   What?

Mother   I don't know. Something nice.

Chris (*wryly*)   She means do you go out much?

Mother   Oh, shut up.

Keller   And are any of them serious?

Mother (*laughing, sits in her chair*)   Why don't you both choke?

Keller   Annie, you can't go into a restaurant with that woman any more. In five minutes thirty-nine strange people are sitting at the table telling her their life story.

Mother   If I can't ask Annie a personal question—

Keller   Askin' is all right, but don't beat her over the head. You're beatin' her, you're beatin' her. (*They are laughing.*)

Ann *takes pan of beans off stool, puts them on floor under chair and sits.*

Ann (*to* **Mother**)   Don't let them bulldoze you. Ask me anything you like. What do you want to know, Kate? Come on, let's gossip.

Mother (*to* **Chris** *and* **Keller**)   She's the only one is got any sense. (*To* **Ann**:) Your mother—she's not getting a divorce, heh?

Ann   No, she's calmed down about it now. I think when he gets out they'll probably live together. In New York, of course.

Mother   That's fine. Because your father is still—I mean he's a decent man after all is said and done.

Ann   I don't care. She can take him back if she likes.

Mother   And you? You—(*Shakes her head negatively*)—go out much? (*Slight pause.*)

Ann (*delicately*)   You mean am I still waiting for him?

Mother   Well, no. I don't expect you to wait for him but—

Ann (*kindly*)   But that's what you mean, isn't it?

Mother   Well . . . yes.

Ann   Well, I'm not, Kate.

Mother (*faintly*)   You're not?

Ann   Isn't it ridiculous? You don't really imagine he's—?

Mother   I know, dear, but don't say it's ridiculous, because the papers were full of it; I don't know about New York, but there was half a page about a man missing even longer than Larry, and he turned up from Burma.

Chris (*coming to* **Ann**)   He couldn't have wanted to come home very badly, Mom.

Mother   Don't be so smart.

Chris   You can have a helluva time in Burma.

Ann (*rises and swings around in back of* **Chris**)   So I've heard.

Chris   Mother, I'll bet you money that you're the only woman in the country who after three years is still—

Mother   You're sure?

Chris   Yes, I am.

Mother   Well, if you're sure then you're sure. (*She turns her head away an instant.*) They don't say it on the radio but I'm sure that in the dark at night they're still waiting for their sons.

Chris   Mother, you're absolutely—

Mother (*waving him off*)   Don't be so damned smart! Now stop it! (*Slight pause.*) There are just a few things you *don't* know. All of you. And I'll tell you one of them, Annie. Deep, deep in your heart you've always been waiting for him.

Ann (*resolutely*)   No, Kate.

Mother (*with increasing demand*)   But deep in your heart, Annie!

Chris   She ought to know, shouldn't she?

Mother   Don't let them tell you what to think. Listen to your heart. Only your heart.

Ann   Why does your heart tell you he's alive?

Mother   Because he has to be.

Ann   But why, Kate?

Mother (*going to her*)   Because certain things have to be, and certain things can never be. Like the sun has to rise, it has to be. That's why there's God. Otherwise anything could happen. But there's God, so certain things can never happen. I would know, Annie—just like I knew the day he (*indicates* **Chris**) went into that terrible battle. Did he write me? Was it in the papers? No, but that morning I couldn't raise my head off the pillow. Ask Joe. Suddenly, I knew. I knew! And he was nearly killed that day. Ann, you *know* I'm right!

Ann *stands there in silence, then turns trembling, going upstage.*

Ann   No, Kate.

Mother   I have to have some tea.

Frank *appears, carrying ladder.*

Frank   Annie! (*Coming down:*) How are you, gee whiz!

Ann (*taking his hand*)   Why, Frank, you're losing your hair.

Keller   He's got responsibility.

Frank   Gee whiz!

Keller   Without Frank the stars wouldn't know when to come out.

Frank (*laughs; to* **Ann**)   You look more womanly. You've matured. You—

Keller   Take it easy, Frank, you're a married man.

Ann (*as they laugh*)   You still haberdashering?

Frank   Why not? Maybe I too can get to be president. How's your brother? Got his degree, I hear.

Ann   Oh, George has his own office now!

Frank   Don't say! (*Funereally:*) And your dad? Is he—?

Ann (*abruptly*)   Fine. I'll be in to see Lydia.

Frank (*sympathetically*)   How about it, does Dad expect a parole soon?

Ann (*with growing ill-ease*)   I really don't know, I—

Frank (*staunchly defending her father for her sake*)   I mean because I feel, y'know, that if an intelligent man like your father is put in prison, there ought to be a law that says either you execute him, or let him go after a year.

Chris (*interrupting*)   Want a hand with that ladder, Frank?

Frank (*taking cue*)   That's all right, I'll—(*Picks up ladder.*) I'll finish the horoscope tonight, Kate. (*Embarrassed:*) See you later, Ann, you look wonderful. (*He exits. They look at* **Ann**.)

Ann (*to* **Chris**, *as she sits slowly on stool*)   Haven't they stopped talking about Dad?

Chris (*comes down and sits on arm of chair*)   Nobody talks about him any more.

Keller (*rises and comes to her*)   Gone and forgotten, kid.

Ann   Tell me. Because I don't want to meet anybody on the block if they're going to—

Chris   I don't want you to worry about it.

Ann (*to* **Keller**)   Do they still remember the case, Joe? Do they talk about you?

Keller   The only one still talks about it is my wife.

Mother   That's because you keep on playing policeman with the kids. All their parents hear out of you is jail, jail, jail.

Keller   Actually what happened was that when I got home from the penitentiary the kids got very interested in me. You know kids. I was (laughs) like the expert on the jail situation. And as time passed they got it confused and . . . I ended up a detective.

Laughs.

Mother   Except that *they* didn't get it confused. (*To* **Ann**.) He hands out police badges from the Post Toasties boxes. (*They laugh.*)

Ann *rises and comes to* **Keller***, putting her arm around his shoulder.*

Ann (*wondrously at them, happy*)   Gosh, it's wonderful to hear you laughing about it.

Chris   Why, what'd you expect?

Ann   The last thing I remember on this block was one word— "Murderers!" Remember that, Kate?—Mrs. Hammond standing in front of our house and yelling that word? She's still around, I suppose?

Mother   They're all still around.

Keller   Don't listen to her. Every Saturday night the whole gang is playin' poker in this arbor. All the ones who yelled murderer takin' my money now.

Mother   Don't, Joe; she's a sensitive girl, don't fool her. (*To* **Ann**.) They still remember about Dad. It's different with him. (*Indicates* **Joe**.) He was exonerated, your father's still there. That's why I wasn't so enthusiastic about your coming. Honestly, I know how sensitive you are, and I told Chris, I said—

Keller   Listen, you do like I did and you'll be all right. The day I come home, I got out of my car—but not in front of the house . . . on the corner. You should've been here, Annie, and you too, Chris; you'd-a seen something. Everybody knew I was getting out that day; the porches were loaded. Picture it now; none of them believed I was innocent. The story was, I pulled a fast one getting myself exonerated. So I get out of my car, and I walk down the street. But very slow. And with a smile. The beast! I was the beast; the guy who sold cracked cylinder heads to the Army Air Force; the guy who made twenty-one P-40s crash in Australia. Kid, walkin' down the street that day I was guilty as hell. Except I wasn't, and there was a court paper in my pocket to prove I wasn't, and I walked . . . past . . . the porches. Result? Fourteen months later I had one of the best shops in the state again, a respected man again; bigger than ever.

Chris (*with admiration*)   Joe McGuts.

Keller (*now with great force*)   That's the only way you lick 'em is guts! (*To* **Ann**:) The worst thing you did was to move away from here. You made it tough for your father when he gets out. That's why I tell you, I like to see him move back right on this block.

Mother (*pained*)   How could they move back?

Keller   It ain't gonna end *till* they move back! (*To* **Ann**:) Till people play cards with him again, and talk with him, and smile with him—you play cards with a man you know he can't be a murderer. And the next time you write him I like you to tell him just what I said. (**Ann** *simply stares at him.*) You hear me?

Ann (*surprised*)   Don't you hold anything against him?

Keller   Annie, I never believed in crucifying people.

Ann (*mystified*)   But he was your partner, he dragged you through the mud.

Keller   Well, he ain't my sweetheart, but you gotta forgive, don't you?

Ann   You, either, Kate? Don't you feel any—?

Keller (*to* **Ann**)   The next time you write Dad—

Ann   I don't write him.

Keller (*struck*)   Well, every now and then you—

Ann (*a little shamed, but determined*)   No, I've *never* written to him. Neither has my brother. (*To* **Chris**:) Say, do you feel this way, too?

Chris   He murdered twenty-one pilots.

Keller   What the hell kinda talk is that?

Mother   That's not a thing to say about a man.

Ann   What else can you say? When they took him away I followed him, went to him every visiting day. I was crying all the time. Until the news came about Larry. Then I realized. It's wrong to pity a man like that. Father or no father, there's only one way to look at him. He knowingly shipped out parts that would crash an airplane. And how do you know Larry wasn't one of them?

Mother   I was waiting for that. (*Going to her:*) As long as you're here, Annie, I want to ask you never to say that again.

Ann   You surprise me. I thought you'd be mad at him.

Mother   What your father did had nothing to do with Larry. Nothing.

Ann   But we can't know that.

Monter (*striving for control*)   As long as you're here!

Ann (*perplexed*)   But, Kate—

Mother   Put that out of your head!

Keller   Because—

Mother (*quickly to* **Keller**)   That's all, that's enough. (*Places her hand on her head:*) Come inside now, and have some tea with me. (*She turns and goes up steps.*)

Keller (*to* **Ann**)   The one thing you—

Mother (*sharply*)   He's not dead, so there's no argument! Now come!

Keller (*angrily*)   In a minute! (**Mother** *turns and goes into house.*) Now look, Annie—

Chris   All right, Dad, forget it.

Keller   No, she dasn't feel that way. Annie—

Chris   I'm sick of the whole subject, now cut it out.

Keller   You want her to go on like this? (*To* **Ann**:) Those cylinder heads went into P-40s only. What's the matter with you? You know Larry never flew a P-40.

Chris   So who flew those P-40s, pigs?

Keller   The man was a fool, but don't make a murderer out of him. You got no sense? Look what it does to her! (*To* **Ann**:) Listen, you gotta appreciate what was doin' in that shop in the war. The both of you! It was a madhouse. Every half hour the Major callin' for cylinder heads, they were whippin' us with the telephone. The trucks were hauling them away hot, damn near. I mean just try to see it human, see it human. All of a sudden a batch comes out with a crack. That happens, that's the business. A fine, hairline crack. All right, so—so he's a little man, your father, always scared of loud voices. What'll the Major say?—Half a day's production shot. . . . What'll I say? You know what I mean? Human. (*He pauses.*) So he takes out his tools and he—covers over the cracks. All right—that's bad, it's wrong, but that's what a little man does. If I could have gone in that day I'd a told him—junk 'em, Steve, we can afford it. But alone he was afraid. But I know he meant no harm. He believed they'd hold up a hundred per cent. That's a mistake, but it ain't murder. You mustn't feel that way about him. You understand me? It ain't right.

Ann (*she regards him a moment*)   Joe, let's forget it.

Keller   Annie, the day the news came about Larry he was in the next cell to mine—Dad. And he cried, Annie—he cried half the night.

Ann (*touched*)   He shoulda cried all night. (*Slight pause.*)

Keller (*almost angered*)   Annie, I do not understand why you—!

Chris (*breaking in—with nervous urgency*)   Are you going to stop it?

Ann   Don't yell at him. He just wants everybody happy.

Keller (*clasps her around waist, smiling*)   That's my sentiments. Can you stand steak?

Chris   And champagne!

Keller   Now you're operatin'! I'll call Swanson's for a table! Big time tonight, Annie!

Ann   Can't scare me.

Keller (*to* **Chris**, *pointing at* **Ann**)   I like that girl. Wrap her up. (*They laugh. Goes up porch.*) You got nice legs, Annie! . . . I want to see everybody drunk tonight. (*Pointing to* **Chris**:) Look at him, he's blushin'! (*He exits, laughing, into house.*)

Chris (*calling after him*)   Drink your tea, Casanova. (*He turns to* **Ann**:) Isn't he a great guy?

Ann   You're the only one I know who loves his parents.

Chris   I know. It went out of style, didn't it?

Ann (*with a sudden touch of sadness*)   It's all right. It's a good thing. (*She looks about.*) You know? It's lovely here. The air is sweet.

Chris (*hopefully*)   You're not sorry you came?

Ann   Not sorry, no. But I'm—not going to stay.

Chris   Why?

Ann   In the first place, your mother as much as told me to go.

Chris   Well—

Ann   You saw that—and then you—you've been kind of—

Chris   What?

Ann   Well . . . kind of embarrassed ever since I got here.

Chris   The trouble is I planned on kind of sneaking up on you over a period of a week or so. But they take it for granted that we're all set.

Ann   I knew they would. Your mother anyway.

Chris   How did you know?

Ann   From *her* point of view, why else would I come?

Chris   Well . . . would you want to? (**Ann** *still studies him.*) I guess you know this is why I asked you to come.

Ann   I guess this is why I came.

Chris   Ann, I love you. I love you a great deal. (*Finally:*) I love you. (*Pause. She waits.*) I have no imagination . . . that's all I know to tell you. (**Ann** *is waiting, ready.*) I'm embarrassing you. I didn't want to tell it to you here. I wanted some place we'd never been; a place where we'd be brand new to each other . . . You feel it's wrong here, don't you? This yard, this chair? I want you to be ready for me. I don't want to win you away from anything.

Ann (*putting her arms around him*)   Oh, Chris, I've been ready a long, long time!

Chris   Then he's gone forever. You're sure.

Ann   I almost got married two years ago.

Chris   Why didn't you?

Ann   You started to write to me—(*Slight pause.*)

Chris   You felt something that far back?

Ann   Every day since!

Chris   Ann, why didn't you let me know?

Ann   I was waiting for you, Chris. Till then you never wrote. And when you did, what did you say? You sure can be ambiguous, you know.

Chris (*looks toward house, then at her, trembling*)   Give me a kiss, Ann. Give me a— (*They kiss.*) God, I kissed you, Annie, I kissed Annie. How long, how long I've been waiting to kiss you!

Ann   I'll never forgive you. Why did you wait all these years? All I've done is sit and wonder if I was crazy for thinking of you.

Chris   Annie, we're going to live now! I'm going to make you so happy. (*He kisses her, but without their bodies touching.*)

Ann (*a little embarrassed*)   Not like that you're not.

Chris   I kissed you . . .

Ann   Like Larry's brother. Do it like you, Chris. (*He breaks away from her abruptly.*) What is it, Chris?

Chris   Let's drive some place . . . I want to be alone with you.

Ann   No . . . what is it, Chris, your mother?

Chris   No—nothing like that.

Ann   Then what's wrong? Even in your letters, there was something ashamed.

Chris   Yes. I suppose I have been. But it's going from me.

Ann   You've got to tell me—

Chris   I don't know how to start. (*He takes her hand.*)

Ann   It wouldn't work this way. (*Slight pause.*)

Chris (*speaks quietly, factually at first*)   It's all mixed up with so many other things . . . You remember, overseas, I was in command of a company?

Ann   Yeah, sure.

Chris   Well, I lost them.

Ann   How many?

Chris   Just about all.

Ann   Oh, gee!

Chris   It takes a little time to toss that off. Because they weren't just men. For instance, one time it'd been raining several days and this kid came to me, and gave me his last pair of dry socks. Put them in my pocket. That's only a little thing—but . . . that's the kind of guys I had. They didn't die; they killed themselves for each other. I mean that exactly; a little more selfish and they'd 've been here today. And I got an idea—watching them go down. Everything was being destroyed, see, but it seemed to me that one new thing was made. A kind of—responsibility. Man for man. You understand me?—To show that, to bring that onto the earth again like some kind of a monument and everyone would feel it standing there, behind him, and it would make a difference to him. (*Pause.*) And then I came home and it was incredible. I—there was no meaning in it here; the whole thing to them was a kind of a—bus accident. I went to work with Dad, and that rat-race again. I felt—what you said—ashamed somehow. Because nobody was changed at all. It seemed to make suckers out of a lot of guys. I felt wrong to be alive, to open the bank-book, to drive the new car, to see the new refrigerator. I mean you can take those things out of a war, but when you drive that car you've got to know that it came out of the love a man can have for a man, you've got to be a little better because of that. Otherwise what you have is really loot, and there's blood on it. I didn't want to take any of it. And I guess that included you.

Ann   And you still feel that way?

Chris   I want you now, Annie.

Ann   Because you mustn't feel that way any more. Because you have a right to whatever you have. Everything, Chris, understand that? To me, too . . . And the money, there's nothing wrong in your money. Your father put hundreds of planes in the air, you should be proud. A man should be paid for that . . .

Chris   Oh Annie, Annie . . . I'm going to make a fortune for you!

Keller (*offstage*)   Hello . . . Yes. Sure.

Ann (*laughing softly*)   What'll I do with a fortune?

They kiss. **Keller** *enters from house.*

Keller (*thumbing toward house*)   Hey, Ann, your brother—(*They step apart shyly.* **Keller** *comes down, and wryly:*) What is this, Labor Day?

Chris (*waving him away, knowing the kidding will be endless*)   All right, all right.

Ann   You shouldn't burst out like that.

Keller   Well, nobody told me it was Labor Day. (*Looks around.*) Where's the hot dogs?

Chris (*loving it*)   All right. You said it once.

Keller   Well, as long as I know it's Labor Day from now on, I'll wear a bell around my neck.

Ann (*affectionately*)   He's so subtle!

Chris   George Bernard Shaw as an elephant.

Keller   George!—hey, you kissed it out of my head—your brother's on the phone.

Ann (*surprised*)   My brother?

Keller   Yeah, George. Long distance.

Ann   What's the matter, is anything wrong?

Keller   I don't know, Kate's talking to him. Hurry up, she'll cost him five dollars.

Ann (*takes a step upstage, then comes down toward* **Chris**)   I wonder if we ought to tell your mother yet? I mean I'm not very good in an argument.

Chris   We'll wait till tonight. After dinner. Now don't get tense, just leave it to me.

Keller   What're you telling her?

Chris   Go ahead, Ann. (*With misgivings,* **Ann** *goes up and into house.*) We're getting married, Dad. (**Keller** *nods indecisively.*) Well, don't you say anything?

Keller (*distracted*)   I'm glad, Chris, I'm just—George is calling from Columbus.

Chris   Columbus!

Keller   Did Annie tell you he was going to see his father today?

Chris   No, I don't think she knew anything about it.

Keller (*asking uncomfortably*)   Chris! You—you think you know her pretty good?

Chris (*hurt and apprehensive*)   What kind of a question?

Keller   I'm just wondering. All these years George don't go to see his father. Suddenly he goes . . . and she comes here.

Chris   Well, what about it?

Keller   It's crazy, but it comes to my mind. She don't hold nothin' against me, does she?

Chris (*angry*)   I don't know what you're talking about.

Keller (*a little more combatively*)   I'm just talkin'. To his last day in court the man blamed it all on me; and this is his daughter. I mean if she was sent here to find out something?

Chris (*angered*)   Why? What is there to find out?

Ann (*on phone, offstage*)   Why are you so excited, George? What happened there?

Keller   I mean if they want to open up the case again, for the nuisance value, to hurt us?

Chris   Dad . . . how could you think that of her?

Ann (*still on phone*)   But what did he say to you, for God's sake?

Keller   It couldn't be, heh. You know.

Chris   Dad, you amaze me . . .

Keller (*breaking in*)   All right, forget it, forget it. (*With great force, moving about.*) I want a clean start for you, Chris. I want a new sign over the plant—Christopher Keller, Incorporated.

Chris (*a little uneasily*)   J. O. Keller is good enough.

Keller   We'll talk about it. I'm going to build you a house, stone, with a driveway from the road. I want you to spread out, Chris, I want you to use what I made for you. (*He is close to him now.*) I mean, with joy, Chris, without shame . . . with joy.

Chris (*touched*)   I will, Dad.

Keller (*with deep emotion*)   Say it to me.

Chris   Why?

Keller   Because sometimes I think you're . . . ashamed of the money.

Chris   No, don't feel that.

Keller   Because it's good money, there's nothing wrong with that money.

Chris (*a little frightened*)   Dad, you don't have to tell me this.

Keller (*with overriding affection and self-confidence now. He grips* **Chris** *by the back of the neck, and with laughter between his determined jaws*)   Look, Chris, I'll go to work on Mother for you. We'll get her so drunk tonight we'll all get married! (*Steps away, with a wide gesture of his arm.*) There's gonna be a wedding, kid, like there never was seen! Champagne, tuxedos—!

He breaks off as **Ann**'s *voice comes out loud from the house where she is still talking on phone.*

Ann   Simply because when you get excited you don't control yourself . . . (**Mother** *comes out of house.*) Well, what did he tell you for God's sake? (*Pause.*) All right, come then. (*Pause.*) Yes, they'll all be here. Nobody's running away from you. And try to get hold of yourself, will you? (*Pause.*) All right, all right. Good-by. (*There is a brief pause as* **Ann** *hangs up receiver, then comes out of kitchen.*)

Chris   Something happen?

Keller   He's coming here?

Ann   On the seven o'clock. He's in Columbus. (*To* **Mother***:*) I told him it would be all right.

Keller   Sure, fine! Your father took sick?

Ann (*mystified*)   No, George didn't say he was sick. I—(*Shaking it off:*) I don't know, I suppose it's something stupid, you know my brother— (*She comes to* **Chris**.) Let's go for a drive, or something . . .

Chris   Sure. Give me the keys, Dad.

Mother   Drive through the park. It's beautiful now.

Chris   Come on, Ann. (*To them:*) Be back right away.

Ann (*as she and* **Chris** *exit up driveway*)   See you.

Mother *comes down toward* **Keller***, her eyes fixed on him.*

Keller   Take your time. (*To* **Mother***:*) What does George want?

Mother   He's been in Columbus since this morning with Steve. He's gotta see Annie right away, he says.

Keller   What for?

Mother   I don't know. (*She speaks with warning:*) He's a lawyer now, Joe. George is a lawyer. All these years he never even sent a postcard to Steve. Since he got back from the war, not a postcard.

Keller   So what?

Mother (*her tension breaking out*)   Suddenly he takes an airplane from New York to see him. An airplane!

Keller   Well? So?

Mother (*trembling*)   Why?

Keller   I don't read minds. Do you?

Mother   Why, Joe? What has Steve suddenly got to tell him that he takes an airplane to see him?

Keller   What do I care what Steve's got to tell him?

Mother   You're sure, Joe?

Keller (*frightened, but angry*)   Yes, I'm sure.

Mother (*sits stiffly in a chair*)   Be smart now, Joe. The boy is coming. Be smart.

Keller (*desperately*)   Once and for all, did you hear what I said? I said I'm sure!

Mother (*nods weakly*)   All right, Joe. (*He straightens up.*) Just . . . be smart.

Keller, *in hopeless fury, looks at her, turns around, goes up to porch and into house, slamming screen door violently behind him.* **Mother** *sits in chair downstage, stiffly, staring, seeing.*

Curtain.

Act Two

As twilight falls, that evening.

On the rise, **Chris** *is discovered sawing the broken-off tree, leaving stump standing alone. He is dressed in good pants, white shoes, but without a shirt. He disappears with tree up the alley when* **Mother** *appears on porch. She comes down and stands watching him. She has on a dressing gown, carries a tray of grape-juice drink in a pitcher, and glasses with sprigs of mint in them.*

Mother (*calling up alley*) Did you have to put on good pants to do that? (*She comes downstage and puts tray on table in the arbor. Then looks around uneasily, then feels pitcher for coolness.* **Chris** *enters from alley brushing off his hands:*) You notice there's more light with that thing gone?

Chris Why aren't you dressing?

Mother It's suffocating upstairs. I made a grape drink for Georgie. He always liked grape. Come and have some.

Chris (*impatiently*) Well, come on, get dressed. And what's Dad sleeping so much for? (*He goes to table and pours a glass of juice.*)

Mother He's worried. When he's worried he sleeps. (*Pauses. Looks into his eyes.*) We're dumb, Chris. Dad and I are stupid people. We don't know anything. You've got to protect us.

Chris You're silly; what's there to be afraid of?

Mother To his last day in court Steve never gave up the idea that Dad made him do it. If they're going to open the case again I won't live through it.

Chris George is just a damn fool, Mother. How can you take him seriously?

Mother That family hates us. Maybe even Annie—

Chris Oh, now, Mother . . .

Mother You think just because you like everybody, they like you!

Chris All right, stop working yourself up. Just leave everything to me.

Mother When George goes home tell her to go with him.

Chris (*noncommittally*) Don't worry about Annie.

Mother   Steve is her father, too.

Chris   Are you going to cut it out? Now, come.

Mother (*going upstage with him*)   You don't realize how people can hate, Chris, they can hate so much they'll tear the world to pieces.

Ann, *dressed up, appears on porch.*

Chris   Look! She's dressed already. (*As he and* **Mother** *mount porch:*) I've just got to put on a shirt.

Ann (*in a preoccupied way*)   Are you feeling well, Kate?

Mother   What's the difference, dear. There are certain people, y'know, the sicker they get the longer they live. (*She goes into house.*)

Chris   You look nice.

Ann   We're going to tell her tonight.

Chris   Absolutely, don't worry about it.

Ann   I wish we could tell her now. I can't stand scheming. My stomach gets hard.

Chris   It's not scheming, we'll just get her in a better mood.

Mother (*offstage, in the house*)   Joe, are you going to sleep all day!

Ann (*laughing*)   The only one who's relaxed is your father. He's fast asleep.

Chris   I'm relaxed.

Ann   Are you?

Chris   Look. (*He holds out his hand and makes it shake.*) Let me know when George gets here.

He goes into the house. **Ann** *moves aimlessly, and then is drawn toward tree stump. She goes to it, hesitantly touches broken top in the hush of her thoughts. Offstage* **Lydia** *calls, "Johnny! Come get your supper!"* **Sue** *enters, and halts, seeing* **Ann**.

Sue   Is my husband—?

Ann (*turns, startled*)   Oh!

Sue   I'm terribly sorry.

Ann   It's all right, I—I'm a little silly about the dark.

Sue (*looks about*)   It is getting dark.

Ann   Are you looking for your husband?

Sue   As usual. (*Laughs tiredly.*) He spends so much time here, they'll be charging him rent.

Ann   Nobody was dressed so he drove over to the depot to pick up my brother.

Sue   Oh, your brother's in?

Ann   Yeah, they ought to be here any minute now. Will you have a cold drink?

Sue   I will, thanks. (**Ann** *goes to table and pours.*) My husband. Too hot to drive me to beach. Men are like little boys; for the neighbors they'll always cut the grass.

Ann   People like to do things for the Kellers. Been that way since I can remember.

Sue   It's amazing. I guess your brother's coming to give you away, heh?

Ann (*giving her drink*)   I don't know. I suppose.

Sue   You must be all nerved up.

Ann   It's always a problem getting yourself married, isn't it?

Sue   That depends on your shape, of course. I don't see why you should have had a problem.

Ann   I've had chances—

Sue   I'll bet. It's romantic . . . it's very unusual to me, marrying the brother of your sweetheart.

Ann   I don't know. I think it's mostly that whenever I need somebody to tell me the truth I've always thought of Chris. When he tells you something you know it's so. He relaxes me.

Sue   And he's got money. That's important, you know.

Ann   It wouldn't matter to me.

Sue   You'd be surprised. It makes all the difference. I married an intern. On my salary. And that was bad, because as soon as a woman supports a man he owes her something. You can never owe somebody without resenting them. (**Ann** *laughs.*) That's true, you know.

Ann   Underneath, I think the doctor is very devoted.

Sue   Oh, certainly. But it's bad when a man always sees the bars in front of him. Jim thinks he's in jail all the time.

Ann   Oh . . .

Sue   That's why I've been intending to ask you a small favor, Ann. It's something very important to me.

Ann   Certainly, if I can do it.

Sue   You can. When you take up housekeeping, try to find a place away from here.

Ann   Are you fooling?

Sue   I'm very serious. My husband is unhappy with Chris around.

Ann   How is that?

Sue   Jim's a successful doctor. But he's got an idea he'd like to do medical research. Discover things. You see?

Ann   Well, isn't that good?

Sue   Research pays twenty-five dollars a week minus laundering the hair shirt. You've got to give up your life to go into it.

Ann   How does Chris—

Sue (*with growing feeling*)   Chris makes people want to be better than it's possible to be. He does that to people.

Ann   Is that bad?

Sue   My husband has a family, dear. Every time he has a session with Chris he feels as though he's compromising by not giving up everything for research. As though Chris or anybody else isn't compromising. It happens with Jim every couple of years. He meets a man and makes a statue out of him.

Ann   Maybe he's right. I don't mean that Chris is a statue, but—

Sue   Now darling, you know he's not right.

Ann   I don't agree with you. Chris—

Sue   Let's face it, dear. Chris is working with his father, isn't he? He's taking money out of that business every week in the year.

Ann   What of it?

Sue   You ask me what of it?

Ann   I certainly do. (*She seems about to burst out.*) You oughtn't cast aspersions like that, I'm surprised at you.

Sue   You're surprised at me!

Ann   He'd never take five cents out of that plant if there was anything wrong with it.

Sue   You know that.

Ann   I know it. I resent everything you've said.

Sue (*moving toward her*)   You know what I resent, dear?

Ann   Please, I don't want to argue.

Sue   I resent living next door to the Holy Family. It makes me look like a bum, you understand?

Ann   I can't do anything about that.

Sue   Who is he to ruin a man's life? Everybody knows Joe pulled a fast one to get out of jail.

Ann   That's not true!

Sue   Then why don't you go out and talk to people? Go on, talk to them. There's not a person on the block who doesn't know the truth.

Ann   That's a lie. People come here all the time for cards and—

Sue   So what? They give him credit for being smart. I do, too, I've got nothing against Joe. But if Chris wants people to put on the hair shirt let him take off his broadcloth. He's driving my husband crazy with that phony idealism of his, and I'm at the end of my rope on it! (**Chris** *enters on porch, wearing shirt and tie now. She turns quickly, hearing. With a smile:*) Hello, darling. How's Mother?

Chris   I thought George came.

Sue   No, it was just us.

Chris (*coming down to them*)   Susie, do me a favor, heh? Go up to Mother and see if you can calm her. She's all worked up.

Sue   She still doesn't know about you two?

Chris (*laughs a little*)   Well, she senses it, I guess. You know my mother.

Sue (*going up to porch*)   Oh, yeah, she's psychic.

Chris   Maybe there's something in the medicine chest.

Sue   I'll give her one of everything. (*On porch:*) Don't worry about Kate; couple of drinks, dance her around a little . . . She'll love Ann. (*To* **Ann**:) Because you're the female version of him. (**Chris** *laughs.*) Don't be alarmed, I said version. (*She goes into house.*)

Chris   Interesting woman, isn't she?

Ann   Yeah, she's very interesting.

Chris   She's a great nurse, you know, she—

Ann (*in tension, but trying to control it*)   Are you still doing that?

Chris (*sensing something wrong, but still smiling*)   Doing what?

Ann   As soon as you get to know somebody you find a distinction for them. How do you know she's a great nurse?

Chris   What's the matter, Ann?

Ann   The woman hates you. She despises you!

Chris   Hey . . . What's hit you?

Ann   Gee, Chris—

Chris   What happened here?

Ann   You never—Why didn't you tell me?

Chris   Tell you what?

Ann   She says they think Joe is guilty.

Chris   What difference does it make what they think?

Ann   I don't care what they think, I just don't understand why you took the trouble to deny it. You said it was all forgotten.

Chris   I didn't want you to feel there was anything wrong in you coming here, that's all. I know a lot of people think my father was guilty, and I assumed there might be some question in your mind.

Ann   But I never once said I suspected him.

Chris   Nobody says it.

Ann   Chris, I know how much you love him, but it could never—

Chris   Do you think I could forgive him if he'd done that thing?

Ann   I'm not here out of a blue sky, Chris. I turned my back on my father, if there's anything wrong here now—

Chris   I know that, Ann.

Ann   George is coming from Dad, and I don't think it's with a blessing.

Chris   He's welcome here. You've got nothing to fear from George.

Ann   Tell me that . . . Just tell me that.

Chris   The man is innocent, Ann. Remember he was falsely accused once and it put him through hell. How would you behave if you were faced with the same thing again? Annie, believe me, there's nothing wrong for you here, believe me, kid.

Ann   All right, Chris, all right. (*They embrace as* **Keller** *appears quietly on porch.* **Ann** *simply studies him.*)

Keller   Every time I come out here it looks like Playland! (*They break and laugh in embarrassment.*)

Chris   I thought you were going to shave?

Keller (*sitting on bench*)   In a minute. I just woke up, I can't see nothin'.

Ann   You look shaved.

Keller   Oh, no. (*Massages his jaw.*) Gotta be extra special tonight. Big night, Annie. So how's it feel to be a married woman?

Ann (*laughs*)   I don't know, yet.

Keller (*to* **Chris**)   What's the matter, you slippin'? (*He takes a little box of apples from under the bench as they talk.*)

Chris   The great roué!

Keller   What is that, roué?

Chris   It's French.

Keller   Don't talk dirty. (*They laugh.*)

Chris (*to* **Ann**)   You ever meet a bigger ignoramus?

Keller   Well, somebody's got to make a living.

Ann (*as they laugh*)   That's telling him.

Keller   I don't know, everybody's gettin' so goddam educated in this country there'll be nobody to take away the garbage. (*They laugh.*) It's gettin' so the only dumb ones left are the bosses.

Ann   You're not so dumb, Joe.

Keller   I know, but you go into our plant, for instance. I got so many lieutenants, majors and colonels that I'm ashamed to ask somebody to sweep the floor. I gotta be careful I'll insult somebody. No kiddin'. It's a tragedy: you stand on the street today and spit, you're gonna hit a college man.

Chris   Well, don't spit.

Keller (*breaks apple in half, passing it to* **Ann** *and* **Chris**)   I mean to say, it's comin' to a pass. (*He takes a breath.*) I been thinkin', Annie . . . your brother, George. I been thinkin' about your brother George. When he comes I like you to brooch something to him.

Chris   Broach.

Keller   What's the matter with brooch?

Chris (*smiling*)   It's not English.

Keller   When I went to night school it was brooch.

Ann (*laughing*)   Well, in day school it's broach.

Keller   Don't surround me, will you? Seriously, Ann . . . You say he's not well. George, I been thinkin', why should he knock himself out in New York with that cut-throat competition, when I got so many friends here; I'm very friendly with some big lawyers in town. I could set George up here.

Ann   That's awfully nice of you, Joe.

Keller   No, kid, it ain't nice of me. I want you to understand me. I'm thinking of Chris. (*Slight pause.*) See . . . this is what I mean. You get older, you want to feel that you—accomplished something. My only accomplishment is my son. I ain't brainy. That's all I accomplished. Now, a year, eighteen months, your father'll be a free man. Who is he going to come to, Annie? His baby. You. He'll come, old, mad, into your house.

Ann   That can't matter any more, Joe.

Keller   I don't want that to come between us. (*Gestures between* **Chris** *and himself.*)

Ann   I can only tell you that that could never happen.

Keller   You're in love now, Annie, but believe me, I'm older than you and I know—a daughter is a daughter, and a father is a father. And it could happen. (*He pauses.*) I like you and George to go to him in prison and tell him . . . "Dad, Joe wants to bring you into the business when you get out."

Ann (*surprised, even shocked*)   You'd have him as a partner?

Keller   No, no partner. A good job. (*Pause. He sees she is shocked, a little mystified. He gets up, speaks more nervously.*) I want him to know, Annie . . . while he's sitting there I want him to know that when he gets out he's got a place waitin' for him. It'll take his bitterness away. To know you got a place . . . it sweetens you.

Ann   Joe, you owe him nothing.

Keller   I owe him a good kick in the teeth, but he's your father.

Chris   Then kick him in the teeth! I don't want him in the plant, so that's that! You understand? And besides, don't talk about him like that. People misunderstand you!

Keller   And I don't understand why she has to crucify the man.

Chris   Well, it's her father, if she feels—

Keller   No, no.

Chris (*almost angrily*)   What's it to you? Why—?

Keller (*a commanding outburst in high nervousness*)   A father is a father! (*As though the outburst had revealed him, he looks about, wanting to retract it. His hand goes to his cheek.*) I better—I better shave. (*He turns and a smile is on his face. To* **Ann***:*) I didn't mean to yell at you, Annie.

Ann   Let's forget the whole thing, Joe.

Keller   Right. (*To* **Chris***:*) She's likeable.

Chris (*a little peeved at the man's stupidity*)   Shave, will you?

Keller   Right again.

As he turns to porch **Lydia** *comes hurrying from her house.*

Lydia   I forgot all about it. (*Seeing* **Chris** *and* **Ann***:*) Hya. (*To* **Joe***:*) I promised to fix Kate's hair for tonight. Did she comb it yet?

Keller   Always a smile, hey, Lydia?

Lydia   Sure, why not?

Keller (*going up on porch*)   Come on up and comb my Katie's hair.

(**Lydia** *goes up on porch:*) She's got a big night, make her beautiful.

Lydia   I will.

Keller (*holds door open for her and she goes into kitchen. To* **Chris** *and* **Ann**)   Hey, that could be a song. (*He sings softly:*)

Come on up and comb my Katie's hair . . .
Oh, come on up, 'cause she's my lady fair—

(*To* **Ann***:*) How's that for one year of night school? (*He continues singing as he goes into kitchen.*)

Oh, come on up, come on up, and comb my lady's hair—

Jim Bayliss *rounds corner of driveway, walking rapidly.* **Jim** *crosses to* **Chris**, *motions him and pulls him down excitedly.* **Keller** *stands just inside kitchen door, watching them.*

Chris   What's the matter? Where is he?

Jim   Where's your mother?

Chris   Upstairs, dressing.

Ann (*crossing to them rapidly*)   What happened to George?

Jim   I asked him to wait in the car. Listen to me now. Can you take some advice? (*They wait.*) Don't bring him in here.

Ann   Why?

Jim   Kate is in bad shape, you can't explode this in front of her.

Ann   Explode what?

Jim   You know why he's here, don't try to kid it away. There's blood in his eye; drive him somewhere and talk to him alone.

Ann *turns to go up drive, takes a couple of steps, sees* **Keller**, *and stops. He goes quietly on into house.*

Chris (*shaken, and therefore angered*)   Don't be an old lady.

Jim   He's come to take her home. What does that mean? (*To* **Ann***:*) You know what that means. Fight it out with him some place else.

Ann (*comes back down toward* **Chris**)   I'll drive . . . him somewhere.

Chris (*goes to her*)   No.

Jim   Will you stop being an idiot?

Chris   Nobody's afraid of him here. Cut that out!

He starts for driveway, but is brought up short by **George***, who enters there.* **George** *is* **Chris***'s age, but a paler man, now on the edge of his self-restraint. He speaks quietly, as though afraid to find himself screaming. An instant's hesitation and* **Chris** *steps up to him, hand extended, smiling.*

Chris   Helluva way to do; what're you sitting out there for?

George   Doctor said your mother isn't well, I—

Chris   So what? She'd want to see you, wouldn't she? We've been waiting for you all afternoon. (*He puts his hand on* **George***'s arm, but* **George** *pulls away, coming across toward* **Ann***.*)

Ann (*touching his collar*)   This is filthy, didn't you bring another shirt?

George *breaks away from her, and moves down, examining the yard. Door opens, and he turns rapidly, thinking it is* **Kate***, but it's* **Sue***. She looks at him; he turns away and moves to fence. He looks over it at his former home.* **Sue** *comes downstage.*

Sue (*annoyed*)   How about the beach, Jim?

Jim   Oh, it's too hot to drive.

Sue   How'd you get to the station—Zeppelin?

Chris   This is Mrs. Bayliss, George. (*Calling, as* **George** *pays no attention, staring at house:*) George! (**George** *turns.*) Mrs. Bayliss.

Sue   How do you do.

George (*removing his hat*)   You're the people who bought our house, aren't you?

Sue   That's right. Come and see what we did with it before you leave.

George (*walks down and away from her*)   I liked it the way it was.

Sue (*after a brief pause*)   He's frank, isn't he?

Jim (*pulling her off*)   See you later . . . Take it easy, fella. (*They exit.*)

Chris (*calling after them*)   Thanks for driving him! (*Turning to* **George***:*) How about some grape juice? Mother made it especially for you.

George (*with forced appreciation*)   Good old Kate, remembered my grape juice.

Chris   You drank enough of it in this house. How've you been, George?—Sit down.

George (*keeps moving*)   It takes me a minute. (*Looking around:*) It seems impossible.

Chris   What?

George   I'm back here.

Chris   Say, you've gotten a little nervous, haven't you?

George   Yeah, toward the end of the day. What're you, big executive now?

Chris   Just kind of medium. How's the law?

George   I don't know. When I was studying in the hospital it seemed sensible, but outside there doesn't seem to be much of a law. The trees got thick, didn't they? (*Points to stump:*) What's that?

Chris   Blew down last night. We had it there for Larry. You know.

George   Why, afraid you'll forget him?

Chris (*starts for* **George**)   Kind of a remark is that?

Ann (*breaking in, putting a restraining hand on* **Chris**)   When did you start wearing a hat?

George (*discovers hat in his hand*)   Today. From now on I decided to look like a lawyer, anyway. (*He holds it up to her:*) Don't you recognize it?

Ann   Why? Where—?

George   Your father's—He asked me to wear it.

Ann   How is he?

George   He got smaller.

Ann   Smaller?

George   Yeah, little. (*Holds out his hand to measure:*) He's a little man. That's what happens to suckers, you know. It's good I went to him in time—another year there'd be nothing left but his smell.

Chris   What's the matter, George, what's the trouble?

George   The trouble? The trouble is when you make suckers out of people once, you shouldn't try to do it twice.

Chris   What does that mean?

George (*to* **Ann**)   You're not married yet, are you?

Ann   George, will you sit down and stop—?

George   Are you married yet?

Ann   No, I'm not married yet.

George   You're not going to marry him.

Ann   Why am I not going to marry him?

George   Because his father destroyed your family.

Chris   Now look, George . . .

George   Cut it short, Chris. Tell her to come home with me. Let's not argue, you know what I've got to say.

Chris   George, you don't want to be the voice of God, do you?

George   I'm—

Chris   That's been your trouble all your life, George, you dive into things. What kind of a statement is that to make? You're a big boy now.

George   I'm a big boy now.

Chris   Don't come bulling in here. If you've got something to say, be civilized about it.

George   Don't civilize me!

Ann   Shhh!

Chris (*ready to hit him*)   Are you going to talk like a grown man or aren't you?

Ann (*quickly, to forestall an outburst*)   Sit down, dear. Don't be angry, what's the matter? (*He allows her to seat him, looking at her.*) Now what happened? You kissed me when I left, now you—

George (*breathlessly*)   My life turned upside down since then. I couldn't go back to work when you left. I wanted to go to Dad and tell him you were going to be married. It seemed impossible not to tell him. He loved you so much. (*He pauses.*) Annie—we did a terrible thing. We can never be forgiven. Not even to send him a card at Christmas. I didn't see him once since I got home from the war! Annie, you don't know what was done to that man. You don't know what happened.

Ann (*afraid*) Of course I know.

George You can't know, you wouldn't be here. Dad came to work that day. The night foreman came to him and showed him the cylinder heads . . . they were coming out of the process with defects. There was something wrong with the process. So Dad went directly to the phone and called here and told Joe to come down right away. But the morning passed. No sign of Joe. So Dad called again. By this time he had over a hundred defectives. The Army was screaming for stuff and Dad didn't have anything to ship. So Joe told him . . . on the phone he told him to weld, cover up the cracks in any way he could, and ship them out.

Chris Are you through now?

George (*surging up at him*) I'm not through now! (*Back to* **Ann***:*) Dad was afraid. He wanted Joe there if he was going to do it. But Joe can't come down . . . He's sick. Sick! He suddenly gets the flu! Suddenly! But he promised to take responsibility. Do you understand what I'm saying? On the telephone you can't have responsibility! In a court you can always deny a phone call and that's exactly what he did. They knew he was a liar the first time, but in the appeal they believed that rotten lie and now Joe is a big shot and your father is the patsy. (*He gets up.*) Now what're you going to do? Eat his food, sleep in his bed? Answer me; what're you going to do?

Chris What're you going to do, George?

George He's too smart for me, I can't prove a phone call.

Chris Then how dare you come in here with that rot?

Ann George, the court—

George The court didn't know your father! But you know him. You know in your heart Joe did it.

Chris (*whirling him around*) Lower your voice or I'll throw you out of here!

George She knows. She knows.

Chris (*to* **Ann**) Get him out of here, Ann. Get him out of here.

Ann George, I know everything you've said. Dad told that whole thing in court, and they—

George (*almost a scream*) The court did not know him, Annie!

Ann   Shhh!—But he'll say anything, George. You know how quick he can lie.

George (*turning to* **Chris**, *with deliberation*)   I'll ask you something, and look me in the eye when you answer me.

Chris   I'll look you in the eye.

George   You know your father—

Chris   I know him well.

George   And he's the kind of boss to let a hundred and twenty-one cylinder heads be repaired and shipped out of his shop without even knowing about it?

Chris   He's that kind of boss.

George   And that's the same Joe Keller who never left his shop without first going around to see that all the lights were out.

Chris (*with growing anger*)   The same Joe Keller.

George   The same man who knows how many minutes a day his workers spend in the toilet.

Chris   The same man.

George   And my father, that frightened mouse who'd never buy a shirt without somebody along—that man would dare do such a thing on his own?

Chris   On his own. And because he's a frightened mouse this is another thing he'd do—throw the blame on somebody else because he's not man enough to take it himself. He tried it in court but it didn't work, but with a fool like you it works!

George   Oh, Chris, you're a liar to yourself!

Ann (*deeply shaken*)   Don't talk like that!

Chris (*sits facing* **George**)   Tell me, George. What happened? The court record was good enough for you all these years, why isn't it good now? Why did you believe it all these years?

George (*after a slight pause*)   Because you believed it . . . That's the truth, Chris. I believed everything, because I thought you did. But today I heard it from his mouth. From his mouth it's altogether different than the record. Anyone who knows him, and knows your father, will believe it from his mouth. Your Dad took everything we have. I can't beat that. But she's one item he's not going to grab. (*He turns to* **Ann**.) Get your things. Everything they have is covered with blood. You're not the kind of a girl who can live with that. Get your things.

Chris   Ann . . . you're not going to believe that, are you?

Ann (*goes to him*)   You know it's not true, don't you?

George   How can he tell you? It's his father. (*To* **Chris**:) None of these things ever even cross your mind?

Chris   Yes, they crossed my mind. Anything can cross your mind!

George   *He knows*, Annie. He knows!

Chris   The voice of God!

George   Then why isn't your name on the business? Explain that to her!

Chris   What the hell has that got to do with—?

George   Annie, why isn't his name on it?

Chris   Even when I don't own it!

George   Who're you kidding? Who gets it when he dies? (*To* **Ann**:) Open your eyes, you know the both of them, isn't that the first thing they'd do, the way they love each other?—J. O. Keller and Son? (*Pause.* **Ann** *looks from him to* **Chris**.) I'll settle it. Do you want to settle it, or are you afraid to?

Chris   What do you mean?

George   Let me go up and talk to your father. In ten minutes you'll have the answer. Or are you afraid of the answer?

Chris   I'm not afraid of the answer. I know the answer. But my mother isn't well and I don't want a fight here now.

George   Let me go to him.

Chris   You're not going to start a fight here now.

George (*to* **Ann**)   What more do you want! (*There is a sound of footsteps in the house.*)

Ann (*turns her head suddenly toward house*)   Someone's coming.

Chris (*to* **George**, *quietly*)   You won't say anything now.

Ann   You'll go soon. I'll call a cab.

George   You're coming with me.

Ann   And don't mention marriage, because we haven't told her yet.

George   You're coming with me.

Ann   You understand? Don't—George, you're not going to start anything now! (*She hears footsteps.*) Shsh!

Mother *enters on porch. She is dressed almost formally; her hair is fixed. They are all turned toward her. On seeing* **George** *she raises both hands, comes down toward him.*

Mother   Georgie, Georgie.

George (*he has always liked her*)   Hello, Kate.

Mother (*cups his face in her hands*)   They made an old man out of you. (*Touches his hair.*) Look, you're gray.

George (*her pity, open and unabashed, reaches into him, and he smiles sadly*)   I know, I—

Mother   I told you when you went away, don't try for medals.

George (*laughs, tiredly*)   I didn't try, Kate. They made it very easy for me.

Mother (*actually angry*)   Go on. You're all alike. (*To* **Ann***:*) Look at him, why did you say he's fine? He looks like a ghost.

George (*relishing her solicitude*)   I feel all right.

Mother   I'm sick to look at you. What's the matter with your mother, why don't she feed you?

Ann   He just hasn't any appetite.

Mother   If he ate in my house he'd have an appetite. (*To* **Ann***:*) I pity your husband! (*To* **George***:*) Sit down. I'll make you a sandwich.

George (*sits with an embarrassed laugh*)   I'm really not hungry.

Mother   Honest to God, it breaks my heart to see what happened to all the children. How we worked and planned for you, and you end up no better than us.

George (*with deep feeling for her*)   You . . . you haven't changed at all, you know that, Kate?

Mother   None of us changed, Georgie. We all love you. Joe was just talking about the day you were born and the water got shut off. People were carrying basins from a block away—a stranger would have thought the whole neighborhood was on fire! (*They laugh. She sees the juice. To* **Ann***:*) Why didn't you give him some juice!

Ann (*defensively*)   I offered it to him.

Mother (*scoffingly*)   You offered it to him! (*Thrusting glass into* **George***'s hand:*) Give it to him! (*To* **George***, who is laughing:*) And now you're going to sit here and drink some juice . . . and look like something!

George (*sitting*)   Kate, I feel hungry already.

Chris (*proudly*)   She could turn Mahatma Gandhi into a heavy-weight!

Mother (*to* **Chris***, with great energy*)   Listen, to hell with the restaurant! I got a ham in the icebox, and frozen strawberries, and avocados, and—

Ann   Swell, I'll help you!

George   The train leaves at eight-thirty, Ann.

Mother (*to* **Ann**)   You're leaving?

Chrts   No, Mother, she's not—

Ann (*breaking through it, going to* **George**)   You hardly got here; give yourself a chance to get acquainted again.

Chris   Sure, you don't even know us any more.

Mother   Well, Chris, if they can't stay, don't—

Chris   No, it's just a question of George, Mother, he planned on—

George (*gets up politely, nicely, for* **Kate***'s sake*)   Now wait a minute, Chris . . .

Chris (*smiling and full of command, cutting him off*)   If you want to go, I'll drive you to the station now, but if you're staying, no arguments while you're here.

Mother (*at last confessing the tension*)   Why should he argue? (*She goes to him. With desperation and compassion, stroking his hair:*) Georgie and us have no argument. How could we have an argument, Georgie? We all got hit by the same lightning, how can you—? Did you see what happened to Larry's tree, Georgie? (*She has taken his arm, and unwillingly he moves across stage with her.*) Imagine? While I was dreaming of him in the middle of the night, the wind came along and—

Lydia *enters on porch. As soon as she sees him:*

Lydia   Hey, Georgie! Georgie! Georgie! Georgie! Georgie! (*She comes down to him eagerly. She has a flowered hat in her hand, which* **Kate** *takes from her as she goes to* **George**.)

George (*as they shake hands eagerly, warmly*)   Hello, Laughy. What'd you do, grow?

Lydia   I'm a big girl now.

Mother   Look what she can do to a hat!

Ann (*to* **Lydia**, *admiring the hat*)   Did you make that?

Mother   In ten minutes! (*She puts it on.*)

Lydia (*fixing it on her head*)   I only rearranged it.

George   You still make your own clothes?

Chris (*of* **Mother**)   Ain't she classy! All she needs now is a Russian wolfhound.

Mother (*moving her head*)   It feels like somebody is sitting on my head.

Ann   No, it's beautiful, Kate.

Mother (*kisses* **Lydia**. *To* **George**)   She's a genius! You should've married her. (*They laugh.*) This one can feed you!

Lydia (*strangely embarrassed*)   Oh, stop that, Kate.

George (*to* **Lydia**)   Didn't I hear you had a baby?

Mother   You don't hear so good. She's got three babies.

George (*a little hurt by it—to* **Lydia**)   No kidding, three?

Lydia   Yeah, it was one, two, three—You've been away a long time, Georgie.

George   I'm beginning to realize.

Mother (*to* **Chris** *and* **George**)   The trouble with you kids is you (*think*) too much.

Lydia   Well, we think, too.

Mother   Yes, but not all the time.

George (*with almost obvious envy*)   They never took Frank, heh?

Lydia (*a little apologetically*)   No, he was always one year ahead of the draft.

Mother   It's amazing. When they were calling boys twenty-seven Frank was just twenty-eight, when they made it twenty-eight he was just twenty-nine. That's why he took up astrology. It's all in when you were born, it just goes to show.

Chris   What does it go to show?

Mother (*to* **Chris**)   Don't be so intelligent. Some superstitions are very nice! (*To* **Lydia***:*) Did he finish Larry's horoscope?

Lydia   I'll ask him now, I'm going in. (*To* **George***, a little sadly, almost embarrassed:*) Would you like to see my babies? Come on.

George   I don't think so, Lydia.

Lydia (*understanding*)   All right. Good luck to you, George.

George   Thanks. And to you . . . And Frank. (*She smiles at him, turns and goes off to her house.* **George** *stands staring after her.*)

Lydia (*as she runs off*)   Oh, Frank!

Mother (*reading his thoughts*)   She got pretty, heh?

George (*sadly*)   Very pretty.

Mother (*as a reprimand*)   She's beautiful, you damned fool!

George (*looks around longingly; and softly, with a catch in his throat*)   She makes it seem so nice around here.

Mother (*shaking her finger at him*)   Look what happened to you because you wouldn't listen to me! I told you to marry that girl and stay out of the war!

George (*laughs at himself*)   She used to laugh too much.

Mother   And you didn't laugh enough. While you were getting mad about Fascism Frank was getting into her bed.

George (*to* **Chris**)   He won the war, Frank.

Chris   All the battles.

Mother (*in pursuit of this mood*)   The day they started the draft, Georgie, I told you you loved that girl.

Chris (*laughs*)   And truer love hath no man!

Mother   I'm smarter than any of you.

Georgie (*laughing*)   She's wonderful!

Mother   And now you're going to listen to me, George. You had big principles, Eagle Scouts the three of you; so now I got a tree, and this one (*indicating* **Chris**) when the weather gets bad he can't stand on his feet; and that big dope (*pointing to* **Lydia**'s *house*) next door who never reads anything but Andy Gump has three children and his house paid off. Stop being a philosopher, and look after yourself. Like Joe was just saying—you move back here, he'll help you get set, and I'll find you a girl and put a smile on your face.

George   Joe? Joe wants me here?

Ann (*eagerly*)   He asked me to tell you, and I think it's a good idea.

Mother   Certainly. Why must you make believe you hate us? Is that another principle?—that you have to hate us? You don't hate us, George, I know you, you can't fool me, I diapered you. (*Suddenly, to* **Ann**:) You remember Mr. Marcy's daughter?

Ann (*laughing, to* **George**)   She's got you hooked already! (**George** *laughs, is excited.*)

Mother   You look her over, George; you'll see she's the most beautiful—

Chris   She's got warts, George.

Mother (*to* **Chris**)   She hasn't got warts! (*To* **George**:) So the girl has a little beauty mark on her chin—

Chris   And two on her nose.

Mother   You remember. Her father's the retired police inspector.

Chris   Sergeant, George.

Mother   He's a very kind man!

Chris   He looks like a gorilla.

Mother (*to* **George**)   He never shot anybody.

They all burst out laughing, as **Keller** *appears in doorway.* **George** *rises abruptly and stares at* **Keller***, who comes rapidly down to him.*

Keller (*the laughter stops. With strained joviality*)   Well! Look who's here! (*Extending his hand:*) Georgie, good to see ya.

George (*shaking hands—somberly*)   How're you, Joe?

Keller   So-so. Gettin' old. You comin' out to dinner with us?

George   No, got to be back in New York.

Ann   I'll call a cab for you. (*She goes up into the house.*)

Keller   Too bad you can't stay, George. Sit down. (*To* **Mother***:*) He looks fine.

Mother   He looks terrible.

Keller   That's what I said, you look terrible, George. (*They laugh.*) I wear the pants and she beats me with the belt.

George   I saw your factory on the way from the station. It looks like General Motors.

Keller   I wish it was General Motors, but it ain't. Sit down, George. Sit down. (*Takes cigar out of his pocket.*) So you finally went to see your father, I hear?

George   Yes, this morning. What kind of stuff do you make now?

Keller   Oh, little of everything. Pressure cookers, an assembly for washing machines. Got a nice, flexible plant now. So how'd you find Dad? Feel all right?

George (*searching* **Keller***, speaking indecisively*)   No, he's not well, Joe.

Keller (*lighting his cigar*)   Not his heart again, is it?

George   It's everything, Joe. It's his soul.

Keller (*blowing out smoke*)   Uh huh—

Chris   How about seeing what they did with your house?

Keller   Leave him be.

George (*to* **Chris***, indicating* **Keller***)   I'd like to talk to him.

Keller   Sure, he just got here. That's the way they do, George. A little man makes a mistake and they hang him by the thumbs; the big ones become ambassadors. I wish you'd-a told me you were going to see Dad.

George (*studying him*)   I didn't know you were interested.

Keller   In a way, I am. I would like him to know, George, that as far as I'm concerned, any time he wants, he's got a place with me. I would like him to know that.

George   He hates your guts, Joe. Don't you know that?

Keller   I imagined it. But that can change, too.

Mother   Steve was never like that.

George   He's like that now. He'd like to take every man who made money in the war and put him up against a wall.

Chris   He'll need a lot of bullets.

George   And he'd better not get any.

Keller   That's a sad thing to hear.

George (*with bitterness dominant*)   Why? What'd you expect him to think of you?

Keller (*the force of his nature rising, but under control*)   I'm sad to see he hasn't changed. As long as I know him, twenty-five years, the man never learned how to take the blame. You know that, George.

George (*he does*)   Well, I—

Keller   But you do know it. Because the way you come in here you don't look like you remember it. I mean like in nineteen thirty-seven when we had the shop on Flood Street. And he damn near blew us all up with that heater he left burning for two days without water. He wouldn't admit that was his fault, either. I had to fire a mechanic to save his face. You remember that.

George   Yes, but—

Keller   I'm just mentioning it, George. Because this is just another one of a lot of things. Like when he gave Frank that money to invest in oil stock.

George (*distressed*)   I know that, I—

Keller (*driving in, but restrained*)   But it's good to remember those things, kid. The way he cursed Frank because the stock went down. Was that Frank's fault? To listen to him Frank was a swindler. And all the man did was give him a bad tip.

George (*gets up, moves away*)   I know those things . . .

Keller   Then remember them, remember them. (**Ann** *comes out of house.*) There are certain men in the world who rather see everybody hung before they'll take blame. You understand me, George?

They stand facing each other, **George** *trying to judge him.*

Ann (*coming downstage*)   The cab's on its way. Would you like to wash?

Mother (*with the thrust of hope*)   Why must he go? Make the midnight, George.

Keller   Sure, you'll have dinner with us!

Ann   How about it? Why not? We're eating at the lake, we could have a swell time.

A long pause, as **George** *looks at* **Ann**, **Chris**, **Keller**, *then back to her.*

George   All right.

Mother   Now you're talking.

Chris   I've got a shirt that'll go right with that suit.

Mother   Size fifteen and a half, right, George?

George   Is Lydia—? I mean—Frank and Lydia coming?

Mother   I'll get you a date that'll make her look like a—(*She starts upstage.*)

George (*laughing*)   No, I don't want a date.

Chris   I know somebody just for you! Charlotte Tanner! (*He starts for the house.*)

Keller   Call Charlotte, that's right.

Mother   Sure, call her up. (**Chris** *goes into house.*)

Ann   You go up and pick out a shirt and tie.

George (*stops, looks around at them and the place*)   I never felt at home anywhere but here. I feel so—(*He nearly laughs, and turns away from them.*) Kate, you look so young, you know? You didn't change at all. It . . . rings an old bell. (*Turns to* **Keller**.) You too, Joe, you're amazingly the same. The whole atmosphere is.

Keller   Say, I ain't got time to get sick.

Mother   He hasn't been laid up in fifteen years.

Keller   Except my flu during the war.

Mother   Huhh?

Keller   My flu, when I was sick during . . . the war.

Mother   Well, sure . . . (*To* **George***:*) I mean except for that flu. (**George** *stands perfectly still.*) Well, it slipped my mind, don't look at me that way. He wanted to go to the shop but he couldn't lift himself off the bed. I thought he had pneumonia.

George   Why did you say he's never—?

Keller   I know how you feel, kid, I'll never forgive myself. If I could've gone in that day I'd never allow Dad to touch those heads.

George   She said you've never been sick.

Mother   I said he was sick, George.

George (*going to* **Ann**)   Ann, didn't you hear her say—?

Mother   Do you remember every time you were sick?

George   I'd remember pneumonia. Especially if I got it just the day my partner was going to patch up cylinder heads . . . What happened that day, Joe?

Frank *enters briskly from driveway, holding* **Larry***'s horoscope in his hand. He comes to* **Kate***.*

Frank   Kate! Kate!

Mother   Frank, did you see George?

Frank (*extending his hand*)   Lydia told me, I'm glad to . . . you'll have to pardon me. (*Pulling* **Mother** *over:*) I've got something amazing for you, Kate, I finished Larry's horoscope.

Mother   You'd be interested in this, George. It's wonderful the way he can understand the—

Chris (*entering from house*)   George, the girl's on the phone—

Mother (*desperately*)   He finished Larry's horoscope!

Chris   Frank, can't you pick a better time than this?

Frank   The greatest men who ever lived believed in the stars!

Chris   Stop filling her head with that junk!

Frank   Is it junk to feel that there's a greater power than ourselves? I've studied the stars of his life! I won't argue with you, I'm telling you. Somewhere in this world your brother is alive!

Mother (*instantly to* **Chris**)   Why isn't it possible?

Chris   Because it's insane.

Frank   Just a minute now. I'll tell you something and you can do as you please. Just let me say it. He was supposed to have died on November twenty-fifth. But November twenty-fifth was his favorable day.

Chris   Mother!

Mother   Listen to him!

Frank   It was a day when everything good was shining on him, the kind of day he should've married on. You can laugh at a lot of it, I can understand you laughing. But the odds are a million to one that a man won't die on his favorable day. That's known, that's known, Chris!

Mother   Why isn't it possible, why isn't it possible, Chris!

George (*to* **Ann**)   Don't you understand what she's saying? She just told you to go. What are you waiting for now?

Chris   Nobody can tell her to go. (*A car horn is heard.*)

Mother (*to* **Frank**)   Thank you, darling, for your trouble. Will you tell him to wait, Frank?

Frank (*as he goes*)   Sure thing.

Mother (*calling out*)   They'll be right out, driver!

Chris   She's not leaving, Mother.

George   You heard her say it, he's never been sick!

Mother   He misunderstood me, Chris! (**Chris** *looks at her, struck.*)

George (*to* **Ann**)   He simply told your father to kill pilots, and covered himself in bed!

Chris   You'd better answer him, Annie. Answer him.

Mother   I packed your bag, darling.

Chris   What?

Mother   I packed your bag. All you've got to do is close it.

Ann   I'm not closing anything. He asked me here and I'm staying till he tells me to go. (*To* **George**:) Till Chris tells me!

Chris   That's all! Now get out of here, George!

Mother (*to* **Chris**)   But if that's how he feels—

Chris   That's all, nothing more till Christ comes, about the case or Larry as long as I'm here! (*To* **George***:*) Now get out of here, George!

George (*to* **Ann**)   You tell me. I want to hear you tell me.

Ann   Go, George!

They disappear up the driveway, **Ann** *saying, "Don't take it that way, Georgie! Please don't take it that way."*

Chris (*turning to his mother*)   What do you mean, you packed her bag? How dare you pack her bag?

Mother   Chris—

Chris   How dare you pack her bag?

Mother   She doesn't belong here.

Chris   Then I don't belong here.

Mother   She's Larry's girl.

Chris   And I'm his brother and he's dead, and I'm marrying his girl.

Mother   Never, never in this world!

Keller   You lost your mind?

Mother   You have nothing to say!

Keller (*cruelly*)   I got plenty to say. Three and a half years you been talking like a maniac—

Mother *smashes him across the face.*

Mother   Nothing. You have nothing to say. Now I say. He's coming back, and everybody has got to wait.

Chris   Mother, Mother—

Mother   Wait, wait—

Chris   How long? How long?

Mother (*rolling out of her*)   Till he comes; forever and ever till he comes!

Chris (*as an ultimatum*)   Mother, I'm going ahead with it.

Mother   Chris, I've never said no to you in my life, now I say no!

Chris   You'll never let him go till I do it.

Mother   I'll never let him go and you'll never let him go!

Chris   I've let him go. I've let him go a long—

Mother (*with no less force, but turning from him*)   Then let your father go. (*Pause.* **Chris** *stands transfixed.*)

Keller   She's out of her mind.

Mother   Altogether! (*To* **Chris**, *but not facing them:*) Your brother's alive, darling, because if he's dead, your father killed him. Do you understand me now? As long as you live, that boy is alive. God does not let a son be killed by his father. Now you see, don't you? Now you see. (*Beyond control, she hurries up and into house.*)

Keller (**Chris** *has not moved. He speaks insinuatingly, questioningly*)   She's out of her mind.

Chris (*in a broken whisper*)   Then . . . you did it?

Keller (*with the beginning of plea in his voice*)   He never flew a P-40—

Chris (*struck; deadly*)   But the others.

Keller (*insistently*)   She's out of her mind. (*He takes a step toward* **Chris**, *pleadingly.*)

Chris (*unyielding*)   Dad . . . you did it?

Keller   He never flew a P-40, what's the matter with you?

Chris (*still asking, and saying*)   Then you did it. To the others.

Both hold their voices down.

Keller (*afraid of him, his deadly insistence*)   What's the matter with you? What the hell is the matter with you?

Chris (*quietly, incredibly*)   How could you do that? How?

Keller   What's the matter with you!

Chris   Dad . . . Dad, you killed twenty-one men!

Keller   What, killed?

Chris   You killed them, you murdered them.

Keller (*as though throwing his whole nature open before* **Chris**)   How could I kill anybody?

Chris   Dad! Dad!

Keller (*trying to hush him*)   I didn't kill anybody!

Chris   Then explain it to me. What did you do? Explain it to me or I'll tear you to pieces!

Keller (*horrified at his overwhelming fury*)   Don't, Chris, don't—

Chris   I want to know what you did, now what did you do? You had a hundred and twenty cracked engine-heads, now what did you do?

Keller   If you're going to hang me then I—

Chris   I'm listening. God Almighty, I'm listening!

Keller (*their movements now are those of subtle pursuit and escape.* **Keller** *keeps a step out of* **Chris**'s *range as he talks*)   You're a boy, what could I do! I'm in business, a man is in business; a hundred and twenty cracked, you're out of business; you got a process, the process don't work you're out of business; you don't know how to operate, your stuff is no good; they close you up, they tear up your contracts, what the hell's it to them? You lay forty years into a business and they knock you out in five minutes, what could I do, let them take forty years, let them take my life away? (*His voice cracking:*) I never thought they'd install them. I swear to God. I thought they'd stop 'em before anybody took off.

Chris   Then why'd you ship them out?

Keller   By the time they could spot them I thought I'd have the process going again, and I could show them they needed me and they'd let it go by. But weeks passed and I got no kick-back, so I was going to tell them.

Chris   Then why didn't you tell them?

Keller   It was too late. The paper, it was all over the front page, twenty-one went down, it was too late. They came with handcuffs into the shop, what could I do? (*He sits on bench.*) Chris . . . Chris, I did it for you, it was a chance and I took it for you. I'm sixty-one years old, when would I have another chance to make something for you? Sixty-one years old you don't get another chance, do ya?

Chris   You even knew they wouldn't hold up in the air.

Keller   I didn't say that.

Chris   But you were going to warn them not to use them—

Keller   But that don't mean—

Chris   It means you knew they'd crash.

Keller   It don't mean that.

Chris   Then you *thought* they'd crash.

Keller   I was afraid maybe—

Chris   You were afraid maybe! God in heaven, what kind of a man are you? Kids were hanging in the air by those heads. You knew that!

Keller   For you, a business for you!

Chris (*with burning fury*)   For me! Where do you live, where have you come from? For me!—I was dying every day and you were killing my boys and you did it for me? What the hell do you think I was thinking of, the goddam business? Is that as far as your mind can see, the business? What is that, the world—the business? What the hell do you mean, you did it for me? Don't you have a country? Don't you live in the world? What the hell are you? You're not even an animal, no animal kills his own, what are you? What must I do to you? I ought to tear the tongue out of your mouth, what must I do? (*With his fist he pounds down upon his father's shoulder. He stumbles away, covering his face as he weeps.*) What must I do, Jesus God, what must I do?

Keller   Chris . . . My Chris . . .

Curtain.

Act Three

Two o'clock the following morning, **Mother** *is discovered on the rise, rocking ceaselessly in a chair, staring at her thoughts. It is an intense, slight, sort of rocking. A light shows from upstairs bedroom, lower floor windows being dark. The moon is strong and casts its bluish light.*

Presently **Jim**, *dressed in jacket and hat, appears, and seeing her, goes up beside her.*

Jim   Any news?

Mother   No news.

Jim (*gently*)   You can't sit up all night, dear, why don't you go to bed?

Mother   I'm waiting for Chris. Don't worry about me, Jim, I'm perfectly all right.

Jim   But it's almost two o'clock.

Mother   I can't sleep. (*Slight pause.*) You had an emergency?

Jim (*tiredly*)   Somebody had a headache and thought he was dying. (*Slight pause.*) Half of my patients are quite mad. Nobody realizes how many people are walking around loose, and they're cracked as coconuts. Money. Money-money-money-money. You say it long enough it doesn't mean anything. (*She smiles, makes a silent laugh.*) Oh, how I'd love to be around when that happens!

Mother (*shaking her head*)   You're so childish, Jim! Sometimes you are.

Jim (*looks at her a moment*)   Kate. (*Pause.*) What happened?

Mother   I told you. He had an argument with Joe. Then he got in the car and drove away.

Jim   What kind of an argument?

Mother   An argument, Joe . . . He was crying like a child, before.

Jim   They argued about Ann?

Mother (*after slight hesitation*)   No, not Ann. Imagine? (*Indicates lighted window above.*) She hasn't come out of that room since he left. All night in that room.

Jim (*looks at window, then at her*)   What'd Joe do, tell him?

Mother (*stops rocking*)   Tell him what?

Jim   Don't be afraid, Kate, I know. I've always known.

Mother   How?

Jim   It occurred to me a long time ago.

Mother   I always had the feeling that in the back of his head, Chris . . . almost knew. I didn't think it would be such a shock.

Jim (*gets up*)   Chris would never know how to live with a thing like that. It takes a certain talent—for lying. You have it, and I do. But not him.

Mother   What do you mean . . . He's not coming back?

Jim   Oh, no, he'll come back. We all come back, Kate. These private little revolutions always die. The compromise is always made. In a peculiar way. Frank is right—every man does have a star. The star of one's honesty. And you spend your life groping for it, but once it's out it never lights again. I don't think he went very far. He probably just wanted to be alone to watch his star go out.

Mother   Just as long as he comes back.

Jim   I wish he wouldn't, Kate. One year I simply took off, went to New Orleans; for two months I lived on bananas and milk, and studied a certain disease. It was beautiful. And then she came, and she cried. And I went back home with her. And now I live in the usual darkness; I can't find myself; it's even hard sometimes to remember the kind of man I wanted to be. I'm a good husband; Chris is a good son—he'll come back.

Keller *comes out on porch in dressing gown and slippers. He goes upstage—to alley.* **Jim** *goes to him.*

Jim   I have a feeling he's in the park. I'll look around for him. Put her to bed, Joe; this is no good for what she's got. (**Jim** *exits up driveway.*)

Keller (*coming down*)   What does he want here?

Mother   His friend is not home.

Keller (*comes down to her. His voice is husky*)   I don't like him mixing in so much.

Mother   It's too late, Joe. He knows.

Keller (*apprehensively*)   How does he know?

Mother   He guessed a long time ago.

Keller   I don't like that.

Mother (*laughs dangerously, quietly into the line*)   What you don't like.

Keller   Yeah, what I don't like.

Mother   You can't bull yourself through this one, Joe, you better be smart now. This thing—this thing is not over yet.

Keller (*indicating lighted window above*)   And what is she doing up there? She don't come out of the room.

Mother   I don't know, what is she doing? Sit down, stop being mad. You want to live? You better figure out your life.

Keller   She don't know, does she?

Mother   She saw Chris storming out of here. It's one and one—she knows how to add.

Keller   Maybe I ought to talk to her?

Mother   Don't ask me, Joe.

Keller (*almost an outburst*)   Then who do I ask? But I don't think she'll do anything about it.

Mother   You're asking me again.

Keller   I'm askin' you. What am I, a stranger? I thought I had a family here. What happened to my family?

Mother   You've got a family. I'm simply telling you that I have no strength to think any more.

Keller   You have no strength. The minute there's trouble you have no strength.

Mother   Joe, you're doing the same thing again; all your life whenever there's trouble you yell at me and you think that settles it.

Keller   Then what do I do? Tell me, talk to me, what do I do?

Mother   Joe . . . I've been thinking this way. If he comes back—

Keller   What do you mean "if"? He's comin' back!

Mother   I think if you sit him down and you—explain yourself. I mean you ought to make it clear to him that you know you did a terrible thing. (*Not looking into his eyes:*) I mean if he saw that you realize what you did. You see?

Keller   What ice does that cut?

Mother (*a little fearfully*)   I mean if you told him that you want to pay for what you did.

Keller (*sensing . . . quietly*)   How can I pay?

Mother   Tell him—you're willing to go to prison. (*Pause.*)

Keller (*struck, amazed*)   I'm willing to—?

Mother (*quickly*)   You wouldn't go, he wouldn't ask you to go. But if you told him you wanted to, if he could feel that you wanted to pay, maybe he would forgive you.

Keller   He would forgive me! For what?

Mother   Joe, you know what I mean.

Keller   I don't know what you mean! You wanted money, so I made money. What must I be forgiven? You wanted money, didn't you?

Mother   I didn't want it that way.

Keller   I didn't want it that way, either! What difference is it what you want? I spoiled the both of you. I should've put him out when he was ten like I was put out, and make him earn his keep. Then he'd know how a buck is made in this world. Forgiven! I could live on a quarter a day myself, but I got a family so I—

Mother   Joe, Joe . . . It don't excuse it that you did it for the family.

Keller   It's got to excuse it!

Mother   There's something bigger than the family to him.

Keller   Nothin' is bigger!

Mother   There is to him.

Keller   There's nothin' he could do that I wouldn't forgive. Because he's my son. Because I'm his father and he's my son.

Mother   Joe, I tell you—

Keller   Nothin's bigger than that. And you're goin' to tell him, you understand? I'm his father and he's my son, and if there's something bigger than that I'll put a bullet in my head!

Mother   You stop that!

Keller   You heard me. Now you know what to tell him. (*Pause. He moves from her—halts.*) But he wouldn't put me away though . . . He wouldn't do that . . . Would he?

Mother   He loved you, Joe, you broke his heart.

Keller   But to put me away . . .

Mother   I don't know. I'm beginning to think we don't really know him. They say in the war he was such a killer. Here he was always afraid of mice. I don't know him. I don't know what he'll do.

Keller   Goddam, if Larry was alive he wouldn't act like this. He understood the way the world is made. He listened to me. To him the world had a forty-foot front, it ended at the building line. This one, everything bothers him. You make a deal, overcharge two cents, and his hair falls out. He don't understand money. Too easy, it came too easy. Yes, sir. Larry. That was a boy we lost. Larry. Larry. (*He slumps on chair in front of her.*) What am I gonna do, Kate?

Mother   Joe, Joe, please . . . You'll be all right, nothing is going to happen.

Keller (*desperately, lost*)   For you, Kate, for both of you, that's all I ever lived for . . .

Mother   I know, darling, I know. (**Ann** *enters from house. They say nothing, waiting for her to speak.*)

Ann   Why do you stay up? I'll tell you when he comes.

Keller (*rises, goes to her*)   You didn't eat supper, did you? (*To* **Mother***:*) Why don't you make her something?

Mother   Sure, I'll—

Ann   Never mind, Kate, I'm all right. (*They are unable to speak to each other.*) There's something I want to tell you. (*She starts, then halts.*) I'm not going to do anything about it.

Mother   She's a good girl! (*To* **Keller***:*) You see? She's a—

Ann   I'll do nothing about Joe, but you're going to do something for me. (*Directly to* **Mother***:*) You made Chris feel guilty with me. Whether you wanted to or not, you've crippled him in front of me. I'd like you to tell him that Larry is dead and that you know it. You understand me? I'm not going out of here alone. There's no life for me that way. I want to set him free. And then I promise you, everything will end, and we'll go away, and that's all.

Keller   You'll do that. You'll tell him.

Ann   I know what I'm asking, Kate. You had two sons. But you've only got one now.

Keller   You'll tell him.

Ann   And you've got to say it to him so he knows you mean it.

Mother   My dear, if the boy was dead, it wouldn't depend on my words to make Chris know it . . . The night he gets into your bed, his heart will dry up. Because he knows and you know. To his dying day he'll wait for his brother! No, my dear, no such thing. You're going in the morning, and you're going alone. That's your life, that's your lonely life. (*She goes to porch, and starts in.*)

Ann   Larry is dead, Kate.

Mother (*she stops*)   Don't speak to me.

Ann   I said he's dead. I know! He crashed off the coast of China November twenty-fifth! His engine didn't fail him. But he died. I know . . .

Mother   How did he die? You're lying to me. If you know, how did he die?

Ann   I loved him. You know I loved him. Would I have looked at anyone else if I wasn't sure? That's enough for you.

Mother (*moving on her*)   What's enough for me? What're you talking about? (*She grasps* **Ann***'s wrists.*)

Ann   You're hurting my wrists.

Mother   What are you talking about! (*Pause. She stares at* **Ann** *a moment, then turns and goes to* **Keller**.)

Ann   Joe, go in the house.

Keller   Why should I—

Ann   Please go.

Keller   Lemme know when he comes. (**Keller** *goes into house.*)

Mother (*as she sees* **Ann** *taking a letter from her pocket*)   What's that?

Ann   Sit down. (**Mother** *moves left to chair, but does not sit.*) First you've got to understand. When I came, I didn't have any idea that Joe—I had nothing against him or you. I came to get married. I hoped . . . So I didn't bring this to hurt you. I thought I'd show it to you only if there was no other way to settle Larry in your mind.

Mother   Larry? (*Snatches letter from* **Ann***'s hand.*)

Ann   He wrote it to me just before he—(**Mother** *opens and begins to read letter.*) I'm not trying to hurt you, Kate. You're making me do this, now remember you're—Remember. I've been so lonely, Kate . . . I can't leave here alone again. (*A long, low moan comes from* **Mother**'*s throat as she reads.*) You made me show it to you. You wouldn't believe me. I told you a hundred times, why wouldn't you believe me!

Mother   Oh, my God . . .

Ann (*with pity and fear*)   Kate, please, please . . .

Mother   My God, my God . . .

Ann   Kate, dear, I'm so sorry . . . I'm so sorry.

Chris *enters from driveway. He seems exhausted.*

Chris   What's the matter—?

Ann   Where were you? . . . You're all perspired. (**Mother** *doesn't move.*) Where were you?

Chris   Just drove around a little. I thought you'd be gone.

Ann   Where do I go? I have nowhere to go.

Chris (*to* **Mother**)   Where's Dad?

Ann   Inside lying down.

Chris   Sit down, both of you. I'll say what there is to say.

Mother   I didn't hear the car . . .

Chris   I left it in the garage.

Mother   Jim is out looking for you.

Chris   Mother . . . I'm going away. There are a couple of firms in Cleveland, I think I can get a place. I mean, I'm going away for good. (*To* **Ann** *alone:*) I know what you're thinking, Annie. It's true. I'm yellow. I was made yellow in this house because I suspected my father and I did nothing about it, but if I knew that night when I came home what I know now, he'd be in the district attorney's office by this time, and I'd have brought him there. Now if I look at him, all I'm able to do is cry.

Mother   What are you talking about? What else can you do?

Chris   I could jail him! I could jail him, if I were human any more. But I'm like everybody else now. I'm practical now. You made me practical.

Mother   But you have to be.

Chris   The cats in that alley are practical, the bums who ran away when we were fighting were practical. Only the dead ones weren't practical. But now I'm practical, and I spit on myself. I'm going away. I'm going now.

Ann (*going up to him*)   I'm coming with you.

Chris   No, Ann.

Ann   Chris, I don't ask you to do anything about Joe.

Chris   You do, you do.

Ann   I swear I never will.

Chris   In your heart you always will.

Ann   Then do what you have to do!

Chris   Do what? What is there to do? I've looked all night for a reason to make him suffer.

Ann   There's reason, there's reason!

Chris   What? Do I raise the dead when I put him behind bars? Then what'll I do it for? We used to shoot a man who acted like a dog, but honor was real there, you were protecting something. But here? This is the land of the great big dogs, you don't love a man here, you eat him! That's the principle; the only one we live by—it just happened to kill a few people this time, that's all. The world's that way, how can I take it out on him? What sense does that make? This is a zoo, a zoo!

Ann (*to* **Mother**)   You know what he's got to do! Tell him!

Mother   Let him go.

Ann   I won't let him go. You'll tell him what he's got to do . . .

Mother   Annie!

Ann   Then I will!

Keller *enters from house.* **Chris** *sees him, goes down near arbor.*

Keller   What's the matter with you? I want to talk to you.

Chris   I've got nothing to say to you.

Keller (*taking his arm*)   I want to talk to you!

Chris (*pulling violently away from him*)   Don't do that, Dad. I'm going to hurt you if you do that. There's nothing to say, so say it quick.

Keller   Exactly what's the matter? What's the matter? You got too much money? Is that what bothers you?

Chris (*with an edge of sarcasm*)   It bothers me.

Keller   If you can't get used to it, then throw it away. You hear me? Take every cent and give it to charity, throw it in the sewer. Does that settle it? In the sewer, that's all. You think I'm kidding? I'm tellin' you what to do, if it's dirty then burn it. It's your money, that's not my money. I'm a dead man, I'm an old dead man, nothing's mine. Well, talk to me! What do you want to do!

Chris   It's not what I want to do. It's what you want to do.

Keller   What should I want to do? (**Chris** *is silent.*) Jail? You want me to go to jail? If you want me to go, say so! Is that where I belong? Then tell me so! (*Slight pause.*) What's the matter, why can't you tell me? (*Furiously.*) You say everything else to me, say that! (*Slight pause.*) I'll tell you why you can't say it. Because you know I don't belong there. Because you know! (*With growing emphasis and passion, and a persistent tone of desperation:*) Who worked for nothin' in that war? When they work for nothin', I'll work for nothin'. Did they ship a gun or a truck outa Detroit before they got their price? Is that clean? It's dollars and cents, nickels and dimes; war and peace, it's nickels and dimes, what's clean? Half the goddam country is gotta go if I go! That's why you can't tell me.

Chris   That's exactly why.

Keller   Then . . . why am *I* bad?

Chris   *I* know you're no worse than most men but I thought you were better. I never saw you as a man. I saw you as my father. (*Almost breaking:*) I can't look at you this way, I can't look at myself!

He turns away, unable to face **Keller**. **Ann** *goes quickly to* **Mother**, *takes letter from her and starts for* **Chris**. **Mother** *instantly rushes to intercept her.*

Mother   Give me that!

Ann   He's going to read it! (*She thrusts letter into* **Chris**'s *hand.*) Larry. He wrote it to me the day he died.

Keller   Larry!

Mother   Chris, it's not for you. (*He starts to read.*) Joe . . . go away . . .

Keller (*mystified, frightened*)   Why'd she say, Larry, what—?

Mother (*desperately pushes him toward alley, glancing at* **Chris**)   Go
to the street, Joe, go to the street! (*She comes down beside* **Keller**.)
Don't, Chris . . . (*Pleading from her whole soul:*) Don't tell him.

Chris (*quietly*)   Three and one half years . . . talking, talking. Now you
tell me what you must do. . . . This is how he died, now tell me where
you belong.

Keller (*pleading*)   Chris, a man can't be a Jesus in this world!

Chris   I know all about the world. I know the whole crap story. Now
listen to this, and tell me what a man's got to be! (*Reads:*) "My dear Ann:
. . ." You listening? He wrote this the day he died. Listen, don't cry . . .
Listen! "My dear Ann: It is impossible to put down the things I feel. But
I've got to tell you something. Yesterday they flew in a load of papers
from the States and I read about Dad and your father being convicted. I
can't express myself. I can't tell you how I feel—I can't bear to live any
more. Last night I circled the base for twenty minutes before I could
bring myself in. How could he have done that? Every day three or four
men never come back and he sits back there doing business . . . I don't
know how to tell you what I feel . . . I can't face anybody . . . I'm going
out on a mission in a few minutes. They'll probably report me missing. If
they do, I want you to know that you mustn't wait for me. I tell you,
Ann, if I had him there now I could kill him—" (**Keller** *grabs letter from*
Chris*'s hand and reads it. After a long pause:*) Now blame the world. Do
you understand that letter?

Keller (*speaking almost inaudibly*)   I think I do. Get the car. I'll put on
my jacket. (*He turns and starts slowly for the house.* **Mother** *rushes to
intercept him.*)

Mother   Why are you going? You'll sleep, why are you going?

Keller   I can't sleep here. I'll feel better if I go.

Mother   You're so foolish. Larry was your son too, wasn't he? You
know he'd never tell you to do this.

Keller (*looking at letter in his hand*)   Then what is this if it isn't telling
me? Sure, he was my son. But I think to him they were all my sons. And
I guess they were, I guess they were. I'll be right down. (*Exits into
house.*)

Mother (*to* **Chris***, with determination*)   You're not going to take him!

Chris   I'm taking him.

Mother   It's up to you, if you tell him to stay he'll stay. Go and tell him!

Chris   Nobody could stop him now.

Mother   You'll stop him! How long will he live in prison? Are you trying to kill him?

Chris (*holding out letter*)   I thought you read this!

Mother (*of* **Larry**, *the letter*)   The war is over! Didn't you hear? It's over!

Chris   Then what was Larry to you? A stone that fell into the water? It's not enough for him to be sorry. Larry didn't kill himself to make you and Dad sorry.

Mother   What more can we be!

Chris   You can be better! Once and for all you can know there's a universe of people outside and you're responsible to it, and unless you know that, you threw away your son because that's why he died.

A shot is heard in the house. They stand frozen for a brief second. **Chris** *starts for porch, pauses at step, turns to* **Ann**.

Chris   Find Jim! (*He goes on into the house and* **Ann** *runs up driveway.* **Mother** *stands alone, transfixed.*)

Mother (*softly, almost moaning*)   Joe . . . Joe . . . Joe . . . Joe . . . (**Chris** *comes out of house, down to* **Mother**'*s arms.*)

Chris (*almost crying*)   Mother, I didn't mean to—

Mother   Don't dear. Don't take it on yourself. Forget now. Live. (**Chris** *stirs as if to answer.*) Shhh . . . (*She puts his arms down gently and moves toward porch.*) Shhh . . . (*As she reaches porch steps she begins sobbing.*)

Curtain.

Death of a Salesman

Certain Private Conversations in
Two Acts and a Requiem

The Characters

Willy Loman	**Charley**
Linda	**Uncle Ben**
Biff	**Howard Wagner**
Happy	**Jenny**
Bernard	**Stanley**
The Woman	**Miss Forsythe**
Letta	

The action takes place in Willy Loman's house and yard and in various places he visits in the New York and Boston of today.

Act One

A melody is heard, played upon a flute. It is small and fine, telling of grass and trees and the horizon. The curtain rises.

Before us is the Salesman's house. We are aware of towering, angular shapes behind it, surrounding it on all sides. Only the blue light of the sky falls upon the house and forestage; the surrounding area shows an angry glow of orange. As more light appears, we see a solid vault of apartment houses around the small, fragile-seeming home. An air of the dream clings to the place, a dream rising out of reality. The kitchen at center seems actual enough, for there is a kitchen table with three chairs, and a refrigerator. But no other fixtures are seen. At the back of the kitchen there is a draped entrance, which leads to the living-room. To the right of the kitchen, on a level raised two feet, is a bedroom furnished only with a brass bedstead and a straight chair. On a shelf over the bed a silver athletic trophy stands. A window opens onto the apartment house at the side.

Behind the kitchen, on a level raised six and a half feet, is the boys' bedroom, at present barely visible. Two beds are dimly seen, and at the back of the room a dormer window. (This bedroom is above the unseen living-room.) At the left a stairway curves up to it from the kitchen.

*The entire setting is wholly or, in some places, partially transparent. The roof-line of the house is one-dimensional; under and over it we see the apartment buildings. Before the house lies an apron, curving beyond the forestage into the orchestra. This forward area serves as the back yard as well as the locale of all **Willy**'s imaginings and of his city scenes. Whenever the action is in the present the actors observe the imaginary wall-lines, entering the house only through its door at the left. But in the scenes of the past these boundaries are broken, and characters enter or leave a room by stepping "through" a wall onto the forestage.*

*From the right, **Willy Loman**, the Salesman, enters, carrying two large sample cases. The flute plays on. He hears but is not aware of it. He is past sixty years of age, dressed quietly. Even as he crosses the stage to the doorway of the house, his exhaustion is apparent. He unlocks the door, comes into the kitchen, and thankfully lets his burden down, feeling the soreness of his palms. A word-sigh escapes his lips—it might be "Oh, boy, oh, boy." He closes the door, then carries his cases out into the living-room, through the draped kitchen doorway.*

Linda, *his wife, has stirred in her bed at the right. She gets out and puts on a robe, listening. Most often jovial, she has developed an iron repression of her exceptions to* **Willy***'s behavior—she more than loves him, she admires him, as though his mercurial nature, his temper, his massive dreams and little cruelties, served her only as sharp reminders of the turbulent longings within him, longings which she shares but lacks the temperament to utter and follow to their end.*

Linda (*hearing* **Willy** *outside the bedroom, calls with some trepidation*)   Willy!

Willy   It's all right. I came back.

Linda   Why? What happened? (*Slight pause.*) Did something happen, Willy?

Willy   No, nothing happened.

Linda   You didn't smash the car, did you?

Willy (*with casual irritation*)   I said nothing happened. Didn't you hear me?

Linda   Don't you feel well?

Willy   I'm tired to the death. (*The flute has faded away. He sits on the bed beside her, a little numb.*) I couldn't make it. I just couldn't make it, Linda.

Linda (*very carefully, delicately*)   Where were you all day? You look terrible.

Willy   I got as far as a little above Yonkers. I stopped for a cup of coffee. Maybe it was the coffee.

Linda   What?

Willy (*after a pause*)   I suddenly couldn't drive any more. The car kept going off onto the shoulder, y'know?

Linda (*helpfully*)   Oh. Maybe it was the steering again. I don't think Angelo knows the Studebaker.

Willy   No, it's me, it's me. Suddenly I realize I'm goin' sixty miles an hour and I don't remember the last five minutes. I'm—I can't seem to— keep my mind to it.

Linda   Maybe it's your glasses. You never went for your new glasses.

Willy   No, I see everything. I came back ten miles an hour. It took me nearly four hours from Yonkers.

Linda (*resigned*)   Well, you'll just have to take a rest, Willy, you can't continue this way.

Willy   I just got back from Florida.

Linda   But you didn't rest your mind. Your mind is overactive, and the mind is what counts, dear.

Willy   I'll start out in the morning. Maybe I'll feel better in the morning. (*She is taking off his shoes.*) These goddam arch supports are killing me.

Linda   Take an aspirin. Should I get you an aspirin? It'll soothe you.

Willy (*with wonder*)   I was driving along, you understand? And I was fine. I was even observing the scenery. You can imagine, me looking at scenery, on the road every week of my life. But it's so beautiful up there, Linda, the trees are so thick, and the sun is warm. I opened the windshield and just let the warm air bathe over me. And then all of a sudden I'm goin' off the road! I'm tellin' ya, I absolutely forgot I was driving. If I'd've gone the other way over the white line I might've killed somebody. So I went on again—and five minutes later I'm dreamin' again, and I nearly—(*He presses two fingers against his eyes.*) I have such thoughts, I have such strange thoughts.

Linda   Willy, dear. Talk to them again. There's no reason why you can't work in New York.

Willy   They don't need me in New York. I'm the New England man. I'm vital in New England.

Linda   But you're sixty years old. They can't expect you to keep traveling every week.

Willy   I'll have to send a wire to Portland. I'm supposed to see Brown and Morrison tomorrow morning at ten o'clock to show the line. Goddammit, I could sell them! (*He starts putting on his jacket.*)

Linda (*taking the jacket from him*)   Why don't you go down to the place tomorrow and tell Howard you've simply got to work in New York? You're too accommodating, dear.

Willy   If old man Wagner was alive I'd a been in charge of New York now! That man was a prince, he was a masterful man. But that boy of his, that Howard, he don't appreciate. When I went north the first time, the Wagner Company didn't know where New England was!

Linda   Why don't you tell those things to Howard, dear?

Willy (*encouraged*)   I will, I definitely will. Is there any cheese?

Linda   I'll make you a sandwich.

Willy   No, go to sleep. I'll take some milk. I'll be up right away. The boys in?

Linda   They're sleeping. Happy took Biff on a date tonight.

Willy (*interested*)   That so?

Linda   It was so nice to see them shaving together, one behind the other, in the bathroom. And going out together. You notice? The whole house smells of shaving lotion.

Willy   Figure it out. Work a lifetime to pay off a house. You finally own it, and there's nobody to live in it.

Linda   Well, dear, life is a casting off. It's always that way.

Willy   No, no, some people—some people accomplish something. Did Biff say anything after I went this morning?

Linda   You shouldn't have criticized him, Willy, especially after he just got off the train. You mustn't lose your temper with him.

Willy   When the hell did I lose my temper? I simply asked him if he was making any money. Is that a criticism?

Linda   But, dear, how could he make any money?

Willy (*worried and angered*)   There's such an undercurrent in him. He became a moody man. Did he apologize when I left this morning?

Linda   He was crestfallen, Willy. You know how he admires you. I think if he finds himself, then you'll both be happier and not fight any more.

Willy   How can he find himself on a farm? Is that a life? A farmhand? In the beginning, when he was young, I thought, well, a young man, it's good for him to tramp around, take a lot of different jobs. But it's more than ten years now and he has yet to make thirty-five dollars a week!

Linda   He's finding himself, Willy.

Willy   Not finding yourself at the age of thirty-four is a disgrace!

Linda   Shh!

Willy   The trouble is he's lazy, goddammit!

Linda   Willy, please!

Willy   Biff is a lazy bum!

Linda   They're sleeping. Get something to eat. Go on down.

Willy   Why did he come home? I would like to know what brought him home.

Linda   I don't know. I think he's still lost, Willy. I think he's very lost.

Willy   Biff Loman is lost. In the greatest country in the world a young man with such—personal attractiveness, gets lost. And such a hard worker. There's one thing about Biff—he's not lazy.

Linda   Never.

Willy (*with pity and resolve*)   I'll see him in the morning; I'll have a nice talk with him. I'll get him a job selling. He could be big in no time. My God! Remember how they used to follow him around in high school? When he smiled at one of them their faces lit up. When he walked down the street . . . (*He loses himself in reminiscences.*)

Linda (*trying to bring him out of it*)   Willy, dear, I got a new kind of American-type cheese today. It's whipped.

Willy   Why do you get American when I like Swiss?

Linda   I just thought you'd like a change—

Willy   I don't want a change! I want Swiss cheese. Why am I always being contradicted?

Linda (*with a covering laugh*)   I thought it would be a surprise.

Willy   Why don't you open a window in here, for God's sake?

Linda (*with infinite patience*)   They're all open, dear.

Willy   The way they boxed us in here. Bricks and windows, windows and bricks.

Linda   We should've bought the land next door.

Willy   The street is lined with cars. There's not a breath of fresh air in the neighborhood. The grass don't grow any more, you can't raise a carrot in the back yard. They should've had a law against apartment houses. Remember those two beautiful elm trees out there? When I and Biff hung the swing between them?

Linda   Yeah, like being a million miles from the city.

Willy   They should've arrested the builder for cutting those down. They massacred the neighborhood. (*Lost:*) More and more I think of those days, Linda. This time of year it was lilac and wisteria. And then the peonies would come out, and the daffodils. What fragrance in this room!

Linda   Well, after all, people had to move somewhere.

Willy   No, there's more people now.

Linda   I don't think there's more people. I think—

Willy   There's more people! That's what ruining this country! Population is getting out of control. The competition is maddening! Smell the stink from that apartment house! And another one on the other side . . . How can they whip cheese?

On **Willy**'s *last line,* **Biff** *and* **Happy** *raise themselves up in their beds, listening.*

Linda   Go down, try it. And be quiet.

Willy (*turning to* **Linda**, *guiltily*)   You're not worried about me, are you, sweetheart?

Biff   What's the matter?

Happy   Listen!

Linda   You've got too much on the ball to worry about.

Willy   You're my foundation and my support, Linda.

Linda   Just try to relax, dear. You make mountains out of mole-hills.

Willy   I won't fight with him any more. If he wants to go back to Texas, let him go.

Linda   He'll find his way.

Willy   Sure. Certain men just don't get started till later in life. Like Thomas Edison, I think. Or B. F. Goodrich. One of them was deaf. (*He starts for the bedroom doorway.*) I'll put my money on Biff.

Linda   And Willy—if it's warm Sunday we'll drive in the country. And we'll open the windshield, and take lunch.

Willy   No, the windshields don't open on the new cars.

Linda   But you opened it today.

Willy   Me? I didn't. (*He stops.*) Now isn't that peculiar! Isn't that a remarkable—(*He breaks off in amazement and fright as the flute is heard distantly.*)

Linda   What, darling?

Willy   That is the most remarkable thing.

Linda   What, dear?

Willy   I was thinking of the Chevvy. (*Slight pause.*) Nineteen twenty-eight . . . when I had that red Chevvy—(*Breaks off.*) That funny? I coulda sworn I was driving that Chevvy today.

Linda   Well, that's nothing. Something must've reminded you.

Willy   Remarkable. Ts. Remember those days? The way Biff used to simonize that car? The dealer refused to believe there was eighty thousand miles on it. (*He shakes his head.*) Heh! (*To* **Linda***:*) Close your eyes, I'll be right up. (*He walks out of the bedroom.*)

Happy (*to* **Biff**)   Jesus, maybe he smashed up the car again!

Linda (*calling after* **Willy**)   Be careful on the stairs, dear! The cheese is on the middle shelf! (*She turns, goes over to the bed, takes his jacket, and goes out of the bedroom.*)

Light has risen on the boys' room. Unseen, **Willy** *is heard talking to himself, "Eighty thousand miles," and a little laugh.* **Biff** *gets out of bed, comes downstage a bit, and stands attentively.* **Biff** *is two years older than his brother* **Happy***, well built, but in these days bears a worn air and seems less self-assured. He has succeeded less, and his dreams are stronger and less acceptable than* **Happy***'s.* **Happy** *is tall, powerfully made. Sexuality is like a visible color on him, or a scent that many women have discovered. He, like his brother, is lost, but in a different way, for he has never allowed himself to turn his face toward defeat and is thus more confused and hard-skinned, although seemingly more content.*

Happy (*getting out of bed*)   He's going to get his license taken away if he keeps that up. I'm getting nervous about him, y'know, Biff?

Biff   His eyes are going.

Happy   No, I've driven with him. He sees all right. He just doesn't keep his mind on it. I drove into the city with him last week. He stops at a green light and then it turns red and he goes. (*He laughs.*)

Biff   Maybe he's color-blind.

Happy   Pop? Why he's got the finest eye for color in the business. You know that.

Biff (*sitting down on his bed*)   I'm going to sleep.

Happy   You're not still sour on Dad, are you, Biff?

Biff   He's all right, I guess.

Willy (*underneath them, in the living-room*)   Yes, sir, eighty thousand miles—eighty-two thousand!

Biff   You smoking?

Happy (*holding out a pack of cigarettes*)   Want one?

Biff (*taking a cigarette*)   I can never sleep when I smell it.

Willy   What a simonizing job, heh!

Happy (*with deep sentiment*)   Funny, Biff, y'know? Us sleeping in here again? The old beds. (*He pats his bed affectionately.*) All the talk that went across those two beds, huh? Our whole lives.

Biff   Yeah. Lotta dreams and plans.

Happy (*with a deep and masculine laugh*)   About five hundred women would like to know what was said in this room.

They share a soft laugh.

Biff   Remember that big Betsy something—what the hell was her name—over on Bushwick Avenue?

Happy (*combing his hair*)   With the collie dog!

Biff   That's the one. I got you in there, remember?

Happy   Yeah, that was my first time—I think. Boy, there was a pig! (*They laugh, almost crudely.*) You taught me everything I know about women. Don't forget that.

Biff   I bet you forgot how bashful you used to be. Especially with girls.

Happy   Oh, I still am, Biff.

Biff   Oh, go on.

Happy   I just control it, that's all. I think I got less bashful and you got more so. What happened, Biff? Where's the old humor, the old confidence? (*He shakes* **Biff**'*s knee.* **Biff** *gets up and moves restlessly about the room.*) What's the matter?

Biff   Why does Dad mock me all the time?

Happy   He's not mocking you, he—

Biff   Everything I say there's a twist of mockery on his face. I can't get near him.

Happy   He just wants you to make good, that's all. I wanted to talk to you about Dad for a long time, Biff. Something's—happening to him. He—talks to himself.

Biff   I noticed that this morning. But he always mumbled.

Happy   But not so noticeable. It got so embarrassing I sent him to Florida. And you know something? Most of the time he's talking to you.

Biff   What's he say about me?

Happy   I can't make it out.

Biff   What's he say about me?

Happy   I think the fact that you're not settled, that you're still kind of up in the air . . .

Biff   There's one or two other things depressing him, Happy.

Happy   What do you mean?

Biff   Never mind. Just don't lay it all to me.

Happy   But I think if you just got started—I mean—is there any future for you out there?

Biff   I tell ya, Hap, I don't know what the future is. I don't know—what I'm supposed to want.

Happy   What do you mean?

Biff   Well, I spent six or seven years after high school trying to work myself up. Shipping clerk, salesman, business of one kind or another. And it's a measly manner of existence. To get on that subway on the hot mornings in summer. To devote your whole life to keeping stock, or making phone calls, or selling or buying. To suffer fifty weeks of the year for the sake of a two-week vacation, when all you really desire is to be outdoors, with your shirt off. And always to have to get ahead of the next fella. And still—that's how you build a future.

Happy   Well, you really enjoy it on a farm? Are you content out there?

Biff (*with rising agitation*)   Hap, I've had twenty or thirty different kinds of jobs since I left home before the war, and it always turns out the same. I just realized it lately. In Nebraska when I herded cattle, and the Dakotas, and Arizona, and now in Texas. It's why I came home now,

I guess, because I realized it. This farm I work on, it's spring there now, see? And they've got about fifteen new colts. There's nothing more inspiring or—beautiful than the sight of a mare and a new colt. And it's cool there now, see? Texas is cool now, and it's spring. And whenever spring comes to where I am, I suddenly get the feeling, my God, I'm not gettin' anywhere! What the hell am I doing, playing around with horses, twenty-eight dollars a week! I'm thirty-four years old, I oughta be makin' my future. That's when I come running home. And now, I get here, and I don't know what to do with myself. (*After a pause:*) I've always made a point of not wasting my life, and everytime I come back here I know that all I've done is to waste my life.

Happy   You're a poet, you know that, Biff? You're a—you're an idealist!

Biff   No, I'm mixed up very bad. Maybe I oughta get married. Maybe I oughta get stuck into something. Maybe that's my trouble. I'm like a boy. I'm not married, I'm not in business, I just—I'm like a boy. Are you content, Hap? You're a success, aren't you? Are you content?

Happy   Hell, no!

Biff   Why? You're making money, aren't you?

Happy (*moving about with energy, expressiveness*)   All I can do now is wait for the merchandise manager to die. And suppose I get to be merchandise manager? He's a good friend of mine, and he just built a terrific estate on Long Island. And he lived there about two months and sold it, and now he's building another one. He can't enjoy it once it's finished. And I know that's just what I would do. I don't know what the hell I'm workin' for. Sometimes I sit in my apartment—all alone. And I think of the rent I'm paying. And it's crazy. But then, it's what I always wanted. My own apartment, a car, and plenty of women. And still, goddammit, I'm lonely.

Biff (*with enthusiasm*)   Listen, why don't you come out West with me?

Happy   You and I, heh?

Biff   Sure, maybe we could buy a ranch. Raise cattle, use our muscles. Men built like we are should be working out in the open.

Happy (*avidly*)   The Loman Brothers, heh?

Biff (*with vast affection*)   Sure, we'd be known all over the counties!

Happy (*enthralled*)   That's what I dream about, Biff. Sometimes I want to just rip my clothes off in the middle of the store and outbox that goddam merchandise manager. I mean I can outbox, outrun, and outlift anybody in that store, and I have to take orders from those common, petty sons-of-bitches till I can't stand it any more.

Biff   I'm tellin' you, kid, if you were with me I'd be happy out there.

Happy (*enthused*)   See, Biff, everybody around me is so false that I'm constantly lowering my ideals . . .

Biff   Baby, together we'd stand up for one another, we'd have someone to trust.

Happy   If I were around you—

Biff   Hap, the trouble is we weren't brought up to grub for money. I don't know how to do it.

Happy   Neither can I!

Biff   Then let's go!

Happy   The only thing is—what can you make out there?

Biff   But look at your friend. Builds an estate and then hasn't the peace of mind to live in it.

Happy   Yeah, but when he walks into the store the waves part in front of him. That's fifty-two thousand dollars a year coming through the revolving door, and I got more in my pinky finger than he's got in his head.

Biff   Yeah, but you just said—

Happy   I gotta show some of those pompous, self-important executives over there that Hap Loman can make the grade. I want to walk into the store the way he walks in. Then I'll go with you, Biff. We'll be together yet, I swear. But take those two we had tonight. Now weren't they gorgeous creatures?

Biff   Yeah, yeah, most gorgeous I've had in years.

Happy   I get that any time I want, Biff. Whenever I feel disgusted. The only trouble is, it gets like bowling or something. I just keep knockin' them over and it doesn't mean anything. You still run around a lot?

Biff   Naa. I'd like to find a girl—steady, somebody with substance.

Happy   That's what I long for.

Biff   Go on! You'd never come home.

Happy   I would! Somebody with character, with resistance! Like Mom, y'know? You're gonna call me a bastard when I tell you this. That girl

Charlotte I was with tonight is engaged to be married in five weeks. (*He tries on his new hat.*)

Biff   No kiddin'!

Happy   Sure, the guy's in line for the vice-presidency of the store. I don't know what gets into me, maybe I just have an overdeveloped sense of competition or something, but I went and ruined her, and furthermore I can't get rid of her. And he's the third executive I've done that to. Isn't that a crummy characteristic? And to top it all, I go to their weddings! (*Indignantly, but laughing:*) Like I'm not supposed to take bribes. Manufacturers offer me a hundred-dollar bill now and then to throw an order their way. You know how honest I am, but it's like this girl, see. I hate myself for it. Because I don't want the girl, and, still, I take it and—I love it!

Biff   Let's go to sleep.

Happy   I guess we didn't settle anything, heh?

Biff   I just got one idea that I think I'm going to try.

Happy   What's that?

Biff   Remember Bill Oliver?

Happy   Sure, Oliver is very big now. You want to work for him again?

Biff   No, but when I quit he said something to me. He put his arm on my shoulder, and he said, "Biff, if you ever need anything, come to me."

Happy   I remember that. That sounds good.

Biff   I think I'll go to see him. If I could get ten thousand or even seven or eight thousand dollars I could buy a beautiful ranch.

Happy   I bet he'd back you. 'Cause he thought highly of you, Biff. I mean, they all do. You're well liked, Biff. That's why I say to come back here, and we both have the apartment. And I'm tellin' you, Biff, any babe you want . . .

Biff   No, with a ranch I could do the work I like and still be something. I just wonder though. I wonder if Oliver still thinks I stole that carton of basketballs.

Happy   Oh, he probably forgot that long ago. It's almost ten years. You're too sensitive. Anyway, he didn't really fire you.

Biff   Well, I think he was going to. I think that's why I quit. I was never sure whether he knew or not. I know he thought the world of me, though. I was the only one he'd let lock up the place.

Willy (*below*)   You gonna wash the engine, Biff?

Happy   Shh!

Biff *looks at* **Happy**, *who is gazing down, listening.* **Willy** *is mumbling in the parlor.*

Happy   You hear that?

They listen. **Willy** *laughs warmly.*

Biff (*growing angry*)   Doesn't he know Mom can hear that?

Willy   Don't get your sweater dirty, Biff!

A look of pain crosses **Biff**'s *face.*

Happy   Isn't that terrible? Don't leave again, will you? You'll find a job here. You gotta stick around. I don't know what to do about him, it's getting embarrassing.

Willy   What a simonizing job!

Biff   Mom's hearing that!

Willy   No kiddin', Biff, you got a date? Wonderful!

Happy   Go on to sleep. But talk to him in the morning, will you?

Biff (*reluctantly getting into bed*)   With her in the house. Brother!

Happy (*getting into bed*)   I wish you'd have a good talk with him.

The light on their room begins to fade.

Biff (*to himself in bed*)   That selfish, stupid . . .

Happy   Sh . . . Sleep, Biff.

Their light is out. Well before they have finished speaking, **Willy**'s *form is dimly seen below in the darkened kitchen. He opens the refrigerator, searches in there, and takes out a bottle of milk. The apartment houses are fading out, and the entire house and surroundings become covered with leaves. Music insinuates itself as the leaves appear.*

Willy   Just wanna be careful with those girls, Biff, that's all. Don't make any promises. No promises of any kind. Because a girl, y'know, they always believe what you tell 'em, and you're very young, Biff, you're too young to be talking seriously to girls.

Light rises on the kitchen. **Willy**, *talking, shuts the refrigerator door and comes downstage to the kitchen table. He pours milk into a glass. He is totally immersed in himself, smiling faintly.*

Willy   Too young entirely, Biff. You want to watch your schooling first. Then when you're all set, there'll be plenty of girls for a boy like you. (*He smiles broadly at a kitchen chair.*) That so? The girls pay for you? (*He laughs.*) Boy, you must really be makin' a hit.

Willy *is gradually addressing—physically—a point offstage, speaking through the wall of the kitchen, and his voice has been rising in volume to that of a normal conversation.*

Willy   I been wondering why you polish the car so careful. Ha! Don't leave the hubcaps, boys. Get the chamois to the hubcaps. Happy, use newspaper on the windows, it's the easiest thing. Show him how to do it, Biff! You see, Happy? Pad it up, use it like a pad. That's it, that's it, good work. You're doin' all right, Hap. (*He pauses, then nods in approbation for a few seconds, then looks upward.*) Biff, first thing we gotta do when we get time is clip that big branch over the house. Afraid it's gonna fall in a storm and hit the roof. Tell you what. We get a rope and sling her around, and then we climb up there with a couple of saws and take her down. Soon as you finish the car, boys, I wanna see ya. I got a surprise for you, boys.

Biff (*offstage*)   Whatta ya got, Dad?

Willy   No, you finish first. Never leave a job till you're finished— remember that. (*Looking toward the "big trees":*) Biff, up in Albany I saw a beautiful hammock. I think I'll buy it next trip, and we'll hang it right between those two elms. Wouldn't that be something? Just swingin' there under those branches. Boy, that would be . . .

Young Biff *and* **Young Happy** *appear from the direction* **Willy** *was addressing.* **Happy** *carries rags and a pail of water.* **Biff**, *wearing a sweater with a block "S," carries a football.*

Biff (*pointing in the direction of the car offstage*)   How's that, Pop, professional?

Willy   Terrific. Terrific job, boys. Good work, Biff.

Happy   Where's the surprise, Pop?

Willy   In the back seat of the car.

Happy   Boy! (*He runs off.*)

Biff   What is it, Dad? Tell me, what'd you buy?

Willy (*laughing, cuffs him*)   Never mind, something I want you to have.

Biff (*turns and starts off*)   What is it, Hap?

Happy (*offstage*)   It's a punching bag!

Biff   Oh, Pop!

Willy   It's got Gene Tunney's signature on it!

Happy *runs onstage with a punching bag.*

Biff   Gee, how'd you know we wanted a punching bag?

Willy   Well, it's the finest thing for the timing.

Happy (*lies down on his back and pedals with his feet*)   I'm losing weight, you notice, Pop?

Willy (*to* **Happy**)   Jumping rope is good too.

Biff   Did you see the new football I got?

Willy (*examining the ball*)   Where'd you get a new ball?

Biff   The coach told me to practice my passing.

Willy   That so? And he gave you the ball, heh?

Biff   Well, I borrowed it from the locker room. (*He laughs confidentially.*)

Willy (*laughing with him at the theft*)   I want you to return that.

Happy   I told you he wouldn't like it!

Biff (*angrily*)   Well, I'm bringing it back!

Willy (*stopping the incipient argument, to* **Happy**)   Sure, he's gotta practice with a regulation ball, doesn't he? (*To* **Biff***:*) Coach'll probably congratulate you on your initiative!

Biff   Oh, he keeps congratulating my initiative all the time, Pop.

Willy   That's because he likes you. If somebody else took that ball there'd be an uproar. So what's the report, boys, what's the report?

Biff   Where'd you go this time, Dad? Gee we were lonesome for you.

Willy (*pleased, puts an arm around each boy and they come down to the apron*)   Lonesome, heh?

Biff   Missed you every minute.

Willy   Don't say? Tell you a secret, boys. Don't breathe it to a soul. Someday I'll have my own business, and I'll never have to leave home any more.

Happy　Like Uncle Charley, heh?

Willy　Bigger than Uncle Charley! Because Charley is not—liked. He's liked, but he's not—well liked.

Biff　Where'd you go this time, Dad?

Willy　Well, I got on the road, and I went north to Providence. Met the Mayor.

Biff　The Mayor of Providence!

Willy　He was sitting in the hotel lobby.

Biff　What'd he say?

Willy　He said, "Morning!" And I said, "You got a fine city here, Mayor." And then he had coffee with me. And then I went to Waterbury. Waterbury is a fine city. Big clock city, the famous Waterbury clock. Sold a nice bill there. And then Boston—Boston is the cradle of the Revolution. A fine city. And a couple of other towns in Mass., and on to Portland and Bangor and straight home!

Biff　Gee, I'd love to go with you sometime, Dad.

Willy　Soon as summer comes.

Happy　Promise?

Willy　You and Hap and I, and I'll show you all the towns. America is full of beautiful towns and fine, upstanding people. And they know me, boys, they know me up and down New England. The finest people. And when I bring you fellas up, there'll be open sesame for all of us, 'cause one thing, boys: I have friends. I can park my car in any street in New England, and the cops protect it like their own. This summer, heh?

Biff and **Happy** (*together*)　Yeah! You bet!

Willy　We'll take our bathing suits.

Happy　We'll carry your bags, Pop!

Willy　Oh, won't that be something! Me comin' into the Boston stores with you boys carryin' my bags. What a sensation!

Biff *is prancing around, practicing passing the ball.*

Willy　You nervous, Biff, about the game?

Biff　Not if you're gonna be there.

Willy   What do they say about you in school, now that they made you captain?

Happy   There's a crowd of girls behind him everytime the classes change.

Biff (*taking* **Willy***'s hand*)   This Saturday, Pop, this Saturday—just for you, I'm going to break through for a touchdown.

Happy   You're supposed to pass.

Biff   I'm takin' one play for Pop. You watch me, Pop, and when I take off my helmet, that means I'm breakin' out. Then you watch me crash through that line!

Willy (*kisses* **Biff**)   Oh, wait'll I tell this in Boston!

Bernard *enters in knickers. He is younger than* **Biff***, earnest and loyal, a worried boy.*

Bernard   Biff, where are you? You're supposed to study with me today.

Willy   Hey, looka Bernard. What're you lookin' so anemic about, Bernard?

Bernard   He's gotta study, Uncle Willy. He's got Regents next week.

Happy (*tauntingly, spinning* **Bernard** *around*)   Let's box, Bernard!

Bernard   Biff! (*He gets away from* **Happy***.*) Listen, Biff, I heard Mr. Birnbaum say that if you don't start studyin' math he's gonna flunk you, and you won't graduate. I heard him!

Willy   You better study with him, Biff. Go ahead now.

Bernard   I heard him!

Biff   Oh, Pop, you didn't see my sneakers! (*He holds up a foot for* **Willy** *to look at.*)

Willy   Hey, that's a beautiful job of printing!

Bernard (*wiping his glasses*)   Just because he printed University of Virginia on his sneakers doesn't mean they've got to graduate him, Uncle Willy!

Willy (*angrily*)   What're you talking about? With scholarships to three universities they're gonna flunk him?

Bernard   But I heard Mr. Birnbaum say—

Willy   Don't be a pest, Bernard! (*To his boys:*) What an anemic!

Bernard   Okay, I'm waiting for you in my house, Biff.

Bernard *goes off. The* **Lomans** *laugh.*

Willy   Bernard is not well liked, is he?

Biff   He's liked, but he's not well liked.

Happy   That's right, Pop.

Willy   That's just what I mean. Bernard can get the best marks in school, y'understand, but when he gets out in the business world, y'understand, you are going to be five times ahead of him. That's why I thank Almighty God you're both built like Adonises. Because the man who makes an appearance in the business world, the man who creates personal interest, is the man who gets ahead. Be liked and you will never want. You take me, for instance. I never have to wait in line to see a buyer. "Willy Loman is here!" That's all they have to know, and I go right through.

Biff   Did you knock them dead, Pop?

Willy   Knocked 'em cold in Providence, slaughtered 'em in Boston.

Happy (*on his back, pedaling again*)   I'm losing weight, you notice, Pop?

Linda *enters, as of old, a ribbon in her hair, carrying a basket of washing.*

Linda (*with youthful energy*)   Hello, dear!

Willy   Sweetheart!

Linda   How'd the Chevvy run?

Willy   Chevrolet, Linda, is the greatest car ever built. (*To the boys:*) Since when do you let your mother carry wash up the stairs?

Biff   Grab hold there, boy!

Happy   Where to, Mom?

Linda   Hang them up on the line. And you better go down to your friends, Biff. The cellar is full of boys. They don't know what to do with themselves.

Biff   Ah, when Pop comes home they can wait!

Willy (*laughs appreciatively*)   You better go down and tell them what to do, Biff.

Biff   I think I'll have them sweep out the furnace room.

Willy   Good work, Biff.

Biff (*goes through wall-line of kitchen to doorway at back and calls down*)   Fellas! Everybody sweep out the furnace room! I'll be right down!

Voices   All right! Okay, Biff.

Biff   George and Sam and Frank, come out back! We're hangin' up the wash! Come on, Hap, on the double! (*He and* **Happy** *carry out the basket.*)

Linda   The way they obey him!

Willy   Well, that's training, the training. I'm tellin' you, I was sellin' thousands and thousands, but I had to come home.

Linda   Oh, the whole block'll be at that game. Did you sell anything?

Willy   I did five hundred gross in Providence and seven hundred gross in Boston.

Linda   No! Wait a minute, I've got a pencil. (*She pulls pencil and paper out of her apron pocket.*) That makes your commission . . . Two hundred—my God! Two hundred and twelve dollars!

Willy   Well, I didn't figure it yet, but . .

Linda   How much did you do?

Willy   Well, I—I did—about a hundred and eighty gross in Providence. Well, no—it came to—roughly two hundred gross on the whole trip.

Linda (*without hesitation*)   Two hundred gross. That's . . . (*She figures.*)

Willy   The trouble was that three of the stores were half closed for inventory in Boston. Otherwise I would a broke records.

Linda   Well, it makes seventy dollars and some pennies. That's very good.

Willy   What do we owe?

Linda   Well, on the first there's sixteen dollars on the refrigerator—

Willy   Why sixteen?

Linda   Well, the fan belt broke, so it was a dollar eighty.

Willy   But it's brand new.

Linda   Well, the man said that's the way it is. Till they work themselves in, y'know.

They move through the wall-line into the kitchen.

Willy   I hope we didn't get stuck on that machine.

Linda   They got the biggest ads of any of them!

Willy   I know, it's a fine machine. What else?

Linda   Well, there's nine-sixty for the washing machine. And for the vacuum cleaner there's three and a half due on the fifteenth. Then the roof, you got twenty-one dollars remaining.

Willy   It don't leak, does it?

Linda   No, they did a wonderful job. Then you owe Frank for the carburetor.

Willy   I'm not going to pay that man! That goddam Chevrolet, they ought to prohibit the manufacture of that car!

Linda   Well, you owe him three and a half. And odds and ends, comes to around a hundred and twenty dollars by the fifteenth.

Willy   A hundred and twenty dollars! My God, if business don't pick up I don't know what I'm gonna do!

Linda   Well, next week you'll do better.

Willy   Oh, I'll knock 'em dead next week. I'll go to Hartford. I'm very well liked in Hartford. You know, the trouble is, Linda, people don't seem to take to me.

They move onto the forestage.

Linda   Oh, don't be foolish.

Willy   I know it when I walk in. They seem to laugh at me.

Linda   Why? Why would they laugh at you? Don't talk that way, Willy.

Willy *moves to the edge of the stage.* **Linda** *goes into the kitchen and starts to darn stockings.*

Willy   I don't know the reason for it, but they just pass me by. I'm not noticed.

Linda   But you're doing wonderful, dear. You're making seventy to a hundred dollars a week.

Willy   But I gotta be at it ten, twelve hours a day. Other men—I don't know—they do it easier. I don't know why—I can't stop myself—I talk too much. A man oughta come in with a few words. One thing about Charley. He's a man of few words, and they respect him.

Linda   You don't talk too much, you're just lively.

Willy   (*smiling*)   Well, I figure, what the hell, life is short, a couple of jokes. (*To himself:*) I joke too much! (*The smile goes.*)

Linda   Why? You're—

Willy   I'm fat. I'm very—foolish to look at, Linda. I didn't tell you, but Christmas time I happened to be calling on F. H. Stewarts, and a salesman I know, as I was going in to see the buyer I heard him say something about—walrus. And I—I cracked him right across the face. I won't take that. I simply will not take that. But they do laugh at me. I know that.

Linda   Darling . . .

Willy   I gotta overcome it. I know I gotta overcome it. I'm not dressing to advantage, maybe.

Linda   Willy, darling, you're the handsomest man in the world—

Willy   Oh, no, Linda.

Linda   To me you are. (*Slight pause.*) The handsomest.

From the darkness is heard the laughter of a woman. **Willy** *doesn't turn to it, but it continues through* **Linda***'s lines.*

Linda   And the boys, Willy. Few men are idolized by their children the way you are.

Music is heard as behind a scrim, to the left of the house, **The Woman***, dimly seen, is dressing.*

Willy   (*with great feeling*)   You're the best there is, Linda, you're a pal, you know that? On the road—on the road I want to grab you sometimes and just kiss the life outa you.

The laughter is loud now, and he moves into a brightening area at the left, where **The Woman** *has come from behind the scrim and is standing, putting on her hat, looking into a "mirror" and laughing.*

Willy   'Cause I get so lonely—especially when business is bad and there's nobody to talk to. I get the feeling that I'll never sell anything again, that I won't make a living for you, or a business, a business for the boys. (*He talks through* **The Woman**'s *subsiding laughter!* **The Woman** *primps at the "mirror."*) There's so much I want to make for—

The Woman   Me? You didn't make me, Willy. I picked you.

Willy (*pleased*)   You picked me?

The Woman (*who is quite proper-looking,* **Willy**'s *age*)   I did. I've been sitting at that desk watching all the salesmen go by, day in, day out. But you've got such a sense of humor, and we do have such a good time together, don't we?

Willy   Sure, sure. (*He takes her in his arms.*) Why do you have to go now?

The Woman   It's two o'clock . . .

Willy   No, come on in! (*He pulls her.*)

The Woman   . . . my sisters'll be scandalized. When'll you be back?

Willy   Oh, two weeks about. Will you come up again?

The Woman   Sure thing. You do make me laugh. It's good for me. (*She squeezes his arm, kisses him.*) And I think you're a wonderful man.

Willy   You picked me, heh?

The Woman   Sure. Because you're so sweet. And such a kidder.

Willy   Well, I'll see you next time I'm in Boston.

The Woman   I'll put you right through to the buyers.

Willy (*slapping her bottom*)   Right. Well, bottoms up!

The Woman (*slaps him gently and laughs*)   You just kill me, Willy. (*He suddenly grabs her and kisses her roughly.*) You kill me. And thanks for the stockings. I love a lot of stockings. Well, good night.

Willy   Good night. And keep your pores open!

The Woman   Oh, Willy!

The Woman *bursts out laughing, and* **Linda**'s *laughter blends in.* **The Woman** *disappears into the dark. Now the area at the kitchen table brightens.* **Linda** *is sitting where she was at the kitchen table, but now is mending a pair of her silk stockings.*

Linda   You are, Willy. The handsomest man. You've got no reason to feel that—

Willy (*coming out of* **The Woman**'s *dimming area and going over to* **Linda**)   I'll make it all up to you, Linda, I'll—

Linda   There's nothing to make up, dear. You're doing fine, better than—

Willy (*noticing her mending*)   What's that?

Linda   Just mending my stockings. They're so expensive—

Willy (*angrily, taking them from her*)   I won't have you mending stockings in this house! Now throw them out!

Linda *puts the stockings in her pocket.*

Bernard (*entering on the run*)   Where is he? If he doesn't study!

Willy (*moving to the forestage, with great agitation*)   You'll give him the answers!

Bernard   I do, but I can't on a Regents! That's a state exam! They're liable to arrest me!

Willy   Where is he? I'll whip him, I'll whip him!

Linda   And he'd better give back that football, Willy, it's not nice.

Willy   Biff! Where is he? Why is he taking everything?

Linda   He's too rough with the girls, Willy. All the mothers are afraid of him!

Willy   I'll whip him!

Bernard   He's driving the car without a license!

The Woman's *laugh is heard.*

Willy   Shut up!

Linda   All the mothers—

Willy   Shut up!

Bernard (*backing quietly away and out*)   Mr. Birnbaum says he's stuck up.

Willy   Get outa here!

Bernard   If he doesn't buckle down he'll flunk math! (*He goes off.*)

Linda   He's right, Willy, you've gotta—

Willy (*exploding at her*)   There's nothing the matter with him! You want him to be a worm like Bernard? He's got spirit, personality . . .

As he speaks, **Linda***, almost in tears, exits into the living-room.* **Willy** *is alone in the ktichen, wilting and staring. The leaves are gone. It is night again, and the apartment houses look down from behind.*

Willy   Loaded with it. Loaded! What is he stealing? He's giving it back, isn't he? Why is he stealing? What did I tell him? I never in my life told him anything but decent things.

Happy *in pajamas has come down the stairs;* **Willy** *suddenly becomes aware of* **Happy**'*s presence.*

Happy   Let's go now, come on.

Willy (*sitting down at the kitchen table*)   Huh! Why did she have to wax the floors herself? Everytime she waxes the floors she keels over. She knows that!

Happy   Shh! Take it easy. What brought you back tonight?

Willy   I got an awful scare. Nearly hit a kid in Yonkers. God! Why didn't I go to Alaska with my brother Ben that time! Ben! That man was a genius, that man was success incarnate! What a mistake! He begged me to go.

Happy   Well, there's no use in—

Willy   You guys! There was a man started with the clothes on his back and ended up with diamond mines!

Happy   Boy, someday I'd like to know how he did it.

Willy   What's the mystery? The man knew what he wanted and went out and got it! Walked into a jungle, and comes out, the age of twenty-one, and he's rich! The world is an oyster, but you don't crack it open on a mattress!

Happy   Pop, I told you I'm gonna retire you for life.

Willy   You'll retire me for life on seventy goddam dollars a week? And your women and your car and your apartment, and you'll retire me for life! Christ's sake, I couldn't get past Yonkers today! Where are you guys, where are you? The woods are burning! I can't drive a car!

Charley *has appeared in the doorway. He is a large man, slow of speech, laconic, immovable. In all he says, despite what he says, there is pity, and, now, trepidation. He has a robe over pajamas, slippers on his feet. He enters the kitchen.*

Charley   Everything all right?

Happy   Yeah, Charley, everything's . . .

Willy   What's the matter?

Charley   I heard some noise. I thought something happened. Can't we do something about the walls? You sneeze in here, and in my house hats blow off.

Happy   Let's go to bed, Dad. Come on.

Charley *signals to* **Happy** *to go.*

Willy   You go ahead, I'm not tired at the moment.

Happy (*to* **Willy**)   Take it easy, huh? (*He exits.*)

Willy   What're you doin' up?

Charley (*sitting down at the kitchen table opposite* **Willy**)   Couldn't sleep good. I had a heartburn.

Willy   Well, you don't know how to eat.

Charley   I eat with my mouth.

Willy   No, you're ignorant. You gotta know about vitamins and things like that.

Charley   Come on, let's shoot. Tire you out a little.

Willy (*hesitantly*)   All right. You got cards?

Charley (*taking a deck from his pocket*)   Yeah, I got them. Someplace. What is it with those vitamins?

Willy (*dealing*)   They build up your bones. Chemistry.

Charley   Yeah, but there's no bones in a heartburn.

Willy   What are you talkin' about? Do you know the first thing about it?

Charley   Don't get insulted.

Willy   Don't talk about something you don't know anything about.

They are playing. Pause.

Charley   What're you doin' home?

Willy   A little trouble with the car.

Charley   Oh. (*Pause.*) I'd like to take a trip to California.

Willy   Don't say.

Charley   You want a job?

Willy   I got a job, I told you that. (*After a slight pause:*) What the hell are you offering me a job for?

Charley   Don't get insulted.

Willy   Don't insult me.

Charley   I don't see no sense in it. You don't have to go on this way.

Willy   I got a good job. (*Slight pause.*) What do you keep comin' in here for?

Charley   You want me to go?

Willy (*after a pause, withering*)   I can't understand it. He's going back to Texas again. What the hell is that?

Charley   Let him go.

Willy   I got nothin' to give him, Charley, I'm clean, I'm clean.

Charley   He won't starve. None a them starve. Forget about him.

Willy   Then what have I got to remember?

Charley   You take it too hard. To hell with it. When a deposit bottle is broken you don't get your nickel back.

Willy   That's easy enough for you to say.

Charley   That ain't easy for me to say.

Willy   Did you see the ceiling I put up in the living-room?

Charley   Yeah, that's a piece of work. To put up a ceiling is a mystery to me. How do you do it?

Willy   What's the difference?

Charley   Well, talk about it.

Willy   You gonna put up a ceiling?

Charley   How could I put up a ceiling?

Willy   Then what the hell are you bothering me for?

Charley   You're insulted again.

Willy   A man who can't handle tools is not a man. You're disgusting.

Charley   Don't call me disgusting, Willy.

Uncle Ben, *carrying a valise and an umbrella, enters the forestage from around the right corner of the house. He is a stolid man, in his sixties,* *with a mustache and an authoritative air. He is utterly certain of his destiny, and there is an aura of far places about him. He enters exactly as* **Willy** *speaks.*

Willy   I'm getting awfully tired, Ben.

Ben's *music is heard.* **Ben** *looks around at everything.*

Charley   Good, keep playing; you'll sleep better. Did you call me Ben?

Ben *looks at his watch.*

Willy   That's funny. For a second there you reminded me of my brother Ben.

Ben   I only have a few minutes. (*He strolls, inspecting the place.* **Willy** *and* **Charley** *continue playing.*)

Charley   You never heard from him again, heh? Since that time?

Willy   Didn't Linda tell you? Couple of weeks ago we got a letter from his wife in Africa. He died.

Charley   That so.

Ben (*chuckling*)   So this is Brooklyn, eh?

Charley   Maybe you're in for some of his money.

Willy   Naa, he had seven sons. There's just one opportunity I had with that man . . .

Ben   I must make a train, William. There are several properties I'm looking at in Alaska.

Willy   Sure, sure! If I'd gone with him to Alaska that time, everything would've been totally different.

Charley   Go on, you'd froze to death up there.

Willy   What're you talking about?

Ben   Opportunity is tremendous in Alaska, William. Surprised you're not up there.

Willy   Sure, tremendous.

Charley   Heh?

Willy   There was the only man I ever met who knew the answers.

Charley   Who?

Ben   How are you all?

Willy (*taking a pot, smiling*)   Fine, fine.

Charley   Pretty sharp tonight.

Ben   Is Mother living with you?

Willy   No, she died a long time ago.

Charley   Who?

Ben   That's too bad. Fine specimen of a lady, Mother.

Willy (*to* **Charley**)   Heh?

Ben   I'd hoped to see the old girl.

Charley   Who died?

Ben   Heard anything from Father, have you?

Willy (*unnerved*)   What do you mean, who died?

Charley (*taking a pot*)   What're you talkin' about?

Ben (*looking at his watch*)   William, it's half-past eight!

Willy (*as though to dispel his confusion he angrily stops* **Charley**'s *hand*)   That's my build!

Charley   I put the ace—

Willy   If you don't know how to play the game I'm not gonna throw my money away on you!

Charley (*rising*)   It was my ace, for God's sake!

Willy   I'm through, I'm through!

Ben   When did Mother die?

Willy   Long ago. Since the beginning you never knew how to play cards.

Charley (*picks up the cards and goes to the door*)   All right! Next time I'll bring a deck with five aces.

Willy   I don't play that kind of game!

Charley (*turning to him*)   You ought to be ashamed of yourself!

Willy   Yeah?

Charley   Yeah! (*He goes out.*)

Willy (*slamming the door after him*)   Ignoramus!

Ben (*as* **Willy** *comes toward him through the wall-line of the kitchen*)   So you're William.

Willy (*shaking* **Ben**'*s hand*)   Ben! I've been waiting for you so long! What's the answer? How did you do it?

Ben   Oh, there's a story in that.

Linda *enters the forestage, as of old, carrying the wash basket.*

Linda   Is this Ben?

Ben (*gallantly*)   How do you do, my dear.

Linda   Where've you been all these years? Willy's always wondered why you—

Willy (*pulling* **Ben** *away from her impatiently*)   Where is Dad? Didn't you follow him? How did you get started?

Ben   Well, I don't know how much you remember.

Willy   Well, I was just a baby, of course, only three or four years old—

Ben   Three years and eleven months.

Willy   What a memory, Ben!

Ben   I have many enterprises, William, and I have never kept books.

Willy   I remember I was sitting under the wagon in—was it Nebraska?

Ben   It was South Dakota, and I gave you a bunch of wild flowers.

Willy   I remember you walking away down some open road.

Ben (*laughing*)   I was going to find Father in Alaska.

Willy   Where is he?

Ben   At that age I had a very faulty view of geography, William. I discovered after a few days that I was heading due south, so instead of Alaska, I ended up in Africa.

Linda   Africa!

Willy   The Gold Coast!

Ben   Principally diamond mines.

Linda   Diamond mines!

Ben   Yes, my dear. But I've only a few minutes—

Willy   No! Boys! Boys! (*Young* **Biff** *and* **Happy** *appear.*) Listen to this. This is your Uncle Ben, a great man! Tell my boys, Ben!

Ben   Why, boys, when I was seventeen I walked into the jungle, and when I was twenty-one I walked out. (*He laughs.*) And by God I was rich.

Willy (*to the boys*)   You see what I been talking about? The greatest things can happen!

Ben (*glancing at his watch*)   I have an appointment in Ketchikan Tuesday week.

Willy   No, Ben! Please tell about Dad. I want my boys to hear. I want them to know the kind of stock they spring from. All I remember is a man with a big beard, and I was in Mamma's lap, sitting around a fire, and some kind of high music.

Ben   His flute. He played the flute.

Willy   Sure, the flute, that's right!

New music is heard, a high, rollicking tune.

Ben   Father was a very great and a very wild-hearted man. We would start in Boston, and he'd toss the whole family into the wagon, and then he'd drive the team right across the country; through Ohio, and Indiana, Michigan, Illinois, and all the Western states. And we'd stop in the towns and sell the flutes that he'd made on the way. Great inventor, Father. With one gadget he made more in a week than a man like you could make in a lifetime.

Willy   That's just the way I'm bringing them up, Ben—rugged, well liked, all-around.

Ben   Yeah? (*To* **Biff**:) Hit that, boy—hard as you can. (*He pounds his stomach.*)

Biff   Oh, no, sir!

Ben (*taking boxing stance*)   Come on, get to me! (*He laughs.*)

Willy   Go to it, Biff! Go ahead, show him!

Biff   Okay! (*He cocks his fists and starts in.*)

Linda (*to* **Willy**)   Why must he fight, dear?

Ben (*sparring with* **Biff**)   Good boy! Good boy!

Willy   How's that, Ben, heh?

Happy   Give him the left, Biff!

Linda   Why are you fighting?

Ben   Good boy! (*Suddenly comes in, trips* **Biff**, *and stands over him, the point of his umbrella poised over* **Biff***'s eye.*)

Linda   Look out, Biff!

Biff   Gee!

Ben (*patting* **Biff***'s knee*)   Never fight fair with a stranger, boy. You'll never get out of the jungle that way. (*Taking* **Linda***'s hand and bowing:*) It was an honor and a pleasure to meet you, Linda.

Linda (*withdrawing her hand coldly, frightened*)   Have a nice—trip.

Ben (*to* **Willy**)   And good luck with your—what do you do?

Willy   Selling.

Ben   Yes. Well . . . (*He raises his hand in farewell to all.*)

Willy   No, Ben, I don't want you to think . . . (*He takes* **Ben***'s arm to show him.*) It's Brooklyn, I know, but we hunt too.

Ben   Really, now.

Willy   Oh, sure, there's snakes and rabbits and—that's why I moved out here. Why, Biff can fell any one of these trees in no time! Boys! Go right over to where they're building the apartment house and get some sand. We're gonna rebuild the entire front stoop right now! Watch this, Ben!

Biff   Yes, sir! On the double, Hap!

Happy (*as he and* **Biff** *run off*)   I lost weight, Pop, you notice?

Charley *enters in knickers, even before the boys are gone.*

Charley   Listen, if they steal any more from that building the watchman'll put the cops on them!

Linda (*to* **Willy**)   Don't let Biff . . .

Ben *laughs lustily.*

Willy   You shoulda seen the lumber they brought home last week. At least a dozen six-by-tens worth all kinds a money.

Charley   Listen, if that watchman—

Willy   I gave them hell, understand. But I got a couple of fearless characters there.

Charley   Willy, the jails are full of fearless characters.

Ben (*clapping* **Willy** *on the back, with a laugh at* **Charley**)   And the stock exchange, friend!

Willy (*joining in* **Ben***'s laughter*)   Where are the rest of your pants?

Charley   My wife bought them.

Willy   Now all you need is a golf club and you can go upstairs and go to sleep. (*To* **Ben***:*) Great athlete! Between him and his son Bernard they can't hammer a nail!

Bernard (*rushing in*)   The watchman's chasing Biff!

Willy (*angrily*)   Shut up! He's not stealing anything!

Linda (*alarmed, hurrying off left*)   Where is he? Biff, dear! (*She exits.*)

Willy (*moving toward the left, away from* **Ben**)   There's nothing wrong. What's the matter with you?

Ben   Nervy boy. Good!

Willy (*laughing*)   Oh, nerves of iron, that Biff!

Charley   Don't know what it is. My New England man comes back and he's bleedin', they murdered him up there.

Willy   It's contacts, Charley, I got important contacts!

Charley (*sarcastically*)   Glad to hear it, Willy. Come in later, we'll shoot a little casino. I'll take some of your Portland money. (*He laughs at* **Willy** *and exits.*)

Willy (*turning to* **Ben**)   Business is bad, it's murderous. But not for me, of course.

Ben   I'll stop by on my way back to Africa.

Willy (*longingly*)   Can't you stay a few days? You're just what I need, Ben, because I—I have a fine position here, but I—well, Dad left when I was such a baby and I never had a chance to talk to him and I still feel— kind of temporary about myself.

Ben   I'll be late for my train.

They are at opposite ends of the stage.

Willy   Ben, my boys—can't we talk? They'd go into the jaws of hell for me, see, but I—

Ben   William, you're being first-rate with your boys. Outstanding, manly chaps!

Willy (*hanging on to his words*)   Oh, Ben, that's good to hear! Because sometimes I'm afraid that I'm not teaching them the right kind of—Ben, how should I teach them?

Ben (*giving great weight to each word, and with a certain vicious audacity*)   William, when I walked into the jungle, I was seventeen. When I walked out I was twenty-one. And, by God, I was rich! (*He goes off into darkness around the right corner of the house.*)

Willy   . . . was rich! That's just the spirit I want to imbue them with! To walk into a jungle! I was right! I was right! I was right!

Ben *is gone, but* **Willy** *is still speaking to him as* **Linda**, *in nightgown and robe, enters the kitchen, glances around for* **Willy**, *then goes to the door of the house, looks out and sees him. Comes down to his left. He looks at her.*

Linda   Willy, dear? Willy?

Willy   I was right!

Linda   Did you have some cheese? (*He can't answer.*) It's very late, darling. Come to bed, heh?

Willy (*looking straight up*)   Gotta break your neck to see a star in this yard.

Linda   You coming in?

Willy   Whatever happened to that diamond watch fob? Remember? When Ben came from Africa that time? Didn't he give me a watch fob with a diamond in it?

Linda   You pawned it, dear. Twelve, thirteen years ago. For Biff's radio correspondence course.

Willy   Gee, that was a beautiful thing. I'll take a walk.

Linda   But you're in your slippers.

Willy (*starting to go around the house at the left*)   I was right! I was! (*Half to* **Linda**, *as he goes, shaking his head:*) What a man! There was a man worth talking to. I was right!

Linda (*calling after* **Willy**)   But in your slippers, Willy!

Willy *is almost gone when* **Biff**, *in his pajamas, comes down the stairs and enters the kitchen.*

Biff   What is he doing out there?

Linda   Sh!

Biff   God Almighty, Mom, how long has he been doing this?

Linda   Don't, he'll hear you.

Biff   What the hell is the matter with him?

Linda   It'll pass by morning.

Biff   Shouldn't we do anything?

Linda   Oh, my dear, you should do a lot of things, but there's nothing to do, so go to sleep.

Happy *comes down the stair and sits on the steps.*

Happy   I never heard him so loud, Mom.

Linda   Well, come around more often; you'll hear him. (*She sits down at the table and mends the lining of* **Willy**'s *jacket.*)

Biff   Why didn't you ever write me about this, Mom?

Linda   How would I write to you? For over three months you had no address.

Biff   I was on the move. But you know I thought of you all the time. You know that, don't you, pal?

Linda   I know, dear, I know. But he likes to have a letter. Just to know that there's still a possibility for better things.

Biff   He's not like this all the time, is he?

Linda   It's when you come home he's always the worst.

Biff   When I come home?

Linda   When you write you're coming, he's all smiles, and talks about the future, and—he's just wonderful. And then the closer you seem to come, the more shaky he gets, and then, by the time you get here, he's arguing, and he seems angry at you. I think it's just that maybe he can't bring himself to—to open up to you. Why are you so hateful to each other? Why is that?

Biff (*evasively*)   I'm not hateful, Mom.

Linda   But you no sooner come in the door than you're fighting!

Biff   I don't know why. I mean to change. I'm tryin', Mom; you understand?

Linda   Are you home to stay now?

Biff   I don't know. I want to look around, see what's doin'.

Linda   Biff, you can't look around all your life, can you?

Biff   I just can't take hold, Mom. I can't take hold of some kind of a life.

Linda   Biff, a man is not a bird, to come and go with the spring-time.

Biff   Your hair . . . (*He touches her hair.*) Your hair got so gray.

Linda   Oh, it's been gray since you were in high school. I just stopped dyeing it, that's all.

Biff   Dye it again, will ya? I don't want my pal looking old. (*He smiles.*)

Linda   You're such a boy! You think you can go away for a year and . . . You've got to get it into your head now that one day you'll knock on this door and there'll be strange people here—

Biff   What are you talking about? You're not even sixty, Mom.

Linda   But what about your father?

Biff (*lamely*)   Well, I meant him too.

Happy   He admires Pop.

Linda   Biff, dear, if you don't have any feeling for him, then you can't have any feeling for me.

Biff   Sure I can, Mom.

Linda   No. You can't just come to see me, because I love him. (*With a threat, but only a threat, of tears:*) He's the dearest man in the world to me, and I won't have anyone making him feel unwanted and low and blue. You've got to make up your mind now, darling, there's no leeway any more. Either he's your father and you pay him that respect, or else you're not to come here. I know he's not easy to get along with—nobody knows that better than me—but . . .

Willy (*from the left, with a laugh*)   Hey, hey, Biffo!

Biff (*starting to go out after* **Willy**)   What the hell is the matter with him? (**Happy** *stops him.*)

Linda   Don't—don't go near him!

Biff   Stop making excuses for him! He always, always wiped the floor with you. Never had an ounce of respect for you.

Happy   He's always had respect for—

Biff   What the hell do you know about it?

Happy (*surlily*)   Just don't call him crazy!

Biff   He's got no character—Charley wouldn't do this. Not in his own house—spewing out that vomit from his mind.

Happy   Charley never had to cope with what he's got to.

Biff   People are worse off than Willy Loman. Believe me, I've seen them!

Linda   Then make Charley your father, Biff. You can't do that, can you? I don't say he's a great man. Willy Loman never made a lot of money. His name was never in the paper. He's not the finest character that ever lived. But he's a human being, and a terrible thing is happening to him. So attention must be paid. He's not to be allowed to fall into his grave like an old dog. Attention, attention must be finally paid to such a person. You called him crazy—

Biff   I didn't mean—

Linda   No, a lot of people think he's lost his—balance. But you don't have to be very smart to know what his trouble is. The man is exhausted.

Happy   Sure!

Linda   A small man can be just as exhausted as a great man. He works for a company thirty-six years this March, opens up unheard of territories to their trademark, and now in his old age they take his salary away.

Happy (*indignantly*)   I didn't know that, Mom.

Linda   You never asked, my dear! Now that you get your spending money someplace else you don't trouble your mind with him.

Happy   But I gave you money last—

Linda   Christmas time, fifty dollars! To fix the hot water it cost ninety-seven fifty! For five weeks he's been on straight commission, like a beginner, an unknown!

Biff   Those ungrateful bastards!

Linda   Are they any worse than his sons? When he brought them business, when he was young, they were glad to see him. But now his old friends, the old buyers that loved him so and always found some order to hand him in a pinch—they're all dead, retired. He used to be able to make six, seven calls a day in Boston. Now he takes his valises out of the car and puts them back and takes them out again and he's exhausted. Instead of walking he talks now. He drives seven hundred miles, and when he gets there no one knows him any more, no one welcomes him. And what goes through a man's mind, driving seven hundred miles home without having earned a cent? Why shouldn't he talk to himself? Why? When he has to go to Charley and borrow fifty dollars a week and pretend to me that it's his pay? How long can that go on? How long? You see what I'm sitting here and waiting for? And you tell me he has no character? The man who never worked a day but for your benefit? When does he get the medal for that? Is this his reward—to turn around at the age of sixty-three and find his sons, who he loved better than his life, one a philandering bum—

Happy   Mom!

Linda   That's all you are, my baby! (*To* **Biff**:) And you! What happened to the love you had for him? You were such pals! How you used to talk to him on the phone every night! How lonely he was till he could come home to you!

Biff   All right, Mom. I'll live here in my room, and I'll get a job. I'll keep away from him, that's all.

Linda   No, Biff. You can't stay here and fight all the time.

Biff   He threw me out of this house, remember that.

Linda   Why did he do that? I never knew why.

Biff   Because I know he's a fake and he doesn't like anybody around who knows!

Linda   Why a fake? In what way? What do you mean?

Biff   Just don't lay it all at my feet. It's between me and him—that's all I have to say. I'll chip in from now on. He'll settle for half my pay check. He'll be all right. I'm going to bed. (*He starts for the stairs.*)

Linda   He won't be all right.

Biff (*turning on the stairs, furiously*)   I hate this city and I'll stay here. Now what do you want?

Linda   He's dying, Biff.

Happy *turns quickly to her, shocked.*

Biff (*after a pause*)   Why is he dying?

Linda   He's been trying to kill himself.

Biff (*with great horror*)   How?

Linda   I live from day to day.

Biff   What're you talking about?

Linda   Remember I wrote you that he smashed up the car again? In February?

Biff   Well?

Linda   The insurance inspector came. He said that they have evidence. That all these accidents in the last year—weren't—weren't—accidents.

Happy   How can they tell that? That's a lie.

Linda   It seems there's a woman . . . (*She takes a breath as*)

Biff (*sharply but contained*)}   What woman?

Linda (*simultaneously*)}   . . . and this woman . . .

Linda   What?

Biff   Nothing. Go ahead.

Linda   What did you say?

Biff   Nothing. I just said what woman?

Happy   What about her?

Linda   Well, it seems she was walking down the road and saw his car. She says that he wasn't driving fast at all, and that he didn't skid. She says he came to that little bridge, and then deliberately smashed into the railing, and it was only the shallowness of the water that saved him.

Biff   Oh, no, he probably just fell asleep again.

Linda   I don't think he fell asleep.

Biff   Why not?

Linda   Last month . . . (*With great difficulty:*) Oh, boys, it's so hard to say a thing like this! He's just a big stupid man to you, but I tell you there's more good in him than in many other people. (*She chokes, wipes* *her eyes.*) I was looking for a fuse. The lights blew out, and I went down the cellar. And behind the fuse box—it happened to fall out—was a length of rubber pipe—just short.

Happy   No kidding?

Linda   There's a little attachment on the end of it. I knew right away. And sure enough, on the bottom of the water heater there's a new little nipple on the gas pipe.

Happy (*angrily*)   That—jerk.

Biff   Did you have it taken off?

Linda   I'm—I'm ashamed to. How can I mention it to him? Every day I go down and take away that little rubber pipe. But, when he comes home, I put it back where it was. How can I insult him that way? I don't know what to do. I live from day to day, boys. I tell you, I know every thought in his mind. It sounds so old-fashioned and silly, but I tell you he put his whole life into you and you've turned your backs on him. (*She is bent over in the chair, weeping, her face in her hands.*) Biff, I swear to God! Biff, his life is in your hands!

Happy (*to* **Biff**)   How do you like that damned fool!

Biff (*kissing her*)   All right, pal, all right. It's all settled now. I've been remiss. I know that, Mom. But now I'll stay, and I swear to you, I'll apply myself. (*Kneeling in front of her, in a fever of self-reproach:*) It's just—you see, Mom, I don't fit in business. Not that I won't try. I'll try, and I'll make good.

Happy   Sure you will. The trouble with you in business was you never tried to please people.

Biff   I know, I—

Happy   Like when you worked for Harrison's. Bob Harrison said you were tops, and then you go and do some damn fool thing like whistling whole songs in the elevator like a comedian.

Biff (*against* **Happy**)   So what? I like to whistle sometimes.

Happy   You don't raise a guy to a responsible job who whistles in the elevator!

Linda   Well, don't argue about it now.

Happy   Like when you'd go off and swim in the middle of the day instead of taking the line around.

Biff (*his resentment rising*)   Well, don't you run off? You take off sometimes, don't you? On a nice summer day?

Happy   Yeah, but I cover myself!

Linda   Boys!

Happy   If I'm going to take a fade the boss can call any number where I'm supposed to be and they'll swear to him that I just left. I'll tell you something that I hate to say, Biff, but in the business world some of them think you're crazy.

Biff (*angered*)   Screw the business world!

Happy   All right, screw it! Great, but cover yourself!

Linda   Hap, Hap!

Biff   I don't care what they think! They've laughed at Dad for years, and you know why? Because we don't belong in this nut-house of a city! We should be mixing cement on some open plain, or—or carpenters. A carpenter is allowed to whistle!

Willy *walks in from the entrance of the house, at left.*

Willy   Even your grandfather was better than a carpenter. (*Pause. They watch him.*) You never grew up. Bernard does not whistle in the elevator, I assure you.

Biff (*as though to laugh* **Willy** *out of it*)   Yeah, but you do, Pop.

Willy   I never in my life whistled in an elevator! And who in the business world thinks I'm crazy?

Biff   I didn't mean it like that, Pop. Now don't make a whole thing out of it, will ya?

Willy   Go back to the West! Be a carpenter, a cowboy, enjoy yourself!

Linda   Willy, he was just saying—

Willy   I heard what he said!

Happy (*trying to quiet* **Willy**)   Hey, Pop, come on now . . .

Willy (*continuing over* **Happy**'s *line*)   They laugh at me, heh? Go to Filene's, go to the Hub, go to Slattery's, Boston. Call out the name Willy Loman and see what happens! Big shot!

Biff   All right, Pop.

Willy   Big!

Biff   All right!

Willy   Why do you always insult me?

Biff   I didn't say a word. (*To* **Linda***:*) Did I say a word?

Linda   He didn't say anything, Willy.

Willy (*going to the doorway of the living-room*)   All right, good night, good night.

Linda   Willy, dear, he just decided . . .

Willy (*to* **Biff**)   If you get tired hanging around tomorrow, paint the ceiling I put up in the living-room.

Biff   I'm leaving early tomorrow.

Happy   He's going to see Bill Oliver, Pop.

Willy (*interestedly*)   Oliver? For what?

Biff (*with reserve, but trying, trying*)   He always said he'd stake me. I'd like to go into business, so maybe I can take him up on it.

Linda   Isn't that wonderful?

Willy   Don't interrupt. What's wonderful about it? There's fifty men in the City of New York who'd stake him. (*To* **Biff***:*) Sporting goods?

Biff   I guess so. I know something about it and—

Willy   He knows something about it! You know sporting goods better than Spalding, for God's sake! How much is he giving you?

Biff   I don't know, I didn't even see him yet, but—

Willy   Then what're you talkin' about?

Biff (*getting angry*)   Well, all I said was I'm gonna see him, that's all!

Willy (*turning away*)   Ah, you're counting your chickens again.

Biff (*starting left for the stairs*)   Oh, Jesus, I'm going to sleep!

Willy (*calling after him*)   Don't curse in this house!

Biff (*turning*)   Since when did you get so clean?

Happy (*trying to stop them*)   Wait a . . .

Willy   Don't use that language to me! I won't have it!

Happy (*grabbing* **Biff***, shouts*)   Wait a minute! I got an idea. I got a feasible idea. Come here, Biff, let's talk this over now, let's talk some sense here. When I was down in Florida last time, I thought of a great idea to sell sporting goods. It just came back to me. You and I, Biff—we have a line, the Loman Line. We train a couple of weeks, and put on a couple of exhibitions, see?

Willy   That's an idea!

Happy   Wait! We form two basketball teams, see? Two waterpolo teams. We play each other. It's a million dollars' worth of publicity. Two brothers, see? The Loman Brothers. Displays in the Royal Palms—all the hotels. And banners over the ring and the basketball court: "Loman Brothers." Baby, we could sell sporting goods!

Willy   That is a one-million-dollar idea!

Linda   Marvelous!

Biff   I'm in great shape as far as that's concerned.

Happy   And the beauty of it is, Biff, it wouldn't be like a business. We'd be out playin' ball again . . .

Biff (*enthused*)   Yeah, that's . . .

Willy   Million-dollar . . .

Happy   And you wouldn't get fed up with it, Biff. It'd be the family again. There'd be the old honor, and comradeship, and if you wanted to go off for a swim or somethin'—well, you'd do it! Without some smart cooky gettin' up ahead of you!

Willy   Lick the world! You guys together could absolutely lick the civilized world.

Biff   I'll see Oliver tomorrow. Hap, if we could work that out . . .

Linda   Maybe things are beginning to—

Willy (*wildly enthused, to* **Linda**)   Stop interrupting! (*To* **Biff**:) But don't wear sport jacket and slacks when you see Oliver.

Biff   No, I'll—

Willy   A business suit, and talk as little as possible, and don't crack any jokes.

Biff   He did like me. Always liked me.

Linda   He loved you!

Willy (*to* **Linda**)   Will you stop! (*To* **Biff**:) Walk in very serious. You are not applying for a boy's job. Money is to pass. Be quiet, fine, and serious. Everybody likes a kidder, but nobody lends him money.

Happy   I'll try to get some myself, Biff. I'm sure I can.

Willy   I see great things for you kids, I think your troubles are over. But remember, start big and you'll end big. Ask for fifteen. How much you gonna ask for?

Biff   Gee, I don't know—

Willy   And don't say "Gee." "Gee" is a boy's word. A man walking in for fifteen thousand dollars does not say "Gee!"

Biff   Ten, I think, would be top though.

Willy   Don't be so modest. You always started too low. Walk in with a big laugh. Don't look worried. Start off with a couple of your good stories to lighten things up. It's not what you say, it's how you say it— because personality always wins the day.

Linda   Oliver always thought the highest of him—

Willy   Will you let me talk?

Biff   Don't yell at her, Pop, will ya?

Willy (*angrily*)   I was talking, wasn't I?

Biff   I don't like you yelling at her all the time, and I'm tellin' you, that's all.

Willy   What're you, takin' over this house?

Linda   Willy—

Willy (*turning on her*)   Don't take his side all the time, goddammit!

Biff (*furiously*)   Stop yelling at her!

Willy (*suddenly pulling on his cheek, beaten down, guilt ridden*)   Give my best to Bill Oliver—he may remember me. (*He exits through the living-room doorway.*)

Linda (*her voice subdued*)   What'd you have to start that for? (**Biff** *turns away.*) You see how sweet he was as soon as you talked hopefully? (*She goes over to* **Biff**.) Come up and say good night to him. Don't let him go to bed that way.

Happy   Come on, Biff, let's buck him up.

Linda   Please, dear. Just say good night. It takes so little to make him happy. Come. (*She goes through the living-room doorway, calling upstairs from within the living-room:*) Your pajamas are hanging in the bathroom, Willy!

Happy (*looking toward where* **Linda** *went out*)   What a woman! They broke the mold when they made her. You know that, Biff?

Biff   He's off salary. My God, working on commission!

Happy   Well, let's face it: he's no hot-shot selling man. Except that sometimes, you have to admit, he's a sweet personality.

Biff (*deciding*)   Lend me ten bucks, will ya? I want to buy some new ties.

Happy   I'll take you to a place I know. Beautiful stuff. Wear one of my striped shirts tomorrow.

Biff   She got gray. Mom got awful old. Gee, I'm gonna go in to Oliver tomorrow and knock him for a—

Happy   Come on up. Tell that to Dad. Let's give him a whirl. Come on.

Biff (*steamed up*)   You know, with ten thousand bucks, boy!

Happy (*as they go into the living-room*)   That's the talk, Biff, that's the first time I've heard the old confidence out of you! (*From within the living-room, fading off:*) You're gonna live with me, kid, and any babe you want just say the word . . . (*The last lines are hardly heard. They are mounting the stairs to their parents' bedroom.*)

Linda (*entering her bedroom and addressing* **Willy***, who is in the bathroom. She is straightening the bed for him*)   Can you do anything about the shower? It drips.

Willy (*from the bathroom*)   All of a sudden everything falls to pieces! Goddam plumbing, oughta be sued, those people. I hardly finished putting it in and the thing . . . (*His words rumble off.*)

Linda   I'm just wondering if Oliver will remember him. You think he might?

Willy (*coming out of the bathroom in his pajamas*)   Remember him? What's the matter with you, you crazy? If he'd've stayed with Oliver he'd be on top by now! Wait'll Oliver gets a look at him. You don't know the average caliber any more. The average young man today (*he is getting into bed*) is got a caliber of zero. Greatest thing in the world for him was to bum around.

Biff *and* **Happy** *enter the bedroom. Slight pause.*

Willy (*stops short, looking at* **Biff**)   Glad to hear it, boy.

Happy   He wanted to say good night to you, sport.

Willy (*to* **Biff**)   Yeah. Knock him dead, boy. What'd you want to tell me?

Biff   Just take it easy, Pop. Good night. (*He turns to go.*)

Willy (*unable to resist*)   And if anything falls off the desk while you're talking to him—like a package or something—don't you pick it up. They have office boys for that.

Linda   I'll make a big breakfast—

Willy   Will you let me finish? (*To* **Biff**:) Tell him you were in the business in the West. Not farm work.

Biff   All right, Dad.

Linda   I think everything—

Willy (*going right through her speech*)   And don't undersell yourself. No less than fifteen thousand dollars.

Biff (*unable to bear him*)   Okay. Good night, Mom. (*He starts moving.*)

Willy   Because you got a greatness in you, Biff, remember that. You got all kinds a greatness . . . (*He lies back, exhausted.* **Biff** *walks out.*)

Linda (*calling after* **Biff**)   Sleep well, darling!

Happy   I'm gonna get married, Mom. I wanted to tell you.

Linda   Go to sleep, dear.

Happy (*going*)   I just wanted to tell you.

Willy   Keep up the good work. (**Happy** *exits.*) God . . . remember that Ebbets Field game? The championship of the city?

Linda   Just rest. Should I sing to you?

Willy   Yeah. Sing to me. (**Linda** *hums a soft lullaby.*) When that team came out—he was the tallest, remember?

Linda   Oh, yes. And in gold.

Biff *enters the darkened kitchen, takes a cigarette, and leaves the house. He comes downstage into a golden pool of light. He smokes, staring at the night.*

Willy   Like a young god. Hercules—something like that. And the sun, the sun all around him. Remember how he waved to me? Right up from the field, with the representatives of three colleges standing by? And the buyers I brought, and the cheers when he came out—Loman, Loman, Loman! God Almighty, he'll be great yet. A star like that, magnificent, can never really fade away!

The light on **Willy** *is fading. The gas heater begins to glow through the kitchen wall, near the stairs, a blue flame beneath red coils.*

Linda (*timidly*)   Willy dear, what has he got against you?

Willy   I'm so tired. Don't talk any more.

Biff *slowly returns to the kitchen. He stops, stares toward the heater.*

Linda   Will you ask Howard to let you work in New York?

Willy   First thing in the morning. Everything'll be all right.

Biff *reaches behind the heater and draws out a length of rubber tubing. He is horrified and turns his head toward* **Willy**'*s room, still dimly lit, from which the strains of* **Linda**'*s desperate but monotonous humming rise.*

Willy (*staring through the window into the moonlight*)   Gee, look at the moon moving between the buildings!

Biff *wraps the tubing around his hand and quickly goes up the stairs.*

Curtain.

Act Two

Music is heard, gay and bright. The curtain rises as the music fades away. **Willy**, *in shirt sleeves, is sitting at the kitchen table, sipping coffee, his hat in his lap.* **Linda** *is filling his cup when she can.*

Willy   Wonderful coffee. Meal in itself.

Linda   Can I make you some eggs?

Willy   No. Take a breath.

Linda   You look so rested, dear.

Willy   I slept like a dead one. First time in months. Imagine, sleeping till ten on a Tuesday morning. Boys left nice and early, heh?

Linda   They were out of here by eight o'clock.

Willy   Good work!

Linda   It was so thrilling to see them leaving together. I can't get over the shaving lotion in this house!

Willy (*smiling*)   Mmm—

Linda   Biff was very changed this morning. His whole attitude seemed to be hopeful. He couldn't wait to get downtown to see Oliver.

Willy   He's heading for a change. There's no question, there simply are certain men that take longer to get—solidified. How did he dress?

Linda   His blue suit. He's so handsome in that suit. He could be a—anything in that suit!

Willy *gets up from the table.* **Linda** *holds his jacket for him.*

Willy   There's no question, no question at all. Gee, on the way home tonight I'd like to buy some seeds.

Linda (*laughing*)   That'd be wonderful. But not enough sun gets back there. Nothing'll grow any more.

Willy   You wait, kid, before it's all over we're gonna get a little place out in the country, and I'll raise some vegetables, a couple of chickens . . .

Linda   You'll do it yet, dear.

Willy *walks out of his jacket.* **Linda** *follows him.*

Willy   And they'll get married, and come for a weekend. I'd build a little guest house. 'Cause I got so many fine tools, all I'd need would be a little lumber and some peace of mind.

Linda (*joyfully*)   I sewed the lining . . .

Willy   I could build two guest houses, so they'd both come. Did he decide how much he's going to ask Oliver for?

Linda (*getting him into the jacket*)   He didn't mention it, but I imagine ten or fifteen thousand. You going to talk to Howard today?

Willy   Yeah. I'll put it to him straight and simple. He'll just have to take me off the road.

Linda   And Willy, don't forget to ask for a little advance, because we've got the insurance premium. It's the grace period now.

Willy   That's a hundred . . .?

Linda   A hundred and eight, sixty-eight. Because we're a little short again.

Willy   Why are we short?

Linda   Well, you had the motor job on the car . . .

Willy   That goddam Studebaker!

Linda   And you got one more payment on the refrigerator . . .

Willy   But it just broke again!

Linda   Well, it's old, dear.

Willy   I told you we should've bought a well-advertised machine. Charley bought a General Electric and it's twenty years old and it's still good, that son-of-a-bitch.

Linda   But, Willy—

Willy   Whoever heard of a Hastings refrigerator? Once in my life I would like to own something outright before it's broken! I'm always in a race with the junkyard! I just finished paying for the car and it's on its last legs. The refrigerator consumes belts like a goddam maniac. They time those things. They time them so when you finally paid for them, they're used up.

Linda (*buttoning up his jacket as he unbuttons it*)   All told, about two hundred dollars would carry us, dear. But that includes the last payment on the mortgage. After this payment, Willy, the house belongs to us.

Willy   It's twenty-five years!

Linda   Biff was nine years old when we bought it.

Willy   Well, that's a great thing. To weather a twenty-five-year mortgage is—

Linda   It's an accomplishment.

Willy   All the cement, the lumber, the reconstruction I put in this house! There ain't a crack to be found in it any more.

Linda   Well, it served its purpose.

Willy   What purpose? Some stranger'll come along, move in, and that's that. If only Biff would take this house, and raise a family . . . (*He starts to go.* Good-by, I'm late.

Linda (*suddenly remembering*)   Oh, I forgot! You're supposed to meet them for dinner.

Willy   Me?

Linda   At Frank's Chop House on Forty-eighth near Sixth Avenue.

Willy   Is that so! How about you?

Linda   No, just the three of you. They're gonna blow you to a big meal!

Willy   Don't say! Who thought of that?

Linda   Biff came to me this morning, Willy, and he said, "Tell Dad, we want to blow him to a big meal." Be there six o'clock. You and your two boys are going to have dinner.

Willy   Gee whiz! That's really somethin'. I'm gonna knock Howard for a loop, kid. I'll get an advance, and I'll come home with a New York job. Goddammit, now I'm gonna do it!

Linda   Oh, that's the spirit, Willy!

Willy   I will never get behind a wheel the rest of my life!

Linda   It's changing, Willy, I can feel it changing!

Willy   Beyond a question. G'by, I'm late. (*He starts to go again.*)

Linda (*calling after him as she runs to the kitchen table for a handkerchief*)   You got your glasses?

Willy (*feels for them, then comes back in*)   Yeah, yeah, got my glasses.

Linda (*giving him the handkerchief*)   And a handkerchief.

Willy   Yeah, handkerchief.

Linda   And your saccharine?

Willy   Yeah, my saccharine.

Linda   Be careful on the subway stairs.

She kisses him, and a silk stocking is seen hanging from her hand. **Willy** *notices it.*

Willy   Will you stop mending stockings? At least while I'm in the house. It gets me nervous. I can't tell you. Please.

Linda *hides the stocking in her hand as she follows* **Willy** *across the forestage in front of the house.*

Linda   Remember, Frank's Chop House.

Willy (*passing the apron*)   Maybe beets would grow out there.

Linda (*laughing*)   But you tried so many times.

Willy   Yeah. Well, don't work hard today. (*He disappears around the right corner of the house.*)

Linda   Be careful!

As **Willy** *vanishes,* **Linda** *waves to him. Suddenly the phone rings. She runs across the stage and into the kitchen and lifts it.*

Linda   Hello? Oh, Biff! I'm so glad you called, I just . . . Yes, sure, I just told him. Yes, he'll be there for dinner at six o'clock, I didn't forget. Listen, I was just dying to tell you. You know that little rubber pipe I told you about? That he connected to the gas heater? I finally decided to go down the cellar this morning and take it away and destroy it. But it's gone! Imagine? He took it away himself, it isn't there! (*She listens.*) When? Oh, then you took it. Oh—nothing, it's just that I'd hoped he'd taken it away himself. Oh, I'm not worried, darling, because this morning he left in such high spirits, it was like the old days! I'm not afraid any more. Did Mr. Oliver see you? . . . Well, you wait there then. And make a nice impression on him, darling. Just don't perspire too much before you see him. And have a nice time with Dad. He may have big news too! . . . That's right, a New York job. And be sweet to him tonight, dear. Be loving to him. Because he's only a little boat looking for a harbor. (*She is trembling with sorrow and joy.*) Oh, that's wonderful, Biff, you'll save his life. Thanks, darling. Just put your arm around him when he comes into the restaurant. Give him a smile. That's the boy . . . Good-by, dear. . . . You got your comb? . . . That's fine. Good-by, Biff dear.

In the middle of her speech, **Howard Wagner**, *thirty-six, wheels on a small typewriter table on which is a wire-recording machine and proceeds to plug it in. This is on the left forestage. Light slowly fades on* **Linda** *as it rises on* **Howard**. **Howard** *is intent on threading the machine and only glances over his shoulder as* **Willy** *appears.*

Willy   Pst! Pst!

Howard   Hello, Willy, come in.

Willy   Like to have a little talk with you, Howard.

Howard   Sorry to keep you waiting. I'll be with you in a minute.

Willy   What's that, Howard?

Howard   Didn't you ever see one of these? Wire recorder.

Willy   Oh. Can we talk a minute?

Howard   Records things. Just got delivery yesterday. Been driving me crazy, the most terrific machine I ever saw in my life. I was up all night with it.

Willy   What do you do with it?

Howard   I bought it for dictation, but you can do anything with it. Listen to this. I had it home last night. Listen to what I picked up. The first one is my daughter. Get this. (*He flicks the switch and "Roll out the Barrel" is heard being whistled.*) Listen to that kid whistle.

Willy   That is lifelike, isn't it?

Howard   Seven years old. Get that tone.

Willy   Ts, ts. Like to ask a little favor if you . . .

The whistling breaks off, and the voice of **Howard**'*s daughter is heard.*

His Daughter   "Now you, Daddy."

Howard   She's crazy for me! (*Again the same song is whistled.*) That's me! Ha! (*He winks.*)

Willy   You're very good!

The whistling breaks off again. The machine runs silent for a moment.

Howard   Sh! Get this now, this is my son.

His Son   "The capital of Alabama is Montgomery; the capital of Arizona is Phoenix; the capital of Arkansas is Little Rock; the capital of California is Sacramento . . ." (*and on, and on.*)

Howard (*holding up five fingers*)   Five years old, Willy!

Willy   He'll make an announcer some day!

His Son (*continuing*)   "The capital . . ."

Howard   Get that—alphabetical order! (*The machine breaks off suddenly.*) Wait a minute. The maid kicked the plug out.

Willy   It certainly is a—

Howard   Sh, for God's sake!

His Son   "It's nine o'clock, Bulova watch time. So I have to go to sleep."

Willy   That really is—

Howard   Wait a minute! The next is my wife.

They wait.

Howard's Voice   "Go on, say something." (*Pause.*) "Well, you gonna talk?"

His Wife   "I can't think of anything."

Howard's Voice   "Well, talk—it's turning."

His Wife (*shyly, beaten*)   "Hello." (*Silence.*) "Oh, Howard, I can't talk into this . . ."

Howard (*snapping the machine off*)   That was my wife.

Willy   That is a wonderful machine. Can we—

Howard   I tell you, Willy, I'm gonna take my camera, and my bandsaw, and all my hobbies, and out they go. This is the most fascinating relaxation I ever found.

Willy   I think I'll get one myself.

Howard   Sure, they're only a hundred and a half. You can't do without it. Supposing you wanna hear Jack Benny, see? But you can't be at home at that hour. So you tell the maid to turn the radio on when Jack Benny comes on, and this automatically goes on with the radio . . .

Willy   And when you come home you . . .

Howard   You can come home twelve o'clock, one o'clock, any time you like, and you get yourself a Coke and sit yourself down, throw the switch, and there's Jack Benny's program in the middle of the night!

Willy   I'm definitely going to get one. Because lots of time I'm on the road, and I think to myself, what I must be missing on the radio!

Howard   Don't you have a radio in the car?

Willy   Well, yeah, but who ever thinks of turning it on?

Howard   Say, aren't you supposed to be in Boston?

Willy   That's what I want to talk to you about, Howard. You got a minute? (*He draws a chair in from the wing.*)

Howard   What happened? What're you doing here?

Willy   Well . . .

Howard   You didn't crack up again, did you?

Willy   Oh, no. No . . .

Howard   Geez, you had me worried there for a minute. What's the trouble?

Willy   Well, tell you the truth, Howard. I've come to the decision that I'd rather not travel any more.

Howard   Not travel! Well, what'll you do?

Willy   Remember, Christmas time, when you had the party here? You said you'd try to think of some spot for me here in town.

Howard   With us?

Willy   Well, sure.

Howard   Oh, yeah, yeah. I remember. Well, I couldn't think of anything for you, Willy.

Willy   I tell ya, Howard. The kids are all grown up, y'know. I don't need much any more. If I could take home—well, sixty-five dollars a week, I could swing it.

Howard   Yeah, but Willy, see I—

Willy   I tell ya why, Howard. Speaking frankly and between the two of us, y'know—I'm just a little tired.

Howard   Oh, I could understand that, Willy. But you're a road man, Willy, and we do a road business. We've only got a half-dozen salesmen on the floor here.

Willy   God knows, Howard, I never asked a favor of any man. But I was with the firm when your father used to carry you in here in his arms.

Howard   I know that, Willy, but—

Willy   Your father came to me the day you were born and asked me what I thought of the name of Howard, may he rest in peace.

Howard   I appreciate that, Willy, but there just is no spot here for you. If I had a spot I'd slam you right in, but I just don't have a single solitary spot.

He looks for his lighter. **Willy** *has picked it up and gives it to him. Pause.*

Willy (*with increasing anger*)   Howard, all I need to set my table is fifty dollars a week.

Howard   But where am I going to put you, kid?

Willy   Look, it isn't a question of whether I can sell merchandise, is it?

Howard   No, but it's a business, kid, and everybody's gotta pull his own weight.

Willy (*desperately*)   Just let me tell you a story, Howard—

Howard   'Cause you gotta admit, business is business.

Willy (*angrily*)   Business is definitely business, but just listen for a minute. You don't understand this. When I was a boy—eighteen, nineteen—I was already on the road. And there was a question in my mind as to whether selling had a future for me. Because in those days I had a yearning to go to Alaska. See, there were three gold strikes in one month in Alaska, and I felt like going out. Just for the ride, you might say.

Howard (*barely interested*)   Don't say.

Willy   Oh, yeah, my father lived many years in Alaska. He was an adventurous man. We've got quite a little streak of self-reliance in our family. I thought I'd go out with my older brother and try to locate him, and maybe settle in the North with the old man. And I was almost decided to go, when I met a salesman in the Parker House. His name was Dave Singleman. And he was eighty-four years old, and he'd drummed merchandise in thirty-one states. And old Dave, he'd go up to his room, y'understand, put on his green velvet slippers—I'll never forget—and pick up his phone and call the buyers, and without ever leaving his room, at the age of eighty-four, he made his living. And when I saw that, I realized that selling was the greatest career a man could want. 'Cause what could be more satisfying than to be able to go, at the age of eighty-four, into twenty or thirty different cities, and pick up a phone, and be remembered and loved and helped by so many different people? Do you know? when he died—and by the way he died the death of a salesman, in his green velvet slippers in the smoker of the New York, New Haven and Hartford, going into Boston—when he died, hundreds of salesmen and buyers were at his funeral. Things were sad on a lotta trains for months after that. (*He stands up.* **Howard** *has not looked at him.*) In those days there was personality in it, Howard. There was respect, and comradeship, and gratitude in it. Today, it's all cut and dried, and there's no chance for bringing friendship to bear—or personality. You see what I mean? They don't know me any more.

Howard (*moving away, toward the right*)   That's just the thing, Willy.

Willy   If I had forty dollars a week—that's all I'd need. Forty dollars, Howard.

Howard   Kid, I can't take blood from a stone, I—

Willy (*desperation is on him now*)   Howard, the year Al Smith was nominated, your father came to me and—

Howard (*starting to go off*)   I've got to see some people, kid.

Willy (*stopping him*)   I'm talking about your father! There were promises made across this desk! You mustn't tell me you've got people to see—I put thirty-four years into this firm, Howard, and now I can't pay my insurance! You can't eat the orange and throw the peel away—a man is not a piece of fruit! (*After a pause:*) Now pay attention. Your father—in 1928 I had a big year. I averaged a hundred and seventy dollars a week in commissions.

Howard (*impatiently*)   Now, Willy, you never averaged—

Willy (*banging his hand on the desk*)   I averaged a hundred and seventy dollars a week in the year of 1928! And your father came to me—or rather, I was in the office here—it was right over this desk—and he put his hand on my shoulder—

Howard (*getting up*)   You'll have to excuse me, Willy, I gotta see some people. Pull yourself together. (*Going out:*) I'll be back in a little while.

On **Howard**'s *exit, the light on his chair grows very bright and strange.*

Willy   Pull myself together! What the hell did I say to him? My God, I was yelling at him! How could I! (**Willy** *breaks off, staring at the light, which occupies the chair, animating it. He approaches this chair, standing across the desk from it.*) Frank, Frank, don't you remember what you told me that time? How you put your hand on my shoulder, and Frank . . . (*He leans on the desk and as he speaks the dead man's name he accidentally switches on the recorder, and instantly*)

Howard's Son   ". . . of New York is Albany. The capital of Ohio is Cincinnati, the capital of Rhode Island is . . ." (*The recitation continues.*)

Willy (*leaping away with fright, shouting*)   Ha! Howard! Howard! Howard!

Howard (*rushing in*)   What happened?

Willy (*pointing at the machine, which continues nasally, childishly, with the capital cities*)   Shut it off! Shut it off!

Howard (*pulling the plug out*)   Look, Willy . . .

Willy (*pressing his hands to his eyes*)   I gotta get myself some coffee. I'll get some coffee . . .

Willy *starts to walk out.* **Howard** *stops him.*

Howard (*rolling up the cord*)   Willy, look . . .

Willy   I'll go to Boston.

Howard   Willy, you can't go to Boston for us.

Willy   Why can't I go?

Howard   I don't want you to represent us. I've been meaning to tell you for a long time now.

Willy   Howard, are you firing me?

Howard   I think you need a good long rest, Willy.

Willy   Howard—

Howard   And when you feel better, come back, and we'll see if we can work something out.

Willy   But I gotta earn money, Howard. I'm in no position to—

Howard   Where are your sons? Why don't your sons give you a hand?

Willy   They're working on a very big deal.

Howard   This is no time for false pride, Willy. You go to your sons and you tell them that you're tired. You've got two great boys, haven't you?

Willy   Oh, no question, no question, but in the meantime . . .

Howard   Then that's that, heh?

Willy   All right, I'll go to Boston tomorrow.

Howard   No, no.

Willy   I can't throw myself on my sons. I'm not a cripple!

Howard   Look, kid, I'm busy this morning.

Willy (*grasping* **Howard**'s *arm*)   Howard, you've got to let me go to Boston!

Howard (*hard, keeping himself under control*)   I've got a line of people to see this morning. Sit down, take five minutes, and pull yourself together, and then go home, will ya? I need the office, Willy. (*He starts to go, turns, remembering the recorder, starts to push off the table holding the recorder.*) Oh, yeah. Whenever you can this week, stop by and drop off the samples. You'll feel better, Willy, and then come back and we'll talk. Pull yourself together, kid, there's people outside.

Howard *exits, pushing the table off left.* **Willy** *stares into space, exhausted. Now the music is heard—***Ben**'s *music—first distantly, then closer, closer. As* **Willy** *speaks, Ben enters from the right. He carries valise and umbrella.*

Willy   Oh, Ben, how did you do it? What is the answer? Did you wind up the Alaska deal already?

Ben   Doesn't take much time if you know what you're doing. Just a short business trip. Boarding ship in an hour. Wanted to say good-by.

Willy   Ben, I've got to talk to you.

Ben (*glancing at his watch*)   Haven't the time, William.

Willy (*crossing the apron to* **Ben**)   Ben, nothing's working out. I don't know what to do.

Ben   Now, look here, William. I've bought timberland in Alaska and I need a man to look after things for me.

Willy   God, timberland! Me and my boys in those grand outdoors!

Ben   You've a new continent at your doorstep, William. Get out of these cities, they're full of talk and time payments and courts of law. Screw on your fists and you can fight for a fortune up there.

Willy   Yes, yes! Linda, Linda!

Linda *enters as of old, with the wash.*

Linda   Oh, you're back?

Ben   I haven't much time.

Willy   No, wait! Linda, he's got a proposition for me in Alaska.

Linda   But you've got— (*To* **Ben***:*) He's got a beautiful job here.

Willy   But in Alaska, kid, I could—

Linda   You're doing well enough, Willy!

Ben (*to* **Linda**)   Enough for what, my dear?

Linda (*frightened of* **Ben** *and angry at him*)   Don't say those things to him! Enough to be happy right here, right now. (*To* **Willy***, while* **Ben** *laughs:*) Why must everybody conquer the world? You're well liked, and the boys love you, and someday (*to* **Ben***:*) why, old man Wagner told him just the other day that if he keeps it up he'll be a member of the firm, didn't he, Willy?

Willy   Sure, sure. I am building something with this firm, Ben, and if a man is building something he must be on the right track, mustn't he?

Ben   What are you building? Lay your hand on it. Where is it?

Willy (*hesitantly*)   That's true, Linda, there's nothing.

Linda   Why? (*To* **Ben***:*) There's a man eighty-four years old—

Willy   That's right, Ben, that's right. When I look at that man I say, what is there to worry about?

Ben   Bah!

Willy   It's true, Ben. All he has to do is go into any city, pick up the phone, and he's making his living and you know why?

Ben (*picking up his valise*)   I've got to go.

Willy (*holding* **Ben** *back*)   Look at this boy!

Biff*, in his high school sweater, enters carrying suitcase.* **Happy** *carries* **Biff***'s shoulder guards, gold helmet, and football pants.*

Willy   Without a penny to his name, three great universities are begging for him, and from there the sky's the limit, because it's not what you do, Ben. It's who you know and the smile on your face! It's contacts, Ben, contacts! The whole wealth of Alaska passes over the lunch table at the Commodore Hotel, and that's the wonder, the wonder of this country, that a man can end with diamonds here on the basis of being liked! (*He turns to* **Biff**.) And that's why when you get out on that field today it's important. Because thousands of people will be rooting for you and loving you. (*To* **Ben**, *who has again begun to leave:*) And Ben! when he walks into a business office his name will sound out like a bell and all the doors will open to him! I've seen it, Ben, I've seen it a thousand times! You can't feel it with your hand like timber, but it's there!

Ben   Good-by, William.

Willy   Ben, am I right? Don't you think I'm right? I value your advice.

Ben   There's a new continent at your doorstep, William. You could walk out rich. Rich! (*He is gone.*)

Willy   We'll do it here, Ben! You hear me? We're gonna do it here!

Young Bernard *rushes in. The gay music of the boys is heard.*

Bernard   Oh, gee, I was afraid you left already!

Willy   Why? What time is it?

Bernard   It's half-past one!

Willy   Well, come on, everybody! Ebbets Field next stop! Where's the pennants? (*He rushes through the wall-line of the kitchen and out into the living-room.*)

Linda (*to* **Biff**)   Did you pack fresh underwear?

Biff (*who has been limbering up*)   I want to go!

Bernard   Biff, I'm carrying your helmet, ain't I?

Happy   No, I'm carrying the helmet.

Bernard   Oh, Biff, you promised me.

Happy   I'm carrying the helmet.

Bernard   How am I going to get in the locker room?

Linda   Let him carry the shoulder guards. (*She puts her coat and hat on in the kitchen.*)

Bernard   Can I, Biff? 'Cause I told everybody I'm going to be in the locker room.

Happy   In Ebbets Field it's the clubhouse.

Bernard   I meant the clubhouse. Biff!

Happy   Biff!

Biff (*grandly, after a slight pause*)   Let him carry the shoulder guards.

Happy (*as he gives* **Bernard** *the shoulder guards*)   Stay close to us now.

Willy *rushes in with the pennants.*

Willy (*handing them out*)   Everybody wave when Biff comes out on the field. (**Happy** *and* **Bernard** *run off.*) You set now, boy?

The music has died away.

Biff   Ready to go, Pop. Every muscle is ready.

Willy (*at the edge of the apron*)   You realize what this means?

Biff   That's right, Pop.

Willy (*feeling* **Biff***'s muscles*)   You're comin' home this afternoon captain of the All-Scholastic Championship Team of the City of New York.

Biff   I got it, Pop. And remember, pal, when I take off my helmet, that touchdown is for you.

Willy   Let's go! (*He is starting out, with his arm around* **Biff**, *when* **Charley** *enters, as of old, in knickers.*) I got no room for you, Charley.

Charley   Room? For what?

Willy   In the car.

Charley   You goin' for a ride? I wanted to shoot some casino.

Willy (*furiously*)   Casino! (*Incredulously:*) Don't you realize what today is?

Linda   Oh, he knows, Willy. He's just kidding you.

Willy   That's nothing to kid about!

Charley   No, Linda, what's goin' on?

Linda   He's playing in Ebbets Field.

Charley   Baseball in this weather?

Willy   Don't talk to him. Come on, come on! (*He is pushing them out.*)

Charley   Wait a minute, didn't you hear the news?

Willy   What?

Charley   Don't you listen to the radio? Ebbets Field just blew up.

Willy   You go to hell! (**Charley** *laughs. Pushing them out:*) Come on, come on! We're late.

Charley (*as they go*)   Knock a homer, Biff, knock a homer!

Willy (*the last to leave, turning to* **Charley**)   I don't think that was funny, Charley. This is the greatest day of his life.

Charley   Willy, when are you going to grow up?

Willy   Yeah, heh? When this game is over, Charley, you'll be laughing out of the other side of your face. They'll be calling him another Red Grange. Twenty-five thousand a year.

Charley (*kidding*)   Is that so?

Willy   Yeah, that's so.

Charley   Well, then, I'm sorry, Willy. But tell me something.

Willy   What?

Charley   Who is Red Grange?

Willy   Put up your hands. Goddam you, put up your hands!

Charley, *chuckling, shakes his head and walks away, around the left corner of the stage.* **Willy** *follows him. The music rises to a mocking frenzy.*

Willy   Who the hell do you think you are, better than everybody else? You don't know everything, you big, ignorant, stupid . . . Put up your hands!

Light rises, on the right side of the forestage, on a small table in the reception room of **Charley**'*s office. Traffic sounds are heard.* **Bernard**, *now mature, sits whistling to himself. A pair of tennis rackets and an overnight bag are on the floor beside him.*

Willy (*offstage*)   What are you walking away for? Don't walk away! If you're going to say something say it to my face! I know you laugh at me behind my back. You'll laugh out of the other side of your goddam face after this game. Touchdown! Touchdown! Eighty thousand people! Touchdown! Right between the goal posts.

Bernard *is a quiet, earnest, but self-assured young man.* **Willy**'s *voice is coming from right upstage now.* **Bernard** *lowers his feet off the table and listens.* **Jenny**, *his father's secretary, enters.*

Jenny (*distressed*)   Say, Bernard, will you go out in the hall?

Bernard   What is that noise? Who is it?

Jenny   Mr. Loman. He just got off the elevator.

Bernard (*getting up*)   Who's he arguing with?

Jenny   Nobody. There's nobody with him. I can't deal with him any more, and your father gets all upset everytime he comes. I've got a lot of typing to do, and your father's waiting to sign it. Will you see him?

Willy (*entering*)   Touchdown! Touch— (*He sees* **Jenny**.) Jenny, Jenny, good to see you. How're ya? Workin'? Or still honest?

Jenny   Fine. How've you been feeling?

Willy   Not much any more, Jenny. Ha, ha! (*He is surprised to see the rackets.*)

Bernard   Hello, Uncle Willy.

Willy (*almost shocked*)   Bernard! Well, look who's here! (*He comes quickly, guiltily, to* **Bernard** *and warmly shakes his hand.*)

Bernard   How are you? Good to see you.

Willy   What are you doing here?

Bernard   Oh, just stopped by to see Pop. Get off my feet till my train leaves. I'm going to Washington in a few minutes.

Willy   Is he in?

Bernard   Yes, he's in his office with the accountant. Sit down.

Willy (*sitting down*)   What're you going to do in Washington?

Bernard   Oh, just a case I've got there, Willy.

Willy   That so? (*Indicating the rackets:*) You going to play tennis there?

Bernard   I'm staying with a friend who's got a court.

Willy   Don't say. His own tennis court. Must be fine people, I bet.

Bernard   They are, very nice. Dad tells me Biff's in town.

Willy (*with a big smile*)   Yeah, Biff's in. Working on a very big deal, Bernard.

Bernard   What's Biff doing?

Willy   Well, he's been doing very big things in the West. But he decided to establish himself here. Very big. We're having dinner. Did I hear your wife had a boy?

Bernard   That's right. Our second.

Willy   Two boys! What do you know!

Bernard   What kind of a deal has Biff got?

Willy   Well, Bill Oliver—very big sporting-goods man—he wants Biff very badly. Called him in from the West. Long distance, carte blanche, special deliveries. Your friends have their own private tennis court?

Bernard   You still with the old firm, Willy?

Willy (*after a pause*)   I'm—I'm overjoyed to see how you made the grade, Bernard, overjoyed. It's an encouraging thing to see a young man really—really—Looks very good for Biff—very—(*He breaks off, then:*) Bernard—(*He is so full of emotion, he breaks off again.*)

Bernard   What is it, Willy?

Willy (*small and alone*)   What—what's the secret?

Bernard   What secret?

Willy   How—how did you? Why didn't he ever catch on?

Bernard   I wouldn't know that, Willy.

Willy (*confidentially, desperately*)   You were his friend, his boyhood friend. There's something I don't understand about it. His life ended after that Ebbets Field game. From the age of seventeen nothing good ever happened to him.

Bernard   He never trained himself for anything.

Willy   But he did, he did. After high school he took so many correspondence courses. Radio mechanics; television; God knows what, and never made the slightest mark.

Bernard (*taking off his glasses*)   Willy, do you want to talk candidly?

Willy (*rising, faces* **Bernard**)   I regard you as a very brilliant man, Bernard. I value your advice.

Bernard   Oh, the hell with the advice, Willy. I couldn't advise you. There's just one thing I've always wanted to ask you. When he was supposed to graduate, and the math teacher flunked him—

Willy   Oh, that son-of-a-bitch ruined his life.

Bernard   Yeah, but, Willy, all he had to do was go to summer school and make up that subject.

Willy   That's right, that's right.

Bernard   Did you tell him not to go to summer school?

Willy   Me? I begged him to go. I ordered him to go!

Bernard   Then why wouldn't he go?

Willy   Why? Why! Bernard, that question has been trailing me like a ghost for the last fifteen years. He flunked the subject, and laid down and died like a hammer hit him!

Bernard   Take it easy, kid.

Willy   Let me talk to you—I got nobody to talk to. Bernard, Bernard, was it my fault? Y'see? It keeps going around in my mind, maybe I did something to him. I got nothing to give him.

Bernard   Don't take it so hard.

Willy   Why did he lay down? What is the story there? You were his friend!

Bernard   Willy, I remember, it was June, and our grades came out. And he'd flunked math.

Willy   That son-of-a-bitch!

Bernard   No, it wasn't right then. Biff just got very angry, I remember, and he was ready to enroll in summer school.

Willy (*surprised*)   He was?

Bernard   He wasn't beaten by it at all. But then, Willy, he disappeared from the block for almost a month. And I got the idea that he'd gone up to New England to see you. Did he have a talk with you then?

Willy *stares in silence.*

Bernard   Willy?

Willy (*with a strong edge of resentment in his voice*)   Yeah, he came to Boston. What about it?

Bernard   Well, just that when he came back—I'll never forget this, it always mystifies me. Because I'd thought so well of Biff, even though he'd always taken advantage of me. I loved him, Willy, y'know? And he came back after that month and took his sneakers—remember those sneakers with "University of Virginia" printed on them? He was so proud of those, wore them every day. And he took them down in the cellar, and burned them up in the furnace. We had a fist fight. It lasted at least half an hour. Just the two of us, punching each other down the cellar, and crying right through it. I've often thought of how strange it was that I knew he'd given up his life. What happened in Boston, Willy?

Willy *looks at him as at an intruder.*

Bernard   I just bring it up because you asked me.

Willy (*angrily*)   Nothing. What do you mean, "What happened?" What's that got to do with anything?

Bernard   Well, don't get sore.

Willy   What are you trying to do, blame it on me? If a boy lays down is that my fault?

Bernard   Now, Willy, don't get—

Willy   Well, don't—don't talk to me that way! What does that mean, "What happened?"

Charley *enters. He is in his vest, and he carries a bottle of bourbon.*

Charley   Hey, you're going to miss that train. (*He waves the bottle.*)

Bernard   Yeah, I'm going. (*He takes the bottle.*) Thanks, Pop. (*He picks up his rackets and bag.*) Good-by, Willy, and don't worry about it. You know, "If at first you don't succeed . . ."

Willy   Yes, I believe in that.

Bernard   But sometimes, Willy, it's better for a man just to walk away.

Willy   Walk away?

Bernard   That's right.

Willy   But if you can't walk away?

Bernard (*after a slight pause*)   I guess that's when it's tough. (*Extending his hand:*) Good-by, Willy.

Willy (*shaking* **Bernard***'s hand*)   Good-by, boy.

Charley (*an arm on* **Bernard***'s shoulder*)   How do you like this kid? Gonna argue a case in front of the Supreme Court.

Bernard (*protesting*)   Pop!

Willy (*genuinely shocked, pained, and happy*)   No! The Supreme Court!

Bernard   I gotta run. 'By, Dad!

Charley   Knock 'em dead, Bernard!

Bernard *goes off.*

Willy (*as* **Charley** *takes out his wallet*)   The Supreme Court! And he didn't even mention it!

Charley (*counting out money on the desk*)   He don't have to—he's gonna do it.

Willy   And you never told him what to do, did you? You never took any interest in him.

Charley   My salvation is that I never took any interest in anything. There's some money—fifty dollars. I got an accountant inside.

Willy   Charley, look . . . (*With difficulty:*) I got my insurance to pay. If you can manage it—I need a hundred and ten dollars.

Charley *doesn't reply for a moment; merely stops moving.*

Willy   I'd draw it from my bank but Linda would know, and I . . .

Charley   Sit down, Willy.

Willy (*moving toward the chair*)   I'm keeping an account of everything, remember. I'll pay every penny back. (*He sits.*)

Charley   Now listen to me, Willy.

Willy   I want you to know I appreciate . . .

Charley (*sitting down on the table*)   Willy, what're you doin'? What the hell is goin' on in your head?

Willy   Why? I'm simply . . .

Charley   I offered you a job. You can make fifty dollars a week. And I won't send you on the road.

Willy   I've got a job.

Charley   Without pay? What kind of a job is a job without pay? (*He rises.*) Now, look, kid, enough is enough. I'm no genius but I know when I'm being insulted.

Willy   Insulted!

Charley   Why don't you want to work for me?

Willy   What's the matter with you? I've got a job.

Charley   Then what're you walkin' in here every week for?

Willy (*getting up*)   Well, if you don't want me to walk in here—

Charley   I am offering you a job.

Willy   I don't want your goddam job!

Charley   When the hell are you going to grow up?

Willy (*furiously*)   You big ignoramus, if you say that to me again I'll rap you one! I don't care how big you are! (*He's ready to fight.*)

Pause.

Charley (*kindly, going to him*)   How much do you need, Willy?

Willy   Charley, I'm strapped, I'm strapped. I don't know what to do. I was just fired.

Charley   Howard fired you?

Willy   That snotnose. Imagine that? I named him. I named him Howard.

Charley   Willy, when're you gonna realize that them things don't mean anything? You named him Howard, but you can't sell that. The only thing you got in this world is what you can sell. And the funny thing is that you're a salesman, and you don't know that.

Willy   I've always tried to think otherwise, I guess. I always felt that if a man was impressive, and well liked, that nothing—

Charley   Why must everybody like you? Who liked J. P. Morgan? Was he impressive? In a Turkish bath he'd look like a butcher. But with his pockets on he was very well liked. Now listen, Willy, I know you don't like me, and nobody can say I'm in love with you, but I'll give you a job because—just for the hell of it, put it that way. Now what do you say?

Willy   I—I just can't work for you, Charley.

Charley   What're you, jealous of me?

Willy   I can't work for you, that's all, don't ask me why.

Charley (*angered, takes out more bills*)   You been jealous of me all your life, you damned fool! Here, pay your insurance. (*He puts the money in* **Willy**'s *hand.*)

Willy   I'm keeping strict accounts.

Charley   I've got some work to do. Take care of yourself. And pay your insurance.

Willy (*moving to the right*)   Funny, y'know? After all the highways, and the trains, and the appointments, and the years, you end up worth more dead than alive.

Charley   Willy, nobody's worth nothin' dead. (*After a slight pause:*) Did you hear what I said?

Willy *stands still, dreaming.*

Charley   Willy!

Willy   Apologize to Bernard for me when you see him. I didn't mean to argue with him. He's a fine boy. They're all fine boys, and they'll end up big—all of them. Someday they'll all play tennis together. Wish me luck, Charley. He saw Bill Oliver today.

Charley   Good luck.

Willy (*on the verge of tears*)   Charley, you're the only friend I got. Isn't that a remarkable thing? (*He goes out.*)

Charley   Jesus!

Charley *stares after him a moment and follows. All light blacks out. Suddenly raucous music is heard, and a red glow rises behind the screen at right.* **Stanley**, *a young waiter, appears, carrying a table, followed by* **Happy**, *who is carrying two chairs.*

Stanley (*putting the table down*)   That's all right, Mr. Loman, I can handle it myself. (*He turns and takes the chairs from* **Happy** *and places them at the table.*)

Happy (*glancing around*)   Oh, this is better.

Stanley   Sure, in the front there you're in the middle of all kinds a noise. Whenever you got a party, Mr. Loman, you just tell me and I'll put you back here. Y'know, there's a lotta people they don't like it private, because when they go out they like to see a lotta action around them because they're sick and tired to stay in the house by theirself. But I know you, you ain't from Hackensack. You know what I mean?

Happy (*sitting down*)   So how's it coming, Stanley?

Stanley   Ah, it's a dog's life. I only wish during the war they'd a took me in the Army. I coulda been dead by now.

Happy   My brother's back, Stanley.

Stanley   Oh, he come back, heh? From the Far West.

Happy   Yeah, big cattle man, my brother, so treat him right. And my father's coming too.

Stanley   Oh, your father too!

Happy   You got a couple of nice lobsters?

Stanley   Hundred per cent, big.

Happy   I want them with the claws.

Stanley   Don't worry, I don't give you no mice. (**Happy** *laughs.*) How about some wine? It'll put a head on the meal.

Happy   No. You remember, Stanley, that recipe I brought you from overseas? With the champagne in it?

Stanley   Oh, yeah, sure. I still got it tacked up yet in the kitchen. But that'll have to cost a buck apiece anyways.

Happy   That's all right.

Stanley   What'd you, hit a number or somethin'?

Happy   No, it's a little celebration. My brother is—I think he pulled off a big deal today. I think we're going into business together.

Stanley   Great! That's the best for you. Because a family business, you know what I mean?—that's the best.

Happy   That's what I think.

Stanley   'Cause what's the difference? Somebody steals? It's in the family. Know what I mean? (*Sotto voce:*) Like this bartender here. The boss is goin' crazy what kinda leak he's got in the cash register. You put it in but it don't come out.

Happy (*raising his head*)   Sh!

Stanley   What?

Happy   You notice I wasn't lookin' right or left, was I?

Stanley   No.

Happy   And my eyes are closed.

Stanley   So what's the—?

Happy   Strudel's comin'.

Stanley (*catching on, looks around*)   Ah, no, there's no—

He breaks off as a furred, lavishly dressed girl enters and sits at the next table. Both follow her with their eyes.

Stanley   Geez, how'd ya know?

Happy   I got radar or something. (*Staring directly at her profile:*) Oooooooo . . . Stanley.

Stanley   I think that's for you, Mr. Loman.

Happy   Look at that mouth. Oh, God. And the binoculars.

Stanley   Geez, you got a life, Mr. Loman.

Happy   Wait on her.

Stanley (*going to the girl's table*)   Would you like a menu, ma'am?

Girl   I'm expecting someone, but I'd like a—

Happy   Why don't you bring her—excuse me, miss, do you mind? I sell champagne, and I'd like you to try my brand. Bring her a champagne, Stanley.

Girl   That's awfully nice of you.

Happy   Don't mention it. It's all company money. (*He laughs.*)

Girl   That's a charming product to be selling, isn't it?

Happy   Oh, gets to be like everything else. Selling is selling, y'know.

Girl   I suppose.

Happy   You don't happen to sell, do you?

Girl   No, I don't sell.

Happy   Would you object to a compliment from a stranger? You ought to be on a magazine cover.

Girl (*looking at him a little archly*)   I have been.

Stanley *comes in with a glass of champagne.*

Happy   What'd I say before, Stanley? You see? She's a cover girl.

Stanley   Oh, I could see, I could see.

Happy (*to the* **Girl**)   What magazine?

Girl   Oh, a lot of them. (*She takes the drink.*) Thank you.

Happy   You know what they say in France, don't you? "Champagne is the drink of the complexion"—Hya, Biff!

Biff *has entered and sits with* **Happy**.

Biff   Hello, kid. Sorry I'm late.

Happy   I just got here. Uh, Miss—?

Girl   Forsythe.

Happy   Miss Forsythe, this is my brother.

Biff   Is Dad here?

Happy   His name is Biff. You might've heard of him. Great football player.

Girl   Really? What team?

Happy   Are you familiar with football?

Girl   No, I'm afraid I'm not.

Happy   Bill is quarterback with the New York Giants.

Girl   Well, that is nice, isn't it? (*She drinks.*)

Happy   Good health.

Girl   I'm happy to meet you.

Happy   That's my name. Hap. It's really Harold, but at West Point they called me Happy.

Girl (*now really impressed*)   Oh, I see. How do you do? (*She turns her profile.*)

Biff   Isn't Dad coming?

Happy   You want her?

Biff   Oh, I could never make that.

Happy   I remember the time that idea would never come into your head. Where's the old confidence, Biff?

Biff   I just saw Oliver—

Happy   Wait a minute. I've got to see that old confidence again. Do you want her? She's on call.

Biff   Oh, no. (*He turns to look at the* **Girl**.)

Happy   I'm telling you. (*Watch this. Turning to the* **Girl**:) Honey? (*She turns to him.*) Are you busy?

Girl   Well, I am . . . but I could make a phone call.

Happy   Do that, will you, honey? And see if you can get a friend. We'll be here for a while. Biff is one of the greatest football players in the country.

Girl (*standing up*)   Well, I'm certainly happy to meet you.

Happy   Come back soon.

Girl   I'll try.

Happy   Don't try, honey, try hard.

The **Girl** *exits.* **Stanley** *follows, shaking his head in bewildered admiration.*

Happy   Isn't that a shame now? A beautiful girl like that? That's why I can't get married. There's not a good woman in a thousand. New York is loaded with them, kid!

Biff   Hap, look—

Happy   I told you she was on call!

Biff (*strangely unnerved*)   Cut it out, will ya? I want to say something to you.

Happy   Did you see Oliver?

Biff   I saw him all right. Now look, I want to tell Dad a couple of things and I want you to help me.

Happy   What? Is he going to back you?

Biff   Are you crazy? You're out of your goddam head, you know that?

Happy   Why? What happened?

Biff (*breathlessly*)   I did a terrible thing today, Hap. It's been the strangest day I ever went through. I'm all numb, I swear.

Happy   You mean he wouldn't see you?

Biff   Well, I waited six hours for him, see? All day. Kept sending my name in. Even tried to date his secretary so she'd get me to him, but no soap.

Happy   Because you're not showin' the old confidence, Biff. He remembered you, didn't he?

Biff (*stopping* **Happy** *with a gesture*)   Finally, about five o'clock, he comes out. Didn't remember who I was or anything. I felt like such an idiot, Hap.

Happy   Did you tell him my Florida idea?

Biff   He walked away. I saw him for one minute. I got so mad I could've torn the walls down! How the hell did I ever get the idea I was a salesman there? I even believed myself that I'd been a salesman for him! And then he gave me one look and—I realized what a ridiculous lie my whole life has been! We've been talking in a dream for fifteen years. I was a shipping clerk.

Happy   What'd you do?

Biff (*with great tension and wonder*)   Well, he left, see. And the secretary went out. I was all alone in the waiting-room. I don't know what came over me, Hap. The next thing I know I'm in his office—paneled walls, everything. I can't explain it. I—Hap, I took his fountain pen.

Happy   Geez, did he catch you?

Biff   I ran out. I ran down all eleven flights. I ran and ran and ran.

Happy   That was an awful dumb—what'd you do that for?

Biff (*agonized*)   I don't know, I just—wanted to take something, I don't know. You gotta help me, Hap, I'm gonna tell Pop.

Happy   You crazy? What for?

Biff   Hap, he's got to understand that I'm not the man somebody lends that kind of money to. He thinks I've been spiting him all these years and it's eating him up.

Happy   That's just it. You tell him something nice.

Biff   I can't.

Happy   Say you got a lunch date with Oliver tomorrow.

Biff   So what do I do tomorrow?

Happy   You leave the house tomorrow and come back at night and say Oliver is thinking it over. And he thinks it over for a couple of weeks, and gradually it fades away and nobody's the worse.

Biff   But it'll go on forever!

Happy   Dad is never so happy as when he's looking forward to something!

Willy *enters.*

Happy   Hello, scout!

Willy   Gee, I haven't been here in years!

Stanley *has followed* **Willy** *in and sets a chair for him.* **Stanley** *starts off but* **Happy** *stops him.*

Happy   Stanley!

Stanley *stands by, waiting for an order.*

Biff (*going to* **Willy** *with guilt, as to an invalid*)   Sit down, Pop. You want a drink?

Willy   Sure, I don't mind.

Biff   Let's get a load on.

Willy   You look worried.

Biff   N-no. (*To* **Stanley***:*) Scotch all around. Make it doubles.

Stanley   Doubles, right; (*He goes.*)

Willy   You had a couple already, didn't you?

Biff   Just a couple, yeah.

Willy   Well, what happened, boy? (*Nodding affirmatively, with a smile:*) Everything go all right?

Biff (*takes a breath, then reaches out and grasps* **Willy***'s hand*)   Pal . . . (*He is smiling bravely, and* **Willy** *is smiling too.*) I had an experience today.

Happy   Terrific, Pop.

Willy   That so? What happened?

Biff (*high, slightly alcoholic, above the earth*)   I'm going to tell you everything from first to last. It's been a strange day. (*Silence. He looks around, composes himself as best he can, but his breath keeps breaking* *the rhythm of his voice.*) I had to wait quite a while for him, and—

Willy   Oliver?

Biff   Yeah, Oliver. All day, as a matter of cold fact. And a lot of— instances—facts, Pop, facts about my life came back to me. Who was it, Pop? Who ever said I was a salesman with Oliver?

Willy   Well, you were.

Biff   No, Dad, I was a shipping clerk.

Willy   But you were practically—

Biff (*with determination*)   Dad,I don't know who said it first, but I was never a salesman for Bill Oliver.

Willy   What're you talking about?

Biff   Let's hold on to the facts tonight, Pop. We're not going to get anywhere bullin' around. I was a shipping clerk.

Willy (*angrily*)   All right, now listen to me—

Biff   Why don't you let me finish?

Willy   I'm not interested in stories about the past or any crap of that kind because the woods are burning, boys, you understand? There's a big blaze going on all around. I was fired today.

Biff (*shocked*)   How could you be?

Willy   I was fired, and I'm looking for a little good news to tell your mother, because the woman has waited and the woman has suffered. The gist of it is that I haven't got a story left in my head, Biff. So don't give me a lecture about facts and aspects. I am not interested. Now what've you got to say to me?

Stanley *enters with three drinks. They wait until he leaves.*

Willy   Did you see Oliver?

Biff   Jesus, Dad!

Willy   You mean you didn't go up there?

Happy   Sure he went up there.

Biff   I did. I—saw him. How could they fire you?

Willy (*on the edge of his chair*)   What kind of a welcome did he give you?

Biff   He won't even let you work on commission?

Willy   I'm out! (*Driving:*) So tell me, he gave you a warm welcome?

Happy   Sure, Pop, sure!

Biff (*driven*)   Well, it was kind of—

Willy   I was wondering if he'd remember you. (*To* **Happy***:*) Imagine, man doesn't see him for ten, twelve years and gives him that kind of a welcome!

Happy   Damn right!

Biff (*trying to return to the offensive*)   Pop, look—

Willy   You know why he remembered you, don't you? Because you impressed him in those days.

Biff   Let's talk quietly and get this down to the facts, huh?

Willy (*as though* **Biff** *had been interrupting*)   Well, what happened? It's great news, Biff. Did he take you into his office or'd you talk in the waiting-room?

Biff   Well, he came in, see, and—

Willy (*with a big smile*)   What'd he say? Betcha he threw his arm around you.

Biff   Well, he kinda—

Willy   He's a fine man. (*To* **Happy***:*) Very hard man to see, y'know.

Happy (*agreeing*)   Oh, I know.

Willy (*to* **Biff**)   Is that where you had the drinks?

Biff   Yeah, he gave me a couple of—no, no!

Happy (*cutting in*)   He told him my Florida idea.

Willy   Don't interrupt. (*To* **Biff***:*) How'd he react to the Florida idea?

Biff   Dad, will you give me a minute to explain?

Willy   I've been waiting for you to explain since I sat down here! What happened? He took you into his office and what?

Biff   Well—I talked. And—and he listened, see.

Willy   Famous for the way he listens, y'know. What was his answer?

Biff   His answer was—(*He breaks off, suddenly angry.*) Dad, you're not letting me tell you what I want to tell you!

Willy (*accusing, angered*)   You didn't see him, did you?

Biff   I did see him!

Willy   What'd you insult him or something? You insulted him, didn't you?

Biff   Listen, will you let me out of it, will you just let me out of it!

Happy   What the hell!

Willy   Tell me what happened!

Biff (*to* **Happy**)   I can't talk to him!

A single trumpet note jars the ear. The light of green leaves stains the house, which holds the air of night and a dream. **Young Bernard** *enters and knocks on the door of the house.*

Young Bernard (*frantically*)   Mrs. Loman, Mrs. Loman!

Happy   Tell him what happened!

Biff (*to* **Happy**)   Shut up and leave me alone!

Willy   No, no! You had to go and flunk math!

Biff   What math? What're you talking about?

Young Bernard   Mrs. Loman, Mrs. Loman!

Linda *appears in the house, as of old.*

Willy (*wildly*)   Math, math, math!

Biff   Take it easy, Pop!

Young Bernard   Mrs. Loman!

Willy (*furiously*)   If you hadn't flunked you'd've been set by now!

Biff   Now, look, I'm gonna tell you what happened, and you're going to listen to me.

Young Bernard   Mrs. Loman!

Biff   I waited six hours—

Happy   What the hell are you saying?

Biff   I kept sending in my name but he wouldn't see me. So finally he . . . (*He continues unheard as light fades low on the restaurant.*)

Young Bernard   Biff flunked math!

Linda   No!

Young Bernard   Birnbaum flunked him! They won't graduate him!

Linda   But they have to. He's gotta go to the university. Where is he? Biff! Biff!

Young Bernard   No, he left. He went to Grand Central.

Linda   Grand—You mean he went to Boston!

Young Bernard   Is Uncle Willy in Boston?

Linda   Oh, maybe Willy can talk to the teacher. Oh, the poor, poor boy!

Light on house area snaps out.

Biff (*at the table, now audible, holding up a gold fountain pen*)   . . . so I'm washed up with Oliver, you understand? Are you listening to me?

Willy (*at a loss*)   Yeah, sure. If you hadn't flunked—

Biff   Flunked what? What're you talking about?

Willy   Don't blame everything on me! I didn't flunk math—you did! What pen?

Happy   That was awful dumb, Biff, a pen like that is worth—

Willy (*seeing the pen for the first time*)   You took Oliver's pen?

Biff (*weakening*)   Dad, I just explained it to you.

Willy   You stole Bill Oliver's fountain pen!

Biff   I didn't exactly steal it! That's just what I've been explaining to you!

Happy   He had it in his hand and just then Oliver walked in, so he got nervous and stuck it in his pocket!

Willy   My God, Biff!

Biff   I never intended to do it, Dad!

Operator's Voice   Standish Arms, good evening!

Willy (*shouting*)   I'm not in my room!

Biff (*frightened*)   Dad, what's the matter? (*He and* **Happy** *stand up.*)

Operator   Ringing Mr. Loman for you!

Willy   I'm not there, stop it!

Biff (*horrified, gets down on one knee before* **Willy**)   Dad, I'll make good, I'll make good. (**Willy** *tries to get to his feet.* **Biff** *holds him down.*) Sit down now.

Willy   No, you're no good, you're no good for anything.

Biff   I am, Dad, I'll find something else, you understand? Now don't worry about anything. (*He holds up* **Willy**'*s face:*) Talk to me, Dad.

Operator   Mr. Loman does not answer. Shall I page him?

Willy (*attempting to stand, as though to rush and silence the* **Operator**)   No, no, no!

Happy   He'll strike something, Pop.

Willy   No, no . . .

Biff (*desperately, standing over* **Willy**)   Pop, listen! Listen to me! I'm telling you something good. Oliver talked to his partner about the Florida idea. You listening? He—he talked to his partner, and he came to me . . . I'm going to be all right, you hear? Dad, listen to me, he said it was just a question of the amount!

Willy   Then you . . . got it?

Happy   He's gonna be terrific, Pop!

Willy (*trying to stand*)   Then you got it, haven't you? You got it! You got it!

Biff (*agonized, holds* **Willy** *down*)   No, no. Look, Pop. I'm supposed to have lunch with them tomorrow. I'm just telling you this so you'll know that I can still make an impression, Pop. And I'll make good somewhere, but I can't go tomorrow, see?

Willy   Why not? You simply—

Biff   But the pen, Pop!

Willy   You give it to him and tell him it was an oversight!

Happy   Sure, have lunch tomorrow!

Biff   I can't say that—

Willy   You were doing a crossword puzzle and accidentally used his pen!

Biff   Listen, kid, I took those balls years ago, now I walk in with his fountain pen? That clinches it, don't you see? I can't face him like that! I'll try elsewhere.

Page's Voice   Paging Mr. Loman!

Willy   Don't you want to be anything?

Biff   Pop, how can I go back?

Willy   You don't want to be anything, is that what's behind it?

Biff (*now angry at* **Willy** *for not crediting his sympathy*)   Don't take it that way! You think it was easy walking into that office after what I'd done to him? A team of horses couldn't have dragged me back to Bill Oliver!

Willy   Then why'd you go?

Biff   Why did I go? Why did I go! Look at you! Look at what's become of you!

Off left, **The Woman** *laughs.*

Willy   Biff, you're going to go to that lunch tomorrow, or—

Biff   I can't go. I've got no appointment!

Happy   Biff, for . . .!

Willy   Are you spiting me?

Biff   Don't take it that way! Goddammit!

Willy (*strikes* **Biff** *and falters away from the table*)   You rotten little louse! Are you spiting me?

The Woman   Someone's at the door, Willy!

Biff   I'm no good, can't you see what I am?

Happy (*separating them*)   Hey, you're in a restaurant! Now cut it out, both of you? (*The girls enter.*) Hello, girls, sit down.

The Woman *laughs, off left.*

Miss Forsythe   I guess we might as well. This is Letta.

The Woman   Willy, are you going to wake up?

Biff (*ignoring* **Willy**)   How're ya, miss, sit down. What do you drink?

Miss Forsythe   Letta might not be able to stay long.

Letta   I gotta get up very early tomorrow. I got jury duty. I'm so excited! Were you fellows ever on a jury?

Biff   No, but I been in front of them! (*The girls laugh.*) This is my father.

Letta   Isn't he cute? Sit down with us, Pop.

Happy   Sit him down, Biff!

Biff (*going to him*)   Come on, slugger, drink us under the table. To hell with it! Come on, sit down, pal.

On **Biff**'*s last insistence,* **Willy** *is about to sit.*

The Woman (*now urgently*)   Willy, are you going to answer the door!

The Woman'*s call pulls* **Willy** *back. He starts right, befuddled.*

Biff   Hey, where are you going?

Willy   Open the door.

Biff   The door?

Willy   The washroom . . . the door . . . where's the door?

Biff (*leading* **Willy** *to the left*)   Just go straight down.

Willy *moves left.*

The Woman   Willy, Willy, are you going to get up, get up, get up, get up?

Willy *exits left.*

Letta   I think it's sweet you bring your daddy along.

Miss Forsythe   Oh, he isn't really your father!

Biff (*at left, turning to her resentfully*)   Miss Forsythe, you've just seen a prince walk by. A fine, troubled prince. A hardworking, unappreciated prince. A pal, you understand? A good companion. Always for his boys.

Letta   That's so sweet.

Happy   Well, girls, what's the program? We're wasting time. Come on, Biff. Gather round. Where would you like to go?

Biff   Why don't you do something for him?

Happy   Me!

Biff   Don't you give a damn for him, Hap?

Happy   What're you talking about? I'm the one who—

Biff   I sense it, you don't give a good goddam about him. (*He takes the rolled-up hose from his pocket and puts it on the table in front of*

Happy.) Look what I found in the cellar, for Christ's sake. How can you bear to let it go on?

Happy   Me? Who goes away? Who runs off and—

Biff   Yeah, but he doesn't mean anything to you. You could help him—I can't! Don't you understand what I'm talking about? He's going to kill himself, don't you know that?

Happy   Don't I know it! Me!

Biff   Hap, help him! Jesus . . . help him . . . Help me, help me, I can't bear to look at his face! (*Ready to weep, he hurries out, up right.*)

Happy (*starting after him*)   Where are you going?

Miss Forsythe   What's he so mad about?

Happy   Come on, girls, we'll catch up with him.

Miss Forsythe (*as* **Happy** *pushes her out*)   Say, I don't like that temper of his!

Happy   He's just a little overstrung, he'll be all right!

Willy (*off left, as* **The Woman** *laughs*)   Don't answer! Don't answer!

Letta   Don't you want to tell your father—

Happy   No, that's not my father. He's just a guy. Come on, we'll catch Biff, and, honey, we're going to paint this town! Stanley, where's the check! Hey, Stanley!

They exit. **Stanley** *looks toward left.*

Stanley (*calling to* **Happy** *indignantly*)   Mr. Loman! Mr. Loman!

Stanley *picks up a chair and follows them off. Knocking is heard off left.* **The Woman** *enters, laughing.* **Willy** *follows her. She is in a black slip; he is buttoning his shirt. Raw, sensuous music accompanies their speech.*

Willy   Will you stop laughing? Will you stop?

The Woman   Aren't you going to answer the door? He'll wake the whole hotel.

Willy   I'm not expecting anybody.

The Woman   Whyn't you have another drink, honey, and stop being so damn self-centered?

Willy   I'm so lonely.

The Woman   You know you ruined me, Willy? From now on, whenever you come to the office, I'll see that you go right through to the buyers. No waiting at my desk any more, Willy. You ruined me.

Willy   That's nice of you to say that.

The Woman   Gee, you are self-centered! Why so sad? You are the saddest, self-centeredest soul I ever did see-saw. (*She laughs. He kisses her.*) Come on inside, drummer boy. It's silly to be dressing in the middle of the night. (*As knocking is heard:*) Aren't you going to answer the door?

Willy   They're knocking on the wrong door.

The Woman   But I felt the knocking. And he heard us talking in here. Maybe the hotel's on fire!

Willy (*his terror rising*)   It's a mistake.

The Woman   Then tell him to go away!

Willy   There's nobody there.

The Woman   It's getting on my nerves, Willy. There's somebody standing out there and it's getting on my nerves!

Willy (*pushing her away from him*)   All right, stay in the bathroom here, and don't come out. I think there's a law in Massachusetts about it, so don't come out. It may be that new room clerk. He looked very mean. So don't come out. It's a mistake, there's no fire.

The knocking is heard again. He takes a few steps away from her, and she vanishes into the wing. The light follows him, and now he is facing **Young Biff**, *who carries a suitcase.* **Biff** *steps toward him. The music is gone.*

Biff   Why didn't you answer?

Willy   Biff! What are you doing in Boston?

Biff   Why didn't you answer? I've been knocking for five minutes, I called you on the phone—

Willy   I just heard you. I was in the bathroom and had the door shut. Did anything happen home?

Biff   Dad—I let you down.

Willy   What do you mean?

Biff   Dad . . .

Willy   Biffo, what's this about? (*Putting his arm around* **Biff***:*) Come on, let's go downstairs and get you a malted.

Biff   Dad, I flunked math.

Willy   Not for the term?

Biff   The term. I haven't got enough credits to graduate.

Willy   You mean to say Bernard wouldn't give you the answers?

Biff   He did, he tried, but I only got a sixty-one.

Willy   And they wouldn't give you four points?

Biff   Birnbaum refused absolutely. I begged him, Pop, but he won't give me those points. You gotta talk to him before they close the school. Because if he saw the kind of man you are, and you just talked to him in your way, I'm sure he'd come through for me. The class came right before practice, see, and I didn't go enough. Would you talk to him? He'd like you, Pop. You know the way you could talk.

Willy   You're on. We'll drive right back.

Biff   Oh, Dad, good work! I'm sure he'll change it for you!

Willy   Go downstairs and tell the clerk I'm checkin' out. Go right down.

Biff   Yes, sir! See, the reason he hates me, Pop—one day he was late for class so I got up at the blackboard and imitated him. I crossed my eyes and talked with a lithp.

Willy (*laughing*)   You did? The kids like it?

Biff   They nearly died laughing!

Willy   Yeah? What'd you do?

Biff   The thquare root of thixthy twee is . . . (**Willy** *bursts out laughing;* **Biff** *joins him.*) And in the middle of it he walked in!

Willy *laughs and* **The Woman** *joins in offstage.*

Willy (*without hesitation*)   Hurry downstairs and—

Biff   Somebody in there?

Willy   No, that was next door.

The Woman *laughs offstage.*

Biff   Somebody got in your bathroom!

Willy   No, it's the next room, there's a party—

The Woman (*enters, laughing. She lisps this*)   Can I come in? There's something in the bathtub, Willy, and it's moving!

Willy *looks at* **Biff**, *who is staring open-mouthed and horrified at* **The Woman**.

Willy   Ah—you better go back to your room. They must be finished painting by now. They're painting her room so I let her take a shower here. Go back, go back . . . (*He pushes her.*)

The Woman (*resisting*)   But I've got to get dressed, Willy, I can't—

Willy   Get out of here! Go back, go back . . . (*Suddenly striving for the ordinary:*) This is Miss Francis, Biff, she's a buyer. They're painting her room. Go back, Miss Francis, go back . . .

The Woman   But my clothes, I can't go out naked in the hall!

Willy (*pushing her offstage*)   Get outa here! Go back, go back!

Biff *slowly sits down on his suitcase as the argument continues offstage.*

The Woman   Where's my stockings? You promised me stockings, Willy!

Willy   I have no stockings here!

The Woman   You had two boxes of size nine sheers for me, and I want them!

Willy   Here, for God's sake, will you get outa here!

The Woman (*enters holding a box of stockings*)   I just hope there's nobody in the hall. That's all I—hope. (*To* **Biff**:) Are you football or baseball?

Biff   Football.

The Woman (*angry, humiliated*)   That's me too. G'night. (*She snatches her clothes from* **Willy**, *and walks out.*)

Willy (*after a pause*)   Well, better get going. I want to get to the school first thing in the morning. Get my suits out of the closet. I'll get my valise. (**Biff** *doesn't move.*) What's the matter? (**Biff** *remains motionless, tears falling.*) She's a buyer. Buys for J. H. Simmons. She lives down the hall—they're painting. You don't imagine—(*He breaks off. After a pause:*) Now listen, pal, she's just a buyer. She sees merchandise in her room and they have to keep it looking just so . . . (*Pause. Assuming command:*) All right, get my suits. (**Biff** *doesn't move.*) Now stop crying and do as I say. I gave you an order. Biff, I gave you an order! Is that what you do when I give you an order? How dare you cry! (*Putting his arm around* **Biff**.) Now look, Biff, when you grow up you'll understand about these things. You mustn't—you mustn't overemphasize a thing like this. I'll see Birnbaum first thing in the morning.

Biff   Never mind.

Willy (*getting down beside* **Biff**)   Never mind! He's going to give you those points. I'll see to it.

Biff   He wouldn't listen to you.

Willy   He certainly will listen to me. You need those points for the U. of Virginia.

Biff   I'm not going there.

Willy   Heh? If I can't get him to change that mark you'll make it up in summer school. You've got all summer to—

Biff (*his weeping breaking from him*)   Dad . . .

Willy (*infected by it*)   Oh, my boy . . .

Biff   Dad . . .

Willy   She's nothing to me, Biff. I was lonely, I was terribly lonely.

Biff   You—you gave her Mama's stockings! (*His tears break through and he rises to go.*)

Willy (*grabbing for* **Biff**)   I gave you an order!

Biff   Don't touch me, you—liar!

Willy   Apologize for that!

Biff   You fake! You phony little fake! You fake! (*Overcome, he turns quickly and weeping fully goes out with his suitcase.* **Willy** *is left on the floor on his knees.*)

Willy   I gave you an order! Biff, come back here or I'll beat you! Come back here! I'll whip you!

Stanley *comes quickly in from the right and stands in front of* **Willy**.

Willy (*shouts at* **Stanley**)   I gave you an order . . .

Stanley   Hey, let's pick it up, pick it up, Mr. Loman. (*He helps* **Willy** *to his feet.*) Your boys left with the chippies. They said they'll see you home.

A second waiter watches some distance away.

Willy   But we were supposed to have dinner together.

Music is heard, **Willy**'s *theme.*

Stanley   Can you make it?

Willy   I'll—sure, I can make it. (*Suddenly concerned about his clothes:*) Do I—I look all right?

Stanley   Sure, you look all right. (*He flicks a speck off* **Willy**'s *lapel.*)

Willy   Here—here's a dollar.

Stanley   Oh, your son paid me. It's all right.

Willy (*putting it in* **Stanley**'s *hand*)   No, take it. You're a good boy.

Stanley   Oh, no, you don't have to . . .

Willy   Here—here's some more, I don't need it any more. (*After a slight pause:*) Tell me—is there a seed store in the neighborhood?

Stanley   Seeds? You mean like to plant?

As **Willy** *turns,* **Stanley** *slips the money back into his jacket pocket.*

Willy   Yes. Carrots, peas . . .

Stanley   Well, there's hardware stores on Sixth Avenue, but it may be too late now.

Willy (*anxiously*)   Oh, I'd better hurry. I've got to get some seeds. (*He starts off to the right.*) I've got to get some seeds, right away. Nothing's planted. I don't have a thing in the ground.

Willy *hurries out as the light goes down.* **Stanley** *moves over to the right after him, watches him off. The other waiter has been staring at* **Willy**.

Stanley (*to the waiter*)   Well, whatta you looking at?

The waiter picks up the chairs and moves off right. **Stanley** *takes the table and follows him. The light fades on this area. There is a long pause, the sound of the flute coming over. The light gradually rises on the kitchen, which is empty.* **Happy** *appears at the door of the house, followed by* **Biff**. **Happy** *is carrying a large bunch of long-stemmed roses. He enters the kitchen, looks around for* **Linda**. *Not seeing her, he turns to* **Biff**, *who is just outside the house door, and makes a gesture with his hands, indicating "Not here, I guess." He looks into the living-room and freezes. Inside,* **Linda**, *unseen, is seated,* **Willy**'s *coat on her* *lap. She rises ominously and quietly and moves toward* **Happy**, *who backs up into the kitchen, afraid.*

Happy   Hey, what're you doing up? (**Linda** *says nothing but moves toward him implacably.*) Where's Pop? (*He keeps backing to the right, and now* **Linda** *is in full view in the doorway to the living-room.*) Is he sleeping?

Linda   Where were you?

Happy (*trying to laugh it off*)   We met two girls, Mom, very fine types. Here, we brought you some flowers. (*Offering them to her:*) Put them in your room, Ma.

She knocks them to the floor at **Biff**'s *feet. He has now come inside and closed the door behind him. She stares at* **Biff**, *silent.*

Happy   Now what'd you do that for? Mom, I want you to have some flowers—

Linda (*cutting* **Happy** *off, violently to* **Biff**)   Don't you care whether he lives or dies?

Happy (*going to the stairs*)   Come upstairs, Biff.

Biff (*with a flare of disgust, to* **Happy**)   Go away from me! (*To* **Linda**:) What do you mean, lives or dies? Nobody's dying around here, pal.

Linda   Get out of my sight! Get out of here!

Biff   I wanna see the boss.

Linda   You're not going near him!

Biff   Where is he? (*He moves into the living-room and* **Linda** *follows.*)

Linda (*shouting after* **Biff**)   You invite him for dinner. He looks forward to it all day (**Biff** *appears in his parents' bedroom, looks around, and exits*) and then you desert him there. There's no stranger you'd do that to!

Happy   Why? He had a swell time with us. Listen, when I (**Linda** *comes back into the kitchen*) desert him I hope I don't outlive the day!

Linda   Get out of here!

Happy   Now look, Mom . . .

Linda   Did you have to go to women tonight? You and your lousy rotten whores!

Biff *re-enters the kitchen.*

Happy   Mom, all we did was follow Biff around trying to cheer him up! (*To* **Biff***:*) Boy, what a night you gave me!

Linda   Get out of here, both of you, and don't come back! I don't want you tormenting him any more. Go on now, get your things together! (*To* **Biff***:*) You can sleep in his apartment. (*She starts to pick up the flowers and stops herself.*) Pick up this stuff, I'm not your maid any more. Pick it up, you bum, you!

Happy *turns his back to her in refusal.* **Biff** *slowly moves over and gets down on his knees, picking up the flowers.*

Linda   You're a pair of animals! Not one, not another living soul would have had the cruelty to walk out on that man in a restaurant!

Biff (*not looking at her*)   Is that what he said?

Linda   He didn't have to say anything. He was so humiliated he nearly limped when he came in.

Happy   But, Mom, he had a great time with us—

Biff (*cutting him off violently*)   Shut up!

Without another word, **Happy** *goes upstairs.*

Linda   You! You didn't even go in to see if he was all right!

Biff (*still on the floor in front of* **Linda**, *the flowers in his hand; with self-loathing*)   No. Didn't. Didn't do a damned thing. How do you like that, heh? Left him babbling in a toilet.

Linda   You louse. You . . .

Biff   Now you hit it on the nose! (*He gets up, throws the flowers in the wastebasket.*) The scum of the earth, and you're looking at him!

Linda   Get out of here!

Biff   I gotta talk to the boss, Mom. Where is he?

Linda   You're not going near him. Get out of this house!

Biff (*with absolute assurance, determination*)   No. We're gonna have an abrupt conversation, him and me.

Linda   You're not talking to him!

Hammering is heard from outside the house, off right. **Biff** *turns toward the noise.*

Linda (*suddenly pleading*)   Will you please leave him alone?

Biff   What's he doing out there?

Linda   He's planting the garden!

Biff (*quietly*)   Now? Oh, my God!

Biff *moves outside,* **Linda** *following. The light dies down on them and comes up on the center of the apron as* **Willy** *walks into it. He is carrying a flashlight, a hoe, and a handful of seed packets. He raps the top of the hoe sharply to fix it firmly, and then moves to the left, measuring off the distance with his foot. He holds the flashlight to look at the seed packets, reading off the instructions. He is in the blue of night.*

Willy   Carrots . . . quarter-inch apart. Rows . . . one-foot rows. (*He measures it off.*) One foot. (*He puts down a package and measures off.*) Beets. (*He puts down another package and measures again.*) Lettuce. (*He reads the package, puts it down.*) One foot—(*He breaks off as* **Ben** *appears at the right and moves slowly down to him.*) What a proposition, ts, ts. Terrific, terrific. 'Cause she's suffered, Ben, the woman has suffered. You understand me? A man can't go out the way he came in, Ben, a man has got to add up to something. You can't, you can't—(**Ben** *moves toward him as though to interrupt.*) You gotta consider, now. Don't answer so quick. Remember, it's a guaranteed twenty-thousand-dollar proposition. Now look, Ben, I want you to go through the ins and outs of this thing with me. I've got nobody to talk to, Ben, and the woman has suffered, you hear me?

Ben (*standing still, considering*)   What's the proposition?

Willy   It's twenty thousand dollars on the barrelhead. Guaranteed, gilt-edged, you understand?

Ben   You don't want to make a fool of yourself. They might not honor the policy.

Willy   How can they dare refuse? Didn't I work like a coolie to meet every premium on the nose? And now they don't pay off! Impossible!

Ben   It's called a cowardly thing, William.

Willy   Why? Does it take more guts to stand here the rest of my life ringing up a zero?

Ben (*yielding*)   That's a point, William. (*He moves, thinking, turns.*) And twenty thousand—that (*is*) something one can feel with the hand, it is there.

Willy (*now assured, with rising power*)   Oh, Ben, that's the whole beauty of it! I see it like a diamond, shining in the dark, hard and rough, that I can pick up and touch in my hand. Not like—like an appointment!

This would not be another damned-fool appointment, Ben, and it changes all the aspects. Because he thinks I'm nothing, see, and so he spites me. But the funeral—(*Straightening up:*) Ben, that funeral will be massive! They'll come from Maine, Massachusetts, Vermont, New Hampshire! All the old-timers with the strange license plates—that boy will be thunder-struck, Ben, because he never realized—I am known! Rhode Island, New York, New Jersey—I am known, Ben, and he'll see it with his eyes once and for all. He'll see what I am, Ben! He's in for a shock, that boy!

Ben (*coming down to the edge of the garden*)   He'll call you a coward.

Willy (*suddenly fearful*)   No, that would be terrible.

Ben   Yes. And a damned fool.

Willy   No, no, he mustn't, I won't have that! (*He is broken and desperate.*)

Ben   He'll hate you, William.

The gay music of the boys is heard.

Willy   Oh, Ben, how do we get back to all the great times? Used to be so full of light, and comradeship, the sleigh-riding in winter, and the ruddiness on his cheeks. And always some kind of good news coming up, always something nice coming up ahead. And never even let me carry the valises in the house, and simonizing, simonizing that little red car! Why, why can't I give him something and not have him hate me?

Ben   Let me think about it. (*He glances at his watch.*) I still have a little time. Remarkable proposition, but you've got to be sure you're not making a fool of yourself.

Ben *drifts off upstage and goes out of sight.* **Biff** *comes down from the left.*

Willy (*suddenly conscious of* **Biff***, turns and looks up at him, then begins picking up the packages of seeds in confusion*)   Where the hell is that seed? (*Indignantly:*) You can't see nothing out here! They boxed in the whole goddam neighborhood!

Biff   There are people all around here. Don't you realize that?

Willy   I'm busy. Don't bother me.

Biff (*taking the hoe from* **Willy**)   I'm saying good-by to you, Pop. (**Willy** *looks at him, silent, unable to move.*) I'm not coming back any more.

Willy   You're not going to see Oliver tomorrow?

Biff   I've got no appointment, Dad.

Willy   He put his arm around you, and you've got no appointment?

Biff   Pop, get this now, will you? Everytime I've left it's been a fight that sent me out of here. Today I realized something about myself and I tried to explain it to you and I—I think I'm just not smart enough to make any sense out of it for you. To hell with whose fault it is or anything like that. (*He takes* **Willy**'*s arm.*) Let's just wrap it up, heh? Come on in, we'll tell Mom. (*He gently tries to pull* **Willy** *to left.*)

Willy   (*frozen, immobile, with guilt in his voice*)   No, I don't want to see her.

Biff   Come on! (*He pulls again, and* **Willy** *tries to pull away.*)

Willy   (*highly nervous*)   No, no, I don't want to see her.

Biff   (*tries to look into* **Willy**'*s face, as if to find the answer there*)   Why don't you want to see her?

Willy   (*more harshly now*)   Don't bother me, will you?

Biff   What do you mean, you don't want to see her? You don't want them calling you yellow, do you? This isn't your fault; it's me, I'm a bum. Now come inside! (**Willy** *strains to get away.*) Did you hear what I said to you?

Willy *pulls away and quickly goes by himself into the house.* **Biff** *follows.*

Linda (*to* **Willy**)   Did you plant, dear?

Biff (*at the door, to* **Linda**)   All right, we had it out. I'm going and I'm not writing any more.

Linda (*going to* **Willy** *in the kitchen*)   I think that's the best way, dear. 'Cause there's no use drawing it out, you'll just never get along.

Willy *doesn't respond.*

Biff   People ask where I am and what I'm doing, you don't know, and you don't care. That way it'll be off your mind and you can start brightening up again. All right? That clears it, doesn't it? (**Willy** *is silent, and* **Biff** *goes to him.*) You gonna wish me luck, scout? (*He extends his hand.*) What do you say?

Linda   Shake his hand, Willy.

Willy (*turning to her, seething with hurt*)   There's no necessity to mention the pen at all, y'know.

Biff (*gently*)   I've got no appointment, Dad.

Willy (*erupting fiercely*)   He put his arm around . . .?

Biff   Dad, you're never going to see what I am, so what's the use of arguing? If I strike oil I'll send you a check. Meantime forget I'm alive.

Willy (*to* **Linda**)   Spite, see?

Biff   Shake hands, Dad.

Willy   Not my hand.

Biff   I was hoping not to go this way.

Willy   Well, this is the way you're going. Good-by.

Biff *looks at him a moment, then turns sharply and goes to the stairs.*

Willy (*stops him with*)   May you rot in hell if you leave this house!

Biff (*turning*)   Exactly what is it that you want from me?

Willy   I want you to know, on the train, in the mountains, in the valleys, wherever you go, that you cut down your life for spite!

Biff   No, no.

Willy   Spite, spite, is the word of your undoing! And when you're down and out, remember what did it. When you're rotting somewhere beside the railroad tracks, remember, and don't you dare blame it on me!

Biff   I'm not blaming it on you!

Willy   I won't take the rap for this, you hear?

Happy *comes down the stairs and stands on the bottom step, watching.*

Biff   That's just what I'm telling you!

Willy (*sinking into a chair at the table, with full accusation*)   You're trying to put a knife in me—don't think I don't know what you're doing!

Biff   All right, phony! Then let's lay it on the line. (*He whips the rubber tube out of his pocket and puts it on the table.*)

Happy   You crazy—

Linda   Biff! (*She moves to grab the hose, but* **Biff** *holds it down with his hand.*)

Biff   Leave it there! Don't move it!

Willy (*not looking at it*)   What is that?

Biff   You know goddam well what that is.

Willy (*caged, wanting to escape*)   I never saw that.

Biff   You saw it. The mice didn't bring it into the cellar! What is this supposed to do, make a hero out of you? This supposed to make me sorry for you?

Willy   Never heard of it.

Biff   There'll be no pity for you, you hear it? No pity!

Willy (*to* **Linda**)   You hear the spite!

Biff   No, you're going to hear the truth—what you are and what I am!

Linda   Stop it!

Willy   Spite!

Happy (*coming down toward* **Biff**)   You cut it now!

Biff (*to* **Happy**)   The man don't know who we are! The man is gonna know! (*To* **Willy***:*) We never told the truth for ten minutes in this house!

Happy   We always told the truth!

Biff (*turning on him*)   You big blow, are you the assistant buyer? You're one of the two assistants to the assistant, aren't you?

Happy   Well, I'm practically—

Biff   You're practically full of it! We all are! And I'm through with it. (*To* **Willy***:*) Now hear this, Willy, this is me.

Willy   I know you!

Biff   You know why I had no address for three months? I stole a suit in Kansas City and I was in jail. (*To* **Linda***, who is sobbing:*) Stop crying. I'm through with it.

Linda *turns away from them, her hands covering her face.*

Willy   I suppose that's my fault!

Biff   I stole myself out of every good job since high school!

Willy   And whose fault is that?

Biff   And I never got anywhere because you blew me so full of hot air I could never stand taking orders from anybody! That's whose fault it is!

Willy   I hear that!

Linda   Don't, Biff!

Biff   It's goddam time you heard that! I had to be boss big shot in two weeks, and I'm through with it!

Willy   Then hang yourself! For spite, hang yourself!

Biff   No! Nobody's hanging himself, Willy! I ran down eleven flights with a pen in my hand today. And suddenly I stopped, you hear me? And in the middle of that office building, do you hear this? I stopped in the middle of that building and I saw—the sky. I saw the things that I love in this world. The work and the food and time to sit and smoke. And I looked at the pen and said to myself, what the hell am I grabbing this for? Why am I trying to become what I don't want to be? What am I doing in an office, making a contemptuous, begging fool of myself, when all I want is out there, waiting for me the minute I say I know who I am! Why can't I say that, Willy? (*He tries to make* **Willy** *face him, but* **Willy** *pulls away and moves to the left.*)

Willy (*with hatred, threateningly*)   The door of your life is wide open!

Biff   Pop! I'm a dime a dozen, and so are you!

Willy (*turning on him now in an uncontrolled outburst*)   I am not a dime a dozen! I am Willy Loman, and you are Biff Loman!

Biff *starts for* **Willy**, *but is blocked by* **Happy**. *In his fury,* **Biff** *seems on the verge of attacking his father.*

Biff   I am not a leader of men, Willy, and neither are you. You were never anything but a hard-working drummer who landed in the ash can like all the rest of them! I'm one dollar an hour, Willy! I tried seven states and couldn't raise it. A buck an hour! Do you gather my meaning? I'm not bringing home any prizes any more, and you're going to stop waiting for me to bring them home!

Willy (*directly to* **Biff**)   You vengeful, spiteful mut!

Biff *breaks from* **Happy**. **Willy**, *in fright, starts up the stairs.* **Biff** *grabs him.*

Biff (*at the peak of his fury*)   Pop, I'm nothing! I'm nothing, Pop. Can't you understand that? There's no spite in it any more. I'm just what I am, that's all.

Biff's *fury has spent itself, and he breaks down, sobbing, holding on to* **Willy**, *who dumbly fumbles for* **Biff**'s *face.*

Willy (*astonished*)   What're you doing? What're you doing? (*To* **Linda**:) Why is he crying?

Biff (*crying, broken*)   Will you let me go, for Christ's sake? Will you take that phony dream and burn it before something happens? (*Struggling to contain himself, he pulls away and moves to the stairs.*) I'll go in the morning. Put him—put him to bed. (*Exhausted,* **Biff** *moves up the stairs to his room.*)

Willy (*after a long pause, astonished, elevated*)   Isn't that—isn't that remarkable? Biff—he likes me!

Linda   He loves you, Willy!

Happy (*deeply moved*)   Always did, Pop.

Willy   Oh, Biff! (*Staring wildly:*) He cried! Cried to me. (*He is choking with his love, and now cries out his promise:*) That boy—that boy is going to be magnificent!

Ben *appears in the light just outside the kitchen.*

Ben   Yes, outstanding, with twenty thousand behind him.

Linda (*sensing the racing of his mind, fearfully, carefully*)   Now come to bed, Willy. It's all settled now.

Willy (*finding it difficult not to rush out of the house*)   Yes, we'll sleep. Come on. Go to sleep, Hap.

Ben   And it does take a great kind of a man to crack the jungle.

In accents of dread, **Ben**'s *idyllic music starts up.*

Happy (*his arm around* **Linda**)   I'm getting married, Pop, don't forget it. I'm changing everything. I'm gonna run that department before the year is up. You'll see, Mom. (*He kisses her.*)

Ben   The jungle is dark but full of diamonds, Willy.

Willy *turns, moves, listening to* **Ben**.

Linda   Be good. You're both good boys, just act that way, that's all.

Happy   'Night, Pop. (*He goes upstairs.*)

Linda (*to* **Willy**)   Come, dear.

Ben (*with greater force*)   One must go in to fetch a diamond out.

Willy (*to* **Linda**, *as he moves slowly along the edge of the kitchen, toward the door*)   I just want to get settled down, Linda. Let me sit alone for a little.

Linda (*almost uttering her fear*)   I want you upstairs.

Willy (*taking her in his arms*)   In a few minutes, Linda. I couldn't sleep right now. Go on, you look awful tired. (*He kisses her.*)

Ben   Not like an appointment at all. A diamond is rough and hard to the touch.

Willy   Go on now. I'll be right up.

Linda   I think this is the only way, Willy.

Willy   Sure, it's the best thing.

Ben   Best thing!

Willy   The only way. Everything is gonna be—go on, kid, get to bed. You look so tired.

Linda   Come right up.

Willy   Two minutes.

Linda *goes into the living-room, then reappears in her bedroom.* **Willy** *moves just outside the kitchen door.*

Willy   Loves me. (*Wonderingly:*) Always loved me. Isn't that a remarkable thing? Ben, he'll worship me for it!

Ben (*with promise*)   It's dark there, but full of diamonds.

Willy   Can you imagine that magnificence with twenty thousand dollars in his pocket?

Linda (*calling from her room*)   Willy! Come up!

Willy (*calling into the kitchen*)   Yes! Yes. Coming! It's very smart, you realize that, don't you, sweetheart? Even Ben sees it. I gotta go, baby. 'By! 'By! (*Going over to* **Ben**, *almost dancing:*) Imagine? When the mail comes he'll be ahead of Bernard again!

Ben   A perfect proposition all around.

Willy   Did you see how he cried to me? Oh, if I could kiss him, Ben!

Ben   Time, William, time!

Willy   Oh, Ben, I always knew one way or another we were gonna make it, Biff and I!

Ben (*looking at his watch*)   The boat. We'll be late. (*He moves slowly off into the darkness.*)

Willy (*elegiacally, turning to the house*)   Now when you kick off, boy, I want a seventy-yard boot, and get right down the field under the ball, and when you hit, hit low and hit hard, because it's important, boy. (*He swings around and faces the audience.*) There's all kinds of important people in the stands, and the first thing you know . . . (*Suddenly realizing he is alone:*) Ben! Ben, where do I . . .? (*He makes a sudden movement of search.*) Ben, how do I . . .?

Linda (*calling*)   Willy, you coming up?

Willy (*uttering a gasp of fear, whirling about as if to quiet her*)   Sh! (*He turns around as if to find his way; sounds, faces, voices, seem to be swarming in upon him and he flicks at them, crying.*) Sh! Sh! (*Suddenly music, faint and high, stops him. It rises in intensity, almost to an unbearable scream. He goes up and down on his toes, and rushes off around the house.*) Shhh!

Linda   Willy?

There is no answer. **Linda** *waits.* **Biff** *gets up off his bed. He is still in his clothes.* **Happy** *sits up.* **Biff** *stands listening.*

Linda (*with real fear*)   Willy, answer me! Willy!

There is the sound of a car starting and moving away at full speed.

Linda   No!

Biff (*rushing down the stairs*)   Pop!

As the car speeds off, the music crashes down in a frenzy of sound, which becomes the soft pulsation of a single cello string. **Biff** *slowly returns to his bedroom. He and* **Happy** *gravely don their jackets.* **Linda** *slowly walks out of her room. The music has developed into a dead march. The leaves of day are appearing over everything.* **Charley** *and* **Bernard**, *somberly dressed, appear and knock on the kitchen door.* **Biff** *and* **Happy** *slowly descend the stairs to the kitchen as* **Charley** *and* **Bernard** *enter. All stop a moment when* **Linda**, *in clothes of mourning, bearing a little bunch of roses, comes through the draped doorway into the kitchen. She goes to* **Charley** *and takes his arm. Now all move toward the audience, through the wall-line of the kitchen. At the limit of the apron,* **Linda** *lays down the flowers, kneels, and sits back on her heels. All stare down at the grave.*

Requiem

Charley   It's getting dark, Linda.

Linda *doesn't react. She stares at the grave.*

Biff   How about it, Mom? Better get some rest, heh? They'll be closing the gate soon.

Linda *makes no move. Pause.*

Happy (*deeply angered*)   He had no right to do that. There was no necessity for it. We would've helped him.

Charley (*grunting*)   Hmmm.

Biff   Come along, Mom.

Linda   Why didn't anybody come?

Charley   It was a very nice funeral.

Linda   But where are all the people he knew? Maybe they blame him.

Charley   Naa. It's a rough world, Linda. They wouldn't blame him.

Linda   I can't understand it. At this time especially. First time in thirty-five years we were just about free and clear. He only needed a little salary. He was even finished with the dentist.

Charley   No man only needs a little salary.

Linda   I can't understand it.

Biff   There were a lot of nice days. When he'd come home from a trip; or on Sundays, making the stoop; finishing the cellar; putting on the new porch; when he built the extra bathroom; and put up the garage. You know something, Charley, there's more of him in that front stoop than in all the sales he ever made.

Charley   Yeah. He was a happy man with a batch of cement.

Linda   He was so wonderful with his hands.

Biff   He had the wrong dreams. All, all, wrong.

Happy (*almost ready to fight* **Biff**)   Don't say that!

Biff   He never knew who be was.

Charley (*stopping* **Happy**'s *movement and reply. To* **Biff**)   Nobody dast blame this man. You don't understand: Willy was a salesman. And for a salesman, there is no rock bottom to the life. He don't put a bolt to a nut, he don't tell you the law or give you medicine. He's a man way out there in the blue, riding on a smile and a shoeshine. And when they start not smiling back—that's an earthquake. And then you get yourself a couple of spots on your hat, and you're finished. Nobody dast blame this man. A salesman is got to dream, boy. It comes with the territory.

Biff   Charley, the man didn't know who he was.

Happy (*infuriated*)   Don't say that!

Biff   Why don't you come with me, Happy?

Happy   I'm not licked that easily. I'm staying right in this city, and I'm gonna beat this racket! (*He looks at* **Biff***, his chin set.*) The Loman Brothers!

Biff   I know who I am, kid.

Happy   All right, boy. I'm gonna show you and everybody else that Willy Loman did not die in vain. He had a good dream. It's the only dream you can have—to come out number-one man. He fought it out here, and this is where I'm gonna win it for him.

Biff (*with a hopeless glance at* **Happy***, bends toward his mother*)   Let's go, Mom.

Linda   I'll be with you in a minute. Go on, Charley. (*He hesitates.*) I want to, just for a minute. I never had a chance to say good-by.

Charley *moves away, followed by* **Happy**. **Biff** *remains a slight distance up and left of* **Linda***. She sits there, summoning herself. The flute begins, not far away, playing behind her speech.*

Linda   Forgive me, dear. I can't cry. I don't know what it is, but I can't cry. I don't understand it. Why did you ever do that? Help me, Willy, I can't cry. It seems to me that you're just on another trip. I keep expecting you. Willy, dear, I can't cry. Why did you do it? I search and search and I search, and I can't understand it, Willy. I made the last payment on the house today. Today, dear. And there'll be nobody home. (*A sob rises in her throat.*) We're free and clear. (*Sobbing more fully, released:*) We're free. (**Biff** *comes slowly toward her.*) We're free . . . We're free . . .

Biff *lifts her to her feet and moves out up right with her in his arms.* **Linda** *sobs quietly.* **Bernard** *and* **Charley** *come together and follow them, followed by* **Happy***. Only the music of the flute is left on the darkening stage as over the house the hard towers of the apartment buildings rise into sharp focus.*

Curtain.

The Crucible

A Play in Four Acts

The Characters

Reverend Parris
Betty Parris
Tituba
Abigail Williams
Susanna Walcott
Mrs. Ann Putnam
Thomas Putnam
Mercy Lewis
Mary Warren
John Proctor
Rebecca Nurse

Giles Corey
Reverend John Hale
Elizabeth Proctor
Francis Nurse
Ezekiel Cheever
Marshal Herrick
Judge Hathorne
Deputy Governor Danforth
Sarah Good
Hopkins

A Note on the Historical Accuracy of this Play

This play is not history in the sense in which the word is used by the academic historian. Dramatic purposes have sometimes required many characters to be fused into one; the number of girls involved in the "crying-out" bas been reduced; Abigail's age has been raised; while there were several judges of almost equal authority, I have symbolized them all in Hathorne and Danforth. However, I believe that the reader will discover here the essential nature of one of the strangest and most awful chapters in human history. The fate of each character is exactly that of his historical model, and there is no one in the drama who did not play a similar—and in some cases exactly the same—role in history.

As for the characters of the persons, little is known about most of them excepting what may be surmised from a few letters, the trial record, certain broadsides written at the time, and references to their conduct in sources of varying reliability. They may therefore be taken as creations of my own, drawn to the best of my ability in conformity with their known behavior, except as indicated in the commentary I have written for this text.

Act One

(An Overture)

A small upper bedroom in the home of **Reverend Samuel Parris**, *Salem, Massachusetts, in the spring of the year 1692.*

There is a narrow window at the left. Through its leaded panes the morning sunlight streams. A candle still burns near the bed, which is at the right. A chest, a chair, and a small table are the other furnishings. At the back a door opens on the landing of the stairway to the ground floor. The room gives off an air of clean spareness. The roof rafters are exposed, and the wood colors are raw and unmellowed.

As the curtain rises, **Reverend Parris** *is discovered kneeling beside the bed, evidently in prayer. His daughter,* **Betty Parris**, *aged ten, is lying on the bed, inert.*

At the time of these events Parris was in his middle forties. In history he cut a villainous path, and there is very little good to be said for him. He believed he was being persecuted wherever he went, despite his best efforts to win people and God to his side. In meeting, he felt insulted if someone rose to shut the door without first asking his permission. He was a widower with no interest in children, or talent with them. He regarded them as young adults, and until this strange crisis he, like the rest of Salem, never conceived that the children were anything but thankful for being permitted to walk straight, eyes slightly lowered, arms at the sides, and mouths shut until bidden to speak.

His house stood in the "town"—but we today would hardly call it a village. The meeting house was nearby, and from this point outward—toward the bay or inland—there were a few small-windowed, dark houses snuggling against the raw Massachusetts winter. Salem had been established hardly forty years before. To the European world the whole province was a barbaric frontier inhabited by a sect of fanatics who, nevertheless, were shipping out products of slowly increasing quantity and value.

No one can really know what their lives were like. They had no novelists—and would not have permitted anyone to read a novel if one were handy. Their creed forbade anything resembling a theater or "vain enjoyment." They did not celebrate Christmas, and a holiday from work meant only that they must concentrate even more upon prayer.

Which is not to say that nothing broke into this strict and somber way of life. When a new farmhouse was built, friends assembled to "raise the roof," and there would be special foods cooked and probably some potent cider passed around. There was a good supply of ne'er-do-wells in Salem, who dallied at the shovelboard in Bridget Bishop's tavern. Probably more than the creed, hard work kept the morals of the place from spoiling, for the people were forced to fight the land like heroes for every grain of corn, and no man had very much time for fooling around.

That there were some jokers, however, is indicated by the practice of appointing a two-man patrol whose duty was to "walk forth in the time of God's worship to take notice of such as either lye about the meeting house, without attending to the word and ordinances, or that lye at home or in the fields without giving good account thereof, and to take the names of such persons, and to present them to the magistrates, whereby they may be accordingly proceeded against." This predilection for minding other people's business was time-honored among the people of Salem, and it undoubtedly created many of the suspicions which were to feed the coming madness. It was also, in my opinion, one of the things that a John Proctor would rebel against, for the time of the armed camp had almost passed, and since the country was reasonably—although not wholly—safe, the old disciplines were beginning to rankle. But, as in all such matters, the issue was not clear-cut, for danger was still a possibility, and in unity still lay the best promise of safety.

The edge of the wilderness was close by. The American continent stretched endlessly west, and it was full of mystery for them. It stood, dark and threatening, over their shoulders night and day, for out of it Indian tribes marauded from time to time, and Reverend Parris had parishioners who had lost relatives to these heathen.

The parochial snobbery of these people was partly responsible for their failure to convert the Indians. Probably they also preferred to take land from heathens rather than from fellow Christians. At any rate, very few Indians were converted, and the Salem folk believed that the virgin forest was the Devil's last preserve, his home base and the citadel of his final stand. To the best of their knowledge the American forest was the last place on earth that was not paying homage to God.

For these reasons, among others, they carried about an air of innate resistance, even of persecution. Their fathers had, of course, been persecuted in England. So now they and their church found it necessary to deny any other sect its freedom, lest their New Jerusalem be defiled and corrupted by wrong ways and deceitful ideas.

They believed, in short, that they held in their steady hands the candle that would light the world. We have inherited this belief, and it has helped and hurt us. It helped them with the discipline it gave them. They were a dedicated folk, by and large, and they had to be to survive the life they had chosen or been born into in this country.

The proof of their belief's value to them may be taken from the opposite character of the first Jamestown settlement, farther south, in Virginia. The Englishmen who landed there were motivated mainly by a hunt for profit. They had thought to pick off the wealth of the new country and then return rich to England. They were a band of individualists, and a much more ingratiating group than the Massachusetts men. But Virginia destroyed them. Massachusetts tried to kill off the Puritans, but they combined; they set up a communal society which, in the beginning, was little more than an armed camp with an autocratic and very devoted leadership. It was, however, an autocracy by consent, for they were united from top to bottom by a commonly held ideology whose perpetuation was the reason and justification for all their sufferings. So their self-denial, their purposefulness, their suspicion of all vain pursuits, their hard-handed justice, were altogether perfect instruments for the conquest of this space so antagonistic to man.

But the people of Salem in 1692 were not quite the dedicated folk that arrived on the *Mayflower*. A vast differentiation had taken place, and in their own time a revolution had unseated the royal government and substituted a junta which was at this moment in power. The times, to their eyes, must have been out of joint, and to the common folk must have seemed as insoluble and complicated as do ours today. It is not hard to see how easily many could have been led to believe that the time of confusion had been brought upon them by deep and darkling forces. No hint of such speculation appears on the court record, but social disorder in any age breeds such mystical suspicions, and when, as in Salem, wonders are brought forth from below the social surface, it is too much to expect people to hold back very long from laying on the victims with all the force of their frustrations.

The Salem tragedy, which is about to begin in these pages, developed from a paradox. It is a paradox in whose grip we still live, and there is no prospect yet that we will discover its resolution. Simply, it was this: for good purposes, even high purposes, the people of Salem developed a theocracy, a combine of state and religious power whose function was to keep the community together, and to prevent any kind of disunity that might open it to destruction by material or ideological enemies. It was forged for a necessary purpose and accomplished that purpose. But all organization is and must be grounded on the idea of exclusion and prohibition, just as two objects cannot occupy the same space. Evidently the time came in New England when the repressions of order were heavier than seemed warranted by the dangers against which the order was organized. The witch-hunt was a perverse manifestation of the panic which set in among all classes when the balance began to turn toward greater individual freedom.

When one rises above the individual villainy displayed, one can only pity them all, just as we shall be pitied someday. It is still impossible for man to organize his social life without repressions, and the balance has yet to be struck between order and freedom.

The witch-hunt was not, however, a mere repression. It was also, and as importantly, a long overdue opportunity for everyone so inclined to express publicly his guilt and sins, under the cover of accusations against the victims. It suddenly became possible—and patriotic and holy—for a man to say that Martha Corey had come into his bedroom at night, and that, while his wife was sleeping at his side, Martha laid herself down on his chest and "nearly suffocated him." Of course it was her spirit only, but his satisfaction at confessing himself was no lighter than if it had been Martha herself. One could not ordinarily speak such things in public.

Long-held hatreds of neighbors could now be openly expressed, and vengeance taken, despite the Bible's charitable injunctions. Land-lust which had been expressed before by constant bickering over boundaries and deeds, could now be elevated to the arena of morality; one could cry witch against one's neighbor and feel perfectly justified in the bargain. Old scores could be settled on a plane of heavenly combat between Lucifer and the Lord; suspicions and the envy of the miserable toward the happy could and did burst out in the general revenge.

Reverend Parris *is praying now, and, though we cannot hear his words, a sense of his confusion hangs about him. He mumbles, then seems about to weep; then he weeps, then prays again; but his daughter does not stir on the bed.*

The door opens, and his Negro slave enters. **Tituba** *is in her forties.* **Parris** *brought her with him from Barbados, where he spent some years as a merchant before entering the ministry. She enters as one does who can no longer bear to be barred from the sight of her beloved, but she is also very frightened because her slave sense has warned her that, as always, trouble in this house eventually lands on her back.*

Tituba (*already taking a step backward*)   My Betty be hearty soon?

Parris   Out of here!

Tituba (*backing to the door*)   My Betty not goin' die . . .

Parris (*scrambling to his feet in a fury*)   Out of my sight! (*She is gone.*) Out of my—(*He is overcome with sobs. He clamps his teeth against them and closes the door and leans against it, exhausted.*) Oh, my God! God help me! (*Quaking with fear, mumbling to himself through his sobs, he goes to the bed and gently takes* **Betty**'s *hand.*) Betty. Child. Dear child. Will you wake, will you open up your eyes! Betty, little one . . .

He is bending to kneel again when his niece, **Abigail Williams**, *seventeen, enters—a strikingly beautiful girl, an orphan, with an endless capacity for dissembling. Now she is all worry and apprehension and propriety.*

Abigail   Uncle? (*He looks to her.*) Susanna Walcott's here from Doctor Griggs.

Parris   Oh? Let her come, let her come.

Abigail (*leaning out the door to call to* **Susanna**, *who is down the hall a few steps*)   Come in, Susanna.

Susanna Walcott, *a little younger than* **Abigail**, *a nervous, hurried girl, enters.*

Parris (*eagerly*)   What does the doctor say, child?

Susanna (*craning around* **Parris** *to get a look at* **Betty**)   He bid me come and tell you, reverend sir, that he cannot discover no medicine for it in his books.

Parris   Then he must search on.

Susanna   Aye, sir, he have been searchin' his books since he left you, sir. But he bid me tell you, that you might look to unnatural things for the cause of it.

Parris (*his eyes going wide*)   No—no. There be no unnatural cause here. Tell him I have sent for Reverend Hale of Beverly, and Mr. Hale will surely confirm that. Let him look to medicine and put out all thought of unnatural causes here. There be none.

Susanna   Aye, sir. He bid me tell you. (*She turns to go.*)

Abigail   Speak nothin' of it in the village, Susanna.

Parris   Go directly home and speak nothing of unnatural causes.

Susanna   Aye, sir. I pray for her. (*She goes out.*)

Abigail   Uncle, the rumor of witchcraft is all about; I think you'd best go down and deny it yourself. The parlor's packed with people, sir. I'll sit with her.

Parris (*pressed, turns on her*)   And what shall I say to them? That my daughter and my niece I discovered dancing like heathen in the forest?

Abigail   Uncle, we did dance; let you tell them I confessed it—and I'll be whipped if I must be. But they're speakin' of witchcraft. Betty's not witched.

Parris   Abigail, I cannot go before the congregation when I know you have not opened with me. What did you do with her in the forest?

Abigail   We did dance, uncle, and when you leaped out of the bush so suddenly, Betty was frightened and then she fainted. And there's the whole of it.

Parris   Child. Sit you down.

Abigail (*quavering, as she sits*)   I would never hurt Betty. I love her dearly.

Parris   Now look you, child, your punishment will come in its time. But if you trafficked with spirits in the forest I must know it now, for surely my enemies will, and they will ruin me with it.

Abigail   But we never conjured spirits.

Parris   Then why can she not move herself since midnight? This child is desperate! (**Abigail** *lowers her eyes.*) It must come out—my enemies will bring it out. Let me know what you done there. Abigail, do you understand that I have many enemies?

Abigail   I have heard of it, uncle.

Parris   There is a faction that is sworn to drive me from my pulpit. Do you understand that?

Abigail   I think so, sir.

Parris   Now then, in the midst of such disruption, my own household is discovered to be the very center of some obscene practice. Abominations are done in the forest—

Abigail   It were sport, uncle!

Parris (*pointing at* **Betty**)   You call this sport? (*She lowers her eyes. He pleads:*) Abigail, if you know something that may help the doctor, for

God's sake tell it to me. (*She is silent.*) I saw Tituba waving her arms over the fire when I came on you. Why was she doing that? And I heard a screeching and gibberish coming from her mouth. She were swaying like a dumb beast over that fire!

Abigail   She always sings her Barbados songs, and we dance.

Parris   I cannot blink what I saw, Abigail, for my enemies will not blink it. I saw a dress lying on the grass.

Abigail (*innocently*)   A dress?

Parris (*it is very hard to say*)   Aye, a dress. And I thought I saw— someone naked running through the trees!

Abigail (*in terror*)   No one was naked! You mistake yourself, uncle!

Parris (*with anger*)   I saw it! (*He moves from her. Then, resolved:*) Now tell me true, Abigail. And I pray you feel the weight of truth upon you, for now my ministry's at stake, my ministry and perhaps your cousin's life. Whatever abomination you have done, give me all of it now, for I dare not be taken unaware when I go before them down there.

Abigail   There is nothin' more. I swear it, uncle.

Parris (*studies her, then nods, half convinced*)   Abigail, I have fought here three long years to bend these stiff-necked people to me, and now, just now when some good respect is rising for me in the parish, you compromise my very character. I have given you a home, child, I have put clothes upon your back—now give me upright answer. Your name in the town—it is entirely white, is it not?

Abigail (*with an edge of resentment*)   Why, I am sure it is, sir. There be no blush about my name.

Parris (*to the point*)   Abigail, is there any other cause than you have told me, for your being discharged from Goody Proctor's service? I have heard it said, and I tell you as I heard it, that she comes so rarely to the church this year for she will not sit so close to something soiled. What signified that remark?

Abigail   She hates me, uncle, she must, for I would not be her slave. It's a bitter woman, a lying, cold, sniveling woman, and I will not work for such a woman!

Parris   She may be. And yet it has troubled me that you are now seven month out of their house, and in all this time no other family has ever called for your service.

Abigail   They want slaves, not such as I. Let them send to Barbados for that. I will not black my face for any of them! (*With ill-concealed resentment at him:*) Do you begrudge my bed, uncle?

Parris   No—no.

Abigail (*in a temper*)   My name is good in the village! I will not have it said my name is soiled! Goody Proctor is a gossiping liar!

Enter **Mrs. Ann Putnam**. *She is a twisted soul of forty-five, a death-ridden woman, haunted by dreams.*

Parris (*as soon as the door begins to open*)   No—no, I cannot have anyone. (*He sees her, and a certain deference springs into him, although his worry remains.*) Why, Goody Putnam, come in.

Mrs. Putnam (*full of breath, shiny-eyed*)   It is a marvel. It is surely a stroke of hell upon you.

Parris   No, Goody Putnam, it is—

Mrs. Putnam (*glancing at* **Betty**)   How high did she fly, how high?

Parris   No, no, she never flew—

Mrs. Putnam (*very pleased with it*)   Why, it's sure she did. Mr. Collins saw her goin' over Ingersoll's barn, and come down light as bird, he says!

Parris   Now, look you, Goody Putnam, she never—(*Enter* **Thomas Putnam**, *a well-to-do hard-handed landowner, near fifty.*) Oh, good morning, Mr. Putnam.

Putnam   It is a providence the thing is out now! It is a providence. (*He goes directly to the bed.*)

Parris   What's out, sir, what's—?

Mrs. Putnam *goes to the bed.*

Putnam (*looking down at* **Betty**)   Why, *her* eyes is closed! Look you, Ann.

Mrs. Putnam   Why, that's strange. (*To* **Parris**:) Ours is open.

Parris (*shocked*)   Your Ruth is sick?

Mrs. Putnam (*with vicious certainty*)   I'd not call it sick; the Devil's touch is heavier than sick. It's death, y'know, it's death drivin' into them, forked and hoofed.

Parris   Oh, pray not! Why, how does Ruth ail?

Mrs. Putnam   She ails as she must—she never waked this morning, but her eyes open and she walks, and hears naught, sees naught, and cannot eat. Her soul is taken, surely.

Parris *is struck.*

Putnam (*as though for further details*)   They say you've sent for Reverend Hale of Beverly?

Parris (*with dwindling conviction now*)   A precaution only. He has much experience in all demonic arts, and I—

Mrs. Putnam   He has indeed; and found a witch in Beverly last year, and let you remember that.

Parris   Now, Goody Ann, they only thought that were a witch, and I am certain there be no element of witchcraft here.

Putnam   No witchcraft! Now look you, Mr. Parris—

Parris   Thomas, Thomas, I pray you, leap not to witchcraft. I know that you—you least of all, Thomas, would ever wish so disastrous a charge laid upon me. We cannot leap to witchcraft. They will howl me out of Salem for such corruption in my house.

A word about Thomas Putnam. He was a man with many grievances, at least one of which appears justified. Some time before, his wife's brother-in-law, James Bayley, had been turned down as minister of Salem. Bayley had all the qualifications, and a two-thirds vote into the bargain, but a faction stopped his acceptance, for reasons that are not clear.

Thomas Putnam was the eldest son of the richest man in the village. He had fought the Indians at Narragansett, and was deeply interested in parish affairs. He undoubtedly felt it poor payment that the village should so blatantly disregard his candidate for one of its more important offices, especially since he regarded himself as the intellectual superior of most of the people around him.

His vindictive nature was demonstrated long before the witchcraft began. Another former Salem minister, George Burroughs, had had to borrow money to pay for his wife's funeral, and, since the parish was remiss in his salary, he was soon bankrupt. Thomas and his brother John had Burroughs jailed for debts the man did not owe. The incident is important only in that Burroughs succeeded in becoming minister where Bayley, Thomas Putnam's brother-in-law, had been rejected; the motif of resentment is clear here. Thomas Putnam felt that his own name and the honor of his family had been smirched by the village, and he meant to right matters however he could.

Another reason to believe him a deeply embittered man was his attempt to break his father's will, which left a disproportionate amount to a stepbrother. As with every other public cause in which he tried to force his way, he failed in this.

So it is not surprising to find that so many accusations against people are in the handwriting of Thomas Putnam, or that his name is so often found as a witness corroborating the supernatural testimony, or that his daughter led the crying-out at the most opportune junctures of the trials, especially when—But we'll speak of that when we come to it.

Putnam (*at the moment he is intent upon getting* **Parris***, for whom he has only contempt, to move toward the abyss*)   Mr. Parris, I have taken your part in all contention here, and I would continue; but I cannot if you hold back in this. There are hurtful, vengeful spirits layin' hands on these children.

Parris   But, Thomas, you cannot—

Putnam   Ann! Tell Mr. Parris what you have done.

Mrs. Putnam   Reverend Parris, I have laid seven babies unbaptized in the earth. Believe me, sir, you never saw more hearty babies born. And yet, each would wither in my arms the very night of their birth. I have spoke nothin', but my heart has clamored intimations. And now, this year, my Ruth, my only—I see her turning strange. A secret child she has become this year, and shrivels like a sucking mouth were pullin' on her life too. And so I thought to send her to your Tituba—

Parris   To Tituba! What may Tituba—?

Mrs. Putnam   Tituba knows how to speak to the dead, Mr. Parris.

Parris   Goody Ann, it is a formidable sin to conjure up the dead!

Mrs. Putnam   I take it on my soul, but who else may surely tell us what person murdered my babies?

Parris (*horrified*)   Woman!

Mrs. Putnam   They were murdered, Mr. Parris! And mark this proof! Mark it! Last night my Ruth were ever so close to their little spirits; I know it, sir. For how else is she struck dumb now except some power of darkness would stop her mouth? It is a marvelous sign, Mr. Parris!

Putnam   Don't you understand it, sir? There is a murdering witch among us, bound to keep herself in the dark. (**Parris** *turns to* **Betty**, *a* *frantic terror rising in him.*) Let your enemies make of it what they will, you cannot blink it more.

Parris (*to* **Abigail**)   Then you were conjuring spirits last night.

Abigail (*whispering*)   Not I, sir—Tituba and Ruth.

Parris (*turns now, with new fear, and goes to* **Betty***, looks down at her, and then, gazing off*)   Oh, Abigail, what proper payment for my charity! Now I am undone.

Putnam   You are not undone! Let you take hold here. Wait for no one to charge you—declare it yourself. You have discovered witchcraft—

Parris   In my house? In my house, Thomas? They will topple me with this! They will make of it a—

Enter **Mercy Lewis***, the* **Putnams***'servant, a fat, sly, merciless girl of eighteen.*

Mercy   Your pardons. I only thought to see how Betty is.

Putnam   Why aren't you home? Who's with Ruth?

Mercy   Her grandma come. She's improved a little, I think—she give a powerful sneeze before.

Mrs. Putnam   Ah, there's a sign of life!

Mercy   I'd fear no more, Goody Putnam. It were a grand sneeze; another like it will shake her wits together, I'm sure. (*She goes to the bed to look.*)

Parris   Will you leave me now, Thomas? I would pray a while alone.

Abigail   Uncle, you've prayed since midnight. Why do you not go down and—

Parris   No—no. (*To* **Putnam***:*) I have no answer for that crowd. I'll wait till Mr. Hale arrives. (*To get* **Mrs. Putnam** *to leave:*) If you will, Goody Ann . . .

Putnam   Now look you, sir. Let you strike out against the Devil, and the village will bless you for it! Come down, speak to them—pray with them. They're thirsting for your word, Mister! Surely you'll pray with them.

Parris (*swayed*)   I'll lead them in a psalm, but let you say nothing of witchcraft yet. I will not discuss it. The cause is yet unknown. I have had enough contention since I came; I want no more.

Mrs. Putnam   Mercy, you go home to Ruth, d'y'hear?

Mercy   Aye, mum.

Mrs. Putnam *goes out.*

Parris (*to* **Abigail**)   If she starts for the window, cry for me at once.

Abigail   I will, uncle.

Parris (*to* **Putnam**)   There is a terrible power in her arms today. (*He goes out with* **Putnam**.)

Abigail (*with hushed trepidation*)   How is Ruth sick?

Mercy   It's weirdish, I know not—she seems to walk like a dead one since last night.

Abigail (*turns at once and goes to* **Betty**, *and now, with fear in her voice*)   Betty? (**Betty** *doesn't move. She shakes her.*) Now stop this! Betty! Sit up now!

Betty *doesn't stir.* **Mercy** *comes over.*

Mercy   Have you tried beatin' her? I gave Ruth a good one and it waked her for a minute. Here, let me have her.

Abigail (*holding* **Mercy** *back*)   No, he'll be comin' up. Listen, now; if they be questioning us, tell them we danced—I told him as much already.

Mercy   Aye. And what more?

Abigail   He knows Tituba conjured Ruth's sisters to come out of the grave.

Mercy   And what more?

Abigail   He saw you naked.

Mercy (*clapping her hands together with a frightened laugh*)   Oh, Jesus!

Enter **Mary Warren**, *breathless. She is seventeen, a subservient, naive, lonely girl.*

Mary Warren   What'll we do? The village is out! I just come from the farm; the whole country's talkin' witchcraft! They'll be callin' us witches, Abby!

Mercy (*pointing and looking at* **Mary Warren**)   She means to tell, I know it.

Mary Warren   Abby, we've got to tell. Witchery's a hangin' error, a hangin' like they done in Boston two year ago! We must tell the truth,

Abby! You'll only be whipped for dancin', and the other things!

Abigail   Oh, *we'll* be whipped!

Mary Warren   I never done none of it, Abby. I only looked!

Mercy (*moving menacingly toward* **Mary**)   Oh, you're a great one for lookin', aren't you, Mary Warren? What a grand peeping courage you have!

Betty, *on the bed, whimpers.* **Abigail** *turns to her at once.*

Abigail   Betty? (*She goes to* **Betty**.) Now, Betty, dear, wake up now. It's Abigail. (*She sits* **Betty** *up and furiously shakes her.*) I'll beat you, Betty! (**Betty** *whimpers.*) My, you seem improving. I talked to your papa and I told him everything. So there's nothing to—

Betty (*darts off the bed, frightened of* **Abigail**, *and flattens herself against the wall*)   I want my mama!

Abigail (*with alarm, as she cautiously approaches* **Betty**)   What ails you, Betty? Your mama's dead and buried.

Betty   I'll fly to Mama. Let me fly! (*She raises her arms as though to fly, and streaks for the window, gets one leg out.*)

Abigail (*pulling her away from the window*)   I told him everything; he knows now, he knows everything we—

Betty   You drank blood, Abby! You didn't tell him that!

Abigail   Betty, you never say that again! You will never—

Betty   You did, you did! You drank a charm to kill John Proctor's wife! You drank a charm to kill Goody Proctor!

Abigail (*smashes her across the face*)   Shut it! Now shut it!

Betty (*collapsing on the bed*)   Mama, Mama! (*She dissolves into sobs.*)

Abigail   Now look you. All of you. We danced. And Tituba conjured Ruth Putnam's dead sisters. And that is all. And mark this. Let either of you breathe a word, or the edge of a word, about the other things, and I will come to you in the black of some terrible night and I will bring a pointy reckoning that will shudder you. And you know I can do it; I saw Indians smash my dear parents' heads on the pillow next to mine, and I have seen some reddish work done at night, and I can make you wish you had never seen the sun go down! (*She goes to* **Betty** *and roughly sits her up.*) Now, you—sit up and stop this!

But **Betty** *collapses in her hands and lies inert on the bed.*

Mary Warren (*with hysterical fright*)   What's got her? (**Abigail** *stares in fright at* **Betty**.) Abby, she's going to die! It's a sin to conjure, and we—

Abigail (*starting for* **Mary**)   I say shut it, Mary Warren!

Enter **John Proctor**. *On seeing him,* **Mary Warren** *leaps in fright.*

> Proctor was a farmer in his middle thirties. He need not have been a partisan of any faction in the town, but there is evidence to suggest that he had a sharp and biting way with hypocrites. He was the kind of man—powerful of body, even-tempered, and not easily led—who cannot refuse support to partisans without drawing their deepest resentment. In Proctor's presence a fool felt his foolishness instantly—and a Proctor is always marked for calumny therefore.

> But as we shall see, the steady manner he displays does not spring from an untroubled soul. He is a sinner, a sinner not only against the moral fashion of the time, but against his own vision of decent conduct. These people had no ritual for the washing away of sins. It is another trait we inherited from them, and it has helped to discipline us as well as to breed hypocrisy among us. Proctor, respected and even feared in Salem, has come to regard himself as a kind of fraud. But no hint of this has yet appeared on the surface, and as he enters from the crowded parlor below it is a man in his prime we see, with a quiet confidence and an unexpressed, hidden force. Mary Warren, his servant, can barely speak for embarrassment and fear.

Mary Warren   Oh! I'm just going home, Mr. Proctor.

Proctor   Be you foolish, Mary Warren? Be you deaf? I forbid you leave the house, did I not? Why shall I pay you? I am looking for you more often than my cows!

Mary Warren   I only come to see the great doings in the world.

Proctor   I'll show you a great doin' on your arse one of these days. Now get you home; my wife is waitin' with your work! (*Trying to retain a shred of dignity, she goes slowly out.*)

Mercy Lewis (*both afraid of him and strangely titillated*)   I'd best be off. I have my Ruth to watch. Good morning, Mr. Proctor.

Mercy *sidles out. Since* **Proctor**'*s entrance,* **Abigail** *has stood as though on tiptoe, absorbing his presence, wide-eyed. He glances at her, then goes to* **Betty** *on the bed.*

Abigail   Gah! I'd almost forgot how strong you are, John Proctor!

Proctor (*looking at* **Abigail** *now, the faintest suggestion of a knowing smile on his face*)   What's this mischief here?

Abigail (*with a nervous laugh*)   Oh, she's only gone silly somehow.

Proctor   The road past my house is a pilgrimage to Salem all morning. The town's mumbling witchcraft.

Abigail   Oh, posh! (*Winningly she comes a little closer, with a confidential, wicked air.*) We were dancin' in the woods last night, and my uncle leaped in on us. She took fright, is all.

Proctor (*his smile widening*)   Ah, you're wicked yet, aren't y'! (*A trill of expectant laughter escapes her, and she dares come closer, feverishly looking into his eyes.*) You'll be clapped in the stocks before you're twenty.

He takes a step to go, and she springs into his path.

Abigail   Give me a word, John. A soft word. (*Her concentrated desire destroys his smile.*)

Proctor   No, no, Abby. That's done with.

Abigail (*tauntingly*)   You come five mile to see a silly girl fly? I know you better.

Proctor (*setting her firmly out of his path*)   I come to see what mischief your uncle's brewin' now. (*With final emphasis:*) Put it out of mind, Abby.

Abigail (*grasping his hand before he can release her*)   John—I am waitin' for you every night.

Proctor   Abby, I never give you hope to wait for me.

Abigail (*now beginning to anger—she can't believe it*)   I have something better than hope, I think!

Proctor   Abby, you'll put it out of mind. I'll not be comin' for you more.

Abigail   You're surely sportin' with me.

Proctor   You know me better.

Abigail   I know how you clutched my back behind your house and sweated like a stallion whenever I come near! Or did I dream that? It's she put me out, you cannot pretend it were you. I saw your face when she put me out, and you loved me then and you do now!

Proctor   Abby, that's a wild thing to say—

Abigail   A wild thing may say wild things. But not so wild, I think. I have seen you since she put me out; I have seen you nights.

Proctor   I have hardly stepped off my farm this sevenmonth.

Abigail   I have a sense for heat, John, and yours has drawn me to my window, and I have seen you looking up, burning in your loneliness. Do you tell me you've never looked up at my window?

Proctor   I may have looked up.

Abigail (*now softening*)   And you must. You are no wintry man. I know you, John. I *know* you. (*She is weeping.*) I cannot sleep for dreamin'; I cannot dream but I wake and walk about the house as though I'd find you comin' through some door. (*She clutches him desperately.*)

Proctor (*gently pressing her from him, with great sympathy but firmly*)   Child—

Abigail (*with a flash of anger*)   How do you call me child!

Proctor   Abby, I may think of you softly from time to time. But I will cut off my hand before I'll ever reach for you again. Wipe it out of mind. We never touched, Abby.

Abigail   Aye, but we did.

Proctor   Aye, but we did not.

Abigail (*with a bitter anger*)   Oh, I marvel how such a strong man may let such a sickly wife be—

Proctor (*angered—at himself as well*)   You'll speak nothin' of Elizabeth!

Abigail   She is blackening my name in the village! She is telling lies about me! She is a cold, sniveling woman, and you bend to her! Let her turn you like a—

Proctor (*shaking her*)   Do you look for whippin'?

A psalm is heard being sung below.

Abigail (*in tears*)   I look for John Proctor that took me from my sleep and put knowledge in my heart! I never knew what pretense Salem was, I never knew the lying lessons I was taught by all these Christian women and their covenanted men! And now you bid me tear the light out of my eyes? I will not, I cannot! You loved me, John Proctor, and whatever sin it is, you love me yet! (*He turns abruptly to go out. She rushes to him.*) John, pity me, pity me!

The words "going up to Jesus" are heard in the psalm, and **Betty** *claps her ears suddenly and whines loudly.*

Abigail   Betty? (*She hurries to* **Betty***, who is now sitting up and screaming.* **Proctor** *goes to* **Betty** *as* **Abigail** *is trying to pull her hands down, calling "Betty!"*)

Proctor (*growing unnerved*)   What's she doing? Girl, what ails you? Stop that wailing!

The singing has stopped in the midst of this, and now **Parris** *rushes in.*

Parris   What happened? What are you doing to her? Betty! (*He rushes to the bed, crying, "Betty, Betty!"* **Mrs. Putnam** *enters, feverish with curiosity, and with her* **Thomas Putnam** *and* **Mercy Lewis***.* **Parris***, at the bed, keeps lightly slapping* **Betty***'s face, while she moans and tries to get up.*)

Abigail   She heard you singin' and suddenly she's up and screamin'.

Mrs. Putnam   The psalm! The psalm! She cannot bear to hear the Lord's name!

Parris   No, God forbid. Mercy, run to the doctor! Tell him what's happened here! (**Mercy Lewis** *rushes out.*)

Mrs. Putnam   Mark it for a sign, mark it!

Rebecca Nurse*, seventy-two, enters. She is white-haired, leaning upon her walking-stick.*

Putnam (*pointing at the whimpering* **Betty**)   That is a notorious sign of witchcraft afoot, Goody Nurse, a prodigious sign!

Mrs. Putnam   My mother told me that! When they cannot bear to hear the name of—

Parris (*trembling*)   Rebecca; Rebecca, go to her, we're lost. She suddenly cannot bear to hear the Lord's—

Giles Corey*, eighty-three, enters. He is knotted with muscle, canny, inquisitive, and still powerful.*

Rebecca   There is hard sickness here, Giles Corey, so please to keep the quiet.

Giles   I've not said a word. No one here can testify I've said a word. Is she going to fly again? I hear she flies.

Putnam   Man, be quiet now!

Everything is quiet. **Rebecca** *walks across the room to the bed.*
Gentleness exudes from her. **Betty** *is quietly whimpering, eyes shut.*
Rebecca *simply stands over the child, who gradually quiets.*

And while they are so absorbed, we may put a word in for Rebecca.
Rebecca was the wife of Francis Nurse, who, from all accounts, was
one of those men for whom both sides of the argument had to have
respect. He was called upon to arbitrate disputes as though he were an
unofficial judge, and Rebecca also enjoyed the high opinion most
people had for him. By the time of the delusion, they had three
hundred acres, and their children were settled in separate homesteads
within the same estate. However, Francis had originally rented the
land, and one theory has it that, as he gradually paid for it and raised
his social status, there were those who resented his rise.

Another suggestion to explain the systematic campaign against
Rebecca, and inferentially against Francis, is the land war he fought
with his neighbors, one of whom was a Putnam. This squabble grew
to the proportions of a battle in the woods between partisans of both
sides, and it is said to have lasted for two days. As for Rebecca
herself, the general opinion of her character was so high that to
explain how anyone dared cry her out for a witch—and more, how
adults could bring themselves to lay hands on her—we must look to
the fields and boundaries of that time.

As we have seen, Thomas Putnam's man for the Salem ministry was
Bayley. The Nurse clan had been in the faction that prevented
Bayley's taking office. In addition, certain families allied to the
Nurses by blood or friendship, and whose farms were contiguous with
the Nurse farm or close to it, combined to break away from the Salem
town authority and set up Topsfield, a new and independent entity
whose existence was resented by old Salemites.

That the guiding hand behind the outcry was Putnam's is indicated by
the fact that, as soon as it began, this Topsfield–Nurse faction
absented themselves from church in protest and disbelief. It was
Edward and Jonathan Putnam who signed the first complaint against
Rebecca; and Thomas Putnam's little daughter was the one who fell
into a fit at the hearing and pointed to Rebecca as her attacker. To top
it all, Mrs. Putnam—who is now staring at the bewitched child on the
bed—soon accused Rebecca's spirit of "tempting her to iniquity," a
charge that had more truth in it than Mrs. Putnam could know.

Mrs. Putnam (*astonished*) What have you done?

Rebecca, *in thought, now leaves the bedside and sits.*

Parris (*wondrous and relieved*) What do you make of it, Rebecca?

Putnam (*eagerly*) Goody Nurse, will you go to my Ruth and see if you can wake her?

Rebecca (*sitting*) I think she'll wake in time. Pray calm yourselves. I have eleven children, and I am twenty-six times a grandma, and I have seen them all through their silly seasons, and when it come on them they will run the Devil bowlegged keeping up with their mischief. I think she'll wake when she tires of it. A child's spirit is like a child, you can never catch it by running after it; you must stand still, and, for love, it will soon itself come back.

Proctor Aye, that's the truth of it, Rebecca.

Mrs. Putnam This is no silly season, Rebecca. My Ruth is bewildered, Rebecca; she cannot eat.

Rebecca Perhaps she is not hungered yet. (*To* **Parris**:) I hope you are not decided to go in search of loose spirits, Mr. Parris. I've heard promise of that outside.

Parris A wide opinion's running in the parish that the Devil may be among us, and I would satisfy them that they are wrong.

Proctor Then let you come out and call them wrong. Did you consult the wardens before you called this minister to look for devils?

Parris He is not coming to look for devils!

Proctor Then what's he coming for?

Putnam There be children dyin' in the village, Mister!

Proctor I seen none dyin'. This society will not be a bag to swing around your head, Mr. Putnam. (*To* **Parris**:) Did you call a meeting before you—?

Putnam I am sick of meetings; cannot the man turn his head without he have a meeting?

Proctor He may turn his head, but not to Hell!

Rebecca Pray, John, be calm. (*Pause. He defers to her.*) Mr. Parris, I think you'd best send Reverend Hale back as soon as he come. This will set us all to arguin' again in the society, and we thought to have peace this year. I think we ought rely on the doctor now, and good prayer.

Mrs. Putnam   Rebecca, the doctor's baffled!

Rebecca   If so he is, then let us go to God for the cause of it. There is prodigious danger in the seeking of loose spirits. I fear it, I fear it. Let us rather blame ourselves and—

Putnam   How may we blame ourselves? I am one of nine sons; the Putnam seed have peopled this province. And yet I have but one child left of eight—and now she shrivels!

Rebecca   I cannot fathom that.

Mrs. Putnam (*with a growing edge of sarcasm*)   But I must! You think it God's work you should never lose a child, nor grandchild either, and I bury all but one? There are wheels within wheels in this village, and fires within fires!

Putnam (*to* **Parris**)   When Reverend Hale comes, you will proceed to look for signs of witchcraft here.

Proctor (*to* **Putnam**)   You cannot command Mr. Parris. We vote by name in this society, not by acreage.

Putnam   I never heard you worried so on this society, Mr. Proctor. I do not think I saw you at Sabbath meeting since snow flew.

Proctor   I have trouble enough without I come five mile to hear him preach only hellfire and bloody damnation. Take it to heart, Mr. Parris. There are many others who stay away from church these days because you hardly ever mention God any more.

Parris (*now aroused*)   Why, that's a drastic charge!

Rebecca   It's somewhat true; there are many that quail to bring their children—

Parris   I do not preach for children, Rebecca. It is not the children who are unmindful of their obligations toward this ministry.

Rebecca   Are there really those unmindful?

Parris   I should say the better half of Salem village—

Putnam   And more than that!

Parris   Where is my wood? My contract provides I be supplied with all my firewood. I am waiting since November for a stick, and even in November I had to show my frostbitten hands like some London beggar!

Giles   You are allowed six pound a year to buy your wood, Mr. Parris.

Parris   I regard that six pound as part of my salary. I am paid little enough without I spend six pound on firewood.

Proctor   Sixty, plus six for firewood—

Parris   The salary is sixty-six pound, Mr. Proctor! I am not some preaching farmer with a book under my arm; I am a graduate of Harvard College.

Giles   Aye, and well instructed in arithmetic!

Parris   Mr. Corey, you will look far for a man of my kind at sixty pound a year! I am not used to this poverty; I left a thrifty business in the Barbados to serve the Lord. I do not fathom it, why am I persecuted here? I cannot offer one proposition but there be a howling riot of argument. I have often wondered if the Devil be in it somewhere; I cannot understand you people otherwise.

Proctor   Mr. Parris, you are the first minister ever did demand the deed to this house—

Parris   Man! Don't a minister deserve a house to live in?

Proctor   To live in, yes. But to ask ownership is like you shall own the meeting house itself; the last meeting I were at you spoke so long on deeds and mortgages I thought it were an auction.

Parris   I want a mark of confidence, is all! I am your third preacher in seven years. I do not wish to be put out like the cat whenever some majority feels the whim. You people seem not to comprehend that a minister is the Lord's man in the parish; a minister is not to be so lightly crossed and contradicted—

Putnam   Aye!

Parris   There is either obedience or the church will burn like Hell is burning!

Proctor   Can you speak one minute without we land in Hell again? I am sick of Hell!

Parris   It is not for you to say what is good for you to hear!

Proctor   I may speak my heart, I think!

Parris (*in a fury*)   What, are we Quakers? We are not Quakers here yet, Mr. Proctor. And you may tell that to your followers!

Proctor   My followers!

Parris (*now he's out with it*)   There is a party in this church. I am not blind; there is a faction and a party.

Proctor   Against you?

Putnam   Against him and all authority!

Proctor   Why, then I must find it and join it.

There is shock among the others.

Rebecca   He does not mean that.

Putnam   He confessed it now!

Proctor   I mean it solemnly, Rebecca; I like not the smell of this "authority."

Rebecca   No, you cannot break charity with your minister. You are another kind, John. Clasp his hand, make your peace.

Proctor   I have a crop to sow and lumber to drag home. (*He goes angrily to the door and turns to* **Corey** *with a smile.*) What say you, Giles, let's find the party. He says there's a party.

Giles   I've changed my opinion of this man, John. Mr. Parris, I beg your pardon. I never thought you had so much iron in you.

Parris (*surprised*)   Why, thank you, Giles!

Giles   It suggests to the mind what the trouble be among us all these years. (*To all:*) Think on it. Wherefore is everybody suing everybody else? Think on it now, it's a deep thing, and dark as a pit. I have been six time in court this year—

Proctor (*familiarly, with warmth, although he knows he is approaching the edge of* **Giles***' tolerance with this*)   Is it the Devil's fault that a man cannot say you good morning without you clap him for defamation? You're old, Giles, and you're not hearin' so well as you did.

Giles (*he cannot be crossed*)   John Proctor, I have only last month collected four pound damages for you publicly sayin' I burned the roof off your house, and I—

Proctor (*laughing*)   I never said no such thing, but I've paid you for it, so I hope I can call you deaf without charge. Now come along, Giles, and help me drag my lumber home.

Putnam   A moment, Mr. Proctor. What lumber is that you're draggin', if I may ask you?

Proctor   My lumber. From out my forest by the riverside.

Putnam   Why, we are surely gone wild this year. What anarchy is this? That tract is in my bounds, it's in my bounds, Mr. Proctor.

Proctor   In your bounds! (*Indicating* **Rebecca***.*) I bought that tract from Goody Nurse's husband five months ago.

Putnam   He had no right to sell it. It stands clear in my grandfather's will that all the land between the river and—

Proctor   Your grandfather had a habit of willing land that never belonged to him, if I may say it plain.

Giles   That's God's truth; he nearly willed away my north pasture but he knew I'd break his fingers before he'd set his name to it. Let's get your lumber home, John. I feel a sudden will to work coming on.

Putnam   You load one oak of mine and you'll fight to drag it home!

Giles   Aye, and we'll win too, Putnam—this fool and I. Come on! (*He turns to* **Proctor** *and starts out.*)

Putnam   I'll have my men on you, Corey! I'll clap a writ on you!

Enter **Reverend John Hale** *of Beverly.*

Mr. Hale is nearing forty, a tight-skinned, eager-eyed intellectual. This is a beloved errand for him; on being called here to ascertain witchcraft he felt the pride of the specialist whose unique knowledge has at last been publicly called for. Like almost all men of learning, he spent a good deal of his time pondering the invisible world, especially since he had himself encountered a witch in his parish not long before. That woman, however, turned into a mere pest under his searching scrutiny, and the child she had allegedly been afflicting recovered her normal behavior after Hale had given her his kindness and a few days of rest in his own house. However, that experience never raised a doubt in his mind as to the reality of the underworld or the existence of Lucifer's many-faced lieutenants. And his belief is not to his discredit. Better minds than Hale's were—and still are—convinced that there is a society of spirits beyond our ken. One cannot help noting that one of his lines has never yet raised a laugh in any audience that has seen this play; it is his assurance that "We cannot look to superstition in this. The Devil is precise." Evidently we are not quite certain even now whether diabolism is holy and not to be scoffed at. And it is no accident that we should be so bemused.

Like Reverend Hale and the others on this stage, we conceive the Devil as a necessary part of a respectable view of cosmology. Ours is a divided empire in which certain ideas and emotions and actions are of God, and their opposites are of Lucifer. It is as impossible for most men to conceive of a morality without sin as of an earth without "sky." Since 1692 a great but superficial change has wiped out God's beard and the Devil's horns, but the world is still gripped between two diametrically opposed absolutes. The concept of unity, in which positive and negative are attributes of the same force, in which good and evil are relative, ever-changing, and always joined to the same phenomenon—such a concept is still reserved to the physical sciences and to the few who have grasped the history of ideas. When it is recalled that until the Christian era the underworld was never regarded as a hostile area, that all gods were useful and essentially friendly to man despite occasional lapses; when we see the steady and methodical inculcation into humanity of the idea of man's worthlessness—until redeemed—the necessity of the Devil may become evident as a weapon, a weapon designed and used time and time again in every age to whip men into a surrender to a particular church or church-state.

Our difficulty in believing the—for want of a better word—political inspiration of the Devil is due in great part to the fact that he is called up and damned not only by our social antagonists but by our own side, whatever it may be. The Catholic Church, through its Inquisition, is famous for cultivating Lucifer as the arch-fiend, but the Church's enemies relied no less upon the Old Boy to keep the human mind enthralled. Luther was himself accused of alliance with Hell, and he in turn accused his enemies. To complicate matters further, he believed that he had had contact with the Devil and had argued theology with him. I am not surprised at this, for at my own university a professor of history—a Lutheran, by the way—used to assemble his graduate students, draw the shades, and commune in the classroom with Erasmus. He was never, to my knowledge, officially scoffed at for this, the reason being that the university officials, like most of us, are the children of a history which still sucks at the Devil's teats. At this writing, only England has held back before the temptations of contemporary diabolism. In the countries of the Communist ideology, all resistance of any import is linked to the totally malign capitalist succubi, and in America any man who is not reactionary in his views is open to the charge of alliance with the Red hell. Political opposition, thereby, is given an inhumane overlay which then justifies the abrogation of all normally applied customs of civilized intercourse. A political policy is equated with moral right, and opposition to it with diabolical malevolence. Once such an equation is effectively made, society becomes a congerie of plots and counterplots, and the main role of government changes from that of the arbiter to that of the scourge of God.

The results of this process are no different now from what they ever were, except sometimes in the degree of cruelty inflicted, and not always even in that department. Normally the actions and deeds of a man were all that society felt comfortable in judging. The secret intent of an action was left to the ministers, priests, and rabbis to deal with. When diabolism rises, however, actions are the least important manifests of the true nature of a man. The Devil, as Reverend Hale said, is a wily one, and, until an hour before he fell, even God thought him beautiful in Heaven.

The analogy, however, seems to falter when one considers that, while there were no witches then, there are Communists and capitalists now, and in each camp there is certain proof that spies of each side are at work undermining the other. But this is a snobbish objection and not at all warranted by the facts. I have no doubt that people *were* communing with, and even worshiping, the Devil in Salem, and if the whole truth could be known in this case, as it is in others, we should discover a regular and conventionalized propitiation of the dark spirit. One certain evidence of this is the confession of Tituba, the slave of Reverend Parris, and another is the behavior of the children who were known to have indulged in sorceries with her.

There are accounts of similar *klatches* in Europe, where the daughters of the towns would assemble at night and, sometimes with fetishes, sometimes with a selected young man, give themselves to love, with some bastardly results. The Church, sharpeyed as it must be when gods long dead are brought to life, condemned these orgies as witchcraft and interpreted them, rightly, as a resurgence of the Dionysiac forces it had crushed long before. Sex, sin, and the Devil were early linked, and so they continued to be in Salem, and are today. From all accounts there are no more puritanical mores in the world than those enforced by the Communists in Russia, where women's fashions, for instance, are as prudent and all-covering as any American Baptist would desire. The divorce laws lay a tremendous responsibility on the father for the care of his children. Even the laxity of divorce regulations in the early years of the revolution was undoubtedly a revulsion from the nineteenth-century Victorian immobility of marriage and the consequent hypocrisy that developed from it. If for no other reasons, a state so powerful, so jealous of the uniformity of its citizens, cannot long tolerate the atomization of the family. And yet, in American eyes at least, there remains the conviction that the Russian attitude toward women is lascivious. It is the Devil working again, just as he is working within the Slav who is shocked at the very idea of a woman's disrobing herself in a burlesque show. Our opposites are always robed in sexual sin, and it is from this unconscious conviction that demonology gains both its attractive sensuality and its capacity to infuriate and frighten.

Coming into Salem now, Reverend Hale conceives of himself much as a young doctor on his first call. His painfully acquired armory of symptoms, catchwords, and diagnostic procedures are now to be put to use at last. The road from Beverly is unusually busy this morning, and he has passed a hundred rumors that make him smile at the ignorance of the yeomanry in this most precise science. He feels himself allied with the best minds of Europe—kings, philosophers, scientists, and ecclesiasts of all churches. His goal is light, goodness and its preservation, and he knows the exaltation of the blessed whose intelligence, sharpened by minute examinations of enormous tracts, is finally called upon to face what may be a bloody fight with the Fiend himself.

He appears loaded down with half a dozen heavy books.

Hale   Pray you, someone take these!

Parris (*delighted*)   Mr. Hale! Oh! it's good to see you again! (*Taking some books:*) My, they're heavy!

Hale (*setting down his books*)   They must be; they are weighted with authority.

Parris (*a little scared*)   Well, you do come prepared!

Hale   We shall need hard study if it comes to tracking down the Old Boy. (*Noticing* **Rebecca***:*) You cannot be Rebecca Nurse?

Rebecca   I am, sir. Do you know me?

Hale   It's strange how I knew you, but I suppose you look as such a good soul should. We have all heard of your great charities in Beverly.

Parris   Do you know this gentleman? Mr. Thomas Putnam. And his good wife Ann.

Hale   Putnam! I had not expected such distinguished company, sir.

Putnam (*pleased*)   It does not seem to help us today, Mr. Hale. We look to you to come to our house and save our child.

Hale   Your child ails too?

Mrs. Putnam   Her soul, her soul seems flown away. She sleeps and yet she walks . . .

Putnam   She cannot eat.

Hale   Cannot eat! (*Thinks on it. Then, to* **Proctor** *and* **Giles Corey***:*) Do you men have afflicted children?

Parris   No, no, these are farmers. John Proctor—

Giles Corey   He don't believe in witches.

Proctor (*to* **Hale**)   I never spoke on witches one way or the other. Will you come, Giles?

Giles   No—no, John, I think not. I have some few queer questions of my own to ask this fellow.

Proctor   I've heard you to be a sensible man, Mr. Hale. I hope you'll leave some of it in Salem.

Proctor *goes.* **Hale** *stands embarrassed for an instant.*

Parris (*quickly*)   Will you look at my daughter, sir? (*Leads* **Hale** *to the bed.*) She has tried to leap out the window; we discovered her this morning on the highroad, waving her arms as though she'd fly.

Hale (*narrowing his eyes*)   Tries to fly.

Putnam   She cannot bear to hear the Lord's name, Mr. Hale; that's a sure sign of witchcraft afloat.

Hale (*holding up his hands*)   No, no. Now let me instruct you. We cannot look to superstition in this. The Devil is precise; the marks of his presence are definite as stone, and I must tell you all that I shall not proceed unless you are prepared to believe me if I should find no bruise of hell upon her.

Parris   It is agreed, sir—it is agreed—we will abide by your judgment.

Hale   Good then. (*He goes to the bed, looks down at* **Betty**. *To* **Parris***:*) Now, sir, what were your first warning of this strangeness?

Parris   Why, sir—I discovered her (*indicating* **Abigail**) and my niece and ten or twelve of the other girls, dancing in the forest last night.

Hale (*surprised*)   You permit dancing?

Parris   No, no, it were secret—

Mrs. Putnam (*unable to wait*)   Mr. Parris's slave has knowledge of conjurin', sir.

Parris (*to* **Mrs. Putnam**)   We cannot be sure of that, Goody Ann—

Mrs. Putnam (*frightened, very softly*)   I know it, sir. I sent my child— she should learn from Tituba who murdered her sisters.

Rebecca (*horrified*)   Goody Ann! You sent a child to conjure up the dead?

Mrs. Putnam   Let God blame me, not you, not you, Rebecca! I'll not have you judging me any more! (*To* **Hale**:) Is it a natural work to lose seven children before they live a day?

Parris   Sssh!

Rebecca, *with great pain, turns her face away. There is a pause.*

Hale   Seven dead in childbirth.

Mrs. Putnam (*softly*)   Aye. (*Her voice breaks; she looks up at him. Silence.* **Hale** *is impressed.* **Parris** *looks to him. He goes to his books, opens one, turns pages, then reads. All wait, avidly.*)

Parris (*hushed*)   What book is that?

Mrs. Putnam   What's there, sir?

Hale (*with a tasty love of intellectual pursuit*)   Here is all the invisible world, caught, defined, and calculated. In these books the Devil stands stripped of all his brute disguises. Here are all your familiar spirits—your incubi and succubi; your witches that go by land, by air, and by sea; your wizards of the night and of the day. Have no fear now—we shall find him out if he has come among us, and I mean to crush him utterly if he has shown his face! (*He starts for the bed.*)

Rebecca   Will it hurt the child, sir?

Hale   I cannot tell. If she is truly in the Devil's grip we may have to rip and tear to get her free.

Rebecca   I think I'll go, then. I am too old for this. (*She rises.*)

Parris (*striving for conviction*)   Why, Rebecca, we may open up the boil of all our troubles today!

Rebecca   Let us hope for that. I go to God for you, sir.

Parris (*with trepidation—and resentment*)   I hope you do not mean we go to Satan here! (*Slight pause.*)

Rebecca   I wish I knew. (*She goes out; they feel resentful of her note of moral superiority.*)

Putnam (*abruptly*)   Come, Mr. Hale, let's get on. Sit you here.

Giles   Mr. Hale, I have always wanted to ask a learned man—what signifies the readin' of strange books?

Hale   What books?

Giles   I cannot tell; she hides them.

Hale   Who does this?

Giles   Martha, my wife. I have waked at night many a time and found her in a corner, readin' of a book. Now what do you make of that?

Hale   Why, that's not necessarily—

Giles   It discomfits me! Last night—mark this—I tried and tried and could not say my prayers. And then she close her book and walks out of the house, and suddenly—mark this—I could pray again!

Old Giles must be spoken for, if only because his fate was to be so remarkable and so different from that of all the others. He was in his early eighties at this time, and was the most comical hero in the history. No man has ever been blamed for so much. If a cow was missed, the first thought was to look for her around Corey's house; a fire blazing up at night brought suspicion of arson to his door. He didn't give a hoot for public opinion, and only in his last years—after he had married Martha—did he bother much with the church. That she stopped his prayer is very probable, but he forgot to say that he'd only recently learned any prayers and it didn't take much to make him stumble over them. He was a crank and a nuisance, but withal a deeply innocent and brave man. In court, once, he was asked if it were true that he had been frightened by the strange behavior of a hog and had then said he knew it to be the Devil in an animal's shape. "What frighted you?" he was asked. He forgot everything but the word "frighted," and instantly replied, "I do not know that I ever spoke that word in my life."

Hale   Ah! The stoppage of prayer—that is strange. I'll speak further on that with you.

Giles   I'm not sayin' she's touched the Devil, now, but I'd admire to know what books she reads and why she hides them. She'll not answer me, y' see.

Hale   Aye, we'll discuss it. (*To all:*) Now mark me, if the Devil is in her you will witness some frightful wonders in this room, so please to keep your wits about you. Mr. Putnam, stand close in case she flies. Now, Betty, dear, will you sit up? (**Putnam** *comes in closer, ready-handed.* **Hale** *sits* **Betty** *up, but she hangs limp in his hands.*) Hmmm. (*He observes her carefully. The others watch breathlessly.*) Can you hear me? I am John Hale, minister of Beverly. I have come to help you, dear. Do you remember my two little girls in Beverly? (*She does not stir in his hands.*)

Parris (*in fright*)   How can it be the Devil? Why would he choose my house to strike? We have all manner of licentious people in the village!

Hale   What victory would the Devil have to win a soul already bad? It is the best the Devil wants, and who is better than the minister?

Giles   That's deep, Mr. Parris, deep, deep!

Parris (*with resolution now*)   Betty! Answer Mr. Hale! Betty!

Hale   Does someone afflict you, child? It need not be a woman, mind you, or a man. Perhaps some bird invisible to others comes to you—perhaps a pig, a mouse, or any beast at all. Is there some figure bids you fly? (*The child remains limp in his hands. In silence he lays her back on the pillow. Now, holding out his hands toward her, he intones:*) *In nomine Domini Sabaoth sui filiique ite ad infernos.* (*She does not stir. He turns to* **Abigail***, his eyes narrowing.*) Abigail, what sort of dancing were you doing with her in the forest?

Abigail   Why—common dancing is all.

Parris   I think I ought to say that I—I saw a kettle in the grass where they were dancing.

Abigail   That were only soup.

Hale   What sort of soup were in this kettle, Abigail?

Abigail   Why, it were beans—and lentils, I think, and—

Hale   Mr. Parris, you did not notice, did you, any living thing in the kettle? A mouse, perhaps, a spider, a frog—?

Parris (*fearfully*)   I—do believe there were some movement—in the soup.

Abigail   That jumped in, we never put it in!

Hale (*quickly*)   What jumped in?

Abigail   Why, a very little frog jumped—

Parris   A frog, Abby!

Hale (*grasping* **Abigail**)   Abigail, it may be your cousin is dying. Did you call the Devil last night?

Abigail   I never called him! Tituba, Tituba . . .

Parris (*blanched*)   She called the Devil?

Hale   I should like to speak with Tituba.

Parris   Goody Ann, will you bring her up? (**Mrs. Putnam** *exits.*)

Hale   How did she call him?

Abigail   I know not—she spoke Barbados.

Hale   Did you feel any strangeness when she called him? A sudden cold wind, perhaps? A trembling below the ground?

Abigail   I didn't see no Devil! (*Shaking* **Betty***:*) Betty, wake up. Betty! Betty!

Hale   You cannot evade me, Abigail. Did your cousin drink any of the brew in that kettle?

Abigail   She never drank it!

Hale   Did you drink it?

Abigail   No, sir!

Hale   Did Tituba ask you to drink it?

Abigail   She tried, but I refused.

Hale   Why are you concealing? Have you sold yourself to Lucifer?

Abigail   I never sold myself! I'm a good girl! I'm a proper girl!

Mrs. Putnam *enters with* **Tituba***, and instantly* **Abigail** *points at* **Tituba***.*

Abigail   She made me do it! She made Betty do it!

Tituba (*shocked and angry*)   Abby!

Abigail   She makes me drink blood!

Parris   Blood!!

Mrs. Putnam   My baby's blood?

Tituba   No, no, chicken blood. I give she chicken blood!

Hale   Woman, have you enlisted these children for the Devil?

Tituba   No, no, sir, I don't truck with no Devil!

Hale   Why can she not wake? Are you silencing this child?

Tituba   I love me Betty!

Hale   You have sent your spirit out upon this child, have you not? Are you gathering souls for the Devil?

Abigail   She sends her spirit on me in church; she makes me laugh at prayer!

Parris   She have often laughed at prayer!

Abigail   She comes to me every night to go and drink blood!

Tituba   You beg *me* to conjure! She beg *me* make charm—

Abigail   Don't lie! (*To* **Hale***:*) She comes to me while I sleep; she's always making me dream corruptions!

Tituba   Why you say that, Abby?

Abigail   Sometimes I wake and find myself standing in the open doorway and not a stitch on my body! I always hear her laughing in my sleep. I hear her singing her Barbados songs and tempting me with—

Tituba   Mister Reverend, I never—

Hale (*resolved now*)   Tituba, I want you to wake this child.

Tituba   I have no power on this child, sir.

Hale   You most certainly do, and you will free her from it now! When did you compact with the Devil?

Tituba   I don't compact with no Devil!

Parris   You will confess yourself or I will take you out and whip you to your death, Tituba!

Putnam   This woman must be hanged! She must be taken and hanged!

Tituba (*terrified, falls to her knees*)   No, no, don't hang Tituba! I tell him I don't desire to work for him, sir.

Parris   The Devil?

Hale   Then you saw him! (**Tituba** *weeps.*) Now Tituba, I know that when we bind ourselves to Hell it is very hard to break with it. We are going to help you tear yourself free—

Tituba (*frightened by the coming process*)   Mister Reverend, I do believe somebody else be witchin' these children.

Hale   Who?

Tituba   I don't know, sir, but the Devil got him numerous witches.

Hale   Does he! (*It is a clue.*) Tituba, look into my eyes. Come, look into me. (*She raises her eyes to his fearfully.*) You would be a good Christian woman, would you not, Tituba?

Tituba   Aye, sir, a good Christian woman.

Hale   And you love these little children?

Tituba   Oh, yes, sir, I don't desire to hurt little children.

Hale   And you love God, Tituba?

Tituba   I love God with all my bein'.

Hale   Now, in God's holy name—

Tituba   Bless Him. Bless Him. (*She is rocking on her knees, sobbing in terror.*)

Hale   And to His glory—

Tituba   Eternal glory. Bless Him—bless God . . .

Hale   Open yourself, Tituba—open yourself and let God's holy light shine on you.

Tituba   Oh, bless the Lord.

Hale   When the Devil comes to you does he ever come—with another person? (*She stares up into his face.*) Perhaps another person in the village? Someone you know.

Parris   Who came with him?

Putnam   Sarah Good? Did you ever see Sarah Good with him? Or Osburn?

Parris   Was it man or woman came with him?

Tituba   Man or woman. Was—was woman.

Parris   What woman? A woman, you said. What woman?

Tituba   It was black dark, and I—

Parris   You could see him, why could you—not see her?

Tituba   Well, they was always talking; they was always runnin' round and carryin' on—

Parris   You mean out of Salem? Salem witches?

Tituba   I believe so, yes, sir.

Now **Hale** *takes her hand. She is surprised.*

Hale   Tituba. You must have no fear to tell us who they are, do you understand? We will protect you. The Devil can never overcome a minister. You know that, do you not?

Tituba (*kisses* **Hale***'s hand*)   Aye, sir, oh, I do.

Hale   You have confessed yourself to witchcraft, and that speaks a wish to come to Heaven's side. And we will bless you, Tituba.

Tituba (*deeply relieved*)   Oh, God bless you, Mr. Hale!

Hale (*with rising exaltation*)   You are God's instrument put in our hands to discover the Devil's agents among us. You are selected, Tituba, you are chosen to help us cleanse our village. So speak utterly, Tituba, turn your back on him and face God—face God, Tituba, and God will protect you.

Tituba (*joining with him*)   Oh, God, protect Tituba!

Hale (*kindly*)   Who came to you with the Devil? Two? Three? Four? How many?

Tituba *pants, and begins rocking back and forth again, staring ahead.*

Tituba   There was four. There was four.

Parris (*pressing in on her*)   Who? Who? Their names, their names!

Tituba (*suddenly bursting out*)   Oh, how many times he bid me kill you, Mr. Parris!

Parris   Kill me!

Tituba (*in a fury*)   He say Mr. Parris must be kill! Mr. Parris no goodly man, Mr. Parris mean man and no gentle man, and he bid me rise out of my bed and cut your throat! (*They gasp.*) But I tell him "No! I don't hate that man. I don't want kill that man." But he say, "You work for me, Tituba, and I make you free! I give you pretty dress to wear, and put you way high up in the air, and you gone fly back to Barbados!" And I say, "You lie, Devil, you lie!" And then he come one stormy night to me, and he say, "Look! I have white people belong to me." And I look—and there was Goody Good.

Parris   Sarah Good!

Tituba (*rocking and weeping*)   Aye, sir, and Goody Osburn.

Mrs. Putnam   I knew it! Goody Osburn were midwife to me three times. I begged you, Thomas, did I not? I begged him not to call Osburn because I feared her. My babies always shriveled in her hands!

Hale   Take courage, you must give us all their names. How can you bear to see this child suffering? Look at her, Tituba. (*He is indicating* **Betty** *on the bed.*) Look at her God-given innocence; her soul is so tender; we must protect her, Tituba; the Devil is out and preying on her like a beast upon the flesh of the pure lamb. God will bless you for your help.

Abigail *rises, staring as though inspired, and cries out.*

Abigail I want to open myself! (*They turn to her, startled. She is enraptured, as though in a pearly light.*) I want the light of God, I want the sweet love of Jesus! I danced for the Devil; I saw him; I wrote in his book; I go back to Jesus; I kiss His hand. I saw Sarah Good with the Devil! I saw Goody Osburn with the Devil! I saw Bridget Bishop with the Devil!

As she is speaking, **Betty** *is rising from the bed, a fever in her eyes, and picks up the chant.*

Betty (*staring too*) I saw George Jacobs with the Devil! I saw Goody Howe with the Devil!

Parris She speaks! (*He rushes to embrace* **Betty**.) She speaks!

Hale Glory to God! It is broken, they are free!

Betty (*calling out hysterically and with great relief*) I saw Martha Bellows with the Devil!

Abigail I saw Goody Sibber with the Devil! (*It is rising to a great glee.*)

Putnam The marshal, I'll call the marshal!

Paris *is shouting a prayer of thanksgiving.*

Betty I saw Alice Barrow with the Devil!

The curtain begins to fall.

Hale (*as* **Putnam** *goes out*) Let the marshal bring irons!

Abigail I saw Goody Hawkins with the Devil!

Betty I saw Goody Bibber with the Devil!

Abigail I saw Goody Booth with the Devil!

On their ecstatic cries—

Curtain.

Act Two

The common room of **Proctor**'s *house, eight days later.*

At the right is a door opening on the fields outside. A fireplace is at the left, and behind it a stairway leading upstairs. It is the low, dark, and rather long living room of the time. As the curtain rises, the room is empty. From above, **Elizabeth** *is heard softly singing to the children. Presently the door opens and* **John Proctor** *enters, carrying his gun. He glances about the room as he comes toward the fireplace, then halts for an instant as he hears her singing. He continues on to the fireplace, leans the gun against the wall as he swings a pot out of the fire and smells it. Then he lifts out the ladle and tastes. He is not quite pleased. He reaches to a cupboard, takes a pinch of salt, and drops it into the pot. As he is tasting again, her footsteps are heard on the stair. He swings the pot into the fireplace and goes to a basin and washes his hands and face.* **Elizabeth** *enters.*

Elizabeth   What keeps you so late? It's almost dark.

Proctor   I were planting far out to the forest edge.

Elizabeth   Oh, you're done then.

Proctor   Aye, the farm is seeded. The boys asleep?

Elizabeth   They will be soon. (*And she goes to the fireplace, proceeds to ladle up stew in a dish.*)

Proctor   Pray now for a fair summer.

Elizabeth   Aye.

Proctor   Are you well today?

Elizabeth   I am. (*She brings the plate to the table, and, indicating the food:*) It is a rabbit.

Proctor (*going to the table*)   Oh, is it! In Jonathan's trap?

Elizabeth   No, she walked into the house this afternoon; I found her sittin' in the corner like she come to visit.

Proctor   Oh, that's a good sign walkin' in.

Elizabeth   Pray God. It hurt my heart to strip her, poor rabbit. (*She sits and watches him taste it.*)

Proctor   It's well seasoned.

Elizabeth (*blushing with pleasure*)   I took great care. She's tender?

Proctor   Aye. (*He eats. She watches him.*) I think we'll see green fields soon. It's warm as blood beneath the clods.

Elizabeth   That's well.

Proctor, *eats, then looks up.*

Proctor   If the crop is good I'll buy George Jacob's heifer. How would that please you?

Elizabeth   Aye, it would.

Proctor (*with a grin*)   I mean to please you, Elizabeth.

Elizabeth (*it is hard to say*)   I know it, John.

He gets up, goes to her, kisses her. She receives it. With a certain disappointment, he returns to the table.

Proctor (*as gently as he can*)   Cider?

Elizabeth (*with a sense of reprimanding herself for having forgot*)   Aye! (*She gets up and goes and pours a glass for him. He now arches his back.*)

Proctor   This farm's a continent when you go foot by foot droppin' seeds in it.

Elizabeth (*coming with the cider*)   It must be.

Proctor (*drinks a long draught, then, putting the glass down*)   You ought to bring some flowers in the house.

Elizabeth   Oh! I forgot! I will tomorrow.

Proctor   It's winter in here yet. On Sunday let you come with me, and we'll walk the farm together; I never see such a load of flowers on the earth. (*With good feeling he goes and looks up at the sky through the open doorway.*) Lilacs have a purple smell. Lilac is the smell of nightfall, I think. Massachusetts is a beauty in the spring!

Elizabeth   Aye, it is.

There is a pause. She is watching him from the table as he stands there absorbing the night. It is as though she would speak but cannot. Instead, now, she takes up his plate and glass and fork and goes with them to the basin. Her back is turned to him. He turns to her and watches her. A sense of their separation rises.

Proctor   I think you're sad again. Are you?

Elizabeth (*she doesn't want friction, and yet she must*)   You come so late I thought you'd gone to Salem this afternoon.

Proctor   Why? I have no business in Salem.

Elizabeth   You did speak of going, earlier this week.

Proctor (*he knows what she means*)   I thought better of it since.

Elizabeth   Mary Warren's there today.

Proctor   Why'd you let her? You heard me forbid her go to Salem any more!

Elizabeth   I couldn't stop her.

Proctor (*holding back a full condemnation of her*)   It is a fault, it is a fault, Elizabeth—you're the mistress here, not Mary Warren.

Elizabeth   She frightened all my strength away.

Proctor   How may that mouse frighten you, Elizabeth? You—

Elizabeth   It is a mouse no more. I forbid her go, and she raises up her chin like the daughter of a prince and says to me, "I must go to Salem, Goody Proctor; I am an official of the court!"

Proctor   Court! What court?

Elizabeth   Aye, it is a proper court they have now. They've sent four judges out of Boston, she says, weighty magistrates of the General Court, and at the head sits the Deputy Governor of the Province.

Proctor (*astonished*)   Why, she's mad.

Elizabeth   I would to God she were. There be fourteen people in the jail now, she says. (**Proctor** *simply looks at her, unable to grasp it.*) And they'll be tried, and the court have power to hang them too, she says.

Proctor (*scoffing, but without conviction*)   Ah, they'd never hang—

Elizabeth   The Deputy Governor promise hangin' if they'll not confess, John. The town's gone wild, I think. She speak of Abigail, and I thought she were a saint, to hear her. Abigail brings the other girls into the court, and where she walks the crowd will part like the sea for Israel. And folks are brought before them, and if they scream and howl and fall to the floor—the person's clapped in the jail for bewitchin' them.

Proctor (*wide-eyed*)   Oh, it is a black mischief.

Elizabeth   I think you must go to Salem, John. (*He turns to her.*) I think so. You must tell them it is a fraud.

Proctor (*thinkin beyond this*)   Aye, it is, it is surely.

Elizabeth   Let you go to Ezekiel Cheever—he knows you well. And tell him what she said to you last week in her uncle's house. She said it had naught to do with witchcraft, did she not?

Proctor (*in thought*)   Aye, she did, she did. (*Now, a pause.*)

Elizabeth (*quietly, fearing to anger him by prodding*)   God forbid you keep that from the court, John. I think they must be told.

Proctor (*quietly, struggling with his thought*)   Aye, they must, they must. It is a wonder they do believe her.

Elizabeth   I would go to Salem now, John—let you go tonight.

Proctor   I'll think on it.

Elizabeth (*with her courage now*)   You cannot keep it, John.

Proctor (*angering*)   I know I cannot keep it. I say I will think on it!

Elizabeth (*hurt, and very coldly*)   Good, then, let you think on it. (*She stands and starts to walk out of the room.*)

Proctor   I am only wondering how I may prove what she told me, Elizabeth. If the girl's a saint now, I think it is not easy to prove she's fraud, and the town gone so silly. She told it to me in a room alone—I have no proof for it.

Elizabeth   You were alone with her?

Proctor (*stubbornly*)   For a moment alone, aye.

Elizabeth   Why, then, it is not as you told me.

Proctor (*his anger rising*)   For a moment, I say. The others come in soon after.

Elizabeth (*quietly—she has suddenly lost all faith in him*)   Do as you wish, then. (*She starts to turn.*)

Proctor   Woman. (*She turns to him.*) I'll not have your suspicion any more.

Elizabeth (*a little loftily*)   *I* have no—

Proctor   I'll not have it!

Elizabeth   Then let you not earn it.

Proctor (*with a violent undertone*)   You doubt me yet?

Elizabeth (*with a smile, to keep her dignity*)   John, if it were not Abigail that you must go to hurt, would you falter now? I think not.

Proctor   Now look you—

Elizabeth   I see what I see, John.

Proctor (*with solemn warning*)   You will not judge me more, Elizabeth. I have good reason to think before I charge fraud on Abigail, and I will think on it. Let you look to your own improvement before you go to judge your husband any more. I have forgot Abigail, and—

Elizabeth   And I.

Proctor   Spare me! You forget nothin' and forgive nothin'. Learn charity, woman. I have gone tiptoe in this house all seven month since she is gone. I have not moved from there to there without I think to please you, and still an everlasting funeral marches round your heart. I cannot speak but I am doubted, every moment judged for lies, as though I come into a court when I come into this house!

Elizabeth   John, you are not open with me. You saw her with a crowd, you said. Now you—

Proctor   I'll plead my honesty no more, Elizabeth.

Elizabeth (*now she would justify herself*)   John, I am only—

Proctor   No more! I should have roared you down when first you told me your suspicion. But I wilted, and, like a Christian, I confessed. Confessed! Some dream I had must have mistaken you for God that day. But you're not, you're not, and let you remember it! Let you look sometimes for the goodness in me, and judge me not.

Elizabeth   I do not judge you. The magistrate sits in your heart that judges you. I never thought you but a good man, John (*with a smile*) only somewhat bewildered.

Proctor (*laughing bitterly*)   Oh, Elizabeth, your justice would freeze beer! (*He turns suddenly toward a sound outside. He starts for the door as* **Mary Warren** *enters. As soon as he sees her, he goes directly to her and grabs her by her cloak, furious.*) How do you go to Salem when I forbid it? Do you mock me? (*Shaking her.*) I'll whip you if you dare leave this house again!

Strangely, she doesn't resist him, but hangs limply by his grip.

Mary Warren   I am sick, I am sick, Mr. Proctor. Pray, pray, hurt me not. (*Her strangeness throws him off, and her evident pallor and weakness. He frees her.*) My insides are all shuddery; I am in the proceedings all day, sir.

Proctor (*with draining anger—his curiosity is draining it*)   And what of these proceedings here? When will you proceed to keep this house, as you are paid nine pound a year to do—and my wife not wholly well?

As though to compensate, **Mary Warren** *goes to* **Elizabeth** *with a small rag doll.*

Mary Warren   I made a gift for you today, Goody Proctor. I had to sit long hours in a chair, and passed the time with sewing.

Elizabeth (*perplexed, looking at the doll*)   Why, thank you, it's a fair poppet.

Mary Warren (*with a trembling, decayed voice*)   We must all love each other now, Goody Proctor.

Elizabeth (*amazed at her strangeness*)   Aye, indeed we must.

Mary Warren (*glancing at the room*)   I'll get up early in the morning and clean the house. I must sleep now. (*She turns and starts off.*)

Proctor   Mary. (*She halts.*) Is it true? There be fourteen women arrested?

Mary Warren   No, sir. There be thirty-nine now—(*She suddenly breaks off and sobs and sits down, exhausted.*)

Elizabeth   Why, she's weepin'! What ails you, child?

Mary Warren   Goody Osburn—will hang!

There is a shocked pause, while she sobs.

Proctor   Hang! (*He calls into her face.*) Hang, y'say?

Mary Warren (*through her weeping*)   Aye.

Proctor   The Deputy Governor will permit it?

Mary Warren   He sentenced her. He must. (*To ameliorate it:*) But not Sarah Good. For Sarah Good confessed, y'see.

Proctor   Confessed! To what?

Mary Warren   That she (*in horror at the memory*) she sometimes made a compact with Lucifer, and wrote her name in his black book—with her blood—and bound herself to torment Christians till God's thrown down—and we all must worship Hell forevermore.

Pause.

Proctor   But—surely you know what a jabberer she is. Did you tell them that?

Mary Warren   Mr. Proctor, in open court she near to choked us all to death.

Proctor   How, choked you?

Mary Warren   She sent her spirit out.

Elizabeth   Oh, Mary, Mary, surely you—

Mary Warren (*with an indignant edge*)   She tried to kill me many times, Goody Proctor!

Elizabeth   Why, I never heard you mention that before.

Mary Warren   I never knew it before. I never knew anything before. When she come into the court I say to myself, I must not accuse this woman, for she sleep in ditches, and so very old and poor. But then—then she sit there, denying and denying, and I feel a misty coldness climbin' up my back, and the skin on my skull begin to creep, and I feel a clamp around my neck and I cannot breathe air; and then (*entranced*) I hear a voice, a screamin' voice, and it were my voice—and all at once I remembered everything she done to me!

Proctor   Why? What did she do to you?

Mary Warren (*like one awakened to a marvelous secret insight*)   So many time, Mr. Proctor, she come to this very door, beggin' bread and a cup of cider—and mark this: whenever I turned her away empty, she *mumbled*.

Elizabeth   Mumbled! She may mumble if she's hungry.

Mary Warren   But *what* does she mumble? You must remember, Goody Proctor. Last month—a Monday, I think—she walked away, and I thought my guts would burst for two days after. Do you remember it?

Elizabeth   Why—I do, I think, but—

Mary Warren   And so I told that to Judge Hathorne, and he asks her so. "Goody Osburn," says he, "what curse do you mumble that this girl must fall sick after turning you away?" And then she replies (*mimicking an old crone*) "Why, your excellence, no curse at all. I only say my commandments; I hope I may say my commandments," says she!

Elizabeth   And that's an upright answer.

Mary Warren   Aye, but then Judge Hathorne say, "Recite for us your commandments!" (*leaning avidly toward them*) and of all the ten she could not say a single one. She never knew no commandments, and they had her in a flat lie!

Proctor   And so condemned her?

Mary Warren (*now a little strained, seeing his stubborn doubt*)   Why, they must when she condemned herself.

Proctor   But the proof, the proof!

Mary Warren (*with greater impatience with him*)   I told you the proof. It's hard proof, hard as rock, the judges said.

Proctor (*pauses an instant, then*)   You will not go to court again, Mary Warren.

Mary Warren   I must tell you, sir, I will be gone every day now. I am amazed you do not see what weighty work we do.

Proctor   What work you do! It's strange work for a Christian girl to hang old women!

Mary Warren   But, Mr. Proctor, they will not hang them if they confess. Sarah Good will only sit in jail some time (*recalling*) and here's a wonder for you; think on this. Goody Good is pregnant!

Elizabeth   Pregnant! Are they mad? The woman's near to sixty!

Mary Warren   They had Doctor Griggs examine her, and she's full to the brim. And smokin' a pipe all these years, and no husband either! But she's safe, thank God, for they'll not hurt the innocent child. But be that not a marvel? You must see it, sir, it's God's work we do. So I'll be gone every day for some time. I'm—I am an official of the court, they say, and I—(*She has been edging toward offstage.*)

Proctor   I'll official you! (*He strides to the mantel, takes down the whip hanging there.*)

Mary Warren (*terrified, but coming erect, striving for her authority*)   I'll not stand whipping any more!

Elizabeth (*hurriedly, as* **Proctor** *approaches*)   Mary, promise now you'll stay at home—

Mary Warren (*backing from him, but keeping her erect posture, striving, striving for her way*)   The Devil's loose in Salem, Mr. Proctor; we must discover where he's hiding!

Proctor   I'll whip the Devil out of you! (*With whip raised he reaches out for her, and she streaks away and yells.*)

Mary Warren (*pointing at* **Elizabeth**)   I saved her life today!

Silence. His whip comes down.

Elizabeth (*softly*)   I am accused?

Mary Warren (*quaking*)   Somewhat mentioned. But I said I never see no sign you ever sent your spirit out to hurt no one, and seeing I do live so closely with you, they dismissed it.

Elizabeth   Who accused me?

Mary Warren   I am bound by law, I cannot tell it. (*To* **Proctor**:) I only hope you'll not be so sarcastical no more. Four judges and the King's deputy sat to dinner with us but an hour ago. I—I would have you speak civilly to me, from this out.

Proctor (*in horror, muttering in disgust at her*)   Go to bed.

Mary Warren (*with a stamp of her foot*)   I'll not be ordered to bed no more, Mr. Proctor! I am eighteen and a woman, however single!

Proctor   Do you wish to sit up? Then sit up.

Mary Warren   I wish to go to bed!

Proctor (*in anger*)   Good night, then!

Mary Warren   Good night. (*Dissatisfied, uncertain of herself, she goes out. Wide-eyed, both,* **Proctor** *and* **Elizabeth** *stand staring.*)

Elizabeth (*quietly*)   Oh, the noose, the noose is up!

Proctor   There'll be no noose.

Elizabeth   She wants me dead. I knew all week it would come to this!

Proctor (*without conviction*)   They dismissed it. You heard her say—

Elizabeth   And what of tomorrow? She will cry me out until they take me!

Proctor   Sit you down.

Elizabeth   She wants me dead, John, you know it!

Proctor   I say sit down! (*She sits, trembling. He speaks quietly, trying to keep his wits.*) Now we must be wise, Elizabeth.

Elizabeth (*with sarcasm, and a sense of being lost*)   Oh, indeed. indeed!

Proctor   Fear nothing. I'll find Ezekiel Cheever. I'll tell him she said it were all sport.

Elizabeth   John, with so many in the jail, more than Cheever's help is needed now, I think. Would you favor me with this? Go to Abigail.

Proctor (*his soul hardening as he senses . . .*)   What have I to say to Abigail?

Elizabeth (*delicately*)   John—grant me this. You have a faulty understanding of young girls. There is a promise made in any bed—

Proctor (*striving against his anger*)   What promise!

Elizabeth   Spoke or silent, a promise is surely made. And she may dote on it now—I am sure she does—and thinks to kill me, then to take my place.

Proctor *'s anger is rising; he cannot speak.*

Elizabeth   It is her dearest hope, John, I know it. There be a thousand names; why does she call mine? There be a certain danger in calling such a name—I am no Goody Good that sleeps in ditches, nor Osburn, drunk and half-witted. She'd dare not call out such a farmer's wife but there be monstrous profit in it. She thinks to take my place, John.

Proctor   She cannot think it! (*He knows it is true.*)

Elizabeth (*"reasonably"*)   John, have you ever shown her somewhat of contempt? She cannot pass you in the church but you will blush—

Proctor   I may blush for my sin.

Elizabeth   I think she sees another meaning in that blush.

Proctor   And what see you? What see you, Elizabeth?

Elizabeth (*"conceding"*)   I think you be somewhat ashamed, for I am there, and she so close.

Proctor   When will you know me, woman? Were I stone I would have cracked for shame this seven month!

Elizabeth   Then go and tell her she's a whore. Whatever promise she may sense—break it, John, break it.

Proctor (*between his teeth*)   Good, then. I'll go. (*He starts for his rifle.*)

Elizabeth (*trembling, fearfully*)   Oh, how unwillingly!

Proctor (*turning on her, rifle in hand*)   I will curse her hotter than the oldest cinder in hell. But pray, begrudge me not my anger!

Elizabeth   Your anger! I only ask you—

Proctor   Woman, am I so base? Do you truly think me base?

Elizabeth   I never called you base.

Proctor   Then how do you charge me with such a promise? The promise that a stallion gives a mare I gave that girl!

Elizabeth   Then why do you anger with me when I bid you break it?

Proctor   Because it speaks deceit, and I am honest! But I'll plead no more! I see now your spirit twists around the single error of my life, and I will never tear it free!

Elizabeth (*crying out*)   You'll tear it free—when you come to know that I will be your only wife, or no wife at all! She has an arrow in you yet, John Proctor, and you know it well!

Quite suddenly, as though from the air, a figure appears in the doorway. They start slightly. It is **Mr. Hale**. *He is different now—drawn a little, and there is a quality of deference, even of guilt, about his manner now.*

Hale   Good evening.

Proctor (*still in his shock*)   Why, Mr. Hale! Good evening to you, sir. Come in, come in.

Hale (*to* **Elizabeth**)   I hope I do not startle you.

Elizabeth   No, no, it's only that I heard no horse—

Hale   You are Goodwife Proctor.

Proctor   Aye; Elizabeth.

Hale (*nods, then*)   I hope you're not off to bed yet.

Proctor (*setting down his gun*)   No, no. (**Hale** *comes further into the room. And* **Proctor**, *to explain his nervousness:*) We are not used to visitors after dark, but you're welcome here. Will you sit you down, sir?

Hale   I will. (*He sits.*) Let you sit, Goodwife Proctor.

She does, never letting him out of her sight. There is a pause as **Hale** *looks about the room.*

Proctor (*to break the silence*)   Will you drink cider, Mr. Hale?

Hale   No, it rebels my stomach; I have some further traveling yet tonight. Sit you down, sir. (**Proctor** *sits.*) I will not keep you long, but I have some business with you.

Proctor   Business of the court?

Hale   No—no, I come of my own, without the court's authority. Hear me. (*He wets his lips.*) I know not if you are aware, but your wife's name is—mentioned in the court.

Proctor   We know it, sir. Our Mary Warren told us. We are entirely amazed.

Hale   I am a stranger here, as you know. And in my ignorance I find it hard to draw a clear opinion of them that come accused before the court. And so this afternoon, and now tonight, I go from house to house—I come now from Rebecca Nurse's house and—

Elizabeth (*shocked*)   Rebecca's charged!

Hale   God forbid such a one be charged. She is, however—mentioned somewhat.

Elizabeth (*with an attempt at a laugh*)   You will never believe, I hope, that Rebecca trafficked with the Devil.

Hale   Woman, it is possible.

Proctor (*taken aback*)   Surely you cannot think so.

Hale   This is a strange time, Mister. No man may longer doubt the powers of the dark are gathered in monstrous attack upon this village. There is too much evidence now to deny it. You will agree, sir?

Proctor (*evading*)   I—have no knowledge in that line. But it's hard to think so pious a woman be secretly a Devil's bitch after seventy year of such good prayer.

Hale   Aye. But the Devil is a wily one, you cannot deny it. However, she is far from accused, and I know she will not be. (*Pause.*) I thought, sir, to put some questions as to the Christian character of this house, if you'll permit me.

Proctor (*coldly, resentful*)   Why, we—have no fear of questions, sir.

Hale   Good, then. (*He makes himself more comfortable.*) In the book of record that Mr. Parris keeps, I note that you are rarely in the church on Sabbath Day.

Proctor   No, sir, you are mistaken.

Hale   Twenty-six time in seventeen month, sir. I must call that rare. Will you tell me why you are so absent?

Proctor   Mr. Hale, I never knew I must account to that man for I come to church or stay at home. My wife were sick this winter.

Hale   So I am told. But you, Mister, why could you not come alone?

Proctor   I surely did come when I could, and when I could not I prayed in this house.

Hale   Mr. Proctor, your house is not a church; your theology must tell you that.

Proctor   It does, sir, it does; and it tells me that a minister may pray to God without he have golden candlesticks upon the altar.

Hale   What golden candlesticks?

Proctor   Since we built the church there were pewter candlesticks upon the altar; Francis Nurse made them, y'know, and a sweeter hand never touched the metal. But Parris came, and for twenty week he preach nothin' but golden candlesticks until he had them. I labor the earth from dawn of day to blink of night, and I tell you true, when I look to heaven and see my money glaring at his elbows—it hurt my prayer, sir, it hurt my prayer. I think, sometimes, the man dreams cathedrals, not clapboard meetin' houses.

Hale (*thinks, then*)   And yet, Mister, a Christian on Sabbath Day must be in church. (*Pause.*) Tell me—you have three children?

Proctor   Aye. Boys.

Hale   How comes it that only two are baptized?

Proctor (*starts to speak, then stops, then, as though unable to restrain this*)   I like it not that Mr. Parris should lay his hand upon my baby. I see no light of God in that man. I'll not conceal it.

Hale   I must say it, Mr. Proctor; that is not for you to decide. The man's ordained, therefore the light of God is in him.

Proctor (*flushed with resentment but trying to smile*)   What's your suspicion, Mr. Hale?

Hale   No, no, I have no—

Proctor   I nailed the roof upon the church, I hung the door—

Hale   Oh, did you! That's a good sign, then.

Proctor   It may be I have been too quick to bring the man to book, but you cannot think we ever desired the destruction of religion. I think that's in your mind, is it not?

Hale (*not altogether giving way*)   I—have—there is a softness in your record, sir, a softness.

Elizabeth   I think, maybe, we have been too hard with Mr. Parris. I think so. But sure we never loved the Devil here.

Hale (*nods, deliberating this. Then, with the voice of one administering a secret test*)   Do you know your Commandments, Elizabeth?

Elizabeth (*without hesitation, even eagerly*)   I surely do. There be no mark of blame upon my life, Mr. Hale. I am a convenanted Christian woman.

Hale   And you, Mister?

Proctor (*a trifle unsteadily*)   I—am sure I do, sir.

Hale (*glances at her open face, then at **John**, then*)   Let you repeat them, if you will.

Proctor   The Commandments.

Hale   Aye.

Proctor (*looking off, beginning to sweat*)   Thou shalt not kill.

Hale   Aye.

Proctor (*counting on his fingers*)   Thou shalt not steal. Thou shalt not covet thy neighbor's goods, nor make unto thee any graven image. Thou shalt not take the name of the Lord in vain; thou shalt have no other gods before me. (*With some hesitation:*) Thou shalt remember the Sabbath Day and keep it holy. (*Pause. Then:*) Thou shalt honor thy father and mother. Thou shalt not bear false witness. (*He is stuck. He counts back on his fingers, knowing one is missing.*) Thou shalt not make unto thee any graven image.

Hale   You have said that twice, sir.

Proctor (*lost*)   Aye. (*He is flailing for it.*)

Elizabeth (*delicately*)   *Adultery*, John.

Proctor (*as though a secret arrow had pained his heart*)   Aye. (*Trying to grin it away—to* **Hale**:) You see, sir, between the two of us we do know them all. (**Hale** *only looks at* **Proctor**, *deep in his attempt to define this man.* **Proctor** *grows more uneasy.*) I think it be a small fault.

Hale   Theology, sir, is a fortress; no crack in a fortress may be accounted small. (*He rises; he seems worried now. He paces a little, in deep thought.*)

Proctor   There be no love for Satan in this house, Mister.

Hale   I pray it, I pray it dearly. (*He looks to both of them, an attempt at a smile on his face, but his misgivings are clear.*) Well, then—I'll bid you good night.

Elizabeth (*unable to restrain herself*)   Mr. Hale. (*He turns.*) I do think you are suspecting me somewhat? Are you not?

Hale (*obviously disturbed—and evasive*)   Goody Proctor, I do not judge you. My duty is to add what I may to the godly wisdom of the court. I pray you both good health and good fortune. (*To* **John**:) Good night, sir. (*He starts out.*)

Elizabeth (*with a note of desperation*)   I think you must tell him, John.

Hale   What's that?

Elizabeth (*restraining a call*)   Will you tell him?

Slight pause. **Hale** *looks questioningly at* **John**.

Proctor (*with difficulty*)   I—I have no witness and cannot prove it, except my word be taken. But I know the children's sickness had naught to do with witchcraft.

Hale (*stopped, struck*)   Naught to do—?

Proctor   Mr. Parris discovered them sportin' in the woods. They were startled and took sick.

Pause.

Hale   Who told you this?

Proctor (*hesitates, then*)   Abigail Williams.

Hale   Abigail!

Proctor   Aye.

Hale (*his eyes wide*)   Abigail Williams told you it had naught to do with witchcraft!

Proctor   She told me the day you came, sir.

Hale (*suspiciously*)   Why—why did you keep this?

Proctor   I never knew until tonight that the world is gone daft with this nonsense.

Hale   Nonsense! Mister, I have myself examined Tituba, Sarah Good, and numerous others that have confessed to dealing with the Devil. They have *confessed* it.

Proctor   And why not, if they must hang for denyin' it? There are them that will swear to anything before they'll hang; have you never thought of that?

Hale   I have. I—I have indeed. (*It is his own suspicion, but he resists it. He glances at* **Elizabeth**, *then at* **John**.) And you—would you testify to this in court?

Proctor   I—had not reckoned with goin' into court. But if I must I will.

Hale   Do you falter here?

Proctor   I falter nothing, but I may wonder if my story will be credited in such a court. I do wonder on it, when such a steady-minded minister as you will suspicion such a woman that never lied, and cannot, and the world knows she cannot! I may falter somewhat, Mister; I am no fool.

Hale (*quietly—it has impressed him*)   Proctor, let you open with me now, for I have a rumor that troubles me. It's said you hold no belief that there may even be witches in the world. Is that true, sir?

Proctor (*he knows this is critical, and is striving against his disgust with* **Hale** *and with himself for even answering*)   I know not what I have said, I may have said it. I have wondered if there be witches in the world—although I cannot believe they come among us now.

Hale   Then you do not believe—

Proctor   I have no knowledge of it; the Bible speaks of witches, and I will not deny them.

Hale   And you, woman?

Elizabeth   I—I cannot believe it.

Hale (*shocked*)   You cannot!

Proctor   Elizabeth, you bewilder him!

Elizabeth (*to* **Hale**)   I cannot think the Devil may own a woman's soul, Mr. Hale, when she keeps an upright way, as I have. I am a good woman, I know it; and if you believe I may do only good work in the world, and yet be secretly bound to Satan, then I must tell you, sir, I do not believe it.

Hale   But, woman, you do believe there are witches in—

Elizabeth   If you think that I am one, then I say there are none.

Hale   You surely do not fly against the Gospel, the Gospel—

Proctor   She believe in the Gospel, every word!

Elizabeth   Question Abigail Williams about the Gospel, not myself!

Hale *stares at her.*

Proctor   She do not mean to doubt the Gospel, sir, you cannot think it. This be a Christian house, sir, a Christian house.

Hale   God keep you both; let the third child be quickly baptized, and go you without fail each Sunday in to Sabbath prayer; and keep a solemn, quiet way among you. I think—

Giles Corey *appears in doorway.*

Giles   John!

Proctor   Giles! What's the matter?

Giles   They take my wife.

Francis Nurse *enters.*

Giles   And his Rebecca!

Proctor (*to* **Francis**)   Rebecca's in the *jail*!

Francis   Aye, Cheever come and take her in his wagon. We've only now come from the jail, and they'll not even let us in to see them.

Elizabeth   They've surely gone wild now, Mr. Hale!

Francis (*going to* **Hale**)   Reverend Hale! Can you not speak to the Deputy Governor? I'm sure he mistakes these people—

Hale   Pray calm yourself, Mr. Nurse.

Francis   My wife is the very brick and mortar of the church, Mr. Hale (*indicating* **Giles**) and Martha Corey, there cannot be a woman closer yet to God than Martha.

Hale   How is Rebecca charged, Mr. Nurse?

Francis (*with a mocking, half-hearted laugh*).   For murder, she's charged! (*Mockingly quoting the warrant:*) "For the marvelous and supernatural murder of Goody Putnam's babies." What am I to do, Mr. Hale?

Hale (*turns from* **Francis***, deeply troubled, then*)   Believe me, Mr. Nurse, if Rebecca Nurse be tainted, then nothing's left to stop the whole green world from burning. Let you rest upon the justice of the court; the court will send her home, I know it.

Francis   You cannot mean she will be tried in court!

Hale (*pleading*)   Nurse, though our hearts break, we cannot flinch; these are new times, sir. There is a misty plot afoot so subtle we should be criminal to cling to old respects and ancient friendships. I have seen too many frightful proofs in court—the Devil is alive in Salem, and we dare not quail to follow wherever the accusing finger points!

Proctor (*angered*)   How may such a woman murder children?

Hale (*in great pain*)   Man, remember, until an hour before the Devil fell, God thought him beautiful in Heaven.

Giles   I never said my wife were a witch, Mr. Hale; I only said she were reading books!

Hale   Mr. Corey, exactly what complaint were made on your wife?

Giles   That bloody mongrel Walcott charge her. Y'see, he buy a pig of my wife four or five year ago, and the pig died soon after. So he come dancin' in for his money back. So my Martha, she says to him, "Walcott, If you haven't the wit to feed a pig properly, you'll not live to own many," she says. Now he goes to court and claims that from that day to this he cannot keep a pig alive for more than four weeks because my Martha bewitch them with her books!

Enter **Ezekiel Cheever**. *A shocked silence.*

Cheever   Good evening to you, Proctor.

Proctor   Why, Mr. Cheever. Good evening.

Cheever   Good evening, all. Good evening, Mr. Hale.

Proctor   I hope you come not on business of the court.

Cheever   I do, Proctor, aye. I am clerk of the court now, y'know.

Enter **Marshal Herrick**, *a man in his early thirties, who is somewhat shamefaced at the moment.*

Giles   It's a pity, Ezekiel, that an honest tailor might have gone to Heaven must burn in Hell. You'll burn for this, do you know it?

Cheever   You know yourself I must do as I'm told. You surely know that, Giles. And I'd as lief you'd not be sending me to Hell. I like not the sound of it, I tell you; I like not the sound of it. (*He fears* **Proctor**, *but starts to reach inside his coat.*) Now believe me, Proctor, how heavy be the law, all its tonnage I do carry on my back tonight. (*He takes out a warrant.*) I have a warrant for your wife.

Proctor (*to* **Hale**)   You said she were not charged!

Hale   I know nothin' of it. (*To* **Cheever***:*) When were she charged?

Cheever   I am given sixteen warrant tonight, sir, and she is one.

Proctor   Who charged her?

Cheever   Why, Abigail Williams charge her.

Proctor   On what proof, what proof?

Cheever (*looking about the room*)   Mr. Proctor, I have little time. The court bid me search your house, but I like not to search a house. So will you hand me any poppets that your wife may keep here?

Proctor   Poppets?

Elizabeth   I never kept no poppets, not since I were a girl.

Cheever (*embarrassed, glancing toward the mantel where sits* **Mary Warren***'s poppet*)   I spy a poppet, Goody Proctor.

Elizabeth   Oh! (*Going for it:*) Why, this is Mary's.

Cheever (*shyly*)   Would you please to give it to me?

Elizabeth (*handing it to him, asks* **Hale**)   Has the court discovered a text in poppets now?

Cheever (*carefully holding the poppet*)   Do you keep any others in this house?

Proctor   No, nor this one either till tonight. What signifies a poppet?

Cheever   Why, a poppet (*he gingerly turns the poppet over*) a poppet may signify—Now, woman, will you please to come with me?

Proctor   She will not! (*To* **Elizabeth***:*) Fetch Mary here.

Cheever (*ineptly reaching toward* **Elizabeth**)   No, no, I am forbid to leave her from my sight.

Proctor (*pushing his arm away*)   You'll leave her out of sight and out of mind, Mister. Fetch Mary, Elizabeth. (**Elizabeth** *goes upstairs.*)

Hale   What signifies a poppet, Mr. Cheever?

Cheever (*turning the poppet over in his hands*)   Why, they say it may signify that she—(*He has lifted the poppet's skirt, and his eyes widen in astonished fear.*) Why, this, this—

Proctor (*reaching for the poppet*)   What's there?

Cheever   Why (*he draws out a long needle from the poppet*) it is a needle! Herrick, Herrick, it is a needle!

Herrick *comes toward him.*

Proctor (*angrily, bewildered*)   And what signifies a needle!

Cheever (*his hands shaking*)   Why, this go hard with her, Proctor, this—I had my doubts, Proctor, I had my doubts, but here's calamity. (*To* **Hale***, showing the needle:*) You see it, sir, it is a needle!

Hale   Why? What meanin' has it?

Cheever (*wide-eyed, trembling*)   The girl, the Williams girl, Abigail Williams, sir. She sat to dinner in Reverend Parris's house tonight, and without word nor warnin' she falls to the floor. Like a struck beast, he says, and screamed a scream that a bull would weep to hear. And he goes to save her, and, stuck two inches in the flesh of her belly, he draw a needle out. And demandin' of her how she come to be so stabbed, she (*to* **Proctor** *now*) testify it were your wife's familiar spirit pushed it in.

Proctor   Why, she done it herself! (*To* **Hale***:*) I hope you're not takin' this for proof, Mister!

Hale*, struck by the proof, is silent.*

Cheever   'Tis hard proof! (*To* **Hale***:*) I find here a poppet Goody Proctor keeps. I have found it, sir. And in the belly of the poppet a needle's stuck. I tell you true, Proctor, I never warranted to see such proof of Hell, and I bid you obstruct me not, for I—

Enter **Elizabeth** *with* **Mary Warren***.* **Proctor***, seeing* **Mary Warren***, draws her by the arm to* **Hale***.*

Proctor   Here now! Mary, how did this poppet come into my house?

Mary Warren (*frightened for herself, her voice very small*)   What poppet's that, sir?

Proctor (*impatiently, pointing at the doll in* **Cheever** *'s hand*)   This poppet, this poppet.

Mary Warren (*evasively, looking at it*)   Why, I—I think it is mine.

Proctor   It is your poppet, is it not?

Mary Warren (*not understanding the direction of this*)   It—is, sir.

Proctor   And how did it come into this house?

Mary Warren (*glancing about at the avid faces*)   Why—I made it in the court, sir, and—give it to Goody Proctor tonight.

Proctor (*to* **Hale***:*)   Now, sir—do you have it?

Hale   Mary Warren, a needle have been found inside this poppet.

Mary Warren (*bewildered*)   Why, I meant no harm by it, sir.

Proctor (*quickly*)   You stuck that needle in yourself?

Mary Warren   I—I believe I did, sir, I—

Proctor (*to* **Hale**)   What say you now?

Hale (*watching* **Mary Warren** *closely*)   Child, you are certain this be your natural memory? May it be, perhaps, that someone conjures you even now to say this?

Mary Warren   Conjures me? Why, no, sir, I am entirely myself, I think. Let you ask Susanna Walcott—she saw me sewin' it in court. (*Or better still:*) Ask Abby, Abby sat beside me when I made it.

Proctor (*to* **Hale***, of* **Cheever**)   Bid him begone. Your mind is surely settled now. Bid him out, Mr. Hale.

Elizabeth   What signifies a needle?

Hale   Mary—you charge a cold and cruel murder on Abigail.

Mary Warren   Murder! I charge no—

Hale   Abigail were stabbed tonight; a needle were found stuck into her belly—

Elizabeth   And she charges me?

Hale   Aye.

Elizabeth (*her breath knocked out*)   Why—! The girl is murder! She must be ripped out of the world!

Cheever (*pointing at* **Elizabeth**)   You've heard that, sir! Ripped out of the world! Herrick, you heard it!

Proctor (*suddenly snatching the warrant out of* **Cheever**'s *hands*)   Out with you.

Cheever   Proctor, you dare not touch the warrant.

Proctor (*ripping the warrant*)   Out with you!

Cheever   You've ripped the Deputy Governor's warrant, man!

Proctor   Damn the Deputy Governor! Out of my house!

Hale   Now, Proctor, Proctor!

Proctor   Get y'gone with them! You are a broken minister.

Hale   Proctor, if she is innocent, the court—

Proctor   If *she* is innocent! Why do you never wonder if Parris be innocent, or Abigail? Is the accuser always holy now? Were they born this morning as clean as God's fingers? I'll tell you what's walking Salem—vengeance is walking Salem. We are what we always were in Salem, but now the little crazy children are jangling the keys of the kingdom, and common vengeance writes the law! This warrant's vengeance! I'll not give my wife to vengeance!

Elizabeth   I'll go, John—

Proctor   You will not go!

Herrick   I have nine men outside. You cannot keep her. The law binds me, John, I cannot budge.

Proctor (*to* **Hale**, *ready to break him*)   Will you see her taken?

Hale   Proctor, the court is just—

Proctor   Pontius Pilate! God will not let you wash your hands of this!

Elizabeth   John—I think I must go with them. (*He cannot bear to look at her.*) Mary, there is bread enough for the morning; you will bake, in the afternoon. Help Mr. Proctor as you were his daughter—you owe me that, and much more. (*She is fighting her weeping. To* **Proctor**:) When the children wake, speak nothing of witchcraft—it will frighten them. (*She cannot go on.*)

Proctor   I will bring you home. I will bring you soon.

Elizabeth   Oh, John, bring me soon!

Proctor   I will fall like an ocean on that court! Fear nothing, Elizabeth.

Elizabeth (*with great fear*)   I will fear nothing. (*She looks about the room, as though to fix it in her mind.*) Tell the children I have gone to visit someone sick.

She walks out the door, **Herrick** *and* **Cheever** *behind her. For a moment,* **Proctor** *watches from the doorway. The clank of chain is heard.*

Proctor   Herrick! Herrick, don't chain her! (*He rushes out the door. From outside:*) Damn you, man, you will not chain her! Off with them! I'll not have it! I will not have her chained!

There are other men's voices against his. **Hale***, in a fever of guilt and uncertainty, turns from the door to avoid the sight;* **Mary Warren** *bursts into tears and sits weeping.* **Giles Corey** *calls to* **Hale***.*

Giles   And yet silent, minister? It is fraud, you know it is fraud! What keeps you, man?

Proctor *is half braced, half pushed into the room by two deputies and* **Herrick***.*

Proctor   I'll pay you, Herrick, I will surely pay you!

Herrick (*panting*)   In God's name, John, I cannot help myself. I must chain them all. Now let you keep inside this house till I am gone! (*He goes out with his deputies.*)

Proctor *stands there, gulping air. Horses and a wagon creaking are heard.*

Hale (*in great uncertainty*)   Mr. Proctor—

Proctor   Out of my sight!

Hale   Charity, Proctor, charity. What I have heard in her favor, I will not fear to testify in court. God help me, I cannot judge her guilty or innocent—I know not. Only this consider: the world goes mad, and it profit nothing you should lay the cause to the vengeance of a little girl.

Proctor   You are a coward! Though you be ordained in God's own tears, you are a coward now!

Hale   Proctor, I cannot think God be provoked so grandly by such a petty cause. The jails are packed—our greatest judges sit in Salem now—and hangin's promised. Man, we must look to cause proportionate. Were there murder done, perhaps, and never brought to light? Abomination? Some secret blasphemy that stinks to Heaven? Think on cause, man, and let you help me to discover it. For there's your way, believe it, there is your only way, when such confusion strikes upon the world. (*He goes to* **Giles** *and* **Francis**.) Let you counsel among yourselves; think on your village and what may have drawn from heaven such thundering wrath upon you all. I shall pray God open up our eyes.

Hale *goes out.*

Francis (*struck by* **Hale**'*s mood*)   I never heard no murder done in Salem.

Proctor (*he has been reached by* **Hale**'*s words*)   Leave me, Francis, leave me.

Giles (*shaken*)   John—tell me, are we lost?

Proctor   Go home now, Giles. We'll speak on it tomorrow.

Giles   Let you think on it. We'll come early, eh?

Proctor   Aye. Go now, Giles.

Giles   Good night, then.

Giles *goes out. After a moment:*

Mary Warren (*in a fearful squeak of a voice*)   Mr. Proctor, very likely they'll let her come home once they're given proper evidence.

Proctor   You're coming to the court with me, Mary. You will tell it in the court.

Mary Warren   I cannot charge murder on Abigail.

Proctor (*moving menacingly toward her*)   You will tell the court how that poppet come here and who stuck the needle in.

Mary Warren   She'll kill me for sayin' that! (**Proctor** *continues toward her*.) Abby'll charge lechery on you, Mr. Proctor!

Proctor (*halting*)   She's told you!

Mary Warren   I have known it, sir. She'll ruin you with it, I know she will.

Proctor (*hesitating, and with deep hatred of himself*)   Good. Then her saintliness is done with. (**Mary** *backs from him*.) We will slide together into our pit; you will tell the court what you know.

Mary Warren (*in terror*)   I cannot, they'll turn on me—

Proctor *strides and catches her, and she is repeating, "I cannot, I cannot!"*

Proctor   My wife will never die for me! I will bring your guts into your mouth but that goodness will not die for me!

Mary Warren (*struggling to escape him*)   I cannot do it, I cannot!

Proctor (*grasping her by the throat as though he would strangle her*)   Make your peace with it! Now Hell and Heaven grapple on our backs, and all our old pretense is ripped away—make your peace! (*He throws her to the floor, where she sobs, "I cannot, I cannot . . ." And now, half to himself, staring, and turning to the open door:*) Peace. It is a providence, and no great change; we are only what we always were, but naked now. (*He walks as though toward a great horror, facing the open sky.*) Aye, naked! And the wind, God's icy wind, will blow!

And she is over and over again sobbing, "I cannot, I cannot, I cannot."

Curtain.

Act Three

The vestry room of the Salem meeting house, now serving as the anteroom of the General Court.

As the curtain rises, the room is empty, but for sunlight pouring through two high windows in the back wall. The room is solemn, even forbidding. Heavy beams jut out, boards of random widths make up the walls. At the right are two doors leading into the meeting house proper, where the court is being held. At the left another door leads outside.

There is a plain bench at the left, and another at the right. In the center a rather long meeting table, with stools and a considerable armchair snugged up to it.

Through the partitioning wall at the right we hear a prosecutor's voice, **Judge Hathorne***'s, asking a question; then a woman's voice,* **Martha Corey***'s, replying.*

Hathorne's Voice   Now, Martha Corey, there is abundant evidence in our hands to show that you have given yourself to the reading of fortunes. Do you deny it?

Martha Corey's Voice   I am innocent to a witch. I know not what a witch is.

Hathorne's Voice   How do you know, then, that you are not a witch?

Martha Corey's Voice   If I were, I would know it.

Hathorne's Voice   Why do you hurt these children?

Martha Corey's Voice   I do not hurt them. I scorn it!

Giles' Voice (*roaring*)   I have evidence for the court!

Voices of townspeople rise in excitement.

Danforth's Voice   You will keep your seat!

Giles' Voice   Thomas Putnam is reaching out for land!

Danforth's Voice   Remove that man, Marshal!

Giles' Voice   You're hearing lies, lies!

A roaring goes up from the people.

Hathorne's Voice   Arrest him, excellency!

Giles' Voice   I have evidence. Why will you not hear my evidence?

The door opens and **Giles** *is half carried into the vestry room by* **Herrick**.

Giles   Hands off, damn you, let me go!

Herrick   Giles, Giles!

Giles   Out of my way, Herrick! I bring evidence—

Herrick   You cannot go in there, Giles; it's a court!

Enter **Hale** *from the court.*

Hale   Pray be calm a moment.

Giles   You, Mr. Hale, go in there and demand I speak.

Hale   A moment, sir, a moment.

Giles   They'll be hangin' my wife!

Judge Hathorne *enters. He is in his sixties, a bitter, remorseless Salem judge.*

Hathorne   How do you dare come roarin' into this court! Are you gone daft, Corey?

Giles   You're not a Boston judge yet, Hathorne. You'll not call me daft!

Enter **Deputy Governor Danforth** *and, behind him,* **Ezekiel Cheever** *and* **Parris**. *On his appearance, silence falls.* **Danforth** *is a grave man in his sixties, of some humor and sophistication that does not, however, interfere with an exact loyalty to his position and his cause. He comes down to* **Giles**, *who awaits his wrath.*

Danforth (*looking directly at* **Giles**)   Who is this man?

Parris   Giles Corey, sir, and a more contentious—

Giles (*to* **Parris**)   I am asked the question, and I am old enough to answer it! (*To* **Danforth**, *who impresses him and to whom he smiles through his strain:*) My name is Corey, sir, Giles Corey. I have six hundred acres, and timber in addition. It is my wife you be condemning now. (*He indicates the courtroom.*)

Danforth   And how do you imagine to help her cause with such contemptuous riot? Now be gone. Your old age alone keeps you out of jail for this.

Giles (*beginning to plead*)   They be tellin' lies about my wife, sir, I—

Danforth   Do you take it upon yourself to determine what this court shall believe and what it shall set aside?

Giles   Your Excellency, we mean no disrespect for—

Danforth   Disrespect indeed! It is disruption, Mister. This is the highest court of the supreme government of this province, do you know it?

Giles (*beginning to weep*)   Your Excellency, I only said she were readin' books, sir, and they come and take her out of my house for—

Danforth (*mystified*)   Books! What books?

Giles (*through helpless sobs*)   It is my third wife, sir; I never had no wife that be so taken with books, and I thought to find the cause of it, d'y'see, but it were no witch I blamed her for. (*He is openly weeping.*) I have broke charity with the woman, I have broke charity with her. (*He covers his face, ashamed.* **Danforth** *is respectfully silent.*)

Hale   Excellency, he claims hard evidence for his wife's defense. I think that in all justice you must—

Danforth   Then let him submit his evidence in proper affidavit. You are certainly aware of our procedure here, Mr. Hale. (*To* **Herrick**:) Clear this room.

Herrick   Come now, Giles. (*He gently pushes* **Corey** *out.*)

Francis   We are desperate, sir; we come here three days now and cannot be heard.

Danforth   Who is this man?

Francis   Francis Nurse, Your Excellency.

Hale   His wife's Rebecca that were condemned this morning.

Danforth   Indeed! I am amazed to find you in such uproar. I have only good report of your character, Mr. Nurse.

Hathorne   I think they must both be arrested in contempt, sir.

Danforth (*to* **Francis**)   Let you write your plea, and in due time I will—

Francis   Excellency, we have proof for your eyes; God forbid you shut them to it. The girls, sir, the girls are frauds.

Danforth   What's that?

Francis   We have proof of it, sir. They are all deceiving you.

Danforth *is shocked, but studying* **Francis**.

Hathorne   This is contempt, sir, contempt!

Danforth   Peace, Judge Hathorne. Do you know who I am, Mr. Nurse?

Francis   I surely do, sir, and I think you must be a wise judge to be what you are.

Danforth   And do you know that near to four hundred are in the jails from Marblehead to Lynn, and upon my signature?

Francis   I—

Danforth   And seventy-two condemned to hang by that signature?

Francis   Excellency, I never thought to say it to such a weighty judge, but you are deceived.

Enter **Giles Corey** *from left. All turn to see as he beckons in* **Mary Warren** *with* **Proctor**. **Mary** *is keeping her eyes to the ground;* **Proctor** *has her elbow as though she were near collapse.*

Parris (*on seeing her, in shock*)   Mary Warren! (*He goes directly to bend close to her face.*) What are you about here?

Proctor (*pressing* **Parris** *away from her with a gentle but firm motion of protectiveness*)   She would speak with the Deputy Governor.

Danforth (*shocked by this, turns to* **Herrick**)   Did you not tell me Mary Warren were sick in bed?

Herrick   She were, Your Honor. When I go to fetch her to the court last week, she said she were sick.

Giles   She has been strivin' with her soul all.week, Your Honor; she comes now to tell the truth of this to you.

Danforth   Who is this?

Proctor   John Proctor, sir. Elizabeth Proctor is my wife.

Parris   Beware this man, Your Excellency, this man is mischief.

Hale (*excitedly*)   I think you must hear the girl, sir, she—

Danforth (*who has become very interested in* **Mary** *and only raises a hand toward* **Hale**)   Peace. What would you tell us, Mary Warren?

Proctor *looks at her, but she cannot speak.*

Proctor   She never saw no spirits, sir.

Danforth (*with great alarm and surprise, to* **Mary**)   Never saw no spirits!

Giles (*eagerly*)   Never.

Proctor (*reaching into his jacket*)   She has signed a deposition, sir—

Danforth (*instantly*)   No, no, I accept no depositions. (*He is rapidly calculating this; he turns from her to* **Proctor**.) Tell me, Mr. Proctor, have you given out this story in the village?

Proctor   We have not.

Parris   They've come to overthrow the court, sir! This man is—

Danforth   I pray you, Mr. Parris. Do you know, Mr. Proctor, that the entire contention of the state in these trials is that the voice of Heaven is speaking through the children?

Proctor   I know that, sir.

Danforth (*thinks, staring at* **Proctor**, *then turns to* **Mary Warren**)   And you, Mary Warren, how came you to cry out people for sending their spirits against you?

Mary Warren   It were pretense, sir.

Danforth   I cannot hear you.

Proctor   It were pretense, she says.

Danforth   Ah? And the other girls? Susanna Walcott, and—the others? They are also pretending?

Mary Warren   Aye, sir.

Danforth (*wide-eyed*)   Indeed. (*Pause. He is baffled by this. He turns to study* **Proctor**'s *face.*)

Parris (*in a sweat*)   Excellency, you surely cannot think to let so vile a lie be spread in open court!

Danforth   Indeed not, but it strike hard upon me that she will dare come here with such a tale. Now, Mr. Proctor, before I decide whether I shall hear you or not, it is my duty to tell you this. We burn a hot fire here; it melts down all concealment.

Proctor   I know that, sir.

Danforth   Let me continue. I understand well, a husband's tenderness may drive him to extravagance in defense of a wife. Are you certain in your conscience, Mister, that your evidence is the truth?

Proctor   It is. And you will surely know it.

Danforth   And you thought to declare this revelation in the open court before the public?

Proctor   I thought I would, aye—with your permission.

Danforth (*his eyes narrowing*)   Now, sir, what is your purpose in so doing?

Proctor   Why, I—I would free my wife, sir.

Danforth   There lurks nowhere in your heart, nor hidden in your spirit, any desire to undermine this court?

Proctor (*with the faintest faltering*)   Why, no, sir.

Cheever (*clears his throat, awakening*)   I—Your Excellency.

Danforth   Mr. Cheever.

Cheever   I think it be my duty, sir—(*Kindly, to* **Proctor***:*) You'll not deny it, John. (*To* **Danforth***:*) When we come to take his wife, he damned the court and ripped your warrant.

Parris   Now you have it!

Danforth   He did that, Mr. Hale?

Hale (*takes a breath*)   Aye, he did.

Proctor   It were a temper, sir. I knew not what I did.

Danforth (*studying him*)   Mr. Proctor.

Proctor   Aye, sir.

Danforth (*straight into his eyes*)   Have you ever seen the Devil?

Proctor   No, sir.

Danforth   You are in all respects a Gospel Christian?

Proctor   I am, sir.

Parris   Such a Christian that will not come to church but once in a month!

Danforth (*restrained—he is curious*)   Not come to church?

Proctor   I—I have no love for Mr. Parris. It is no secret. But God I surely love.

Cheever   He plow on Sunday, sir.

Danforth   Plow on Sunday!

Cheever (*apologetically*)   I think it be evidence, John. I am an official of the court, I cannot keep it.

Proctor   I—I have once or twice plowed on Sunday. I have three children, sir, and until last year my land give little.

Giles   You'll find other Christians that do plow on Sunday if the truth be known.

Hale   Your Honor, I cannot think you may judge the man on such evidence.

Danforth   I judge nothing. (*Pause. He keeps watching* **Proctor***, who tries to meet his gaze*.) I tell you straight, Mister—I have seen marvels in this court. I have seen people choked before my eyes by spirits; I have seen them stuck by pins and slashed by daggers. I have until this moment not the slightest reason to suspect that the children may be deceiving me. Do you understand my meaning?

Proctor   Excellency, does it not strike upon you that so many of these women have lived so long with such upright reputation, and—

Parris   Do you read the Gospel, Mr. Proctor?

Proctor   I read the Gospel.

Parris   I think not, or you should surely know that Cain were an upright man, and yet he did kill Abel.

Proctor   Aye, God tells us that. (*To* **Danforth**:) But who tells us Rebecca Nurse murdered seven babies by sending out her spirit on them? It is the children only, and this one will swear she lied to you.

Danforth *considers, then beckons* **Hathorne** *to him.* **Hathorne** *leans in, and he speaks in his ear.* **Hathorne** *nods.*

Hathorne   Aye, she's the one.

Danforth   Mr. Proctor, this morning, your wife send me a claim in which she states that she is pregnant now.

Proctor   My wife pregnant!

Danforth   There be no sign of it—we have examined her body.

Proctor   But if she say she is pregnant, then she must be! That woman will never lie, Mr. Danforth.

Danforth   She will not?

Proctor   Never, sir, never.

Danforth   We have thought it too convenient to be credited. However, if I should tell you now that I will let her be kept another month; and if she begin to show her natural signs, you shall have her living yet another year until she is delivered—what say you to that? (**Proctor** *is struck silent.*) Come now. You say your only purpose is to save your wife. Good, then, she is saved at least this year, and a year is long. What say you, sir? It is done now. (*In conflict,* **Proctor** *glances at* **Francis** *and* **Giles**.) Will you drop this charge?

Proctor   I—I think I cannot.

Danforth (*now an almost imperceptible hardness in his voice*)   Then your purpose is somewhat larger.

Parris   He's come to overthrow this court, Your Honor!

Proctor   These are my friends. Their wives are also accused—

Danforth (*with a sudden briskness of manner*)   I judge you not, sir. I am ready to hear your evidence.

Proctor   I come not to hurt the court; I only—

Danforth (*cutting him off*)   Marshal, go into the court and bid Judge Stoughton and Judge Sewall declare recess for one hour. And let them go to the tavern, if they will. All witnesses and prisoners are to be kept in the building.

Herrick   Aye, sir. (*Very deferentially:*) If I may say it, sir, I know this man all my life. It is a good man, sir.

Danforth (*it is the reflection on himself he resents*)   I am sure of it, Marshal. (**Herrick** *nods, then goes out.*) Now, what deposition do you have for us, Mr. Proctor? And I beg you be clear, open as the sky, and honest.

Proctor (*as he takes out several papers*)   I am no lawyer, so I'll—

Danforth   The pure in heart need no lawyers. Proceed as you will.

Proctor (*handing* **Danforth** *a paper*)   Will you read this first, sir? It's a sort of testament. The people signing it declare their good opinion of Rebecca, and my wife, and Martha Corey. (**Danforth** *looks down at the paper.*)

Parris (*to enlist* **Danforth**'s *sarcasm*)   Their good opinion! (*But* **Danforth** *goes on reading, and* **Proctor** *is heartened.*)

Proctor   These are all landholding farmers, members of the church.

(*Delicately, trying to point out a paragraph:*) If you'll notice, sir—they've known the women many years and never saw no sign they had dealings with the Devil.

Parris *nervously moves over and reads over* **Danforth**'*s shoulder.*

Danforth (*glancing down a long list*)   How many names are here?

Francis   Ninety-one, Your Excellency.

Parris (*sweating*)   These people should be summoned. (**Danforth** *looks up at him questioningly.*) For questioning.

Francis (*trembling with anger*)   Mr. Danforth, I gave them all my word no harm would come to them for signing this.

Parris   This is a clear attack upon the court!

Hale (*to* **Parris**, *trying to contain himself*)   Is every defense an attack upon the court? Can no one—?

Parris   All innocent and Christian people are happy for the courts in Salem! These people are gloomy for it. (*To* **Danforth** *directly:*) And I think you will want to know, from each and every one of them, what discontents them with you!

Hathorne   I think they ought to be examined, sir.

Danforth   It is not necessarily an attack, I think. Yet—

Francis   These are all covenanted Christians, sir.

Danforth   Then I am sure they may have nothing to fear. (*Hands* **Cheever** *the paper.*) Mr. Cheever, have warrants drawn for all of these—arrest for examination. (*To* **Proctor***:*) Now, Mister, what other information do you have for us? (**Francis** *is still standing, horrified.*) You may sit, Mr. Nurse.

Francis   I have brought trouble on these people; I have—

Danforth   No, old man, you have not hurt these people if they are of good conscience. But you must understand, sir, that a person is either with this court or he must be counted against it, there be no road between. This is a sharp time, now, a precise time—we live no longer in the dusky afternoon when evil mixed itself with good and befuddled the world. Now, by God's grace, the shining sun is up, and them that fear not light will surely praise it. I hope you will be one of those. (**Mary Warren** *suddenly sobs.*) She's not hearty, I see.

Proctor   No, she's not, sir. (*To* **Mary***, bending to her, holding her hand, quietly:*) Now remember what the angel Raphael said to the boy Tobias. Remember it.

Mary Warren (*hardly audible*)   Aye.

Proctor   "Do that which is good, and no harm shall come to thee."

Mary Warren   Aye.

Danforth   Come, man, we wait you.

Marshal Herrick *returns, and takes his post at the door.*

Giles   John, my deposition, give him mine.

Proctor   Aye. (*He hands* **Danforth** *another paper.*) This is Mr. Corey's deposition.

Danforth   Oh? (*He looks down at it. Now* **Hathorne** *comes behind him and reads with him.*)

Hathorne (*suspiciously*)   What lawyer drew this, Corey?

Giles   You know I never hired a lawyer in my life, Hathorne.

Danforth (*finishing the reading*)   It is very well phrased. My compliments. Mr. Parris, if Mr. Putnam is in the court, will you bring him in? (**Hathorne** *takes the deposition, and walks to the window with it.* **Parris** *goes into the court.*) You have no legal training, Mr. Corey?

Giles (*very pleased*)   I have the best, sir—I am thirty-three time in court in my life. And always plaintiff, too.

Danforth   Oh, then you're much put-upon.

Giles   I am never put-upon; I know my rights, sir, and I will have them. You know, your father tried a case of mine—might be thirty-five year ago, I think.

Danforth   Indeed.

Giles   He never spoke to you of it?

Danforth   No, I cannot recall it.

Giles   That's strange, he give me nine pound damages. He were a fair judge, your father. Y'see, I had a white mare that time, and this fellow come to borrow the mare—(*Enter* **Parris** *with* **Thomas Putnam***. When he sees* **Putnam***,* **Giles***'ease goes; he is hard.*) Aye, there he is.

Danforth   Mr. Putnam, I have here an accusation by Mr. Corey against you. He states that you coldly prompted your daughter to cry witchery upon George Jacobs that is now in jail.

Putnam   It is a lie.

Danforth (*turning to* **Giles**)   Mr. Putnam states your charge is a lie. What say you to that?

Giles (*furious, his fists clenched*)   A fart on Thomas Putnam, that is what I say to that!

Danforth   What proof do you submit for your charge, sir?

Giles   My proof is there! (*Pointing to the paper.*) If Jacobs hangs for a witch he forfeit up his property—that's law! And there is none but Putnam with the coin to buy so great a piece. This man is killing his neighbors for their land!

Danforth   But proof, sir, proof.

Giles (*pointing at his deposition*)   The proof is there! I have it from an honest man who heard Putnam say it! The day his daughter cried out on Jacobs, he said she'd given him a fair gift of land.

Hathorne   And the name of this man?

Giles (*taken aback*)   What name?

Hathorne   The man that give you this information.

Giles (*hesitates, then*)   Why, I—I cannot give you his name.

Hathorne   And why not?

Giles (*hesitates, then bursts out*)   You know well why not! He'll lay in jail if I give his name!

Hathorne   This is contempt of the court, Mr. Danforth!

Danforth (*to avoid that*)   You will surely tell us the name.

Giles   I will not give you no name. I mentioned my wife's name once and I'll burn in hell long enough for that. I stand mute.

Danforth   In that case, I have no choice but to arrest you for contempt of this court, do you know that?

Giles   This is a hearing; you cannot clap me for contempt of a hearing.

Danforth   Oh, it is a proper lawyer! Do you wish me to declare the court in full session here? Or will you give me good reply?

Giles (*faltering*)   I cannot give you no name, sir, I cannot.

Danforth   You are a foolish old man. Mr. Cheever, begin the record. The court is now in session. I ask you, Mr. Corey—

Proctor (*breaking in*)   Your Honor—he has the story in confidence, sir, and he—

Parris   The Devil lives on such confidences! (*To* **Danforth***.*) Without confidences there could be no conspiracy, Your Honor!

Hathorne   I think it must be broken, sir.

Danforth (*to* **Giles**)   Old man, if your informant tells the truth let him come here openly like a decent man. But if he hide in anonymity I must know why. Now sir, the government and central church demand of you the name of him who reported Mr. Thomas Putnam a common murderer.

Hale   Excellency—

Danforth   Mr. Hale.

Hale   We cannot blink it more. There is a prodigious fear of this court in the country—

Danforth   Then there is a prodigious guilt in the country. Are *you* afraid to be questioned here?

Hale   I may only fear the Lord, sir, but there is fear in the country nevertheless.

Danforth (*angered now*)   Reproach me not with the fear in the country; there is fear in the country because there is a moving plot to topple Christ in the country!

Hale   But it does not follow that everyone accused is part of it.

Danforth   No uncorrupted man may fear this court, Mr. Hale! None! (*To* **Giles***:*) You are under arrest in contempt of this court. Now sit you down and take counsel with yourself, or you will be set in the jail until you decide to answer all questions.

Giles Corey *makes a rush for* **Putnam***.* **Proctor** *lunges and holds him.*

Proctor   No, Giles!

Giles (*over* **Proctor***'s shoulder at* **Putnam**)   I'll cut your throat, Putnam, I'll kill you yet!

Proctor (*forcing him into a chair*)   Peace, Giles, peace. (*Releasing him.*) We'll prove ourselves. Now we will. (*He starts to turn to* **Danforth***.*)

Giles   Say nothin' more, John. (*Pointing at* **Danforth**.) He's only playin' you! You means to hang us all!

Mary Warren *bursts into sobs.*

Danforth   This is a court of law, Mister. I'll have no effrontery here!

Proctor   Forgive him, sir, for his old age. Peace, Giles, we'll prove it all now. (*He lifts up* **Mary**'s *chin.*) You cannot weep, Mary. Remember the angel, what he say to the boy. Hold to it, now; there is your rock. (**Mary** *quiets. He takes out a paper, and turns to* **Danforth**.) This is Mary Warren's deposition. I—I would ask you remember, sir, while you read it, that until two week ago she were no different than the other children are today. (*He is speaking reasonably, restraining all his fears, his anger, his anxiety.*) You saw her scream, she howled, she swore familiar spirits choked her; she even testified that Satan, in the form of women now in jail, tried to win her soul away, and then when she refused—

Danforth   We know all this.

Proctor   Aye, sir. She swears now that she never saw Satan; nor any spirit, vague or clear, that Satan may have sent to hurt her. And she declares her friends are lying now.

Proctor *starts to hand* **Danforth** *the deposition, and* **Hale** *comes up to* **Danforth** *in a trembling state.*

Hale   Excellency, a moment. I think this goes to the heart of the matter.

Danforth (*with deep misgivings*)   It surely does.

Hale   I cannot say he is an honest man; I know him little. But in all justice, sir, a claim so weighty cannot be argued by a farmer. In God's name, sir, stop here; send him home and let him come again with a lawyer—

Danforth (*patiently*)   Now look you, Mr. Hale—

Hale   Excellency, I have signed seventy-two death warrants; I am a minister of the Lord, and I dare not take a life without there be a proof so immaculate no slightest qualm of conscience may doubt it.

Danforth   Mr. Hale, you surely do not doubt my justice.

Hale   I have this morning signed away the soul of Rebecca Nurse, Your Honor. I'll not conceal it, my hand shakes yet as with a wound! I pray you, sir, *this* argument let lawyers present to you.

Danforth   Mr. Hale, believe me; for a man of such terrible learning you are most bewildered—I hope you will forgive me. I have been thirty-two year at the bar, sir, and I should be confounded were I called upon to defend these people. Let you consider, now—(*To* **Proctor** *and the others:*) And I bid you all do likewise. In an ordinary crime, how does one defend the accused? One calls up witnesses to prove his innocence. But witchcraft is *ipso facto*, on its face and by its nature, an invisible crime, is it not? Therefore, who may possibly be witness to it? The witch and the victim. None other. Now we cannot hope the witch will accuse herself; granted? Therefore, we must rely upon her victims—and they do testify, the children certainly do testify. As for the witches, none will deny that we are most eager for all their confessions. Therefore, what is left for a lawyer to bring out? I think I have made my point. Have I not?

Hale   But this child claims the girls are not truthful, and if they are not—

Danforth   That is precisely what I am about to consider, sir. What more may you ask of me? Unless you doubt my probity?

Hale (*defeated*)   I surely do not, sir. Let you consider it, then.

Danforth   And let you put your heart to rest. Her deposition, Mr. Proctor.

Proctor *hands it to him.* **Hathorne** *rises, goes beside* **Danforth**, *and starts reading.* **Parris** *comes to his other side.* **Danforth** *looks at* **John Proctor**, *then proceeds to read.* **Hale** *gets up, finds position near the judge, reads too.* **Proctor** *glances at* **Giles**. **Francis** *prays silently, hands pressed together.* **Cheever** *waits placidly, the sublime official, dutiful.* **Mary Warren** *sobs once.* **John Proctor** *touches her head reassuringly. Presently* **Danforth** *lifts his eyes. stands up, takes out a kerchief and blows his nose. The others stand aside as he moves in thought toward the window.*

Parris (*hardly able to contain his anger and fear*)   I should like to question—

Danforth (*his first real outburst, in which his contempt for* **Parris** *is clear*)   Mr. Parris, I bid you be silent! (*He stands in silence, looking out the window. Now, having established that he will set the gait:*) Mr. Cheever, will you go into the court and bring the children here? (**Cheever** *gets up and goes out upstage.* **Danforth** *now turns to* **Mary**.) Mary Warren, how came you to this turnabout? Has Mr. Proctor threatened you for this deposition?

Mary Warren   No, sir.

Danforth   Has he ever threatened you?

Mary Warren (*weaker*)   No, sir.

Danforth (*sensing a weakening*)   Has he threatened you?

Mary Warren   No, sir.

Danforth   Then you tell me that you sat in my court, callously lying, when you knew that people would hang by your evidence? (*She does not answer.*) Answer me!

Mary Warren (*almost inaudibly*)   I did, sir.

Danforth   How were you instructed in your life? Do you not know that God damns all liars? (*She cannot speak.*) Or is it now that you lie?

Mary Warren   No, sir—I am with God now.

Danforth   You are with God now.

Mary Warren   Aye, sir.

Danforth (*containing himself*)   I will tell you this—you are either lying now, or you were lying in the court, and in either case you have committed perjury and you will go to jail for it. You cannot lightly say you lied, Mary. Do you know that?

Mary Warren   I cannot lie no more. I am with God, I am with God.

But she breaks into sobs at the thought of it, and the right door opens, and enter **Susanna Walcott**, **Mercy Lewis**, **Betty Parris**, *and finally* **Abigail**. **Cheever** *comes to* **Danforth**.

Cheever   Ruth Putnam's not in the court, sir, nor the other children.

Danforth   These will be sufficient. Sit you down, children. (*Silently they sit.*) Your friend, Mary Warren, has given us a deposition in which she swears that she never saw familiar spirits, apparitions, nor any manifest of the Devil. She claims as well that none of you have seen these things either. (*Slight pause.*) Now, children, this is a court of law. The law, based upon the Bible, and the Bible, writ by Almighty God, forbid the practice of witchcraft, and describe death as the penalty thereof. But likewise, children, the law and Bible damn all bearers of false witness. (*Slight pause.*) Now then. It does not escape me that this deposition may be devised to blind us; it may well be that Mary Warren has been conquered by Satan, who sends her here to distract our sacred purpose. If so, her neck will break for it. But if she speak true, I bid you now drop your guile and confess your pretense, for a quick confession will go easier with you. (*Pause.*) Abigail Williams, rise. (**Abigail** *slowly rises.*) Is there any truth in this?

Abigail   No, sir.

Danforth (*thinks, glances at* **Mary**, *then back to* **Abigail**)   Children, a very augur bit will now be turned into your souls until your honesty is proved. Will either of you change your positions now, or do you force me to hard questioning?

Abigail   I have naught to change, sir. She lies.

Danforth (*to* **Mary**)   You would still go on with this?

Mary Warren (*faintly*)   Aye, sir.

Danforth (*turning to* **Abigail**)   A poppet were discovered in Mr. Proctor's house, stabbed by a needle. Mary Warren claims that you sat beside her in the court when she made it, and that you saw her make it and witnessed how she herself stuck her needle into it for safe-keeping. What say you to that?

Abigail (*with a slight note of indignation*)   It is a lie, sir.

Danforth (*after a slight pause*)   While you worked for Mr. Proctor, did you see poppets in that house?

Abigail   Goody Proctor always kept poppets.

Proctor   Your honor, my wife never kept no poppets. Mary Warren confesses it was her poppet.

Cheever   Your Excellency.

Danforth   Mr. Cheever.

Cheever   When I spoke with Goody Proctor in that house, she said she never kept no poppets. But she said she did keep poppets when she were a girl.

Proctor   She has not been a girl these fifteen years, Your Honor.

Hathorne   But a poppet will keep fifteen years, will it not?

Proctor   It will keep if it is kept, but Mary Warren swears she never saw no poppets in my house, nor anyone else.

Parris   Why could there not have been poppets hid where no one ever saw them?

Proctor (*furious*)   There might also be a dragon with five legs in my house, but no one has ever seen it.

Parris   We are here, Your Honor, precisely to discover what no one has ever seen.

Proctor   Mr. Danforth, what profit this girl to turn herself about? What may Mary Warren gain but hard questioning and worse?

Danforth   You are charging Abigail Williams with a marvelous cool plot to murder, do you understand that?

Proctor   I do, sir. I believe she means to murder.

Danforth (*pointing at* **Abigail**, *incredulously*)   This child would murder your wife?

Proctor   It is not a child. Now hear me, sir. In the sight of the congregation she were twice this year put out of this meetin' house for laughter during prayer.

Danforth (*shocked, turning to* **Abigail**)   What's this? Laughter during—!

Parris   Excellency, she were under Tituba's power at that time, but she is solemn now.

Giles   Aye, now she is solemn and goes to hang people!

Danforth   Quiet, man.

Hathorne   Surely it have no bearing on the question, sir. He charges contemplation of murder.

Danforth   Aye. (*He studies* **Abigail** *for a moment, then:*) Continue, Mr. Proctor.

Proctor   Mary. Now tell the Governor how you danced in the woods.

Parris (*instantly*)   Excellency, since I come to Salem this man is blackening my name. He—

Danforth   In a moment, sir. (*To* **Mary Warren**, *sternly, and surprised:*) What is this dancing?

Mary Warren   I—(*She glances at* **Abigail**, *who is staring down at her remorselessly. Then, appealing to* **Proctor**:) Mr. Proctor—

Proctor (*taking it right up*)   Abigail leads the girls to the woods, Your Honor, and they have danced there naked—

Parris   Your Honor, this—

Proctor (*at once*)   Mr. Parris discovered them himself in the dead of night! There's the "child" she is!

Danforth (*it is growing into a nightmare, and he turns, astonished, to* **Parris**)   Mr. Parris—

Parris   I can only say, sir, that I never found any of them naked, and this man is—

Danforth   But you discovered them dancing in the woods? (*Eyes on* **Parris***, he points at* **Abigail***.*) Abigail?

Hale   Excellency, when I first arrived from Beverly, Mr. Parris told me that.

Danforth   Do you deny it, Mr. Parris?

Parris   I do not, sir, but I never saw any of them naked.

Danforth   But she have *danced?*

Parris (*unwillingly*)   Aye, sir.

Danforth*, as though with new eyes, looks at* **Abigail***.*

Hathorne   Excellency, will you permit me? (*He points at* **Mary Warren***.*)

Danforth (*with great worry*)   Pray, proceed.

Hathorne   You say you never saw no spirits, Mary, were never threatened or afflicted by any manifest of the Devil or the Devil's agents.

Mary Warren (*very faintly*)   No, sir.

Hathorne (*with a gleam of victory*)   And yet, when people accused of witchery confronted you in court, you would faint, saying their spirits came out of their bodies and choked you—

Mary Warren   That were pretense, sir.

Danforth   I cannot hear you.

Mary Warren   Pretense, sir.

Parris   But you did turn cold, did you not? I myself picked you up many times, and your skin were icy. Mr. Danforth, you—

Danforth   I saw that many times.

Proctor   She only pretended to faint, Your Excellency. They're all marvelous pretenders.

Hathorne   Then can she pretend to faint now?

Proctor   Now?

Parris   Why not? Now there are no spirits attacking her, for none in this room is accused of witchcraft. So let her turn herself cold now, let her pretend she is attacked now, let her faint. (*He turns to* **Mary Warren**.) Faint!

Mary Warren   Faint?

Parris   Aye, faint. Prove to us how you pretended in the court so many times.

Mary Warren (*looking to* **Proctor**)   I—cannot faint now, sir.

Proctor (*alarmed, quietly*)   Can you not pretend it?

Mary Warren   I—(*She looks about as though searching for the passion to faint.*) I—have no *sense* of it now, I—

Danforth   Why? What is lacking now?

Mary Warren   I—cannot tell, sir, I—

Danforth   Might it be that here we have no afflicting spirit loose, but in the court there were some?

Mary Warren   I never saw no spirits.

Parris   Then see no spirits now, and prove to us that you can faint by your own will, as you claim.

Mary Warren (*stares, searching for the emotion of it, and then shakes her head*)   I—cannot do it.

Parris   Then you will confess, will you not? It were attacking spirits made you faint!

Mary Warren   No, sir, I—

Parris   Your Excellency, this is a trick to blind the court!

Mary Warren   It's not a trick! (*She stands.*) I—I used to faint because I—I thought I saw spirits.

Danforth   *Thought* you saw them!

Mary Warren   But I did not, Your Honor.

Hathorne   How could you think you saw them unless you saw them?

Mary Warren   I—I cannot tell how, but I did. I—I heard the other girls screaming, and you, Your Honor, you seemed to believe them, and I—It were only sport in the beginning, sir, but then the whole world cried spirits, spirits, and I—I promise you, Mr. Danforth, I only thought I saw them but I did not.

Danforth *peers at her.*

Parris (*smiling, but nervous because* **Danforth** *seems to be struck by* **Mary Warren**'s *story*)   Surely Your Excellency is not taken by this simple lie.

Danforth (*turning worriedly to* **Abigial**)   Abigail. I bid you now search your heart and tell me this—and beware of it, child, to God every soul is precious and His vengeance is terrible on them that take life without cause. Is it possible, child, that the spirits you have seen are illusion only, some deception that may cross your mind when—

Abigail   Why, this—this—is a base question, sir.

Danforth   Child, I would have you consider it—

Abigail   I have been hurt, Mr. Danforth; I have seen my blood runnin' out! I have been near to murdered every day because I done my duty pointing out the Devil's people—and this is my reward? To be mistrusted, denied, questioned like a—

Danforth (*weakening*)   Child, I do not mistrust you—

Abigail (*in an open threat*)   Let *you* beware, Mr. Danforth. Think you to be so mighty that the power of Hell may not turn *your* wits? Beware of it! There is—(*Suddenly, from an accusatory attitude, her face turns, looking into the air above—it is truly frightened.*)

Danforth (*apprehensively*)   What is it, child?

Abigail (*looking about in the air, clasping her arms about her as though cold*)   I—I know not. A wind, a cold wind, has come.

Her eyes fall on **Mary Warren**.

Mary Warren (*terrified, pleading*)   Abby!

Mercy Lewis (*shivering*)   Your Honor, I freeze!

Proctor   They're pretending!

Hathorne (*touching* **Abigail's** *hand*)   She is cold, Your Honor, touch her!

Mercy Lewis (*through chattering teeth*)   Mary, do you send this shadow on me?

Mary Warren   Lord, save me!

Susanna Walcott   I freeze, I freeze!

Abigail (*shivering visibly*)   It is a wind, a wind!

Marry Warren   Abby, don't do that!

Danforth (*himself engaged and entered by* **Abigail**)   Mary Warren, do you witch her? I say to you, do you send your spirit out?

With a hysterical cry **Mary Warren** *starts to run.* **Proctor** *catches her.*

Mary Warren (*almost collapsing*)   Let me go. Mr. Proctor, I cannot, I cannot—

Abigail (*crying to Heaven*)   Oh, Heavenly Father, take away this shadow!

Without warning or hesitation, **Proctor** *leaps at* **Abigail** *and, grabbing her by the hair, pulls her to her feet. She screams in pain.* **Danforth**, *astonished, cries, "What are you about?" and* **Hathorne** *and* **Parris** *call, "Take your hands off her!" and out of it all comes* **Proctor**'s *roaring voice.*

Proctor   How do you call Heaven! Whore! Whore!

Herrick *breaks* **Proctor** *from her.*

Herrick   John!

Danforth   Man! Man, what do you—

Proctor (*breathless and in agony*)   It is a whore!

Danforth (*dumfounded*)   You charge—?

Abigail   Mr. Danforth, he is lying!

Proctor   Mark her! Now she'll suck a scream to stab me with but—

Danforth   You will prove this! This will not pass!

Proctor (*trembling, his life collapsing about him*)   I have known her, sir. I have known her.

Danforth   You—you are a lecher?

Francis (*horrified*)   John, you cannot say such a—

Proctor   Oh, Francis, I wish you had some evil in you that you might know me! (*To* **Danforth***:*) A man will not cast away his good name. You surely know that.

Danforth (*dumfounded*)   In—in what time? In what place?

Proctor (*his voice about to break, and his shame great*)   In the proper place—where my beasts are bedded. On the last night of my joy, some eight months past. She used to serve me in my house, sir. (*He has to clamp his jaw to keep from weeping.*) A man may think God sleeps, but God sees everything, I know it now. I beg you, sir, I beg you—see her what she is. My wife, my dear good wife, took this girl soon after, sir, and put her out on the highroad. And being what she is, a lump of vanity, sir—(*He is being overcome.*) Excellency, forgive me, forgive me. (*Angrily against himself, he turns away from the* **Governor** *for a moment. Then, as though to cry out is his only means of speech left:*) She thinks to dance with me on my wife's grave! And well she might, for I thought of her softly. God help me, I lusted, and there *is* a promise in such sweat. But it is a whore's vengeance, and you must see it; I set myself entirely in your hands. I know you must see it now.

Danforth (*blanched, in horror, turning to* **Abigail**)   You deny every scrap and tittle of this?

Abigail   If I must answer that, I will leave and I will not come back again!

Danforth *seems unsteady.*

Proctor   I have made a bell of my honor! I have rung the doom of my good name—you will believe me, Mr. Danforth! My wife is innocent, except she knew a whore when she saw one!

Abigail (*stepping up to* **Danforth**)   What look do you give me? (**Danforth** *cannot speak.*) I'll not have such looks! (*She turns and starts for the door.*)

Danforth   You will remain where you are! (**Herrick** *steps into her path. She comes up short, fire in her eyes.*) Mr. Parris, go into the court and bring Goodwife Proctor out.

Parris (*objecting*)   Your Honor, this is all a—

Danforth (*sharply to* **Parris**)   Bring her out! And tell her not one word of what's been spoken here. And let you knock before you enter. (**Parris** *goes out.*) Now we shall touch the bottom of this swamp. (*To* **Proctor**:) Your wife, you say, is an honest woman.

Proctor   In her life, sir, she have never lied. There are them that cannot sing, and them that cannot weep—my wife cannot lie. I have paid much to learn it, sir.

Danforth   And when she put this girl out of your house, she put her out for a harlot?

Proctor   Aye, sir.

Danforth   And knew her for a harlot?

Proctor   Aye, sir, she knew her for a harlot.

Danforth   Good then. (*To* **Abigail***:*) And if she tell me, child, it were for harlotry, may God spread His mercy on you! (*There is a knock. He calls to the door.*) Hold! (*To* **Abigail***:*) Turn your back. Turn your back. (*To* **Proctor***:*) Do likewise. (*Both turn their backs—***Abigail** *with indignant slowness.*) Now let neither of you turn to face Goody Proctor. No one in this room is to speak one word, or raise a gesture aye or nay. (*He turns toward the door, calls:*) Enter! (*The door opens.* **Elizabeth** *enters with* **Parris**. **Parris** *leaves her. She stands alone, her eyes looking for* **Proctor**.) Mr. Cheever, report this testimony in all exactness. Are you ready?

Cheever   Ready, sir.

Danforth   Come here, woman. (**Elizabeth** *comes to him, glancing at* **Proctor's** *back.*) Look at me only, not at your husband. In my eyes only.

Elizabeth (*faintly*)   Good, sir.

Danforth   We are given to understand that at one time you dismissed your servant, Abigail Williams.

Elizabeth   That is true, sir.

Danforth   For what cause did you dismiss her? (*Slight pause. Then* **Elizabeth** *tries to glance at* **Proctor**.) You will look in my eyes only and not at your husband. The answer is in your memory and you need no help to give it to me. Why did you dismiss Abigail Williams?

Elizabeth (*not knowing what to say, sensing a situation, wetting her lips to stall for time*)   She—dissatisfied me. (*Pause.*) And my husband.

Danforth   In what way dissatisfied you?

Elizabeth   She were—(*She glances at* **Proctor** *for a cue.*)

Danforth   Woman, look at me! (**Elizabeth** *does.*) Were she slovenly? Lazy? What disturbance did she cause?

Elizabeth   Your Honor, I—in that time I were sick. And I—My husband is a good and righteous man. He is never drunk as some are, nor wastin' his time at the shovelboard, but always at his work. But in my sickness—you see, sir, I were a long time sick after my last baby, and I thought I saw my husband somewhat turning from me. And this girl—(*She turns to* **Abigail**.)

Danforth   Look at me.

Elizabeth   Aye, sir. Abigail Williams—(*She breaks off.*)

Danforth   What of Abigail Williams?

Elizaneth   I came to think he fancied her. And so one night I lost my wits, I think, and put her out on the highroad.

Danforth   Your husband—did he indeed turn from you?

Elizabeth (*in agony*)   My husband—is a goodly man, sir.

Danforth   Then he did not turn from you.

Elizabeth (*starting to glance at* **Proctor***:*)   He—

Danforth (*reaches out and holds her face, then*)   Look at me! To your own knowledge, has John Proctor ever committed the crime of lechery? (*In a crisis of indecision she cannot speak.*) Answer my question! Is your husband a lecher!

Elizabeth (*faintly*)   No, sir.

Danforth   Remove her, Marshal.

Proctor   Elizabeth, tell the truth!

Danforth   She has spoken. Remove her!

Proctor (*crying out*)   Elizabeth, I have confessed it!

Elizabeth   Oh, God! (*The door closes behind her.*)

Proctor   She only thought to save my name!

Hale   Excellency, it is a natural lie to tell; I beg you, stop now before another is condemned! I may shut my conscience to it no more—private vengeance is working through this testimony! From the beginning this man has struck me true. By my oath to Heaven, I believe him now, and I pray you call back his wife before we—

Danforth   She spoke nothing of lechery, and this man has lied!

Hale   I believe him! (*Pointing at* **Abigail***:*) This girl has always struck me false! She has—

Abigail*, with a weird, wild, chilling cry, screams up to the ceiling.*

Abigail   You will not! Begone! Begone, I say!

Danforth   What is it, child? (*But* **Abigail***, pointing with fear, is now raising up her frightened eyes, her awed face, toward the ceiling—the girls are doing the same—and now* **Hathorne**, **Hale**, **Putnam**, **Cheever**, **Herrick**, *and* **Danforth** *do the same.*) What's there? (*He lowers his eyes from the ceiling, and now he is frightened; there is real tension in his* voice.) Child! (*She is transfixed—with all the girls, she is whimpering open-mouthed, agape at the ceiling.*) Girls! Why do you—?

Mercy Lewis (*pointing*)   It's on the beam! Behind the rafter!

Danforth (*looking up*)   Where!

Abigail   Why—? (*She gulps.*) Why do you come, yellow bird?

Proctor   Where's a bird? I see no bird!

Abigail (*to the ceiling*)   My face? My face?

Proctor   Mr. Hale—

Danforth   Be quiet!

Proctor (*to* **Hale**)   Do you see a bird?

Danforth   Be quiet!!

Abigail (*to the ceiling, in a genuine conversation with the "bird," as though trying to talk it out of attacking her*)   But God made my face; you cannot want to tear my face. Envy is a deadly sin, Mary.

Mary Warren (*on her feet with a spring, and horrified, pleading*)   Abby!

Abigail (*unperturbed, continuing to the "bird"*)   Oh, Mary, this is a black art to change your shape. No, I cannot, I cannot stop my mouth; it's God's work I do.

Mary Warren   Abby, I'm *here*!

Proctor (*frantically*)   They're pretending, Mr. Danforth!

Abigail (*now she takes a backward step, as though in fear the bird will swoop down momentarily*)   Oh, please, Mary! Don't come down.

Susanna Walcott   Her claws, she's stretching her claws!

Proctor   Lies, lies.

Abigail (*backing further, eyes still fixed above*)   Mary, please don't hurt me!

Mary Warren (*to* **Danforth**)   I'm not hurting her!

Danforth (*to* **Mary Warren**)   Why does she see this vision?

Mary Warren   She sees nothin'!

Abigail (*now staring full front as though hypnotized, and mimicking the exact tone of* **Mary Warren**'*s cry*)   She sees nothin'!

Mary Warren (*pleading*)   Abby, you mustn't!

Abigail and All the Girls (*all transfixed*)   Abby, you mustn't!

Mary Warren (*to all the girls*)   I'm here, I'm here!

Girls   I'm here, I'm here!

Danforth (*horrified*)   Mary Warren! Draw back your spirit out of them!

Mary Warren   Mr. Danforth!

Girls (*cutting her off*)   Mr. Danforth!

Danforth   Have you compacted with the Devil? Have you?

Mary Warren   Never, never!

Girls   Never, never!

Danforth (*growing hysterical*)   Why can they only repeat you?

Proctor   Give me a whip—I'll stop it!

Mary Warren   They're sporting. They—!

Girls   They're sporting!

Mary Warren (*turning on them all hysterically and stamping her feet*)   Abby, stop it!

Girls (*stamping their feet*)   Abby, stop it!

Mary Warren   Stop it!

Girls   Stop it!

Mary Warren (*screaming it out at the top of her lungs, and raising her fists*)   Stop it!!

Girls (*raising their fists*)   Stop it!!

Mary Warren, *utterly confounded, and becoming overwhelmed by* **Abigail**'s—*and the girls'—utter conviction, starts to whimper, hands half raised, powerless, and all the girls begin whimpering exactly as she does.*

Danforth   A little while ago you were afflicted. Now it seems you afflict others; where did you find this power?

Mary Warren (*staring at* **Abigail**)   I—have no power.

Girls   I have no power.

Proctor   They're gulling you, Mister!

Danforth   Why did you turn about this past two weeks? You have seen the Devil, have you not?

Hale (*indicating* **Abigail** *and the girls*)   You cannot believe them!

Mary Warren   I—

Proctor (*sensing her weakening*)   Mary, God damns all liars!

Danforth (*pounding it into her*)   You have seen the Devil, you have made compact with Lucifer, have you not?

Proctor   God damns liars, Mary!

Mary *utters something unintelligible, staring at* **Abigail***, who keeps watching the "bird" above.*

Danforth   I cannot hear you. What do you say? (**Mary** *utters again unintelligibly.*) You will confess yourself or you will hang! (*He turns her roughly to face him.*) Do you know who I am? I say you will hang if you do not open with me!

Proctor   Mary, remember the angel Raphael—do that which is good and—

Abigail (*pointing upward*)   The wings! Her wings are spreading! Mary, please, don't, don't—!

Hale   I see nothing, Your Honor!

Danforth   Do you confess this power! (*He is an inch from her face.*) Speak!

Abigail   She's going to come down! She's walking the beam!

Danforth   Will you speak!

Mary Warren (*staring in horror*)   I cannot!

Girls   I cannot!

Parris   Cast the Devil out! Look him in the face! Trample him! We'll save you, Mary, only stand fast against him and—

Abigail (*looking up*)   Look out! She's coming down!

She and all the girls run to one wall, shielding their eyes. And now, as though cornered, they let out a gigantic scream, and **Mary***, as though infected, opens her mouth and screams with them. Gradually* **Abigail** *and the girls leave off, until only* **Mary** *is left there, staring up at the "bird," screaming madly. All watch her, horrified by this evident fit.* **Proctor** *strides to her.*

Proctor   Mary, tell the Governor what they—(*He has hardly got a word out, when, seeing him coming for her, she rushes out of his reach, screaming in horror.*)

Mary Warren   Don't touch me—don't touch me! (*At which the girls halt at the door.*)

Proctor (*astonished*)   Mary!

Mary Warren (*pointing at* **Proctor**)   You're the Devil's man!

He is stopped in his tracks.

Parris   Praise God!

Girls   Praise God!

Proctor (*numbed*)   Mary, how—?

Mary Warren   I'll not hang with you! I love God, I love God

Danforth (*to* **Mary**)   He bid you do the Devil's work?

Mary Warren (*hysterically, indicating* **Proctor**)   He come at me by night and every day to sign, to sign, to—

Danforth   Sign what?

Parris   The Devil's book? He come with a book?

Mary Warren (*hysterically, pointing at* **Proctor**, *fearful of him*)   My name, he want my name. "I'll murder you," he says, "if my wife hangs! We must go and overthrow the court," he says!

Danforth's *head jerks toward* **Proctor**, *shock and horror in his face.*

Proctor (*turning, appealing to* **Hale**)   Mr. Hale!

Mary Warren (*her sobs beginning*)   He wake me every night, his eyes were like coals and his fingers claw my neck, and I sign, I sign . . .

Hale   Excellency, this child's gone wild!

Proctor (*as* **Danforth**'s *wide eyes pour on him*)   Mary, Mary!

Mary Warren (*screaming at him*)   No, I love God; I go your way no more. I love God, I bless God. (*Sobbing, she rushes to* **Abigail**.) Abby, Abby, I'll never hurt you more! (*They all watch, as* **Abigail**, *out of her*

infinite charity, reaches out and draws the sobbing **Mary** *to her, and then looks up to* **Danforth**.)

Danforth (*to* **Proctor**)   What are you? (**Proctor** *is beyond speech in his anger.*) You are combined with anti-Christ, are you not? I have seen your power; you will not deny it! What say you, Mister?

Hale   Excellency—

Danforth   I will have nothing from you, Mr. Hale! (*To* **Proctor**:) Will you confess yourself befouled with Hell, or do you keep that black allegiance yet? What say you?

Proctor (*his mind wild, breathless*)   I say—I say—God is dead!

Parris   Hear it, hear it!

Proctor (*laughs insanely, then*)   A fire, a fire is burning! I hear the boot of Lucifer, I see his filthy face! And it is my face, and yours, Danforth! For them that quail to bring men out of ignorance, as I have quailed, and as you quail now when you know in all your black hearts that this be fraud—God damns our kind especially, and we will burn, we will burn together!

Danforth   Marshal! Take him and Corey with him to the jail!

Hale (*starting across to the door*)   I denounce these proceedings!

Proctor   You are pulling Heaven down and raising up a whore!

Hale   I denounce these proceedings, I quit this court! (*He slams the door to the outside behind him.*)

Danforth (*calling to him in a fury*)   Mr. Hale! Mr. Hale!

Curtain.

Act Four

A cell in Salem jail, that fall.

At the back is a high barred window; near it, a great, heavy door. Along the walls are two benches.

The place is in darkness but for the moonlight seeping through the bars. It appears empty. Presently footsteps are heard coming down a corridor beyond the wall, keys rattle, and the door swings open. **Marshal Herrick** *enters with a lantern.*

He is nearly drunk, and heavy-footed. He goes to a bench and nudges a bundle of rags lying on it.

Herrick   Sarah, wake up! Sarah Good! (*He then crosses to the other bench.*)

Sarah Good (*rising in her rags*)   Oh, Majesty! Comin', comin'! Tituba, he's here, His Majesty's come!

Herrick   Go to the north cell; this place is wanted now. (*He hangs his lantern on the wall.* **Tituba** *sits up.*)

Tituba   That don't look to me like His Majesty; look to me like the marshal.

Herrick (*taking out a flask*)   Get along with you now, clear this place. (*He drinks, and* **Sarah Good** *comes and peers up into his face.*)

Sarah Good   Oh, is it you, Marshal! I thought sure you be the Devil comin' for us. Could I have a sip of cider for me goin'-away?

Herrick (*handing her the flask*)   And where are you off to, Sarah?

Tituba (*as* **Sarah** *drinks*)   We goin' to Barbados, soon the Devil gits here with the feathers and the wings.

Herrick   Oh? A happy voyage to you.

Sarah Good   A pair of bluebirds wingin' southerly, the two of us! Oh, it be a grand transformation, Marshal! (*She raises the flask to drink again.*)

Herrick (*taking the flask from her lips*)   You'd best give me that or you'll never rise off the ground. Come along now.

Tituba   I'll speak to him for you, if you desires to come along, Marshal.

Herrick   I'd not refuse it, Tituba; it's the proper morning to fly into Hell.

Tituba   Oh, it be no Hell in Barbados. Devil, him be pleasure-man in Barbados, him be singin' and dancin' in Barbados. It's you folks—you riles him up 'round here; it be too cold 'round here for that Old Boy. He freeze his soul in Massachusetts, but in Barbados he just as sweet and—(*A bellowing cow is heard, and* **Tituba** *leaps up and calls to the window:*) Aye, sir! That's him, Sarah!

Sarah Good   I'm here, Majesty! (*They hurriedly pick up their rags as* **Hopkins**, *a guard, enters.*)

Hopkins   The Deputy Governor's arrived.

Herrick (*grabbing* **Tituba**)   Come along, come along.

Tituba (*resisting him*)   No, he comin' for me. I goin' home!

Herrick (*pulling her to the door*)   That's not Satan, just a poor old cow with a hatful of milk. Come along now, out with you!

Tituba (*calling to the window*)   Take me home, Devil! Take me home!

Sarah Good (*following the shouting* **Tituba** *out*)   Tell him I'm goin', Tituba! Now you tell him Sarah Good is goin' too!

In the corridor outside **Tituba** *calls on—"Take me home, Devil; Devil take me home!"—and* **Hopkins**' *voice orders her to move on.* **Herrick** *returns and begins to push old rags and straw into a corner. Hearing footsteps, he turns, and enter* **Danforth** *and* **Judge Hathorne**. *They are in greatcoats and wear hats against the bitter cold. They are followed in by* **Cheever**, *who carries a dispatch case and a flat wooden box containing his writing materials.*

Herrick   Good morning, Excellency.

Danforth   Where is Mr. Parris?

Herrick   I'll fetch him. (*He starts for the door.*)

Danforth   Marshal. (**Herrick** *stops.*) When did Reverend Hale arrive?

Herrick   It were toward midnight, I think.

Danforth (*suspiciously*)   What is he about here?

Herrick   He goes among them that will hang, sir. And he prays with them. He sits with Goody Nurse now. And Mr. Parris with him.

Danforth   Indeed. That man have no authority to enter here, Marshal. Why have you let him in?

Herrick   Why, Mr. Parris command me, sir. I cannot deny him.

Danforth   Are you drunk, Marshal?

Herrick   No, sir; it is a bitter night, and I have no fire here.

Danforth (*containing his anger*)   Fetch Mr. Parris.

Herrick   Aye, sir.

Danforth   There is a prodigious stench in this place.

Herrick   I have only now cleared the people out for you.

Danforth   Beware hard drink, Marshal.

Herrick   Aye, sir. (*He waits an instant for further orders. But* **Danforth**, *in dissatisfaction, turns his back on him, and* **Herrick** *goes out. There is a pause.* **Danforth** *stands in thought.*)

Hathorne   Let you question Hale, Excellency; I should not be surprised he have been preaching in Andover lately.

Danforth   We'll come to that; speak nothing of Andover. Parris prays with him. That's strange. (*He blows on his hands, moves toward the window, and looks out.*)

Hathorne   Excellency, I wonder if it be wise to let Mr. Parris so continuously with the prisoners. (**Danforth** *turns to him, interested.*) I think, sometimes, the man has a mad look these days.

Danforth   Mad?

Hathorne   I met him yesterday coming out of his house, and I bid him good morning—and he wept and went his way. I think it is not well the village sees him so unsteady.

Danforth   Perhaps he have some sorrow.

Cheever (*stamping his feet against the cold*)   I think it be the cows, sir.

Danforth   Cows?

Cheever   There be so many cows wanderin' the highroads, now their masters are in the jails, and much disagreement who they will belong to now. I know Mr. Parris be arguin' with farmers all yesterday—there is great contention, sir, about the cows. Contention make him weep, sir; it were always a man that weep for contention. (*He turns, as do* **Hathorne**

and **Danforth**, *hearing someone coming up the corridor.* **Danforth** *raises his head as* **Parris** *enters. He is gaunt, frightened, and sweating in his greatcoat.*)

Parris (*to Danforth, instantly*)   Oh, good morning, sir, thank you for coming, I beg your pardon wakin' you so early. Good morning, Judge Hathorne.

Danforth   Reverend Hale have no right to enter this—

Parris   Excellency, a moment. (*He hurries back and shuts the door.*)

Hathorne   Do you leave him alone with the prisoners?

Danforth   What's his business here?

Parris (*prayerfully holding up his hands*)   Excellency, hear me. It is a providence. Reverend Hale has returned to bring Rebecca Nurse to God.

Danforth (*surprised*)   He bids her confess?

Parris (*sitting*)   Hear me. Rebecca have not given me a word this three month since she came. Now she sits with him, and her sister and Martha Corey and two or three others—, and he pleads with them, confess their crimes and save their lives.

Danforth   Why—this is indeed a providence. And they soften, they soften?

Parris   Not yet, not yet. But I thought to summon you, sir, that we might think on whether it be not wise, to—(*He dares not say it.*) I had thought to put a question, sir, and I hope you will not—

Danforth   Mr. Parris, be plain, what troubles you?

Parris   There is news, sir, that the court—the court must reckon with. My niece, sir, my niece—I believe she has vanished.

Danforth   Vanished!

Parris   I had thought to advise you of it earlier in the week, but—

Danforth   Why? How long is she gone?

Parris   This be the third night. You see, sir, she told me she would stay a night with Mercy Lewis. And next day, when she does not return, I send to Mr. Lewis to inquire. Mercy told him she would sleep in *my* house for a night.

Danforth   They are both gone?!

Parris (*in fear of him*)   They are, sir.

Danforth (*alarmed*)   I will send a party for them. Where may they be?

Parris   Excellency, I think they be aboard a ship. (**Danforth** *stands agape.*) My daughter tells me how she heard them speaking of ships last week, and tonight I discover my—my strongbox is broke into. (*He presses his fingers against his eyes to keep back tears.*)

Hathorne (*astonished*)   She have robbed you?

Parris   Thirty-one pound is gone. I am penniless. (*He covers his face and sobs.*)

Danforth   Mr. Parris, you are a brainless man! (*He walks in thought, deeply worried.*)

Parris   Excellency, it profit nothing you should blame me. I cannot think they would run off except they fear to keep in Salem any more. (*He is pleading.*) Mark it, sir, Abigail had close knowledge of the town, and since the news of Andover has broken here—

Danforth   Andover is remedied. The court returns there on Friday, and will resume examinations.

Parris   I am sure of it, sir. But the rumor here speaks rebellion in Andover, and it—

Danforth   There is no rebellion in Andover!

Parris   I tell you what is said here, sir. Andover have thrown out the court, they say, and will have no part of witchcraft. There be a faction here, feeding on that news, and I tell you true, sir, I fear there will be riot here.

Hathorne   Riot! Why at every execution I have seen naught but high satisfaction in the town.

Parris   Judge Hathorne—it were another sort that hanged till now. Rebecca Nurse is no Bridget that lived three year with Bishop before she married him. John Proctor is not Isaac Ward that drank his family to ruin. (*To* **Danforth***:*) I would to God it were not so, Excellency, but these people have great weight yet in the town. Let Rebecca stand upon the gibbet and send up some righteous prayer, and I fear she'll wake a vengeance on you.

Hathorne   Excellency, she is condemn a witch. The court have—

Danforth (*in deep concern, raising a hand to* **Hathorne**)   Pray you. (*To* **Parris***:*) How do you propose, then?

Parris   Excellency, I would postpone these hangin's for a time.

Danforth   There will be no postponement.

Parris   Now Mr. Hale's returned, there is hope, I think—for if he bring even one of these to God, that confession surely damns the others in the public eye, and none may doubt more that they are all linked to Hell. This way, unconfessed and claiming innocence, doubts are multiplied, many honest people will weep for them, and our good purpose is lost in their tears.

Danforth (*after thinking a moment, then going to* **Cheever**)   Give me the list.

Cheever *opens the dispatch case, searches.*

Parris   It cannot be forgot, sir, that when I summoned the congregation for John Proctor's excommunication there were hardly thirty people come to hear it. That speak a discontent, I think, and—

Danforth (*studying the list*)   There will be no postponement.

Parris   Excellency—

Danforth   Now, sir—which of these in your opinion may be brought to God? I will myself strive with him till dawn. (*He hands the list to* **Parris**, *who merely glances at it.*)

Parris   There is not sufficient time till dawn.

Danforth   I shall do my utmost. Which of them do you have hope for?

Parris (*not even glancing at the list now, and in a quavering voice, quietly*)   Excellency—a dagger—(*He chokes up.*)

Danforth   What do you say?

Parris   Tonight, when I open my door to leave my house—a dagger clattered to the ground. (*Silence.* **Danforth** *absorbs this. Now* **Parris** *cries out:*) You cannot hang this sort. There is danger for me. I dare not step outside at night!

Reverend Hale *enters. They look at him for an instant in silence.*

He is steeped in sorrow, exhausted, and more direct than he ever was.

Danforth   Accept my congratulations, Reverend Hale; we are gladdened to see you returned to your good work.

Hale (*coming to* **Danforth** *now*)   You must pardon them. They will not budge.

Herrick *enters, waits.*

Danforth (*conciliatory*)   You misunderstand, sir; I cannot pardon these when twelve are already hanged for the same crime. It is not just.

Parris (*with failing heart*)   Rebecca will not confess?

Hale   The sun will rise in a few minutes. Excellency, I must have more time.

Danforth   Now hear me, and beguile yourselves no more. I will not receive a single plea for pardon or postponement. Them that will not confess will hang. Twelve are already executed; the names of these seven are given out, and the village expects to see them die this morning. Postponement now speaks a floundering on my part; reprieve or pardon must cast doubt upon the guilt of them that died till now. While I speak God's law, I will not crack its voice with whimpering. If retaliation is your fear, know this—I should hang ten thousand that dared to rise against the law, and an ocean of salt tears could not melt the resolution of the statutes. Now draw yourselves up like men and help me, as you are bound by Heaven to do. Have you spoken with them all, Mr. Hale?

Hale   All but Proctor. He is in the dungeon.

Danforth (*to* **Herrick**)   What's Proctor's way now?

Herrick   He sits like some great bird; you'd not know he lived except he will take food from time to time.

Danforth (*after thinking a moment*)   His wife—his wife must be well on with child now.

Herrick   She is, sir.

Danforth   What think you, Mr. Parris? You have closer knowledge of this man; might her presence soften him?

Parris   It is possible, sir. He have not laid eyes on her these three months. I should summon her.

Danforth (*to* **Herrick**)   Is he yet adamant? Has he struck at you again?

Herrick   He cannot, sir, he is chained to the wall now.

Danforth (*after thinking on it*)   Fetch Goody Proctor to me. Then let you bring him up.

Herrick   Aye, sir. (**Herrick** *goes. There is silence.*)

Hale   Excellency, if you postpone a week and publish to the town that you are striving for their confessions, that speak mercy on your part, not faltering.

Danforth   Mr. Hale, as God have not empowered me like Joshua to stop this sun from rising, so I cannot withhold from them the perfection of their punishment.

Hale (*harder now*)   If you think God wills you to raise rebellion, Mr. Danforth, you are mistaken!

Danforth (*instantly*)   You have heard rebellion spoken in the town?

Hale   Excellency, there are orphans wandering from house to house; abandoned cattle bellow on the highroads, the stink of rotting crops hangs everywhere, and no man knows when the harlots' cry will end his life—and you wonder yet if rebellion's spoke? Better you should marvel how they do not burn your province!

Danforth   Mr. Hale, have you preached in Andover this month?

Hale   Thank God they have no need of me in Andover.

Danforth   You baffle me, sir. Why have you returned here?

Hale   Why, it is all simple. I come to do the Devil's work. I come to counsel Christians they should belie themselves. (*His sarcasm collapses.*) There is blood on my head! Can you not see the blood on my head!!

Parris   Hush! (*For he has heard footsteps. They all face the door. Herrick enters with Elizabeth. Her wrists are linked by heavy chain, which Herrick now removes. Her clothes are dirty; her face is pale and gaunt. Herrick goes out.*)

Danforth (*very politely*)   Goody Proctor. (*She is silent.*) I hope you are hearty?

Elizabeth (*as a warning reminder*)   I am yet six month before my time.

Danforth   Pray be at your ease, we come not for your life. We— (*Uncertain how to plead, for he is not accustomed to it.*) Mr. Hale, will you speak with the woman?

Hale   Goody Proctor, your husband is marked to hang this morning.

Pause.

Elizabeth (*quietly*)   I have heard it.

Hale   You know, do you not, that I have no connection with the court? (*She seems to doubt it.*) I come of my own, Goody Proctor. I would save your husband's life, for if he is taken I count myself his murderer. Do you understand me?

Elizabeth   What do you want of me?

Hale   Goody Proctor, I have gone this three month like our Lord into the wilderness. I have sought a Christian way, for damnation's doubled on a minister who counsels men to lie.

Hathorne   It is no lie, you cannot speak of lies.

Hale   It is a lie! They are innocent!

Danforth   I'll hear no more of that!

Hale (*continuing to* **Elizabeth**)   Let you not mistake your duty as I mistook my own. I came into this village like a bridegroom to his beloved, bearing gifts of high religion; the very crowns of holy law I brought, and what I touched with my bright confidence, it died; and where I turned the eye of my great faith, blood flowed up. Beware, Goody Proctor—cleave to no faith when faith brings blood. It is mistaken law that leads you to sacrifice. Life, woman, life is God's most precious gift; no principle, however glorious, may justify the taking of it. I beg you, woman, prevail upon your husband to confess. Let him give his lie. Quail not before God's judgment in this, for it may well be God damns a liar less than he that throws his life away for pride. Will you plead with him? I cannot think he will listen to another.

Elizabeth (*quietly*)   I think that be the Devil's argument.

Hale (*with a climactic desperation*)   Woman, before the laws of God we are as swine! We cannot read His will!

Elizabeth   I cannot dispute with you, sir; I lack learning for it.

Danforth (*going to her*)   Goody Proctor, you are not summoned here for disputation. Be there no wifely tenderness within you? He will die with the sunrise. Your husband. Do you understand it? (*She only looks at him.*) What say you? Will you contend with him? (*She is silent.*) Are you stone? I tell you true, woman, had I no other proof of your unnatural life, your dry eyes now would be sufficient evidence that you delivered up your soul to Hell! A very ape would weep at such calamity! Have the devil dried up any tear of pity in you? (*She is silent.*) Take her out. It profit nothing she should speak to him!

Elizabeth (*quietly*)   Let me speak with him, Excellency.

Parris (*with hope*)   You'll strive with him? (*She hesitates.*)

Danforth   Will you plead for his confession or will you not?

Elizabeth   I promise nothing. Let me speak with him.

A sound—the sibilance of dragging feet on stone. They turn. A pause. **Herrick** *enters with* **John Proctor**. *His wrists are chained. He is another man, bearded, filthy, his eyes misty as though webs had overgrown them. He halts inside the doorway, his eye caught by the sight of* **Elizabeth**. *The emotion flowing between them prevents anyone from speaking for an instant. Now* **Hale**, *visibly affected, goes to* **Danforth** *and speaks quietly.*

Hale   Pray, leave them, Excellency.

Danforth (*pressing* **Hale** *impatiently aside*)   Mr. Proctor, you have been notified, have you not? (**Proctor** *is silent, staring at* **Elizabeth**.) I see light in the sky, Mister; let you counsel with your wife, and may God help you turn your back on Hell. (**Proctor** *is silent, staring at* **Elizabeth**.)

Hale (*quietly*)   Excellency, let—

Danforth *brushes past* **Hale** *and walks out.* **Hale** *follows.* **Cheever** *stands and follows,* **Hathorne** *behind.* **Herrick** *goes.* **Parris**, *from a safe distance, offers:*

Parris   If you desire a cup of cider, Mr. Proctor, I am sure I—(**Proctor** *turns an icy stare at him, and he breaks off.* **Parris** *raises his palms toward* **Proctor**.) God lead you now. (**Parris** *goes out.*)

Alone. **Proctor** *walks to her, halts. It is as though they stood in a spinning world. It is beyond sorrow, above it. He reaches out his hand as though toward an embodiment not quite real, and as he touches her, a strange soft sound, half laughter, half amazement, comes from his throat. He pats her hand. She covers his hand with hers. And then, weak, he sits. Then she sits, facing him.*

Proctor   The child?

Elizabeth   It grows.

Proctor   There is no word of the boys?

Elizabeth   They're well. Rebecca's Samuel keeps them.

Proctor   You have not seen them?

Elizabeth   I have not. (*She catches a weakening in herself and downs it.*)

Proctor   You are a—marvel, Elizabeth.

Elizabeth   You—have been tortured?

Proctor   Aye. (*Pause. She will not let herself be drowned in the sea that threatens her.*) They come for my life now.

Elizabeth   I know it.

Pause.

Proctor   None—have yet confessed?

Elizabeth   There be many confessed.

Proctor   Who are they?

Elizabeth   There be a hundred or more, they say. Goody Ballard is one; Isaiah Goodkind is one. There be many.

Proctor   Rebecca?

Elizabeth   Not Rebecca. She is one foot in Heaven now; naught may hurt her more.

Proctor   And Giles?

Elizabeth   You have not heard of it?

Proctor   I hear nothin', where I am kept.

Elizabeth   Giles is dead.

He looks at her incredulously.

Proctor   When were he hanged?

Elizabeth (*quietly, factually*)   He were not hanged. He would not answer aye or nay to his indictment; for if he denied the charge they'd hang him surely, and auction out his property. So he stand mute, and died Christian under the law. And so his sons will have his farm. It is the law, for he could not be condemned a wizard without he answer the indictment, aye or nay.

Proctor   Then how does he die?

Elizabeth (*gently*)   They press him, John.

Proctor   Press?

Elizabeth   Great stones they lay upon his chest until he plead aye or nay. (*With a tender smile for the old man:*) They say he give them but two words. "More weight," he says. And died.

Proctor (*numbed—a thread to weave into his agony*)   "More weight."

Elizabeth   Aye. It were a fearsome man, Giles Corey.

Pause.

Proctor (*with great force of will, but not quite looking at her*)   I have been thinking I would confess to them, Elizabeth. (*She shows nothing.*) What say you? If I give them that?

Elizabeth   I cannot judge you, John.

Pause.

Proctor (*simply—a pure question*)   What would you have me do?

Elizabeth   As you will, I would have it. (*Slight pause:*) I want you living, John. That's sure.

Proctor (*pauses, then with a flailing of hope*)   Giles' wife? Have she confessed?

Elizabeth   She will not.

Pause.

Proctor   It is a pretense, Elizabeth.

Elizabeth   What is?

Proctor   I cannot mount the gibbet like a saint. It is a fraud. I am not that man. (*She is silent.*) My honesty is broke, Elizabeth; I am no good man. Nothing's spoiled by giving them this lie that were not rotten long before.

Elizabeth   And yet you've not confessed till now. That speak, goodness in you.

Proctor   Spite only keeps me silent. It is hard to give a lie to dogs. (*Pause, for the first time he turns directly to her.*) I would have your forgiveness, Elizabeth.

Elizabeth   It is not for me to give, John, I am—

Proctor   I'd have you see some honesty in it. Let them that never lied die now to keep their souls. It is pretense for me, a vanity that will not blind God nor keep my children out of the wind. (*Pause.*) What say you?

Elizabeth (*upon a heaving sob that always threatens*)   John, it come to naught that I should forgive you, if you'll not forgive yourself. (*Now he turns away a little, in great agony.*) It is not my soul, John, it is yours. (*He stands, as though in physical pain, slowly rising to his feet with a* *great immortal longing to find his answer. It is difficult to say, and she is on the verge of tears.*) Only be sure of this, for I know it now: Whatever you will do, it is a good man does it. (*He turns his doubting, searching gaze upon her.*) I have read my heart this three month, John. (*Pause.*) I have sins of my own to count. It needs a cold wife to prompt lechery.

Proctor (*in great pain*)   Enough, enough—

Elizabeth (*now pouring out her heart*)   Better you should know me!

Proctor   I will not hear it! I know you!

Elizabeth   You take my sins upon you, John—

Proctor (*in agony*)   No, I take my own, my own!

Elizabeth   John, I counted myself so plain, so poorly made, no honest love could come to me! Suspicion kissed you when I did; I never knew how I should say my love. It were a cold house I kept! (*In fright, she swerves, as* **Hathorne** *enters.*)

Hathorne   What say you, Proctor? The sun is soon up.

Proctor*, his chest heaving, stares, turns to* **Elizabeth***. She comes to him as though to plead, her voice quaking.*

Elizabeth   Do what you will. But let none be your judge. There be no higher judge under Heaven than Proctor is! Forgive me, forgive me, John—I never knew such goodness in the world! (*She covers her face, weeping.*)

Proctor *turns from her to* **Hathorne***; he is off the earth, his voice hollow.*

Proctor   I want my life.

Hathorne (*electrified, surprised*)   You'll confess yourself?

Proctor   I will have my life.

Hathorne (*with a mystical tone*)   God be praised! It is a providence! (*He rushes out the door, and his voice is heard calling down the corridor:*) He will confess! Proctor will confess!

Proctor (*with a cry, as he strides to the door*)   Why do you cry it? (*In great pain he turns back to her.*) It is evil, is it not? It is evil.

Elizabeth (*in terror, weeping*)   I cannot judge you, John, I cannot!

Proctor   Then who will judge me? (*Suddenly clasping his hands:*) God in Heaven, what is John Proctor, what is John Proctor? (*He moves as an animal, and a jury is riding in him, a tantalized search.*) I think it is honest, I think so; I am no saint. (*As though she had denied this he calls angrily at her*:) Let Rebecca go like a saint; for me it is fraud!

Voices are heard in the hall, speaking together in suppressed excitement.

Elizabeth   I am not your judge, I cannot be. (*As though giving him release:*) Do as you will, do as you will!

Proctor   Would you give them such a lie? Say it. Would you ever give them this? (*She cannot answer.*) You would not; if tongs of fire were singeing you you would not! It is evil. Good, then—it is evil, and I do it!

Hathorne *enters with* **Danforth**, *and, with them,* **Cheever**, **Parris**, *and* **Hale**. *It is a businesslike, rapid entrance, as though the ice had been broken.*

Danforth (*with great relief and gratitude*)   Praise to God, man, praise to God; you shall be blessed in Heaven for this. (**Cheever** *has hurried to the bench with pen, ink, and paper.* **Proctor** *watches him.*) Now then, let us have it. Are you ready, Mr. Cheever?

Proctor (*with a cold, cold horror at their efficiency*)   Why must it be written?

Danforth   Why, for the good instruction of the village, Mister; this we shall post upon the church door! (*To* **Parris**, *urgently:*) Where is the marshal?

Parris (*runs to the door and calls down the corridor*)   Marshal! Hurry!

Danforth   Now, then, Mister, will you speak slowly, and directly to the point, for Mr. Cheever's sake. (*He is on record now, and is really dictating to* **Cheever**, *who writes.*) Mr. Proctor, have you seen the Devil in your life? (**Proctor**'s *jaws lock.*) Come, man, there is light in the sky; the town waits at the scaffold; I would give out this news. Did you see the Devil?

Proctor   I did.

Parris   Praise God!

Danforth   And when he come to you, what were his demand? (**Proctor** *is silent.* **Danforth** *helps.*) Did he bid you to do his work upon the earth?

Proctor   He did.

Danforth   And you bound yourself to his service? (**Danforth** *turns, as* **Rebecca Nurse** *enters, with* **Herrick** *helping to support her. She is barely able to walk.*) Come in, come in, woman!

Rebecca (*brightening as she sees* **Proctor**)   Ah, John! You are well, then, eh?

Proctor *turns his face to the wall.*

Danforth   Courage, man, courage—let her witness your good example that she may come to God herself. Now hear it, Goody Nurse! Say on, Mr. Proctor. Did you bind yourself to the Devil's service?

Rebecca (*astonished*)   Why, John!

Proctor (*through his teeth, his face turned from* **Rebecca**)   I did.

Danforth   Now, woman, you surely see it profit nothin' to keep this conspiracy any further. Will you confess yourself with him?

Rebecca   Oh, John—God send his mercy on you!

Danforth   I say, will you confess yourself, Goody Nurse?

Rebecca   Why, it is a lie, it is a lie; how may I damn myself? I cannot, I cannot.

Danforth   Mr. Proctor. When the Devil came to you did you see Rebecca Nurse in his company? (**Proctor** *is silent.*) Come, man, take courage—did you ever see her with the Devil?

Proctor (*almost inaudibly*)   No.

Danforth, *now sensing trouble, glances at* **John** *and goes to the table, and picks up a sheet—the list of condemned.*

Danforth   Did you ever see her sister, Mary Easty, with the Devil?

Proctor   No, I did not.

Danforth (*his eyes narrow on* **Proctor**)   Did you ever see Martha Corey with the Devil?

Proctor   I did not.

Danforth (*realizing, slowly putting the sheet down*)   Did you ever see anyone with the Devil?

Proctor   I did not.

Danforth   Proctor, you mistake me. I am not empowered to trade your life for a lie. You have most certainly seen some person with the Devil. (**Proctor** *is silent.*) Mr. Proctor, a score of people have already testified they saw this woman with the Devil.

Proctor   Then it is proved. Why must I say it?

Danforth   Why "must" you say it! Why, you should rejoice to say it if your soul is truly purged of any love for Hell!

Proctor   They think to go like saints. I like not to spoil their names.

Danforth (*inquiring, incredulous*)   Mr. Proctor, do you think they go like saints?

Proctor (*evading*)   This woman never thought she done the Devil's work.

Danforth   Look you, sir. I think you mistake your duty here. It matters nothing what she thought—she is convicted of the unnatural murder of children, and you for sending your spirit out upon Mary Warren. Your soul alone is the issue here, Mister, and you will prove its whiteness or you cannot live in a Christian country. Will you tell me now what persons conspired with you in the Devil's company? (**Proctor** *is silent.*) To your knowledge was Rebecca Nurse ever—

Proctor   I speak my own sins; I cannot judge another. (*Crying out, with hatred:*) I have no tongue for it.

Hale (*quickly to* **Danforth**)   Excellency, it is enough he confess himself. Let him sign it, let him sign it.

Parris (*feverishly*)   It is a great service, sir. It is a weighty name; it will strike the village that Proctor confess. I beg you, let him sign it. The sun is up, Excellency!

Danforth (*considers; then with dissatisfaction*)   Come, then, sign your testimony. (*To* **Cheever**:) Give it to him. (**Cheever** *goes to* **Proctor***, the confession and a pen in hand.* **Proctor** *does not look at it.*) Come, man, sign it.

Proctor (*after glancing at the confession*)   You have all witnessed it—it is enough.

Danforth   You will not sign it?

Proctor   You have all witnessed it; what more is needed?

Danforth   Do you sport with me? You will sign your name or it is no confession, Mister! (*His breast heaving with agonized breathing,* **Proctor** *now lays the paper down and signs his name.*)

Parris   Praise be to the Lord!

Proctor *has just finished signing when* **Danforth** *reaches for the paper. But* **Proctor** *snatches it up, and now a wild terror is rising in him, and a boundless anger.*

Danforth (*perplexed, but politely extending his hand*)   If you please, sir.

Proctor   No.

Danforth (*as though* **Proctor** *did not understand*)   Mr. Proctor, I must have—

Proctor   No, no. I have signed it. You have seen me. It is done! You have no need for this.

Parris   Proctor, the village must have proof that—

Proctor   Damn the village! I confess to God, and God has seen my name on this! It is enough!

Danforth   No, sir, it is—

Proctor   You came to save my soul, did you not? Here! I have confessed myself; it is enough!

Danforth   You have not con—

Proctor   I have confessed myself! Is there no good penitence but it be public? God does not need my name nailed upon the church! God sees my name; God knows how black my sins are! It is enough!

Danforth   Mr. Proctor—

Proctor   You will not use me! I am no Sarah Good or Tituba, I am John Proctor! You will not use me! It is no part of salvation that you should use me!

Danforth   I do not wish to—

Proctor   I have three children—how may I teach them to walk like men in the world, and I sold my friends?

Danforth   You have not sold your friends—

Proctor   Beguile me not! I blacken all of them when this is nailed to the church the very day they hang for silence!

Danforth   Mr. Proctor, I must have good and legal proof that you—

Proctor   You are the high court, your word is good enough! Tell them I confessed myself; say Proctor broke his knees and wept like a woman; say what you will, but my name cannot—

Danforth (*with suspicion*)   It is the same, is it not? If I report it or you sign to it?

Proctor (*he knows it is insane*)   No, it is not the same! What others say and what I sign to is not the same!

Danforth   Why? Do you mean to deny this confession when you are free?

Proctor   I mean to deny nothing!

Danforth   Then explain to me, Mr. Proctor, why you will not let—

Proctor (*with a cry of his whole soul*)   Because it is my name! Because I cannot have another in my life! Because I lie and sign myself to lies! Because I am not worth the dust on the feet of them that hang! How may I live without my name? I have given you my soul; leave me my name!

Danforth (*pointing at the confession in* **Proctor***'s hand*)   Is that document a lie? If it is a lie I will not accept it! What say you? I will not deal in lies, Mister! (**Proctor** *is motionless.*) You will give me your honest confession in my hand, or I cannot keep you from the rope. (**Proctor** *does not reply.*) Which way do you go, Mister?

His breast heaving, his eyes staring, **Proctor** *tears the paper and crumples it, and he is weeping in fury, but erect.*

Danforth   Marshal!

Parris (*hysterically, as though the tearing paper were his life*)   Proctor, Proctor!

Hale   Man, you will hang! You cannot!

Proctor (*his eyes full of tears*)   I can. And there's your first marvel, that I can. You have made your magic now, for now I do think I see some shred of goodness in John Proctor. Not enough to weave a banner with, but white enough to keep it from such dogs. (**Elizabeth**, *in a burst of terror, rushes to him and weeps against his hand.*) Give them no tear! Tears pleasure them! Show honor now, show a stony heart and sink them with it! (*He has lifted her, and kisses her now with great passion.*)

Rebecca   Let you fear nothing! Another judgment waits us all!

Danforth   Hang them high over the town! Who weeps for these, weeps for corruption! (*He sweeps out past them.* **Herrick** *starts to lead* **Rebecca**, *who almost collapses, but* **Proctor** *catches her, and she glances up at him apologetically.*)

Rebecca   I've had no breakfast.

Herrick   Come, man.

Herrick *escorts them out,* **Hathorne** *and* **Cheever** *behind them.* **Elizabeth** *stands staring at the empty doorway.*

Parris (*in deadly fear, to* **Elizabeth**)   Go to him, Goody Proctor! There is yet time!

From outside a drumroll strikes the air. **Parris** *is startled.* **Elizabeth** *jerks about toward the window.*

Parris   Go to him! (*He rushes out the door, as though to hold back his fate.*) Proctor! Proctor!

Again, a short burst of drums.

Hale   Woman, plead with him! (*He starts to rush out the door, and then goes back to her.*) Woman! It is pride, it is vanity. (*She avoids his eyes, and moves to the window. He drops to his knees.*) Be his helper!—What profit him to bleed? Shall the dust praise him? Shall the worms declare his truth? Go to him, take his shame away!

Elizabeth (*supporting herself against collapse, grips the bars of the window, and with a cry*)   He have his goodness now. God forbid I take it from him!

The final drumroll crashes, then heightens violently. **Hale** *weeps in frantic prayer, and the new sun is pouring in upon her face, and the drums rattle like bones in the morning air.*

Curtain.

Echoes Down the Corridor

Not long after the fever died, Parris was voted from office, walked out on the highroad, and was never heard of again.

The legend has it that Abigail turned up later as a prostitute in Boston.

Twenty years after the last execution, the government awarded compensation to the victims still living, and to the families of the dead. However, it is evident that some people still were unwilling to admit their total guilt, and also that the factionalism was still alive, for some beneficiaries were actually not victims at all, but informers.

Elizabeth Proctor married again, four years after Proctor's death.

In solemn meeting, the congregation rescinded the excommunications—this in March 1712. But they did so upon orders of the government. The jury, however, wrote a statement praying forgiveness of all who had suffered.

Certain farms which had belonged to the victims were left to ruin, and for more than a century no one would buy them or live on them.

To all intents and purposes, the power of theocracy in Massachusetts was broken.

A Memory of Two Mondays

A Play in One Act

The Characters

Bert	Larry
Raymond	Frank
Agnes	Jerry
Patricia	William
Gus	Tom
Jim	Mechanic
Kenneth	Mr. Eagle

The shipping room of a large auto-parts warehouse. This is but the back of a large loft in an industrial section of New York. The front of the loft, where we cannot see, is filled with office machinery, records, the telephone switchboard, and the counter where customers may come who do not order by letter or phone.

The two basic structures are the long packing table which curves upstage at the left, and the factory-type windows which reach from floor to ceiling and are encrusted with the hard dirt of years. These windows are the background and seem to surround the entire stage.

At the back, near the center, is a door to the toilet; on it are hooks for clothing. The back wall is bare but for a large spindle on which orders are impaled every morning and taken off and filled by the workers all day long. At center there is an ancient desk and chair. Downstage right is a small bench. Boxes, a roll of packing paper on the table, and general untidiness. This place is rarely swept.

The right and left walls are composed of corridor openings, a louverlike effect, leading out into the alleys which are lined with bins reaching to the ceiling. Downstage center there is a large cast-iron floor scale with weights and balance exposed.

The nature of the work is simple. The men take orders off the hook, go out into the bin-lined alleys, fill the orders, bring the merchandise back to the table, where **Kenneth** *packs and addresses everything. The desk is used by* **Gus** *and/or* **Tom Kelly** *to figure postage or express rates on, to eat on, to lean on, or to hide things in. It is just home base, generally.*

A warning: The place must seem dirty and unmanageably chaotic, but since it is seen in this play with two separate visions it is also romantic. It is a little world, a home to which, unbelievably perhaps, these people like to come every Monday morning, despite what they say.

It is a hot Monday morning in summer, just before nine.

The stage is empty for a moment; then **Bert** *enters. He is eighteen. His trousers are worn at the knees but not unrespectable; he has rolled-up sleeves and is tieless. He carries a thick book, a large lunch in a brown paper bag, and a* New York Times. *He stores the lunch behind the packing table, clears a place on the table, sits and opens the paper, reads.*

Enter **Raymond Ryan**, *the manager. He wears a tie, white shirt, pressed pants, carries a clean towel, a tabloid, and in the other hand a sheaf of orders.*

Raymond *is forty, weighed down by responsibilities, afraid to be kind, quite able to be tough. He walks with the suggestion of a stoop.*

He goes directly to a large hook set in the back wall and impales the orders. **Bert** *sees him but, getting no greeting, returns to his paper. Preoccupied,* **Raymond** *walks past* **Bert** *toward the toilet, then halts in thought, turns back to* **Bert**.

Raymond   Tommy Kelly get in yet?

Bert   I haven't seen him, but I just got here myself. (**Raymond** *nods slightly, worried.*) He'll probably make it all right.

Raymond   What are you doing in so early?

Bert   I wanted to get a seat on the subway for once. Boy, it's nice to walk around in the streets before the crowds get out . . .

Raymond (*he has never paid much attention to* **Bert**, *is now curious, has time for it*)   How do you get time to read that paper?

Bert   Well, I've got an hour and ten minutes on the subway. I don't read it all, though. Just reading about Hitler.

Raymond   Who's that?

Bert   He took over the German government last week.

Raymond (*nodding, uninterested*)   Listen, I want you to sweep up that excelsior laying around the freight elevator.

Bert   Okay. I had a lot of orders on Saturday, so I didn't get to it.

Raymond (*self-consciously; thus almost in mockery*)   I hear you're going to go to college. Is that true?

Bert (*embarrassed*)   Oh, I don't know, Mr. Ryan. They may not even let me in, I got such bad marks in high school.

Raymond   *You* did?

Bert   Oh, yeah. I just played ball and fooled around, that's all. I think I wasn't listening, y'know?

Raymond   How much it going to cost you?

Bert   I guess about four, five hundred for the first year. So I'll be here a long time—if I ever do go. You ever go to college?

Raymond (*shaking his head negatively*)   My kid brother went to pharmacy though. What are you going to take up?

Bert   I really don't know. You look through that catalogue—boy, you feel like taking it all, you know?

Raymond   This the same book you been reading?

Bert   Well, it's pretty long, and I fall asleep right after supper.

Raymond (*turning the book up*)   "War and Peace"?

Bert   Yeah, he's supposed to be a great writer.

Raymond   How long it take you to read a book like this?

Bert   Oh, probably about three, four months, I guess. It's hard on the subway, with all those Russian names.

Raymond (*putting the book down*)   What do you get out of a book like that?

Bert   Well, it's—it's literature.

Raymond (*nodding, mystified*)   Be sure to open those three crates of axles that came in Saturday, will you? (*He starts to go toward the toilet.*)

Bert   I'll get to it this morning.

Raymond   And let me know when you decide to leave. I'll have to get somebody—

Bert   Oh, that'll be another year. Don't worry about it. I've got to save it all up first. I'm probably just dreaming anyway.

Raymond   How much do you save?

Bert   About eleven or twelve a week.

Raymond   Out of fifteen?

Bert   Well, I don't buy much. And my mother gives me my lunch.

Raymond   Well, sweep up around the elevator, will you?

Raymond *starts for the toilet as* **Agnes** *enters. She is a spinster in her late forties, always on the verge of laughter.*

Agnes   Morning, Ray!

Raymond   Morning, Agnes. (*He exits into the toilet.*)

Agnes (*to* **Bert**)   Bet you wish you could go swimming, heh?

Bert   Boy, I wouldn't mind. It's starting to boil already.

Agnes   You ought to meet my nephew sometime, Bert. He's a wonderful swimmer. Really, you'd like him. He's very serious.

Bert   How old is he now?

Agnes   He's only thirteen, but he reads the *New York Times* too.

Bert   Yeah?

Agnes (*noticing the book*)   You still reading that book?

Bert (*embarrassed*)   Well, I only get time on the subway, Agnes—

Agnes   Don't let any of them kid you, Bert. You go ahead. You read the *New York Times* and all that. What happened today?

Bert   Hitler took over the German government.

Agnes   Oh, yes; my nephew knows about him. He loves civics. Last week one night he made a regular speech to all of us in the living room, and I realized that everything Roosevelt has done is absolutely illegal. Did you know that? Even my brother-in-law had to admit it, and he's a Democrat.

Enter **Patricia** *on her way to the toilet. She is twenty-three, blankly pretty, dressed just a little too tightly. She is not quite sure who she is yet.*

Patricia   Morning!

Agnes   Morning, Patricia! Where did you get that pin?

Patricia   It was given. (*She glances at* **Bert***, who blushes.*)

Agnes   Oh, Patricia! Which one is he?

Patricia   Oh, somebody. (*She starts past for the toilet;* **Bert** *utters a warning "Ugh," and she remains.*)

Agnes (*she tends to laugh constantly, softly*)   Did you go to the dance Saturday night?

Patricia (*fixing her clothing*)   Well, they're always ending up with six guys in the hospital at that dance, and like that, so we went bowling.

Agnes   Did he give you that pin?

Patricia   No, I had a date after him.

Agnes (*laughing, titillated*)   Pat!

Patricia   Well, I forgot all about him. So when I got home he was still sitting in front of the house in his car. I thought he was going to murder me. But isn't it an unusual pin? (*To* **Bert**, *who has moved off:*) What are you always running away for?

Bert (*embarrassed*)   I was just getting ready to work, that's all.

Enter **Gus**. *He is sixty-eight, a barrel-bellied man, totally bald, with a long, fierce, gray mustache that droops on the right side. He wears a bowler, and his pants are a little too short. He has a ready-made clip-on tie. He wears winter underwear all summer long, changes once a week. There is something neat and dusty about him—a rolling gait, bandy legs, a belly hard as a rock and full of beer. He speaks with a gruff Slavic accent.*

Patricia   Oh, God, here's King Kong. (*She goes out up one of the corridors.*)

Gus (*calling after her halfheartedly—he is not completely sober, not bright yet*)   You let me get my hands on you I give you King Kong!

Agnes (*laughing*)   Oh, Gus, don't say those things!

Gus (*going for her*)   Aggie, you make me crazy for you!

Agnes (*laughing and running from him toward the toilet door*)   Gus!

Gus   Agnes, let's go Atlantic City!

Agnes *starts to open the toilet door.* **Raymond** *emerges from it.*

Agnes (*surprised by* **Raymond**)   Oh!

Raymond (*with plaintive anger*)   Gus! Why don't you cut it out, heh?

Gus   Oh, I'm sick and tired, Raymond.

Agnes *goes into the toilet.*

Raymond   How about getting all the orders shipped out by tonight, heh, Gus—for once?

Gus   What I did? I did something?

Raymond   Where's Jim?

Gus   How do I know where's Jim? Jim is my brother?

Jim *enters, stiff. He is in his mid-seventies, wears bent eye-glasses; has a full head of hair; pads about with careful tread.*

Jim (*dimly*)   Morning, Raymond. (*He walks as though he will fall forward. All watch as* **Jim** *aims his jacket for a hook, then, with a sudden motion, makes it. But he never really sways.*)

Gus   Attaboy, Jim! (*To* **Raymond***:*) What you criticize Jim? Look at that!

Jim (*turning to* **Raymond** *with an apologetic smile*)   Morning, Raymond. Hot day today. (*He goes to the spike and takes orders off it.*)

Raymond   Now look, Gus, Mr. Eagle is probably going to come today, so let's have everything going good, huh?

Gus   You can take Mr. Eagle and you shove him!

Agnes *enters from the toilet.*

Raymond   What's the matter with you? I don't want that language around here any more. I'm not kidding, either. It's getting worse and worse, and we've got orders left over every night. Let's get straightened out here, will you? It's the same circus every Monday morning. (*He goes out.*)

Agnes   How's Lilly? Feeling better?

Gus   She's all the time sick, Agnes. I think she gonna die.

Agnes   Oh, don't say that. Pray to God, Gus.

Gus (*routinely*)   Aggie, come with me Atlantic City. (*He starts taking off his shirt.*)

Agnes (*going from him*)   Oh, how you smell!

Gus (*loudly*)   I stink, Aggie!

Agnes (*closing her ears, laughing*)   Oh, Gus, you're so terrible! (*She rushes out.*)

Gus (*laughs loudly, tauntingly, and turns to* **Bert**)   What are you doin'? It's nine o clock.

Bert   Oh. (*He gets off the bench.*) I've got five to. Is your wife really sick? (*He gets an order from the hook.*)

Gus   You don't see Jim wait till nine o'clock! (*He goes to* **Jim**, *who is looking through the orders, and puts an arm around him.*) Goddam Raymond. You hear what he says to me?

Jim   Ssh, Gus, it's all right. Maybe better call Lilly.

Gus (*grasping* **Jim***'s arm*)   Wanna beer?

Jim (*trying to disengage himself*)   No, Gus, let's behave ourselves. Come on.

Gus (*looking around*)   Oh, boy. Oh, goddam boy. Monday morning. Ach.

Jim (*to* **Bert**, *as he starts out*)   Did you unpack those axles yet?

Gus (*taking the order out of* **Jim**'s *hand*)   What are you doing with axles? Man your age! (*He gives* **Bert Jim**'s *order.*) Bert! Here! You let him pick up heavy stuff I show you something! Go!

Bert   I always take Jim's heavy orders, Gus. (*He goes out with the orders.*)

Gus   Nice girls, heh, Jim?

Jim   Oh, darn nice. Darn nice girls, Gus.

Gus   I keep my promise, hah, Jim?

Jim   You did, Gus. I enjoyed myself. But maybe you ought to call up your wife. She might be wonderin' about you. You been missin' since Saturday, Gus.

Gus (*asking for a reminder*)   Where we was yesterday?

Jim   That's when we went to Staten Island, I think. On the ferry? Remember? With the girls? I think we was on a ferry. So it must've been to Staten Island. You better call her.

Gus   Ach—She don't hear nothing, Jim.

Jim   But if the phone rings, Gus, she'll know you're all right.

Gus   All right, I ring the phone. (*He goes and dials.* **Jim** *leaves with his orders.*)

Patricia *enters.*

Patricia   Morning, Kong!

Gus   Shatap.

She goes into the toilet as **Gus** *listens on the phone. Then he roars: "Hallo! Hallo! Lilly! Gus! Gus! How you feel? Gus! Working! Ya! Ya! Gus! Oh, shatap!" He hangs up the phone angrily, confused.* **Jim** *enters with a few small boxes, which he sets in a pile on the table.*

Jim   You call her?

Gus   Oh, Jim, she don't hear nothing. (*He goes idly to the toilet, opens the door.* **Patricia** *screams within, and* **Gus** *stands there in the open doorway, screaming with her in parody, then lets the door shut.*)

Jim *starts out, examining his order, a pencil in his hand, as* **Kenneth** *enters, lunch in hand.* **Kenneth** *is twenty-six, a strapping, fair-skinned man, with thinning hair, delicately shy, very strong. He has only recently come to the country.*

Jim   Morning, Kenneth.

Kenneth   And how are you this fine exemplary morning, James?

Jim   Oh, comin' along. Goin' to be hot today. (*He goes out.*)

Kenneth *hangs up his jacket and stores his lunch.* **Gus** *is standing in thought, picking his ear with a pencil.*

Kenneth   Havin' yourself a thought this morning, Gus? (**Gus** *just looks at him, then goes back to his thought and his excavation.*) Gus, don't you think something could be done about the dust constantly fallin' through the air of this place? Don't you imagine a thing or two could be done about that?

Gus   Because it's dusty, that's why. (*He goes to the desk, sits.*)

Kenneth   That's what I was sayin'—it's dusty. Tommy Kelly get in?

Gus   No.

Kenneth   Oh, poor Tommy Kelly. (**Bert** *enters.*) Good morning to you, Bert. Have you finished your book yet?

Bert (*setting two heavy axles on the bench*)   Not yet, Kenneth.

Kenneth (*his jacket in his hand*)   Well, don't lose heart. (*He orates:*)

Courage, brother! do not stumble
Though thy path be dark as night;
There's a star to guide the humble;
Trust in God, and do the Right.

By Norman Macleod.

Bert (*with wonder, respect*)   How'd you learn all that poetry?

Kenneth (*hanging up his jacket*)   Why, in Ireland, Bert; there's all kinds of useless occupations in Ireland. "When lilacs last in the dooryard bloomed . . ."

Gus (*from the desk*)   What the hell you doin'? (**Bert** *goes to order hook.*)

Kenneth   Why, it's the poetry hour, Gus, don't you know that? This is the hour all men rise to thank God for the blue of the sky, the roundness of the everlasting globe, and the cheerful cleanliness of the subway system. And here we have some axles. Oh, Bert, I never thought I would end me life wrappin' brown paper around strange axles. (*He wraps.*) And what's the latest in the *New York Times* this morning?

Bert (*looking through orders on the hook*)   Hitler took over the German government.

Kenneth   Oh, did he! Strange, isn't it, about the Germans? A great people they are for mustaches. You take Bismarck, now, or you take Frederick the Great, or even take Gus over here—

Gus   I'm no Heinie.

Kenneth   Why, I always thought you were, Gus. What are you, then?

Gus   American.

Kenneth   I know that, but what *are* you?

Gus   I fought in submarine.

Kenneth   Did you, now? An American submarine?

Gus   What the hell kind of submarine I fight in, Hungarian? (*He turns back to his desk.*)

Kenneth   Well, don't take offense, Gus. There's all kinds of submarines, y'know. (**Bert** *starts out, examining his order.*) How's this to be wrapped, Bert? Express?

Bert   I think that goes parcel post. It's for Skaneateles.

Gus (*erupting at his desk*)   Axles parcel post? You crazy? You know how much gonna cost axles parcel post?

Bert   That's right. I guess it goes express.

Gus   And you gonna go college? Barber college you gonna go!

Bert   Well, I forgot it was axles, Gus.

Gus (*muttering over his desk*)   Stupid.

Kenneth   I've never been to Skaneateles. Where would that be?

Bert   It's a little town upstate. It's supposed to be pretty there.

Kenneth   That a sweet thought? Sendin' these two grimy axles out into the green countryside? I spent yesterday in the park. What did you do, Bert? Go swimmin' again, I suppose?

Gus (*turning*)   You gonna talk all day?

Bert   We're working. (*He goes out.* **Kenneth** *wraps.*)

Kenneth   You're rubbin' that poor kid pretty hard, Gus; he's got other things on his mind than parcel post and—

Gus   What the hell I care what he got on his mind? Axles he gonna send parcel post! (*He returns to his work on the desk.*)

Kenneth (*wraps, then*)   Can you feel the heat rising in this building! If only some of it could be saved for the winter. (*Pause. He is wrapping.*) The fiery furnace. Nebuchadnezzar was the architect. (*Pause.*) What do you suppose would happen, Gus, if a man took it into his head to wash these windows? They'd snatch him off to the nuthouse, heh? (*Pause.*) I wonder if he's only kiddin'—Bert. About goin' to college someday.

Gus (*not turning from his desk*)   Barber college he gonna go.

Kenneth (*he works, thinking*)   He must have a wealthy family. Still and all, he don't spend much. I suppose he's just got some strong idea in his mind. That's the thing, y'know. I often conceive them myself, but I'm all the time losin' them, though. It's the holdin' on—that's what does it. You can almost see it in him, y'know? He's holdin' on to somethin'. (*He shakes his head in wonder, then sings:*)

> Oh, the heat of the summer,
> The cool of the fall.
> The lady went swimming
> With nothing at all.

Ah, that's a filthy song, isn't it! (*Pause. He wraps.*) Gus, you suppose Mr. Roosevelt'll be makin' it any better than it is? (*He sings:*)

> The minstrel boy to the war has gone,
> In the ranks of death . . .

Patricia *enters from the toilet.*

Patricia   Was that an Irish song?

Kenneth (*shyly*)   All Irish here and none of yiz knows an Irish song.

Patricia   You have a terrific voice, Kenneth.

Gus (*to* **Patricia**)   Why don't you make date with him?

Kenneth (*stamping his foot*)   Oh, that's a nasty thing to say in front of a girl, Gus!

Gus *rises.*

Patricia (*backing away from* **Gus**)   Now don't start with me, kid, because—

Gus *lunges for her. She turns to run, and he squeezes her buttocks mercilessly as she runs out and almost collides with* **Larry**, *who is entering.* **Larry** *is thirty-nine, a troubled but phlegmatic man, good-looking. He is carrying a container of coffee and a lighted cigarette. On the collision he spills a little coffee.*

Larry (*with a slight humor*)   Hey! Take it easy.

Patricia (*quite suddenly all concerned for* **Larry**, *to* **Gus**)   Look what you did, you big horse!

Larry *sets the coffee on the table.*

Larry   Jesus, Gus.

Gus   Tell her stop makin' all the men crazy! (*He returns to his desk.*)

Patricia   I'm sorry, Larry. (*She is alone, in effect, with* **Larry**. *Both of them wipe the spot on his shirt.*) Did you buy it?

Larry (*embarrassed but courageous, as though inwardly flaunting his own fears*)   Yeah, I got it yesterday.

Patricia   Gee, I'd love to see it. You ever going to bring it to work?

Larry (*now he meets her eyes*)   I might. On a Saturday, maybe.

Patricia   'Cause I love those Auburns, y'know?

Larry   Yeah, they got nice valves. Maybe I'll drive you home some night. For the ride.

Patricia (*the news stuns her*)   Oh, boy! Well—I'll see ya. (*She goes.*)

Gus   You crazy? Buy Auburn?

Larry (*with depth—a profound conclusion*)   I like the valves, Gus.

Gus   Yeah, but when you gonna go sell it who gonna buy an Auburn?

Larry   Didn't you ever get to where you don't care about that? I *always* liked those valves, and I decided, that's all.

Gus   Yeah, but when you gonna go sell it—

Larry   I don't care.

Gus   You don't care!

Larry   I'm sick of dreaming about things. They've got the most beautifully laid-out valves in the country on that car, and I want it, that's all.

Kenneth *is weighing a package on the scales.*

Gus   Yeah, but when you gonna go sell it—

Larry   I just don't care, Gus. Can't you understand that? (*He stares away, inhaling his cigarette.*)

Kenneth (*stooped over, sliding the scale weights*)   There's a remarkable circumstance, Larry. Raymond's got twins, and now you with the triplets. And both in the same corporation. We ought to send that to the *Daily News* or something. I think they give you a dollar for an item like that.

Bert *enters, puts goods on the table.*

Bert   Gee, I'm getting hungry. Want a sandwich, Kenneth? (*He reaches behind the packing table for his lunch bag.*)

Kenneth   Thank you, Bert. I might take one later.

Gus (*turning from the desk to* **Bert**)   Lunch you gonna eat nine o'clock?

Bert   I got up too early this morning. You want some?

Kenneth   He's only a growing boy, Gus—and by the way, if you care to bend down, Gus (*indicating under the scale platform*) there's more mice than ever under here.

Gus (*without turning*)   Leave them mice alone.

Kenneth   Well, you're always complainin' the number of crayons I'm using, and I'm only tellin' you they're the ones is eatin' them up. (*He turns to* **Larry**.) It's a feast of crayons goin' on here every night, Larry.

Enter **Jim** *with goods, padding along.*

Jim   Goin' to be hot today, Gus.

Gus   Take easy, what you running for? (**Jim** *stops to light his cigar butt.*)

Kenneth (*reading off the scale weights*)   Eighty-one pounds, Gus. For Skaneateles, in the green countryside of upper New York State.

Gus   What? What you want?

Kenneth   I want the express order—eighty-one pounds to Skaneateles, New York.

Gus   Then why don't you say that, goddam Irishman? You talk so much. When you gonna stop talkin'? (*He proceeds to make out the slip.*)

Kenneth   Oh, when I'm rich, Gus, I'll have very little more to say. (**Gus** *is busy making out the slip;* **Kenneth** *turns to* **Larry**.) No sign yet of Tommy Kelly in the place, Larry.

Larry   What'd you, cut a hole in your shoe?

Kenneth   A breath of air for me little toe. I only paid a quarter for them, y'know; feller was sellin' them in Bryant Park. Slightly used, but they're a fine pair of shoes, you can see that.

Larry   They look small for you.

Kenneth   They are at that. But you can't complain for a quarter, I guess.

Gus   Here.

Gus *hands* **Kenneth** *an express slip, which* **Kenneth** *now proceeds to attach to the package on the table. Meanwhile* **Jim** *has been leafing through the orders on the hook and is now leaving with two in his hand.*

Kenneth   How do you keep up your strength, Jim? I'm always exhausted. You never stop movin', do ya? (**Jim** *just shakes his head with a "Heh, heh."*) I bet it's because you never got married, eh?

Jim   No, I guess I done everything there is but that.

Larry   How come you never did get married, Jim?

Jim   Well, I was out West so long, you know, Larry. Out West. (*He starts to go again.*)

Kenneth   Oh, don't they get married much out there?

Jim   Well, the cavalry was amongst the Indians most of the time.

Bert   How old are you now, Jim? No kidding.

Kenneth   I'll bet he's a hundred.

Jim   Me? No. I ain't no hunderd. I ain't near a hunderd. You don't have to be a hunderd to've fought the Indians. They was more Indians was fought than they tells in the schoolbooks, y'know. They was a hell of a lot of fightin' up to McKinley and all in there. I ain't no hunderd. (*He starts out.*)

Kenneth   Well, how old would you say you are, Jim?

Jim   Oh, I'm seventy-four, seventy-five, seventy-six—around in there. But I ain't no hunderd. (*He exits, and* **Kenneth** *sneezes.*)

Bert (*he has put his lunch bag away and is about to leave*)   Boy, I was hungry!

Kenneth (*irritated*)   Larry, don't you suppose a word might be passed to Mr. Eagle about the dust? It's rainin' dust from the ceiling!

Bert *goes out.*

Gus   What the hell Mr. Eagle gonna do about the dust?

Kenneth   Why, he's supposed to be a brilliant man, isn't he? Dartmouth College graduate and all? I've been five and a half months in this country, and I never sneezed so much in my entire life before. My nose is all—

Enter **Frank***, the truckdriver, an impassive, burly man in his thirties.*

Frank   Anything for the West Bronx?

Kenneth   Nothin' yet, Frank. I've only started, though.

Jim *enters with little boxes, which he adds to the pile on the bench.*

Frank   You got anything for West Bronx, Jim? I've got the truck on the elevator.

Gus   What's the hurry?

Frank   I got the truck on the elevator.

Gus   Well, take it off the elevator! You got one little box of bearings for the West Bronx. You can't go West Bronx with one little box.

Frank   Well, I gotta go.

Gus   You got a little pussy in the West Bronx.

Frank   Yeah, I gotta make it before lunch.

Jim (*riffling through his orders*)   I think I got something for the East Bronx.

Frank   No, West Bronx.

Jim (*removing one order from his batch*)   How about Brooklyn?

Frank   What part? (*He takes* **Jim***'s order, reads the address, looks up, thinking.*)

Jim   Didn't you have a girl around Williamsburg?

Frank   I'll have to make a call. I'll be right back.

Gus   You gonna deliver only where you got a woman?

Frank   No, Gus, I go any place you tell me. But as long as I'm goin' someplace I might as well—you know. (*He starts out.*)

Gus   You some truckdriver.

Frank   You said it, Gus. (*He goes out.*)

Gus   Why don't you go with him sometime, Kenneth? Get yourself nice piece ding-a-ling—

Kenneth   Oh, don't be nasty now, Gus. You're only tryin' to be nasty to taunt me.

Raymond *enters.*

Raymond   Didn't Tommy Kelly get here?

Gus   Don't worry for Tommy. Tommy going to be all right.

Larry   Can I see you a minute, Ray? (*He moves with* **Raymond** *over to the left.*)

Raymond   Eagle's coming today, and if he sees him drunk again I don't know what I'm going to do.

Larry   Ray, I'd like you to ask Eagle something for me.

Raymond   What?

Larry   I've got to have more money.

Raymond   You and me both, boy.

Larry   No, I can't make it any more, Ray. I mean it. The car put me a hundred and thirty bucks in the hole. If one of the kids gets sick I'll be strapped.

Raymond   Well, what'd you buy the car for?

Larry   I'm almost forty, Ray. What am I going to be careful for?

Raymond   See, the problem is, Larry, if you go up, I'm only making thirty-eight myself, and I'm the manager, so it's two raises—

Larry   Ray, I hate to make it tough for you, but my wife is driving me nuts. Now—

Enter **Jerry Maxwell** *and* **Willy Hogan**, *both twenty-three.* **Jerry** *has a black eye; both are slick dressers.*

Jerry and Willy   Morning. Morning, Gus.

Raymond   Aren't you late, fellas?

Jerry (*glancing at his gold wristwatch*)   I've got one minute to nine, Mr. Ryan.

Willy   That's Hudson Tubes time, Mr. Ryan.

Gus   The stopwatch twins.

Raymond (*to* **Jerry**)   You got a black eye?

Jerry   Yeah, we went to a dance in Jersey City last night.

Willy   Ran into a wise guy in Jersey City, Mr. Ryan.

Jerry (*with his taunting grin; he is very happy with himself*)   Tried to take his girl away from us.

Raymond   Well, get on the ball. Mr. Eagle's—

Enter **Tom Kelly**. **Gus** *rises from the desk.* **Bert** *enters, stands still.* **Raymond** *and* **Larry** *stand watching.* **Kenneth** *stops wrapping.* **Tom** *is stiff; he moves in a dream to the chair* **Gus** *has left and sits rigidly. He is a slight, graying clerk in his late forties.*

Gus (*to* **Raymond**)   Go 'way, go 'head.

Raymond *comes up and around the desk to face* **Tom**, *who sits there, staring ahead, immobile, his hands in his lap.*

Raymond   Tommy.

Jerry *and* **Willy** *titter.*

Gus (*to them*)   Shatap, goddam bums!

Jerry   Hey, don't call me—

Gus   Shatap, goddamit I break you goddam head! (*He has an axle in his hand, and* **Raymond** *and* **Larry** *are pulling his arm down.* **Jim** *enters and goes directly to him. All are crying, "Gus! Cut it out! Put it down!"*)

Jerry   What'd we do? What'd I say?

Gus   Watch out! Just watch out you make fun of this man! I break you head, both of you! (*Silence. He goes to* **Tom**, *who has not moved since arriving.*) Tommy. Tommy, you hear Gus? Tommy? (**Tom** *is transfixed.*)

Raymond   Mr. Eagle is coming today, Tommy.

Gus (*to all*) Go 'head, go to work, go to work! (*They all move;* **Jerry** *and* **Willy** *go out.*)

Raymond Can you hear me, Tom? Mr. Eagle is coming to look things over today, Tom.

Jim Little shot of whisky might bring him to.

Gus Bert! (*He reaches into his pocket.*) Here, go downstairs bring a shot. Tell him for Tommy. (*He sees what is in his hand.*) I only got ten cents.

Raymond Here. (*He reaches into his pocket as* **Jim**, **Kenneth**, *and* **Larry** *all reach into their own pockets.*)

Bert (*taking a coin from* **Raymond**) Okay, I'll be right up. (*He hurries out.*)

Raymond Well, this is it, Gus. I gave him his final warning.

Gus (*he is worried*) All right, go 'way, go 'way.

Agnes *enters.*

Agnes Is he—?

Raymond You heard me, Agnes. I told him on Saturday, didn't I? (*He starts past her.*)

Agnes But Ray, look how nice and clean he came in today. His hair is all combed, and he's much neater.

Raymond I did my best, Agnes. (*He goes out.*)

Gus (*staring into* **Tom**'*s dead eyes*) Ach. He don't see nothin', Agnes.

Agnes (*looking into* **Tom**'*s face*) And he's supposed to be saving for his daughter's confirmation dress! Oh, Tommy. I'd better cool his face. (*She goes into the toilet.*)

Kenneth (*to* **Larry**) Ah, you can't blame the poor feller; sixteen years of his life in this place.

Larry You said it.

Kenneth There's a good deal of monotony connected with the life, isn't it?

Larry You ain't kiddin'.

Kenneth Oh, there must be a terrible lot of Monday mornings in sixteen years. And no philosophical idea at all, y'know, to pass the time?

Gus (*to* **Kenneth**)   When you gonna shut up?

Agnes *comes from the toilet with a wet cloth. They watch as she washes* **Tom**'*s face.*

Kenneth   Larry, you suppose we could get these windows washed sometime? I've often thought if we could see a bit of the sky now and again it would help matters now and again.

Larry   They've never been washed since I've been here.

Kenneth   I'd do it myself if I thought they wouldn't all be laughin' at me for a greenhorn. (*He looks out through the open window, which only opens out a few inches.*) With all this glass we might observe the clouds and the various signs of approaching storms. And there might even be a bird now and again.

Agnes   Look at that—he doesn't even move. And he's been trying so hard! Nobody gives him credit, but he does try hard. (*To* **Larry**:) See how nice and clean he comes in now?

Jim *enters, carrying parts.*

Jim   Did you try blowing in his ear?

Gus   Blow in his ear?

Jim   Yeah, the Indians used to do that. Here, wait a minute. (*He comes over, takes a deep breath, and blows into* **Tom**'*s ear. A faint smile begins to appear on* **Tom**'*s face, but, as* **Jim** *runs out of breath, it fades.*)

Kenneth   Well, I guess he's not an Indian.

Jim   That's the truth, y'know. Out West, whenever there'd be a drunken Indian, they used to blow in his ear.

Enter **Bert**, *carefully carrying a shotglass of whisky.*

Gus   Here, gimme that. (*He takes it.*)

Bert (*licking his fingers*)   Boy, that stuff is strong.

Gus   Tommy? (*He holds the glass in front of* **Tom**'*s nose.*) Whisky. (**Tom** *doesn't move.*) Mr. Eagle is coming today, Tommy.

Jim   Leave it on the desk. He might wake up to it.

Bert   How's he manage to make it here, I wonder.

Agnes   Oh, he's awake. Somewhere inside, y'know. He just can't show it, somehow. It's not really like being drunk, even.

Kenneth   Well, it's pretty close, though, Agnes.

Agnes *resumes wetting* **Tom**'s *brow.*

Larry   Is that a fact, Jim, about blowing in a guy's ear?

Jim   Oh, sure. Indians always done that. (*He goes to the order hook, leafs through.*)

Kenneth   What did yiz all have against the Indians?

Jim   The Indians? Oh, we didn't have nothin' against the Indians. Just law and order, that's all. Talk about heat, though. It was so hot out there we—

Jim *exits with an order as* **Frank** *enters.*

Frank   All right, I'll go to Brooklyn.

Gus   Where you running? I got nothing packed yet.

Enter **Jerry**, *who puts goods on the table.*

Frank   Well, you beefed that I want to go Bronx, so I'm tellin' you now I'll go to Brooklyn.

Gus   You all fixed up in Brooklyn?

Frank   Yeah, I just made a call.

Agnes (*laughing*)   Oh, you're all so terrible! (*She goes out.*)

Jerry   How you doin', Kenny? You gittin' any?

Kenneth   Is that all two fine young fellas like you is got on your minds?

Jerry   Yeah, that's all. What's on your mind?

Frank *is loading himself with packages.*

Gus (*of* **Tom**)   What am I gonna do with him, Larry? The old man's comin'.

Larry   Tell you the truth, Gus, I'm sick and tired of worrying about him, y'know? Let him take care of himself.

Gus *goes to* **Larry**, *concerned, and they speak quietly.*

Gus   What's the matter with you these days?

Larry   Two years I'm asking for a lousy five-dollar raise. Meantime my brother's into me for fifty bucks for his wife's special shoes; my sister's got me for sixty-five to have her kid's teeth fixed. So I buy a car, and they're all on my back—how'd I dare buy a car! Whose money is it? Y'know, Gus? I mean—

Gus   Yeah, but an Auburn, Larry—

Larry (*getting hot*)   I happen to like the valves! What's so unusual about that?

Enter **Willy** *and* **Jerry** *with goods.*

Willy (*to* **Jerry**)   Here! Ask Frank. (*To* **Frank***:*) Who played shortstop for Pittsburgh in nineteen-twenty-four?

Frank   Pittsburgh? Honus Wagner, wasn't it?

Willy (*to* **Jerry**)   What I tell ya?

Jerry   How could it be Honus Wagner? Honus Wagner—

Raymond *enters with a* **Mechanic***, and* **Willy** *and* **Jerry** *exit, arguing.* **Frank** *goes out with his packages.* **Gus** *returns to his desk.*

Raymond   Larry, you want to help this man? He's got a part here.

Larry *simply turns, silent, with a hurt and angry look. The* **Mechanic** *goes to him, holds out the part; but* **Larry** *does not take it, merely inspects it, for it is greasy, as is the man.*

Raymond (*going to the desk, where* **Gus** *is now seated at work beside* **Tom**)   Did he move at all, Gus?

Gus   He's feeling much better, I can see. Go, go 'way, Raymond.

Raymond *worriedly stands there.*

Larry (*to* **Mechanic**)   Where you from?

Mechanic   I'm mechanic over General Truck.

Larry   What's that off?

Mechanic (*as* **Bert** *stops to watch, and* **Kenneth** *stops packing to observe*)   That's the thing—I don't know. It's a very old coal truck, see, and I thought it was a Mack, because it says Mack on the radiator, see? But I went over to Mack, and they says there's no part like that on any Mack in their whole history, see?

Larry   Is there any name on the engine?

Mechanic   I'm tellin' you; on the engine it says American-LaFrance— must be a replacement engine.

Larry   That's not off a LaFrance.

Mechanic   I know! I went over to American-LaFrance, but they says they never seen nothin' like that in their whole life since the year one.

Raymond *joins them.*

Larry   What is it, off the manifold?

Mechanic   Well, it ain't exactly off the manifold. It like sticks out, see, except it don't stick out, it's like stuck in there—I mean it's like in a little hole there on top of the head, except it ain't exactly a hole, it's a thing that comes up in like a bump, see, and then it goes down. Two days I'm walkin' the streets with this, my boss is goin' crazy.

Larry   Well, go and find out what it is, and if we got it we'll sell it to you.

Raymond   Don't you have any idea, Larry?

Larry   I might, Ray, but I'm not getting paid for being an encyclopedia. There's ten thousand obsolete parts upstairs—it was never my job to keep all that in my head. If the old man wants that service, let him pay somebody to do it.

Raymond   Ah, Larry, the guy's here with the part.

Larry   The guy is always here with the part, Ray. Let him hire somebody to take an inventory up there and see what it costs him.

Raymond (*taking the part off the table*)   Well, I'll see what I can find up there.

Larry   You won't find it, Ray. Put it down. (**Raymond** *does, and* **Larry***, blinking with hurt, turns to the mechanic.*) What is that truck, about nineteen-twenty-two?

Mechanic   That truck? (*He shifts onto his right foot in thought.*)

Larry   Nineteen-twenty?

Mechanic (*in a higher voice, shifting to the left foot*)   That truck?

Larry   Well, it's at least nineteen-twenty, isn't it?

Mechanic   Oh, it's at least. I brung over a couple a friend of mines, and one of them is an old man and he says when he was a boy already that truck was an old truck, and he's an old, old man, that guy. (**Larry** *takes the part now and sets it on the packing bench. Now even* **Gus** *gets up to watch as he stares at the part. There is a hush.* **Raymond** *goes out.*

Larry *turns the part a little and stares at it again. Now he sips his coffee.*) I understand this company's got a lot of old parts from the olden days, heh?

Larry   We may have one left, if it's what I think it is, but you'll have to pay for it.

Mechanic   Oh, I know; that's why my boss says try all the other places first, because he says youse guys charge. But looks to me like we're stuck.

Larry   Bert. (*He stares in thought.*) Get the key to the third floor from Miss Molloy. Go up there, and when you open the door you'll see those Model-T mufflers stacked up.

Bert   Okay.

Larry   You ever been up there?

Bert   No, but I always wanted to go.

Larry   Well, go past the mufflers and you'll see a lot of bins going up to the ceiling. They're full of Marmon valves and ignition stuff.

Bert   Yeah?

Larry   Go past them, and you'll come to a little corridor, see?

Bert   Yeah?

Larry   At the end of the corridor is a pile of crates—I think there's some Maxwell differentials in there.

Bert   Yeah?

Larry   Climb over the crates, but don't keep goin', see. Stand on top of the crates and turn right. Then bend down, and there's a bin—No, I tell you, get off the crates, and you can reach behind them, but to the right, and reach into that bin. There's a lot of Locomobile headnuts in there, but way back—you gotta stick your hand way in, see, and you'll find one of these.

Bert   Geez, Larry, how do you remember all that?

Agnes *rushes in.*

Agnes   Eagle's here! Eagle's here!

Larry (*to the mechanic*)   Go out front and wait at the counter, will ya? (*The* **Mechanic** *nods and leaves.* **Larry** *indicates the glass on the desk.*) Better put that whisky away, Gus.

Gus (*alarmed now*)   What should we do with him?

Larry *goes to* **Tom**, *peeved, and speaks in his ear.*

Larry   Tommy. Tommy!

Agnes   Larry, why don't you put him up on the third floor? He got a dozen warnings already. Eagle's disgusted—

Gus   Maybe he's sick. I never seen him like this.

Jim *enters with goods.*

Jim   Eagle's here.

Larry   Let's try to walk him around. Come on.

Gus *looks for a place to hide the whisky, then drinks it.*

Gus   All right, Tommy, come on, get up. (*They hoist him up to his feet, then let him go. He starts to sag; they catch him.*) I don't think he feel so good.

Larry   Come on, walk him. (*To* **Agnes***:*) Watch out for Eagle. (*She stands looking off and praying silently.*) Let's go, Tom. (*They try to walk* **Tom**, *but he doesn't lift his feet.*)

Agnes (*trembling, watching* **Tom**)   He's so kindhearted, y'see? That's his whole trouble—he's too kindhearted.

Larry (*angering, but restrained, shaking* **Tom**)   For God's sake, Tom, come on! Eagle's here! (*He shakes* **Tom** *more violently.*) Come on! What the hell is the matter with you, you want to lose your job? Goddamit, you a baby or something?

Agnes   Sssh!

They all turn to the left. In the distance is heard the clacking of heel taps on a concrete floor.

Gus   Put him down. Larry! (*They seat* **Tom** *before the desk.* **Agnes** *swipes back his mussed hair.* **Gus** *sets his right hand on top of an invoice on the desk.*) Here, put him like he's writing. Where's my pencil? Who's got pencil? (**Larry**, **Kenneth**, **Agnes** *search themselves for a pencil.*)

Kenneth   Here's a crayon.

Gus   Goddam, who take my pencil! Bert! Where's that Bert! He always take my pencil!

Bert *enters, carrying a heavy axle.*

Bert   Hey, Eagle's here!

Gus   Goddam you, why you take my pencil?

Bert   I haven't got your pencil. This is mine.

Gus *grabs the pencil out of* **Bert**'s *shirt pocket and sticks it upright into* **Tom**'s *hand. They have set him up to look as if he is writing. They step away.* **Tom** *starts sagging toward one side.*

Agnes (*in a loud whisper*)   Here he comes!

She goes to the order spike and pretends she is examining it. **Larry** *meanwhile rushes to* **Tom**, *sets him upright, then walks away, pretending to busy himself. But* **Tom** *starts falling off the chair again, and* **Bert** *rushes and props him up.*

The sound of the heel taps is on us now, and **Bert** *starts talking to* **Tom**, *meantime supporting him with one hand on his shoulder.*

Bert (*overloudly*)   Tommy, the reason I ask, see, is because on Friday I filled an order for the same amount of coils for Scranton, see, and it just seems they wouldn't be ordering the same exact amount again.

During his speech **Eagle** *has entered—a good-looking man in his late forties, wearing palm beach trousers, a shirt and tie, sleeves neatly folded up, a new towel over one arm. He walks across the shipping room, not exactly looking at anyone, but clearly observing everything. He goes into the toilet, past* **Agnes**, *who turns.*

Agnes   Good morning, Mr. Eagle.

Eagle (*nodding*)   Morning. (*He goes into the toilet.*)

Kenneth (*indicating the toilet*)   Keep it up, keep it up now!

Bert (*loudly*)   Ah—another thing that's bothering me, Tommy, is those rear-end gears for Riverhead. I can't find any invoice for Riverhead. I can't find any invoice for gears to Riverhead. (*He is getting desperate, looks to the others, but they only urge him on.*) So what happened to the invoice? That's the thing we're all wondering about, Tommy. What happened to that invoice? You see, Tom? That invoice—it was blue, I remember, blue with a little red around the edges—

Kenneth (*loudly*)   That's right there, Bert, it was a blue invoice—and it had numbers on it—

Suddenly **Tom** *stands, swaying a little, blinking. There is a moment's silence.*

Tom   No, no, Glen Wright was shortstop for Pittsburgh, not Honus Wagner.

Eagle *emerges from the toilet.* **Bert** *goes to the order spike.*

Larry   Morning, sir. (*He goes out.*)

Tom (*half bewildered, shifting from foot to foot*)   Who was talking about Pittsburgh? (*He turns about and almost collides with* **Eagle**.) Morning, Mr. Eagle.

Eagle (*as he passes* **Tom** *he lets his look linger on his face*)   Morning, Kelly.

Eagle *crosses the shipping room and goes out.* **Agnes**, **Kenneth**, *and* **Gus** *wait an instant.* **Jim** *enters, sees* **Tom** *is up.*

Jim   Attaboy, Tommy, knew you'd make it.

Tom   Glen Wright was shortstop. Who asked about that?

Gus (*nodding sternly his approbation to* **Bert**)   Very good, Bert, you done good.

Bert (*wiping his forehead*)   Boy!

Tom   Who was talking about Pittsburgh? (**Agnes** *is heard weeping. They turn.*) Agnes? (*He goes to her.*) What's the matter, Ag?

Agnes   Oh, Tommy, why do you do that?

Patricia (*calling from offstage left*)   Aggie? Your switchboard's ringing.

Agnes   Oh, Tommy! (*Weeping, she hurries out.*)

Tom (*to the others*)   What happened? What is she cryin' for?

Gus (*indicating the desk*)   Why don't you go to work, Tommy? You got lotta parcel post this morning.

Tom *always has a defensive smile. He shifts from foot to foot as he talks, as though he were always standing on a hot stove. He turns to the desk, sees* **Kenneth**. *He wants to normalize everything.*

Tom   Kenny! I didn't even see ya!

Kenneth   Morning, Tommy. Good to see you up and about.

Tom (*with a put-on brogue*)   Jasus, me bye, y'r hair is fallin' like the dew of the evenin'.

Kenneth (*self-consciously wiping his hair*)   Oh, Tommy, now—

Tom   Kenny, bye, y'r gittin' an awful long face to wash!

Kenneth (*gently cuffing him*)   Oh, now, stop that talk!

Tom (*backing toward his desk*)   Why, ya donkey, ya. I bet they had to back you off the boat!

Kenneth (*with mock anger*)   Oh, don't you be callin' me a donkey now!

Enter **Raymond**.

Raymond   Tom? (*He is very earnest, even deadly.*)

Tom (*instantly perceiving his own guilt*)   Oh, mornin', Ray, how's the twins? (*He gasps little chuckles as he sits at his desk, feeling about for a pencil.*)

Raymond *goes up close to the desk and leans over, as the others watch—pretending not to.*

Raymond (*quietly*)   Eagle wants to see you.

Tom (*with foreboding, looking up into* **Raymond**'*s face*)   Eagle? I got a lot of parcel post this morning, Ray. (*He automatically presses down his hair.*)

Raymond   He's in his office waiting for you now, Tom.

Tom   Oh, sure. It's just that there's a lot of parcel post on Monday . . . (*He feels for his tie as he rises, and walks out.* **Raymond** *starts out after him, but* **Gus** *intercedes.*)

Gus (*going up to* **Raymond**)   What Eagle wants?

Raymond   I warned him, Gus, I warned him a dozen times.

Gus   He's no gonna fire him.

Raymond   Look, it's all over, Gus, so there's nothing—

Gus   He gonna fire Tommy?

Raymond   Now don't raise your voice.

Gus   Sixteen year Tommy work here! He got daughter gonna be in church confirmation!

Raymond   Now listen, I been nursing him along for—

Gus   Then you fire me! You fire Tommy, you fire me!

Raymond   Gus!

With a stride **Gus** *goes to the hook, takes his shirt down, thrusts himself into it.*

Gus   Goddam son-of-a-bitch.

Raymond   Now don't be crazy, Gus.

Gus   I show who crazy! Tommy Kelly he gonna fire! (*He grabs his bowler off the hook. Enter* **Agnes**, *agitated.*)

Agnes   Gus! Go to the phone!

Gus (*not noticing her, and with bowler on, to* **Raymond**)   Come on, he gonna fire me now, son-of-a-bitch! (*He starts out, shirttails flying, and* **Agnes** *stops him.*)

Agnes (*indicating the phone*)   Gus, your neighbor's—

Gus (*trying to disengage himself*)   No, he gonna fire me now. He fire Tommy Kelly, he fire me!

Agnes   Lilly, Gus! Your neighbor wants to talk to you. Go, go to the phone.

Gus *halts, looks at* **Agnes**.

Gus   What, Lilly?

Agnes   Something's happened. Go, go to the phone.

Gus   Lilly? (*Perplexed, he goes to the phone.*) Hallo. Yeah, Gus. Ha? (*He listens, stunned. His hand, of itself, goes to his hatbrim as though to doff the hat, but it stays there.* **Jim** *enters, comes to a halt, sensing the attention, and watches* **Gus**.) When? When it happen? (*He listens, and then mumbles:*) Ya. Thank you. I come home right away. (*He hangs up.* **Jim** *comes forward to him questioningly. To* **Jim**, *perplexed:*) My Lilly. Die.

Jim   Oh? Hm!

Larry *enters.* **Gus** *dumbly turns to him.*

Gus (*to* **Larry**)   Die. My Lilly.

Larry   Oh, that's tough, Gus.

Raymond   You better go home. (*Pause.*) Go ahead, Gus. Go home.

Gus *stands blinking.* **Raymond** *takes his jacket from the hook and helps him on with it.* **Agnes** *starts to push his shirttails into his pants.*

Gus   We shouldn't've go to Staten Island, Jim. Maybe she don't feel good yesterday. Ts, I was in Staten Island, maybe she was sick. (**Tom**

enters, goes directly to his desk, sits, his back to the others. Pause. To **Tom***:*) He fire you, Tommy?

Tom (*holding tears back*)   No, Gus, I'm all right.

Gus (*going up next to him*)   Give you another chance?

Tom (*he is speaking with his head lowered*)   Yeah. It's all right, Gus, I'm goin' to be all right from now on.

Gus   Sure. Be a man, Tommy. Don't be no drunken bum. Be a man. You hear? Don't let nobody walk on top you. Be man.

Tom   I'm gonna be all right, Gus.

Gus (*nodding*)   One more time you come in drunk I gonna show you something. (**Agnes** *sobs. He turns to her.*) What for you cry all the time? (*He goes past her and out.* **Agnes** *then goes. A silence.*)

Raymond (*breaking the silence*)   What do you say, fellas, let's get going, heh? (*He claps his hands and walks out as all move about their work. Soon all are gone but* **Tom**, *slumped at his desk;* **Kenneth**, *wrapping; and* **Bert**, *picking an order from the hook. Now* **Kenneth** *faces* **Bert** *suddenly.*)

Kenneth (*he has taken his feeling from the departing* **Gus**, *and turns now to* **Bert**)   Bert? How would you feel about washing these windows—you and I—once and for all? Let a little of God's light in the place?

Bert (*excitedly, happily*)   Would you?

Kenneth   Well, I would if you would.

Bert   Okay, come on! Let's do a little every day; couple of months it'll all be clean! Gee! Look at the sun!

Kenneth   Hey, look down there!
See the old man sitting in a chair?
And roses all over the fence!
Oh, that's a lovely back yard!

A rag in hand, **Bert** *mounts the table; they make one slow swipe of the window before them and instantly all the windows around the stage burst into the yellow light of summer that floods into the room.*

Bert   Boy, they've got a tree!
And all those cats!

Kenneth   It'll be nice to watch the seasons pass.

'That pretty up there now, a real summer sky
And a little white cloud goin' over?
I can just see autumn comin' in
And the leaves falling on the gray days.
You've got to have a sky to look at!

Gradually, as they speak, all light hardens to that of winter, finally.

Bert (*turning to* **Kenneth**)   Kenny, were you ever fired from a job?

Kenneth   Oh, sure; two-three times.

Bert   Did you feel bad?

Kenneth   The first time, maybe. But you have to get used to that, Bert.
I'll bet you never went hungry in your life, did you?

Bert   No, I never did. Did you?

Kenneth   Oh, many and many a time. You get used to that too, though.

Bert (*turning and looking out*)   That tree is turning red.

Kenneth   It must be spectacular out in the country now.

Bert   How does the cold get through these walls?
Feel it, it's almost a wind!

Kenneth   Don't cats walk dainty in the snow!

Bert   Gee, you'd never know it was the same place—
How clean it is when it's white!
Gus doesn't say much any more, y'know?

Kenneth   Well, he's showin' his age. Gus is old.
When do you buy your ticket for the train?

Bert   I did. I've got it.

Kenneth   Oh, then you're off soon!
You'll confound all the professors, I'll bet!
(*He sings softly.*)
   The minstrel boy to the war has gone . . .

Bert *moves a few feet away; thus he is alone.* **Kenneth** *remains at the
window, looking out, polishing, and singing softly.*

Bert   There's something so terrible here!
There always was, and I don't know what.
Gus, and Agnes, and Tommy and Larry, Jim and Patricia—

Why does it make me so sad to see them every morning?
It's like the subway;
Every day I see the same people getting on
And the same people getting off,
And all that happens is that they get older. God!
Sometimes it scares me; like all of us in the world
Were riding back and forth across a great big room,
From wall to wall and back again,
And no end ever! Just no end!

He turns to **Kenneth***, but not quite looking at him, and with a deeper anxiety.*

Didn't you ever want to be anything, Kenneth?

Kenneth   I've never been able to keep my mind on it, Bert . . .
I shouldn't've cut a hole in me shoe.
Now the snow's slushin' in, and me feet's all wet.

Bert   If you studied, Kenneth, if you put your mind to something great,
I know you'd be able to learn anything, because you're clever, you're
much smarter than I am!

Kenneth   You've got something steady in your mind, Bert; Something
far away and steady.
I never could hold my mind on a far-away thing . . .

*His tone changes as though he were addressing a group of men; his
manner is rougher, angrier, less careful of proprieties.*

She's not giving me the heat I'm entitled to.
Eleven dollars a week room and board,
And all she puts in the bag is a lousy pork sandwich,
The same every day and no surprises.
Is that right? Is that right now?
How's a man to live,
Freezing all day in this palace of dust
And night comes with one window and a bed
And the streets full of strangers
And not one of them's read a book through,
Or seen a poem from beginning to end
Or knows a song worth singing.
Oh, this is an ice-cold city, Mother,
And Roosevelt's not makin' it warmer, somehow.

He sits on the table, holding his head.

And here's another grand Monday!

They are gradually appearing in natural light now, but it is a cold wintry light which has gradually supplanted the hot light of summer. **Bert** *goes to the hook for a sweater.*

Jesus, me head'll murder me. I never had the headache till this year.

Bert (*delicately*)   You're not taking up drinking, are you?

Kenneth (*he doesn't reply. Suddenly, as though to retrieve something slipping by, he gets to his feet, and roars out*)

> "The Ship of State," by Walt Whitman!
> "O Captain! my Captain! our fearful trip is done!
> The ship has weathered every wrack,
> The prize we sought is won . . ."

Now what in the world comes after that?

Bert   I don't know that poem.

Kenneth   Dammit all! I don't remember the bloody poems any more the way I did! It's the drinkin' does it, I think. I've got to stop the drinkin'!

Bert   Well, why do you drink, Kenny, if it makes you feel—

Kenneth   Good God, Bert, you can't always be doin' what you're better off to do! There's all kinds of unexpected turns, y'know, and things not workin' out the way they ought! What in hell *is* the next stanza of that poem? "The prize we sought is won . . ." God, I'd never believe I could forget that poem! I'm thinkin', Bert, y'know—maybe I ought to go onto the Civil Service. The only trouble is there's no jobs open except for the guard in the insane asylum. And that'd be a nervous place to work, I think.

Bert   It might be interesting, though.

Kenneth   I suppose it might. They tell me it's only the more intelligent people goes mad, y'know. But it's sixteen hundred a year, Bert, and I've a feelin' I'd never dare leave it, y'know? And I'm not ready for me last job yet, I think. I don't want nothin' to be the last, yet. Still and all . . .

Raymond *enters, going to toilet. He wears a blue button-up sweater.*

Raymond   Morning, boys. (*He impales a batch of orders on the desk.*)

Kenneth (*in a routine way*)   Morning, Mr. Ryan. Have a nice New Year's, did you?

Raymond   Good enough. (*To* **Bert**, *seeing the book on the table.*) Still reading that book?

Bert   Oh, I'm almost finished now. (**Raymond** *nods, continues on.* **Bert** *jumps off the table.*) Mr. Ryan? Can I see you a minute? (*He goes to* **Raymond**.) I wondered if you hired anybody yet, to take my place.

Raymond (*pleasantly surprised*)   Why? Don't you have enough money to go?

Bert   No, I'm going. I just thought maybe I could help you break in the new boy. I won't be leaving till after lunch tomorrow.

Raymond (*with resentment, even an edge of sarcasm*)   We'll break him in all right. Why don't you just get on to your own work? There's a lot of excelsior laying around the freight elevator.

Raymond *turns and goes into the toilet. For an instant* **Bert** *is left staring after him. Then he turns to* **Kenneth**, *perplexed.*

Bert   Is he sore at me?

Kenneth (*deprecatingly*)   Ah, why would he be sore at you? (*He starts busying himself at the table, avoiding* **Bert***'s eyes.* **Bert** *moves toward him, halts.*)

Bert   I hope you're not, are you?

Kenneth (*with an evasive air*)   Me? Ha! Why, Bert, you've got the heartfelt good wishes of everybody in the place for your goin'-away! (*But he turns away to busy himself at the table—and on his line* **Larry** *has entered with a container of coffee and a cigarette.*)

Bert   Morning, Larry. (*He goes to the hook, takes an order.*)

Larry (*leaning against the table*)   Jesus, it'd be just about perfect in here for penguins. (**Bert** *passes him.*) You actually leaving tomorrow?

Bert (*eagerly*)   I guess so, yeah.

Larry (*with a certain embarrassed envy*)   Got all the dough, heh?

Bert   Well, for the first year anyway. (*He grins in embarrassment.*) You mind if I thank you?

Larry   What for?

Bert   I don't know—just for teaching me everything. I'd have been fired the first month without you, Larry.

Larry (*with some wonder, respect*)   Got all your dough, heh?

Bert   Well, that's all I've been doing is saving.

Enter **Tom Kelly**. *He is bright, clean, sober.*

Tom   Morning!

Kenneth (*with an empty kind of heartiness*)   Why, here comes Tommy Kelly!

Tom (*passing to hang up his coat and hat*)   Ah, y're gettin' an awful long face to wash, Kenny, me bye.

Kenneth   Oh, cut it out with me face, Tommy. I'm as sick of it as you are.

Tom   Go on, ya donkey ya, they backed you off the boat.

Kenneth   Why, I'll tear you limb from limb, Tom Kelly! (*He mocks a fury, and* **Tom** *laughs as he is swung about. And then, with a quick hug and a laugh:*) Oh, Tommy, you're the first man I ever heard of done it. How'd you do it, Tom?

Tom   Will power, Kenny. (*He walks to his desk, sits.*) Just made up my mind, that's all.

Kenneth   Y'know the whole world is talking about you, Tom—the way you mixed all the drinks at the Christmas party and never weakened? Y'know, when I heard it was you going to mix the drinks I was prepared to light a candle for you.

Tom   I just wanted to see if I could do it, that's all. When I done that—mixin' the drinks for three hours, and givin' them away—I realized I made it. You don't look so hot to me, you know that?

Kenneth (*with a sigh*)   Oh, I'm all right. It's the sight of Monday, that's all, is got me down.

Tom   You better get yourself a little will power, Kenny. I think you're gettin' a fine taste for the hard stuff.

Kenneth   Ah, no, I'll never be a drunk, Tommy.

Tom   You're a drunk now.

Kenneth   Oh, don't say that, please!

Tom   I'm tellin' you, I can see it comin' on you.

Kenneth (*deeply disturbed*)   You can't either. Don't say that, Tommy!

Agnes *enters.*

Agnes   Morning! (*She wears sheets of brown paper for leggins.*)

Kenneth   Winter's surely here when Agnes is wearin' her leggins.

Agnes (*with her laughter*)   Don't they look awful? But that draft under the switchboard is enough to kill ya.

Larry   This place is just right for penguins.

Agnes   Haven't you got a heavier sweater, Bert? I'm surprised at your mother.

Bert   Oh, it's warm; she knitted it.

Kenneth   Bert's got the idea. Get yourself an education.

Tom   College guys are sellin' ties all over Macy's. Accountancy, Bert, that's my advice to you. You don't even have to go to college for it either.

Bert   Yeah, but I don't want to be an accountant.

Tom (*with a superior grin*)   You don't want to be an accountant?

Larry   What's so hot about an accountant?

Tom   Well, try runnin' a business without one. That's what you should've done, Larry. If you'd a took accountancy, you'd a—

Larry   You know, Tommy, I'm beginning to like you better drunk? (**Tom** *laughs, beyond criticism.*) I mean it. Before, we only had to pick you up all the time; now you got opinions about everything.

Tom   Well, if I happen to know something, why shouldn't I say—

Enter **Raymond** *from the toilet.*

Raymond   What do you say we get on the ball early today, fellas? Eagle's coming today. Bert, how about gettin' those carburetor crates open, will ya?

Bert   I was just going to do that.

Bert *and* **Raymond** *are starting out, and* **Agnes** *is moving to go, when* **Gus** *and* **Jim** *enter. Both of them are on the verge of staggering.* **Gus** *has a bright new suit and checked overcoat, a new bowler, and new shoes. He is carrying upright a pair of Ford fenders, still in their brown paper wrappings—they stand about seven feet in height.* **Jim** *aids him in carefully resting the fenders against the wall.*

Kenneth, *and* **Larry** *watch in silence.*

Patricia *enters and watches. She is wearing leggins.*

Willy *and* **Jerry** *enter in overcoats, all jazzed up.*

Willy   Morning!

Jerry   Morn—(*Both break off and slowly remove their coats as they note the scene and the mood.* **Gus**, *now that the fenders are safely stacked, turns.*)

Gus (*dimly*)   Who's got a hanger?

Kenneth   Hanger? You mean a coat-hanger, Gus?

Gus   Coat-hanger.

Jerry   Here! Here's mine! (*He gives a wire hanger to* **Gus**. **Gus** *is aided by* **Jim** *in removing his overcoat, and they both hang it on the hanger, then on a hook. Both give it a brush or two, and* **Gus** *goes to his chair, sits. He raises his eyes to them all.*)

Gus   So what everybody is looking at?

Bert, **Willy**, **Jerry** *go to work, gradually going out with orders.* **Jim** *also takes orders off the hook, and the pattern of going-and-coming emerges.* **Patricia** *goes to the toilet.* **Tom** *works at the desk.*

Larry (*half-kidding, but in a careful tone*)   What are you all dressed up about?

Gus *simply glowers in his fumes and thoughts.* **Raymond** *goes over to* **Jim**.

Raymond   What's he all dressed up for?

Jim   Oh, don't talk to me about him, Ray, I'm sick and tired of him. Spent all Saturday buyin' new clothes to go to the cemetery; then all the way the hell over to Long Island City to get these damned fenders for that old wreck of a Ford he's got. Never got to the cemetery, never got the fenders on—and we been walkin' around all weekend carryin' them damn things.

Raymond   Eagle'll be here this morning. See if you can get him upstairs. I don't want him to see him crocked again.

Jim   I'd just let him sit there, Ray, if I was you. I ain't goin' to touch him. You know what he went and done? Took all his insurance money outa the bank Saturday. Walkin' around with all that cash in his pocket—I tell ya, I ain't been to sleep since Friday night. 'Cause you can't let him loose with all that money and so low in his mind, y'know . . .

Gus   Irishman! (*All turn to him. He takes a wad out of his pocket, peels one bill off.*) Here. Buy new pair shoes.

Kenneth   Ah, thank you, no, Gus, I couldn't take that.

Raymond   Gus, Eagle's coming this morning; why don't you—

Gus (*stuffing a bill into* **Kenneth**'s *pocket*)   Go buy pair shoes.

Raymond   Gus, he's going to be here right away; why don't you—

Gus   I don't give one goddam for Eagle! Why he don't make one more toilet?

Raymond   What?

Bert *enters with goods.*

Gus   Toilet! That's right? Have one toilet for so many people? That's very bad, Raymond. That's no nice. (*Offering* **Bert** *a bill:*) Here, boy, go—buy book, buy candy.

Larry *goes to* **Gus** *before he gives the bill, puts an arm around him, and walks away from the group.*

Larry   Come on, Gussy, let me take you upstairs.

Gus   I don't care Eagle sees me, I got my money now, goddam. Oh, Larry, Larry, twenty-two year I workin' here.

Larry   Why don't you give me the money, Gus? I'll put in the bank for you.

Gus   What for I put in bank? I'm sixty-eight years old, Larry. I got no children, nothing. What for I put in bank? (*Suddenly, reminded, he turns back to* **Raymond***, pointing at the floor scale.*) Why them goddam mice nobody does nothing?

Raymond (*alarmed by* **Gus**'s *incipient anger*)   Gus, I want you to go upstairs!

Patricia *enters from toilet.*

Gus (*at the scale*)   Twenty-two years them goddam mice! That's very bad, Raymond, so much mice! (*He starts rocking the scale.*) Look at them goddam mice! (**Patricia** *screams as mice come running out from under the scale. A mêlée of shouts begins, everyone dodging mice or swinging brooms and boxes at them.* **Raymond** *is pulling* **Gus** *away from the scale, yelling at him to stop it.* **Agnes** *rushes in and, seeing the mice, screams and rushes out.* **Jerry** *and* **Willy** *rush in and join in chasing the mice, laughing.* **Patricia***, wearing leggins, is helped onto the packing table by* **Larry***, and* **Gus** *shouts up at her.*) Come with me Atlantic City, Patricia! (*He pulls out the wad.*) Five thousand dollars I got for my wife!

Patricia   You rotten thing, you! You dirty rotten thing, Gus!

Gus   I make you happy, Patricia! I make you—(*Suddenly his hand goes to his head; he is dizzy.* **Larry** *goes to him, takes one look.*)

Larry   Come, come on. (*He walks* **Gus** *into the toilet.*)

Patricia (*out of the momentary silence*)   Oh, that louse! Did you see what he did, that louse? (*She gets down off the table, and, glancing angrily toward the toilet, she goes out.*)

Raymond   All right, fellas, what do you say, heh? Let's get going.

Work proceeds—the going and coming.

Tom (*as* **Raymond** *passes him*)   I tried talking to him a couple of times, Ray, but he's got no will power! There's nothing you can do if there's no will power, y'know?

Raymond   Brother! It's a circus around here. Every Monday morning! I never saw anything like . . .

He is gone. **Kenneth** *is packing.* **Tom** *works at his desk.* **Jim** *comes and, leaving goods on the packing table, goes to the toilet, peeks in, then goes out, studying an order.* **Bert** *enters with goods.*

Kenneth   There's one thing you have to say for the Civil Service; it seals the fate and locks the door. A man needn't wonder what he'll do with his life any more.

Jerry *enters with goods.*

Bert (*glancing at the toilet door*)   Gee, I never would've thought Gus liked his wife, would you?

Tom, *studying a letter, goes out.*

Jerry (*looking up and out the window*)   Jesus!

Bert (*not attending to* **Jerry**)   I thought he always hated his wife—

Jerry   Jesus, boy!

Kenneth (*to* **Jerry**)   What're you doin'? What's—?

Jerry   Look at the girls up in there. One, two, three, four windows— full a girls, look at them! Them two is naked!

Willy *enters with goods.*

Kenneth   Oh, my God!

Willy (*rushing to the windows*)   Where? Where?

Kenneth   Well, what're you gawkin' at them for!

Gus *and* **Larry** *enter from the toilet.*

Jerry   There's another one down there! Look at her on the bed! What a beast!

Willy (*overjoyed*)   It's a cathouse! Gus! A whole cathouse moved in!

Willy *and* **Jerry** *embrace and dance around wildly;* **Gus** *stands with* **Larry**, *staring out, as does* **Bert**.

Kenneth   Aren't you ashamed of yourself!!

Tom *enters with his letter.*

Tom   Hey, fellas, Eagle's here.

Jerry (*pointing out*)   There's a new cathouse, Tommy! (**Tom** *goes and looks out the windows.*)

Kenneth   Oh, that's a terrible thing to be lookin' at, Tommy! (**Agnes** *enters;* **Kenneth** *instantly goes to her to get her out.*) Oh, Agnes, you'd best not be comin' back here any more now—

Agnes   What? What's the matter?

Jerry *has opened a window, and he and* **Willy** *whistle sharply through their fingers.* **Agnes** *looks out.*

Kenneth   Don't, Agnes, don't look at that!

Agnes   Well, for heaven's sake! What are all those women doing there?

Gus   That's whorehouse, Aggie.

Kenneth   Gus, for God's sake! (*He walks away in pain.*)

Agnes   What are they sitting on the beds like that for?

Tom   The sun is pretty warm this morning—probably trying to get a little tan.

Agnes   Oh, my heavens. Oh, Bert, it's good you're leaving! (*She turns to them.*) You're not all going, are you? (**Gus** *starts to laugh, then* **Tom**, *then* **Jerry** *and* **Willy**, *then* **Larry**, *and she is unstrung and laughing herself, but shocked.*) Oh, my heavens! (*She is gone, as* **Jim** *enters with goods.*)

Kenneth   All right, now, clear off, all of you. I can't be workin' with a lot of sex maniacs blockin' off me table!

Gus   Look, Jim! (**Jim** *looks out.*)

Jim   Oh, nice.

Jerry   How about it, fellas? Let's all go lunchtime! What do you say, Kenny? I'll pay for you!

Gus *goes to the desk, drags the chair over to the window.*

Kenneth   I'd sooner roll meself around in the horse manure of the gutter!

Jerry   I betcha you wouldn't even know what to do!

Kenneth (*bristling, fists shut*)   I'll show you what I do! I'll show you right now!

Enter **Raymond**, *furious.*

Raymond   What the hell is this? What's going on here?

Gus (*sitting in his chair, facing the windows*)   Whorehouse. (**Raymond** *looks out the windows.*)

Kenneth   You'd better pass a word to Mr. Eagle about this, Raymond, or the corporation's done for. Poor Agnes, she's all mortified, y'know.

Raymond   Oh, my God! (*To all:*) All right, break it up, come on, break it up, Eagle's here. (**Willy**, **Jerry**, **Bert**, *and* **Jim** *disperse, leaving with orders.* **Tommy** *returns to the desk.*) What're you going to do, Gus? You going to sit there? (**Gus** *doesn't answer; sits staring out thoughtfully.*) What's going on with you? Gus! Eagle's here! All right, cook in your own juice. Sit there. (*He glances out the windows.*) Brother, I needed this now! (*He goes out angrily.*)

Larry   Give me the money, Gus, come on. I'll hold it for you.

Gus (*an enormous sadness is on him*)   Go way.

Enter **Patricia**. *She glances at* **Larry** *and* **Gus**, *then looks out the windows.*

Kenneth (*wrapping*)   Ah, Patricia, don't look out there. It's disgraceful.

Tom   It's only a lot of naked women.

Kenneth   Oh, Tommy, now! In front of a girl!

Patricia (*to* **Kenneth**)   What's the matter? Didn't you ever see that before? (*She sees* **Gus** *sitting there.*) Look at Kong, will ya? (*She laughs.*) Rememberin' the old days, heh, Kong?

Larry *is walking toward an exit at left.*

Gus   Oh, shatap!

Patricia (*catching up with* **Larry** *at the edge of the stage, quietly*)   What's Ray sayin' about you sellin' the Auburn?

Larry   Yeah, I'm kinda fed up with it. It's out of my class anyway.

Patricia   That's too bad. I was just gettin' to enjoy it.

Larry (*very doubtfully*)   Yeah?

Patricia   What're you mad at me for?

Larry   Why should I be mad?

Patricia   You're married, what're you—?

Larry   Let me worry about that, will you?

Patricia   Well, I gotta worry about it too, don't I?

Larry   Since when do you worry about anything, Pat?

Patricia   Well, what did you expect me to do? How did I know you were serious?

Gus *goes to his coat, searches in a pocket.*

Larry   What did you think I was telling you all the time?

Patricia   Yeah, but Larry, anybody could say those kinda things.

Larry   I know, Pat. But I never did. (*With a cool, hurt smile:*) You know, kid, you better start believing people when they tell you something. Or else you're liable to end up in there. (*He points out the windows.*)

Patricia (*with quiet fury*)   You take that back! (*He walks away; she goes after him.*) You're going to take that back, Larry!

Eagle *enters, nods to* **Larry** *and* **Patricia**.

Eagle   Morning.

Patricia (*with a mercurial change to sunny charm*)   Good morning, Mr. Eagle!

Larry *is gone, and she exits.* **Eagle** *crosses, noticing* **Gus**, *who is standing beside his coat, drinking out of a pint whisky bottle.*

Eagle   Morning, Gus.

Gus (*lowering the bottle*)   Good morning. (**Eagle** *exits into the toilet.*)

Tom (*to* **Gus**)   You gone nuts?

Gus *returns, holding the bottle, to his chair, where he sits, looking out the window. He is growing sodden and mean.* **Bert** *enters with goods.*

Kenneth (*sotto voce*)   Eagle's in there, and look at him. He'll get the back of it now for sure.

Tom (*going to* **Gus**)   Gimme the bottle, Gus!

Gus   I goin' go someplace, Tommy. I goin' go cemetery. I wasn't one time in cemetery. I go see my Lilly. My Lilly die, I was in Staten Island. All alone she was in the house. Ts! (**Jerry** *enters with goods, sees him, and laughs.*)

Bert   Gus, why don't you give Tommy the bottle?

Gus   Twenty-two years I work here.

Kenneth (*to* **Jerry**, *who is staring out the window*)   Will you quit hangin' around me table, please?

Jerry   Can't I look out the window?

Willy *enters with goods.*

Willy   How's all the little pussies?

Kenneth   Now cut that out! (*They laugh at him.*)

Tom (*sotto voce*)   Eagle's in there!

Kenneth   Is that all yiz know of the world—filthy women and dirty jokes and the ignorance drippin' off your faces? (**Eagle** *enters from the toilet.*) There's got to be somethin' done about this, Mr. Eagle. It's an awful humiliation for the women here. (*He points, and* **Eagle** *looks.*) I mean to say, it's a terrible disorganizing sight starin' a man in the face eight hours a day, sir.

Eagle   Shouldn't have washed the windows, I guess. (*He glances down at* **Gus** *and his bottle and walks out.*)

Kenneth   Shouldn't have washed the windows, he says! (*They are laughing;* **Gus** *is tipping the bottle up.* **Jim** *enters with goods.*)

Jerry   What a donkey that guy is!

Kenneth *lunges for* **Jerry** *and grabs him by the tie, one fist ready.*

Kenneth   I'll donkey you! (**Jerry** *starts a swing at him, and* **Bert** *and* **Tom** *rush to separate them as* **Raymond** *enters.*)

Raymond   Hey! Hey!

Jerry (*as they part*)   All right, donkey, I'll see you later.

Kenneth   You'll see me later, all right—with one eye closed!

Raymond   Cut it out! (**Kenneth**, *muttering, returns to work at his table.* **Jerry** *rips an order off the hook and goes out.* **Willy** *takes an order.* **Bert** *goes out with an order.* **Raymond** *has been looking down at* **Gus**, *who is sitting with the bottle.*) You going to work, Gus? Or you going to do that? (**Gus** *gets up and goes to his coat, takes it off the hanger.*) What're you doing?

Gus   Come on, Jim, we go someplace. Here—put on you coat.

Raymond   Where you going? It's half-past nine in the morning.

Enter **Agnes**.

Agnes   What's all the noise here? (*She breaks off, seeing* **Gus** *dressing.*)

Gus   That's when I wanna go—half-past nine. (*He hands* **Jim** *his coat.*) Here. Put on. Cold outside.

Jim (*quietly*)   Maybe I better go with him, Ray. He's got all his money in—

Bert *enters with goods.*

Raymond (*reasonably, deeply concerned*)   Gus, now look; where you gonna go now? Why don't you lie down upstairs?

Gus (*swaying, to* **Bert**)   Twenty-two years I was here.

Bert   I know, Gus.

Larry *enters, watches.*

Gus   I was here before you was born I was here.

Bert   I know.

Gus   Them mice was here before you was born. (**Bert** *nods uncomfortably, full of sadness.*) When Mr. Eagle was in high school I was already here. When there was Winton Six I was here. When was Minerva car I was here. When was Stanley Steamer I was here, and Stearns Knight, and Marmon was good car; I was here all them times. I was here first day Raymond come; he was young boy; work hard be manager.

When Agnes still think she was gonna get married I was here. When was Locomobile, and Model K Ford and Model N Ford—all them different Fords, and Franklin was good car, Jordan car, Reo car, Pierce Arrow, Cleveland car—all them was good cars. All them times I was here.

Bert   I know.

Gus   You don't know nothing. Come on, Jim. (*He goes and gets a fender.* **Jim** *gets the other.*) Button up you coat, cold outside. Tommy? Take care everything good.

He walks out with **Jim** *behind him, each carrying a fender upright.* **Raymond** *turns and goes out, then* **Larry**. **Agnes** *goes into the toilet. The lights lower as this movement takes place, until* **Bert** *is alone in light, still staring at the point where* **Gus** *left.*

Bert   I don't understand;
I don't know anything:
How is it me that gets out?
I don't know half the poems Kenneth does,
Or a quarter of what Larry knows about an engine.

I don't understand how they come every morning,
Every morning and every morning,
And no end in sight.
That's the thing—there's no end!
Oh, there ought to be a statue in the park—
"To All the Ones That Stay."
One to Larry, to Agnes, Tom Kelly, Gus . . .

Gee, it's peculiar to leave a place—forever!
Still, I always hated coming here;
The same dried-up jokes, the dust;
Especially in spring, walking in from the sunshine,
Or any Monday morning in the hot days.

In the darkness men appear and gather around the packing table, eating lunch out of bags; we see them as ghostly figures, silent.

God, it's so peculiar to leave a place!
I know I'll remember them as long as I live,
As long as I live they'll never die,
And still I know that in a month or two
They'll forget my name, and mix me up
With another boy who worked here once,
And went. Gee, it's a mystery!

As full light rises **Bert** *moves into the group, begins eating from a bag.*

Jerry (*looking out the window*)   You know what's a funny thing? It's a funny thing how you get used to that.

Willy   Tommy, what would you say Cobb's average was for lifetime?

Tom   Cobb? Lifetime? (*He thinks. Pause.* **Kenneth** *sings.*)

Kenneth

>   The minstrel boy to the war has gone—

Patricia *enters, crossing to toilet—*

Kenneth   In the ranks of death you will find him.

Patricia   Is that an Irish song?

Kenneth   All Irish here, and none of yiz knows an Irish song! (*She laughs, exits into the toilet.*)

Tom   I'd say three-eighty lifetime for Ty Cobb. (*To* **Larry***:*) You're foolish sellin' that car with all the work you put in it.

Larry   Well, it was one of those crazy ideas. Funny how you get an idea, and then suddenly you wake up and you look at it and it's like— dead or something. I can't afford a car.

Agnes *enters, going toward the toilet.*

Agnes   I think it's even colder today than yesterday.

Raymond *enters.*

Raymond   It's five after one, fellas; what do you say?

They begin to get up as **Jim** *enters in his overcoat and hat.*

Kenneth   Well! The old soldier returns!

Raymond   Where's Gus, Jim?

Agnes *has opened the toilet door as* **Patricia** *emerges.*

Agnes   Oh! You scared me. I didn't know you were in there!

Jim (*removing his coat*)   He died, Ray.

Raymond   What?

The news halts everyone—but one by one—in midair, as it were.

Larry   He what?

Agnes   What'd you say?

Jim   Gus died.

Kenneth   Gus died!

Bert   Gus?

Agnes (*going to* **Jim**)   Oh, good heavens. When? What happened?

Larry   What'd you have an accident?

Jim   No, we—we went home and got the fenders on all right, and he wanted to go over and start at the bottom, and go right up Third Avenue and hit the bars on both sides. And we got up to about Fourteenth Street, in around there, and we kinda lost track of the car someplace. I have to go back there tonight, see if I can find—

Agnes   Well, what happened?

Jim   Well, these girls got in the cab, y'know, and we seen a lot of places and all that—we was to some real high-class places, forty cents for a cup of coffee and all that; and then he put me in another cab, and we rode around a while; and then he got another cab to follow us. Case one of our cabs got a flat, see? He just didn't want to be held up for a minute, Gus didn't.

Larry   Where were you going?

Jim   Oh, just all over. And we stopped for a light, y'know, and I thought I'd go up and see how he was gettin' along, y'know, and I open his cab door, and—the girl was fast asleep, see—and he—was dead. Right there in the seat. It was just gettin' to be morning.

Agnes   Oh, poor Gus!

Jim   I tell ya, Agnes, he didn't look too good to me since she died, the old lady. I never knowed it. He—liked that woman.

Raymond   Where's his money?

Jim   Oh (*with a wasting wave of the hand*) it's gone, Ray. We was stoppin' off every couple minutes so he call long distance. I didn't even know it, he had a brother someplace in California. Called him half a dozen times. And there was somebody he was talkin' to in Texas someplace, somebody that was in the Navy with him. He was tryin' to call all the guys that was in the submarine with him, and he was callin' all over hell and gone—and givin' big tips, and he bought a new suit, and give the cab driver a wristwatch and all like that. I think he got himself too sweated. Y'know it got pretty cold last night, and he was all sweated up. I kept tellin' him, I says, "Gus," I says, "you're gettin" yourself all sweated, y'know, and it's a cold night," I says; and all he kept sayin' to me all night he says, "Jim," he says, "I'm gonna do it right, Jim." That's all he says practically all night.—"I'm gonna do it right," he says. "I'm gonna do it right." (*Pause.* **Jim** *shakes his head.*) Oh, when I open that cab door I knowed it right away. I takes one look at him and I knowed it. (*There is a moment of silence, and* **Agnes** *turns and goes into the toilet.*) Oh, poor Agnes, I bet she's gonna cry now.

Jim *goes to the order hook, takes an order off, and, putting a cigar into his mouth, he goes out, studying the order.* **Raymond** *crosses and goes out; then* **Patricia** *goes.* **Willy** *and* **Jerry** *exit in different directions with orders in their hands;* **Kenneth** *begins wrapping.* **Tom** *goes to his desk and sits, clasps his hands, and for a moment he prays.*

Bert *goes and gets his jacket. He slowly puts it on.*

Enter **Frank***, the truckdriver.*

Frank   Anything for West Bronx, Tommy?

Tom   There's some stuff for Sullivan's there.

Frank   Okay. (*He pokes through the packages, picks some.*)

Kenneth   Gus died.

Frank   No kiddin'!

Kenneth   Ya, last night.

Frank   What do you know. Hm. (*He goes on picking packages out.*) Is this all for West Bronx, Tom?

Tom   I guess so for now.

Frank (*to* **Kenneth**)   Died.

Kenneth   Yes, Jim was with him. Last night.

Frank   Jesus. (*Pause. He stares, shakes his head.*) I'll take Brooklyn when I get back, Tommy. (*He goes out, loaded with packages.* **Bert** *is buttoning his overcoat.* **Agnes** *comes out of the toilet.*)

Bert   Agnes?

Agnes (*seeing the coat on, the book in his hand*)   Oh, you're leaving, Bert!

Bert   Yeah.

Agnes   Well. You're leaving.

Bert (*expectantly*)   Yeah.

Patricia *enters.*

Patricia   Agnes? Your switchboard's ringing.

Jerry *enters with goods.*

Agnes   Okay! (**Patricia** *goes out.*) Well, good luck. I hope you pass everything.

Bert   Thanks, Aggie. (*She walks across and out, wiping a hair across her forehead.* **Willy** *enters with goods as* **Jerry** *goes out.* **Jim** *enters with goods.*)

Bert *seems about to say good-by to each of them, but they are engrossed and he doesn't quite want to start a scene with them; but now* **Jim** *is putting his goods on the table, so* **Bert** *goes over to him.*

Bert   I'm leaving, **Jim**, so—uh—

Jim   Oh, leavin'? Heh! Well, that's—

Tom (*from his place at the desk, offering an order to* **Jim**)   Jim? See if these transmissions came in yet, will ya? This guy's been ordering them all month.

Jim   Sure, Tom.

Jim *goes out past* **Bert**, *studying his order.* **Bert** *glances at* **Kenneth**, *who is busy wrapping. He goes to* **Tom**, *who is working at the desk.*

Bert   Well, so long, Tommy.

Tom (*turning*)   Oh, you goin', heh?

Bert   Yeah, I'm leavin' right now.

Tom   Well, keep up the will power, y'know. That's what does it.

Bert   Yeah. I—uh—I wanted to—

Raymond *enters.*

Raymond (*handing* **Tom** *an order*)   Tommy, make this a special, will you? The guy's truck broke down in Peekskill. Send it out special today.

Tom   Right.

Raymond *turns to go out, sees* **Bert**, *who seems to expect some moment from him.*

Raymond   Oh! 'By, Bert.

Bert   So long, Raymond, I—(**Raymond** *is already on his way, and he is gone.* **Jim** *enters with goods.* **Bert** *goes over to* **Kenneth** *and touches his back.* **Kenneth** *turns to him.* **Jim** *goes out as* **Willy** *enters with goods—***Jerry** *too, and this work goes on without halt.*) Well, good-by, Kenny.

Kenneth (*he is embarrassed as he turns to* **Bert**)   Well, it's our last look, I suppose, isn't it?

Bert   No, I'll come back sometime. I'll visit you.

Kenneth   Oh, not likely; it'll all be out of mind as soon as you turn the corner. I'll probably not be here anyway.

Bert   You made up your mind for Civil Service?

Kenneth   Well, you've got to keep movin', and—I'll move there, I guess. I done a shockin' thing last night, Bert; I knocked over a bar.

Bert   Knocked it over?

Kenneth   It's disgraceful, what I done. I'm standin' there, havin' a decent conversation, that's all, and before I know it I start rockin' the damned thing, and it toppled over and broke every glass in the place, and the beer spoutin' out of the pipes all over the floor. They took all me money; I'll be six weeks payin' them back. I'm for the Civil Service, I think; I'll get back to regular there, I think.

Bert   Well—good luck, Kenny. (*Blushing:*) I hope you'll remember the poems again.

Kenneth (*as though they were unimportant*)   No, they're gone, Bert. There's too much to do in this country for that kinda stuff.

Willy *enters with goods.*

Tom   Hey, Willy, get this right away; it's a special for Peekskill.

Willy   Okay.

Willy *takes the order and goes, and when* **Bert** *turns back to* **Kenneth** *he is wrapping again. So* **Bert** *moves away from the table.* **Jerry** *enters, leaves; and* **Jim** *enters, drops goods on the table, and leaves.* **Larry** *enters with a container of coffee, goes to the order hook, and checks through the orders.* **Bert** *goes to him.*

Bert   I'm goin', Larry.

Larry (*over his shoulder*)   Take it easy, kid.

Patricia *enters and crosses past* **Bert**, *looking out through the windows.* **Tom** *gets up and bumbles through a pile of goods on the table, checking against an order in his hand. It is as though* **Bert** *wished it could stop for a moment, and as each person enters he looks expectantly, but nothing much happens. And so he gradually moves—almost is moved—toward an exit, and with his book in his hand he leaves.*

Now **Kenneth** *turns and looks about, sees* **Bert** *is gone. He resumes his work and softly sings.*

Kenneth

The minstrel boy to the war has gone! Tommy, I'll be needin' more crayon before the day is out.

Tom (*without turning from the desk*)   I'll get some for you.

Kenneth (*looking at a crayon, peeling it down to a nub*)   Oh, the damn mice. But they've got to live too, I suppose. (*He marks a package and softly sings:*)

. . . in the ranks of death you will find him.
His father's sword he has girded on,
And his wild harp slung behind him.

Curtain.

A View from the Bridge

A Play in Two Acts

The Characters

Louis	**Rodolpho**
Mike	**First Immigration Officer**
Alfieri	**Second Immigration Officer**
Eddie	**Mr. Lipari**
Catherine	**Mrs. Lipari**
Beatrice	**Two "Submarines"**
Marco	**Neighbors**
Tony	

Act One

The street and house front of a tenement building. The front is skeletal entirely. The main acting area is the living room-dining room of **Eddie's** *apartment. It is a worker's flat, clean, sparse, homely. There is a rocker down front; a round dining table at center, with chairs; and a portable phonograph.*

At back are a bedroom door and an opening to the kitchen; none of these interiors are seen.

At the right, forestage, a desk. This is **Mr. Alfieri's** *law office. There is also a telephone booth. This is not used until the last scenes, so it may be covered or left in view.*

A stairway leads up to the apartment, and then farther up to the next story, which is not seen.

Ramps, representing the street, run upstage and off to right and left.

As the curtain rises, **Louis** *and* **Mike**, *longshoremen, are pitching coins against the building at left.*

A distant foghorn blows.

Enter **Alfieri**, *a lawyer in his fifties turning gray; he is portly, good-humored, and thoughtful. The two pitchers nod to him as he passes. He crosses the stage to his desk, removes his hat, runs his fingers through his hair, and grinning, speaks to the audience.*

Alfieri   You wouldn't have known it, but something amusing has just happened. You see how uneasily they nod to me? That's because I am a lawyer. In this neighborhood to meet a lawyer or a priest on the street is unlucky. We're only thought of in connection with disasters, and they'd rather not get too close.

I often think that behind that suspicious little nod of theirs lie three thousand years of distrust. A lawyer means the law, and in Sicily, from where their fathers came, the law has not been a friendly idea since the Greeks were beaten.

I am inclined to notice the ruins in things, perhaps because I was born in Italy . . . I only came here when I was twenty-five. In those days, Al Capone, the greatest Carthaginian of all, was learning his trade on these pavements, and Frankie Yale himself was cut precisely in half by a machine gun on the corner of Union Street, two blocks away. Oh, there were many here who were justly shot by unjust men. Justice is very important here.

But this is Red Hook, not Sicily. This is the slum that faces the bay on the seaward side of Brooklyn Bridge. This is the gullet of New York swallowing the tonnage of the world. And now we are quite civilized, quite American. Now we settle for half, and I like it better. I no longer keep a pistol in my filing cabinet.

And my practice is entirely unromantic.

My wife has warned me, so have my friends; they tell me the people in this neighborhood lack elegance, glamour. After all, who have I dealt with in my life? Longshoremen and their wives, and fathers and grandfathers, compensation cases, evictions, family squabbles—the petty troubles of the poor—and yet . . . every few years there is still a case, and as the parties tell me what the trouble is, the flat air in my office suddenly washes in with the green scent of the sea, the dust in this air is blown away and the thought comes that in some Caesar's year, in Calabria perhaps or on the cliff at Syracuse, another lawyer, quite differently dressed, heard the same complaint and sat there as powerless as I, and watched it run its bloody course.

Eddie *has appeared and has been pitching coins with the men and is highlighted among them. He is forty—a husky, slightly overweight longshoreman.*

This one's name was Eddie Carbone, a longshoreman working the docks from Brooklyn Bridge to the breakwater where the open sea begins.

Alfieri *walks into darkness.*

Eddie (*moving up steps into doorway*) Well, I'll see ya, fellas.

Catherine *enters from kitchen, crosses down to window, looks out.*

Louis You workin' tomorrow?

Eddie Yeah, there's another day yet on that ship. See ya, Louis.

Eddie *goes into the house, as light rises in the apartment.*

Catherine *is waving to* **Louis** *from the window and turns to him.*

Catherine Hi, Eddie!

Eddie *is pleased and therefore shy about it; he hangs up his cap and jacket.*

Eddie Where you goin' all dressed up?

Catherine (*running her hands over her skirt*)   I just got it. You like it?

Eddie   Yeah, it's nice. And what happened to your hair?

Catherine   You like it? I fixed it different. (*Calling to kitchen:*) He's here, B.!

Eddie   Beautiful. Turn around, lemme see in the back. (*She turns for him.*) Oh, if your mother was alive to see you now! She wouldn't believe it.

Catherine   You like it, huh?

Eddie   You look like one of them girls that went to college. Where you goin'?

Catherine (*taking his arm*)   Wait'll B. comes in, I'll tell you something. Here, sit down. (*She is walking him to the armchair. Calling offstage:*) Hurry up, will you, B.?

Eddie (*sitting*)   What's goin' on?

Catherine   I'll get you a beer, all right?

Eddie   Well, tell me what happened. Come over here, talk to me.

Catherine   I want to wait till B. comes in. (*She sits on her heels beside him.*) Guess how much we paid for the skirt.

Eddie   I think it's too short, ain't it?

Catherine (*standing*)   No! not when I stand up.

Eddie   Yeah, but you gotta sit down sometimes.

Catherine   Eddie, it's the style now. (*She walks to show him.*) I mean, if you see me walkin' down the street—

Eddie   Listen, you been givin' me the willies the way you walk down the street, I mean it.

Catherine   Why?

Eddie   Catherine, I don't want to be a pest, but I'm tellin' you you're walkin' wavy.

Catherine   I'm walkin' wavy?

Eddie   Now don't aggravate me, Katie, you are walkin' wavy! I don't like the looks they're givin' you in the candy store. And with them new high heels on the sidewalk—clack, clack, clack. The heads are turnin' like windmills.

Catherine   But those guys look at all the girls, you know that.

Eddie   You ain't "all the girls."

Catherine (*almost in tears because he disapproves*)   What do you want me to do? You want me to—

Eddie   Now don't get mad, kid.

Catherine   Well, I don't know what you want from me.

Eddie   Katie, I promised your mother on her deathbed. I'm responsible for you. You're a baby, you don't understand these things. I mean like when you stand here by the window, wavin' outside.

Catherine   I was wavin' to Louis!

Eddie   Listen, I could tell you things about Louis which you wouldn't wave to him no more.

Catherine (*trying to joke him out of his warning*)   Eddie, I wish there was one guy you couldn't tell me things about!

Eddie   Catherine, do me a favor, will you? You're gettin' to be a big girl now, you gotta keep yourself more, you can't be so friendly, kid. (*Calls:*) Hey, B., what're you doin' in there? (*To* **Catherine***:*) Get her in here, will you? I got news for her.

Catherine (*starting out*)   What?

Eddie   Her cousins landed.

Catherine (*clapping her hands together*)   No! (*She turns instantly and starts for the kitchen.*) B.! Your cousins!

Beatrice *enters, wiping her hands with a towel.*

Beatrice (*in the face of* **Catherine***'s shout*)   What?

Catherine   Your cousins got in!

Beatrice (*astounded, turns to* **Eddie**)   What are you talkin' about? Where?

Eddie   I was just knockin' off work before and Tony Bereli come over to me; he says the ship is in the North River.

Beatrice (*her hands are clasped at her breast; she seems half in fear, half in unutterable joy*)   They're all right?

Eddie   He didn't see them yet, they're still on board. But as soon as they get off he'll meet them. He figures about ten o'clock they'll be here.

Beatrice (*sits, almost weak from tension*)   And they'll let them off the ship all right? That's fixed, heh?

Eddie   Sure, they give them regular seamen papers and they walk off with the crew. Don't worry about it, B., there's nothin' to it. Couple of hours they'll be here.

Beatrice   What happened? They wasn't supposed to be till next Thursday.

Eddie   I don't know; they put them on any ship they can get them out on. Maybe the other ship they was supposed to take there was some danger—What you cryin' about?

Beatrice (*astounded and afraid*)   I'm—I just—I can't believe it! I didn't even buy a new table cloth; I was gonna wash the walls—

Eddie   Listen, they'll think it's a millionaire's house compared to the way they live. Don't worry about the walls. They'll be thankful. (*To* **Catherine***:*) Whyn't you run down buy a table cloth. Go ahead, here. (*He is reaching into his pocket.*)

Catherine   There's no stores open now.

Eddie (*to* **Beatrice**)   You was gonna put a new cover on the chair.

Beatrice   I know—well, I thought it was gonna be next week! I was gonna clean the walls, I was gonna wax the floors. (*She stands disturbed.*)

Catherine (*pointing upward*)   Maybe Mrs. Dondero upstairs—

Beatrice (*of the table cloth*)   No, hers is worse than this one. (*Suddenly:*) My God, I don't even have nothin' to eat for them! (*She starts for the kitchen.*)

Eddie (*reaching out and grabbing her arm*)   Hey, hey! Take it easy.

Beatrice   No, I'm just nervous, that's all. (*To* **Catherine***:*) I'll make the fish.

Eddie   You're savio' their lives, what're you worryin' about the table cloth? They probably didn't see a table cloth in their whole life where they come from.

Beatrice (*looking into his eyes*)   I'm just worried about you, that's all I'm worried.

Eddie   Listen, as long as they know where they're gonna sleep.

Beatrice   I told them in the letters. They're sleepin' on the floor.

Eddie   Beatrice, all I'm worried about is you got such a heart that I'll end up on the floor with you, and they'll be in our bed.

Beatrice   All right, stop it.

Eddie   Because as soon as you see a tired relative, I end up on the floor.

Beatrice   When did you end up on the floor?

Eddie   When your father's house burned down I didn't end up on the floor?

Beatrice   Well, their house burned down!

Eddie   Yeah, but it didn't keep burnin' for two weeks!

Beatrice   All right, look, I'll tell them to go someplace else. (*She starts into the kitchen.*)

Eddie   Now wait a minute. Beatrice! (*She halts. He goes to her.*) I just don't want you bein' pushed around, that's all. You got too big a heart. (*He touches her hand.*) What're you so touchy?

Beatrice   I'm just afraid if it don't turn out good you'll be mad at me.

Eddie   Listen, if everybody keeps his mouth shut, nothin' can happen. They'll pay for their board.

Beatrice   Oh, I told them.

Eddie   Then what the hell. (*Pause. He moves.*) It's an honor, B. I mean it. I was just thinkin' before, comin' home, suppose my father didn't come to this country, and I was starvin' like them over there . . . and I had people in America could keep me a couple of months? The man would be honored to lend me a place to sleep.

Beatrice (*there are tears in her eyes. She turns to* **Catherine**)   You see what he is? (*She turns and grabs* **Eddie**'*s face in her hands.*) Mmm! You're an angel! God'll bless you. (*He is gratefully smiling.*) You'll see, you'll get a blessing for this!

Eddie (*laughing*)   I'll settle for my own bed.

Beatrice   Go, Baby, set the table.

Catherine   We didn't tell him about me yet.

Beatrice   Let him eat first, then we'll tell him. Bring everything in. (*She hurries* **Catherine** *out.*)

Eddie (*sitting at the table*)   What's all that about? Where's she goin'?

Beatrice   Noplace. It's very good news, Eddie. I want you to be happy.

Eddie   What's goin' on?

Catherine *enters with plates, forks.*

Beatrice   She's got a job.

Pause. **Eddie** *looks at* **Catherine**, *then back to* **Beatrice**.

Eddie   What job? She's gonna finish school.

Catherine   Eddie, you won't believe it—

Eddie   No—no, you gonna finish school. What kinda job, what do you mean? All of a sudden you—

Catherine   Listen a minute, it's wonderful.

Eddie   It's not wonderful. You'll never get nowheres unless you finish school. You can't take no job. Why didn't you ask me before you take a job?

Beatrice   She's askin' you now, she didn't take nothin' yet.

Catherine   Listen a minute! I came to school this morning and the principal called me out of the class, see? To go to his office.

Eddie   Yeah?

Catherine   So I went in and he says to me he's got my records, y'know? And there's a company wants a girl right away. It ain't exactly a secretary, it's a stenographer first, but pretty soon you get to be secretary. And he says to me that I'm the best student in the whole class—

Beatrice   You hear that?

Eddie   Well why not? Sure she's the best.

Catherine   I'm the best student, he says, and if I want, I should take the job and the end of the year he'll let me take the examination and he'll give me the certificate. So I'll save practically a year!

Eddie (*strangely nervous*)   Where's the job? What company?

Catherine   It's a big plumbing company over Nostrand Avenue.

Eddie   Nostrand Avenue and where?

Catherine   It's someplace by the Navy Yard.

Beatrice   Fifty dollars a week, Eddie.

Eddie (*to* **Catherine**, *surprised*)   Fifty?

Catherine   I swear.

Pause.

Eddie   What about all the stuff you wouldn't learn this year, though?

Catherine   There's nothin' more to learn, Eddie, I just gotta practice from now on. I know all the symbols and I know the keyboard. I'll just get faster, that's all. And when I'm workin' I'll keep gettin' better and better, you see?

Beatrice   Work is the best practice anyway.

Eddie   That ain't what I wanted, though.

Catherine   Why! It's a great big company—

Eddie   I don't like that neighborhood over there.

Catherine   It's a block and half from the subway, he says.

Eddie   Near the Navy Yard plenty can happen in a block and a half. And a plumbin' company! That's one step over the water front. They're practically longshoremen.

Beatrice   Yeah, but she'll be in the office, Eddie.

Eddie   I know she'll be in the office, but that ain't what I had in mind.

Beatrice   Listen, she's gotta go to work sometime.

Eddie   Listen, B., she'll be with a lotta plumbers? And sailors up and down the street? So what did she go to school for?

Catherine   But it's fifty a week, Eddie.

Eddie   Look, did I ask you for money? I supported you this long I support you a little more. Please, do me a favor, will ya? I want you to be with different kind of people. I want you to be in a nice office. Maybe a lawyer's office someplace in New York in one of them nice buildings. I mean if you're gonna get outa here then get out; don't go practically in the same kind of neighborhood.

Pause. **Catherine** *lowers her eyes.*

Beatrice   Go, Baby, bring in the supper. (**Catherine** *goes out.*) Think about it a little bit, Eddie. Please. She's crazy to start work. It's not a little shop, it's a big company. Some day she could be a secretary. They picked her out of the whole class. (*He is silent, staring down at the tablecloth, fingering the pattern.*) What are you worried about? She could take care of herself. She'll get out of the subway and be in the office in two minutes.

Eddie (*somehow sickened*)   I know that neighborhood, B., I don't like it.

Beatrice   Listen, if nothin' happened to her in this neighborhood it ain't gonna happen noplace else. (*She turns his face to her.*) Look, you gotta get used to it, she's no baby no more. Tell her to take it. (*He turns his head away.*) You hear me? (*She is angering.*) I don't understand you; she's seventeen years old, you gonna keep her in the house all her life?

Eddie (*insulted*)   What kinda remark is that?

Beatrice (*with sympathy but insistent force*)   Well, I don't understand when it ends. First it was gonna be when she graduated high school, so she graduated high school. Then it was gonna be when she learned stenographer, so she learned stenographer. So what're we gonna wait for now? I mean it, Eddie, sometimes I don't understand you; they picked her out of the whole class, it's an honor for her.

Catherine *enters with food, which she silently sets on the table. After a moment of watching her face,* **Eddie** *breaks into a smile, but it almost seems that tears will form in his eyes.*

Eddie   With your hair that way you look like a madonna, you know that? You're the madonna type. (*She doesn't look at him, but continues ladling out food onto the plates.*) You wanna go to work, heh, Madonna?

Catherine (*softly*)   Yeah.

Eddie (*with a sense of her childhood, her babyhood, and the years*)   All right, go to work. (*She looks at him, then rushes and hugs him.*) Hey, hey! Take it easy! (*He holds her face away from him to look at her.*) What're you cryin' about? (*He is affected by her, but smiles his emotion away.*)

Catherine (*sitting at her place*)   I just—(*Bursting out:*) I'm gonna buy all new dishes with my first pay! (*They laugh warmly.*) I mean it. I'll fix up the whole house! I'll buy a rug!

Eddie   And then you'll move away.

Catherine   No, Eddie!

Eddie (*grinning*)   Why not? That's life. And you'll come visit on Sundays, then once a month, then Christmas and New Year's, finally.

Catherine (*grasping his arm to reassure him and to erase the accusation*) No, please!

Eddie (*smiling but hurt*) I only ask you one thing—don't trust nobody. You got a good aunt but she's got too big a heart, you learned bad from her. Believe me.

Beatrice Be the way you are, Katie, don't listen to him.

Eddie (*to* **Beatrice**—*strangely and quickly resentful*) You lived in a house all your life, what do you know about it? You never worked in your life.

Beatrice She likes people. What's wrong with that?

Eddie Because most people ain't people. She's goin' to work; plumbers; they'll chew her to pieces if she don't watch out. (*To* **Catherine***:*) Believe me, Katie, the less you trust, the less you be sorry.

Eddie *crosses himself and the women do the same, and they eat.*

Catherine First thing I'll buy is a rug, heh, B.?

Beatrice I don't mind. (*To* **Eddie***:*) I smelled coffee all day today. You unloadin' coffee today?

Eddie Yeah, a Brazil ship.

Catherine I smelled it too. It smelled all over the neighborhood.

Eddie That's one time, boy, to be a longshoreman is a pleasure. I could work coffee ships twenty hours a day. You go down in the hold, y'know? It's like flowers, that smell. We'll bust a bag tomorrow, I'll bring you some.

Beatrice Just be sure there's no spiders in it, will ya? I mean it. (*She directs this to* **Catherine***, rolling her eyes upward.*) I still remember that spider coming out of that bag he brung home. I nearly died.

Eddie You call that a spider? You oughta see what comes outa the bananas sometimes.

Beatrice Don't talk about it!

Eddie I seen spiders could stop a Buick.

Beatrice (*clapping her hands over her ears*) All right, shut up!

Eddie (*laughing and taking a watch out of his pocket*) Well, who started with spiders?

Beatrice   All right, I'm sorry, I didn't mean it. Just don't bring none home again. What time is it?

Eddie   Quarter nine. (*Puts watch back in his pocket.*)

They continue eating in silence.

Catherine   He's bringin' them ten o'clock, Tony?

Eddie   Around, yeah. (*He eats.*)

Catherine   Eddie, suppose somebody asks if they're livin' here. (*He looks at her as though already she had divulged something publicly. Defensively:*) I mean if they ask.

Eddie   Now look, Baby, I can see we're gettin' mixed up again here.

Catherine   No, I just mean . . . people'll see them goin' in and out.

Eddie   I don't care who sees them goin' in and out as long as you don't see them goin' in and out. And this goes for you too, B. You don't see nothin' and you don't know nothin'.

Beatrice   What do you mean? I understand.

Eddie   You don't understand; you still think you can talk about this to somebody just a little bit. Now lemme say it once and for all, because you're makin' me nervous again, both of you. I don't care if somebody comes in the house and sees them sleepin' on the floor, it never comes out of your mouth who they are or what they're doin' here.

Beatrice   Yeah, but my mother'll know—

Eddie   Sure she'll know, but just don't you be the one who told her, that's all. This is the United States government you're playin' with now, this is the Immigration Bureau. If you said it you knew it, if you didn't say it you didn't know it.

Catherine   Yeah, but Eddie, suppose somebody—

Eddie   I don't care what question it is. You—don't—know—nothin'. They got stool pigeons all over this neighborhood they're payin' them every week for information, and you don't know who they are. It could be your best friend. You hear? (*To* **Beatrice***:*) Like Vinny Bolzano, remember Vinny?

Beatrice   Oh, yeah. God forbid.

Eddie   Tell her about Vinny. (*To* **Catherine***:*) You think I'm blowin' steam here? (*To* **Beatrice***:*) Go ahead, tell her. (*To* **Catherine***:*) You was a baby then. There was a family lived next door to her mother, he was about sixteen—

Beatrice   No, he was no more than fourteen, cause I was to his confirmation in Saint Agnes. But the family had an uncle that they were hidin' in the house, and he snitched to the Immigration.

Catherine   The kid snitched?

Eddie   On his own uncle!

Catherine   What, was he crazy?

Eddie   He was crazy after, I tell you that, boy.

Beatrice   Oh, it was terrible. He had five brothers and the old father. And they grabbed him in the kitchen and pulled him down the stairs—three flights his head was bouncin' like a coconut. And they spit on him in the street, his own father and his brothers. The whole neighborhood was cryin'.

Catherine   Ts! So what happened to him?

Beatrice   I think he went away. (*To* **Eddie***:*) I never seen him again, did you?

Eddie (*rises during this, taking out his watch*)   Him? You'll never see him no more, a guy do a thing like that? How's he gonna show his face? (*To* **Catherine***, as he gets up uneasily:*) Just remember, kid, you can quicker get back a million dollars that was stole than a word that you gave away. (*He is standing now, stretching his back.*)

Catherine   Okay, I won't say a word to nobody, I swear.

Eddie   Gonna rain tomorrow. We'll be slidin' all over the decks. Maybe you oughta put something on for them, they be here soon.

Beatrice   I only got fish, I hate to spoil it if they ate already. I'll wait, it only takes a few minutes; I could broil it.

Catherine   What happens, Eddie, when that ship pulls out and they ain't on it, though? Don't the captain say nothin'?

Eddie (*slicing an apple with his pocket knife*)   Captain's pieced off, what do you mean?

Catherine   Even the captain?

Eddie   What's the matter, the captain don't have to live? Captain gets a piece, maybe one of the mates, piece for the guy in Italy who fixed the papers for them, Tony here'll get a little bite . . .

Beatrice   I just hope they get work here, that's all I hope.

Eddie   Oh, the syndicate'll fix jobs for them; till they pay 'em off they'll get them work every day. It's after the pay-off, then they'll have to scramble like the rest of us.

Beatrice   Well, it be better than they got there.

Eddie   Oh sure, well, listen. So you gonna start Monday, heh, Madonna?

Catherine (*embarrassed*)   I'm supposed to, yeah.

Eddie *is standing facing the two seated women. First* **Beatrice** *smiles, then* **Catherine**, *for a powerful emotion is on him, a childish one and a knowing fear, and the tears show in his eyes—and they are shy before the avowal.*

Eddie (*sadly smiling, yet somehow proud of her*)   Well . . . I hope you have good luck. I wish you the best. You know that, kid.

Catherine (*rising, trying to laugh*)   You sound like I'm goin' a million miles!

Eddie   I know. I guess I just never figured on one thing.

Catherine (*smiling*)   What?

Eddie   That you would ever grow up. (*He utters a soundless laugh at himself, feeling his breast pocket of his shirt.*) I left a cigar in my other coat, I think. (*He starts for the bedroom.*)

Catherine   Stay there! I'll get it for you.

She hurries out. There is a slight pause, and **Eddie** *turns to* **Beatrice**, *who has been avoiding his gaze.*

Eddie   What are you mad at me lately?

Beatrice   Who's mad? (*She gets up, clearing the dishes.*) I'm not mad. (*She picks up the dishes and turns to him.*) You're the one is mad. (*She turns and goes into the kitchen as* **Catherine** *enters from the bedroom with a cigar and a pack of matches.*)

Catherine   Here! I'll light it for you! (*She strikes a match and holds it to his cigar. He puffs. Quietly:*) Don't worry about me, Eddie, heh?

Eddie   Don't burn yourself. (*Just in time she blows out the match.*) You better go in help her with the dishes.

Catherine (*turns quickly to the table, and, seeing the table cleared, she says, almost guiltily*)   Oh! (*She hurries into the kitchen, and as she exits there:*) I'll do the dishes, B.!

Alone, **Eddie** *stands looking toward the kitchen for a moment. Then he takes out his watch, glances at it, replaces it in his pocket, sits in the armchair, and stares at the smoke flowing out of his mouth.*

The lights go down, then come up on **Alfieri***, who has moved onto the forestage.*

Alfieri   He was as good a man as he had to be in a life that was hard and even. He worked on the piers when there was work, he brought home his pay, and he lived. And toward ten o'clock of that night, after they had eaten, the cousins came.

The lights fade on **Alfieri** *and rise on the street.*

Enter **Tony***, escorting* **Marco** *and* **Rodolpho***, each with a valise.* **Tony** *halts, indicates the house. They stand for a moment looking at it.*

Marco (*he is a square-built peasant of thirty-two, suspicious, tender, and quiet-voiced*)   Thank you.

Tony   You're on your own now. Just be careful, that's all. Ground floor.

Marco   Thank you.

Tony (*indicating the house*)   I'll see you on the pier tomorrow. You'll go to work.

Marco *nods.* **Tony** *continues on walking down the street.*

Rodolpho   This will be the first house I ever walked into in America! Imagine! She said they were poor!

Marco   Ssh! Come. (*They go to door.*)

Marco *knocks. The lights rise in the room.* **Eddie** *goes and opens the door. Enter* **Marco** *and* **Rodolpho***, removing their caps.* **Beatrice** *and* **Catherine** *enter from the kitchen. The lights fade in the street.*

Eddie   You Marco?

Marco   Marco.

Eddie   Come on in! (*He shakes* **Marco***'s hand.*)

Beatrice   Here, take the bags!

Marco (*nods, looks to the women and fixes on* **Beatrice**. *Crosses to* **Beatrice**.)   Are you my cousin?

She nods. He kisses her hand.

Beatrice (*above the table, touching her chest with her hand*)   Beatrice. This is my husband, Eddie. (*All nod.*) Catherine, my sister Nancy's daughter. (*The brothers nod.*)

Marco (*indicating* **Rodolpho**)   My brother. Rodolpho. (**Rodolpho** *nods.* **Marco** *comes with a certain formal stiffness to* **Eddie**.) I want to tell you now Eddie—when you say go, we will go.

Eddie   Oh, no . . . (*Takes* **Marco**'s *bag.*)

Marco   I see it's a small house, but soon, maybe, we can have our own house.

Eddie   You're welcome, Marco, we got plenty of room here. Katie, give them supper, heh? (*Exits into bedroom with their bags.*)

Catherine   Come here, sit down. I'll get you some soup.

Marco (*as they go to the table*)   We ate on the ship. Thank you. (*To* **Eddie**, *calling off to bedroom:*) Thank you.

Beatrice   Get some coffee. We'll all have coffee. Come sit down.

Rodolpho *and* **Marco** *sit, at the table.*

Catherine (*wondrously*)   How come he's so dark and you're so light, Rodolpho?

Rodolpho (*ready to laugh*)   I don't know. A thousand years ago, they say, the Danes invaded Sicily.

Beatrice *kisses* **Rodolpho**. *They laugh as* **Eddie** *enters.*

Catherine (*to* **Beatrice**)   He's practically blond!

Eddie   How's the coffee doin'?

Catherine (*brought up*)   I'm gettin' it. (*She hurries out to kitchen.*)

Eddie (*sits on his rocker*)   Yiz have a nice trip?

Marco   The ocean is always rough. But we are good sailors.

Eddie   No trouble gettin' here?

Marco   No. The man brought us. Very nice man.

Rodolpho (*to* **Eddie**)   He says we start to work tomorrow. Is he honest?

Eddie (*laughing*)   No. But as long as you owe them money, they'll get you plenty of work. (*To* **Marco**:) Yiz ever work on the piers in Italy?

Marco   Piers? Ts!—no.

Rodolpho (*smiling at the smallness of his town*)   In our town there are no piers, only the beach, and little fishing boats.

Beatrice   So what kinda work did yiz do?

Marco (*shrugging shyly, even embarrassed*)   Whatever there is, anything.

Rodolpho   Sometimes they build a house, or if they fix the bridge— Marco is a mason and I bring him the cement. (*He laughs.*) In harvest time we work in the fields . . . if there is work. Anything.

Eddie   Still bad there, heh?

Marco   Bad, yes.

Rodolpho (*laughing*)   It's terrible! We stand around all day in the piazza listening to the fountain like birds. Everybody waits only for the train.

Beatrice   What's on the train?

Rodolpho   Nothing. But if there are many passengers and you're lucky you make a few lire to push the taxi up the hill.

Enter **Catherine***; she listens.*

Beatrice   You gotta push a taxi?

Rodolpho (*laughing*)   Oh, sure! It's a feature in our town. The horses in our town are skinnier than goats. So if there are too many passengers we help to push the carriages up to the hotel. (*He laughs.*) In our town the horses are only for show.

Catherine   Why don't they have automobile taxis?

Rodolpho   There is one. We push that too. (*They laugh.*) Everything in our town, you gotta push!

Beatrice (*to* **Eddie**)   How do you like that!

Eddie (*to* **Marco**)   So what're you wanna do, you gonna stay here in this country or you wanna go back?

Marco (*surprised*)   Go back?

Eddie   Well, you're married, ain't you?

Marco   Yes. I have three children.

Beatrice   Three! I thought only one.

Marco   Oh, no. I have three now. Four years, five years, six years.

Beatrice   Ah . . . I bet they're cryin' for you already, heh?

Marco   What can I do? The older one is sick in his chest. My wife—she feeds them from her own mouth. I tell you the truth, if I stay there they will never grow up. They eat the sunshine.

Beatrice   My God. So how long you want to stay?

Marco   With your permission, we will stay maybe a—

Eddie   She don't mean in this house, she means in the country.

Marco   Oh. Maybe four, five, six years, I think.

Rodolpho (*smiling*)   He trusts his wife.

Beatrice   Yeah, but maybe you'll get enough, you'll be able to go back quicker.

Marco   I hope. I don't know. (*To* **Eddie**:) I understand it's not so good here either.

Eddie   Oh, you guys'll be all right—till you pay them off, anyway. After that, you'll have to scramble, that's all. But you'll make better here than you could there.

Rodolpho   How much? We hear all kinds of figures. How much can a man make? We work hard, we'll work all day, all night—

Marco *raises a hand to hush him.*

Eddie (*he is coming more and more to address* **Marco** *only*)   On the average a whole year? Maybe—well, it's hard to say, see. Sometimes we lay off, there's no ships three four weeks.

Marco   Three, four weeks!—Ts!

Eddie   But I think you could probably—thirty, forty a week, over the whole twelve months of the year.

Marco (*rises, crosses to* **Eddie**)   Dollars.

Eddie   Sure dollars.

Marco *puts an arm round* **Rodolpho** *and they laugh.*

Marco   If we can stay here a few months, Beatrice—

Beatrice   Listen, you're welcome, Marco—

Marco   Because I could send them a little more if I stay here.

Beatrice   As long as you want, we got plenty a room.

Marco (*his eyes are showing tears*)   My wife—(*To* **Eddie**:) My wife—I want to send right away maybe twenty dollars—

Eddie   You could send them something next week already.

Marco (*he is near tears*)   Eduardo . . . (*He goes to* **Eddie**, *offering his hand.*)

Eddie   Don't thank me. Listen, what the hell, it's no skin off me. (*To* **Catherine**:) What happened to the coffee?

Catherine   I got it on. (*To* **Rodolpho**:) You married too? No.

Rodolpho (*rises*)   Oh, no . . .

Beatrice (*to* **Catherine**)   I told you he—

Catherine   I know, I just thought maybe he got married recently.

Rodolpho   I have no money to get married. I have a nice face, but no money. (*He laughs.*)

Catherine (*to* **Beatrice**)   He's a real blond!

Beatrice (*to* **Rodolpho**)   You want to stay here too, heh? For good?

Rodolpho   Me? Yes, forever! Me, I want to be an American. And then I want to go back to Italy when I am rich, and I will buy a motorcycle. (*He smiles.* **Marco** *shakes him affectionately.*)

Catherine   A motorcycle!

Rodolpho   With a motorcycle in Italy you will never starve any more.

Beatrice   I'll get you coffee. (*She exits to the kitchen.*)

Eddie   What you do with a motorcycle?

Marco   He dreams, he dreams.

Rodolpho (*to* **Marco**)   Why? (*To* **Eddie**:) Messages! The rich people in the hotel always need someone who will carry a message. But quickly, and with a great noise. With a blue motorcycle I would station myself in the courtyard of the hotel, and in a little while I would have messages.

Marco   When you have no wife you have dreams.

Eddie   Why can't you just walk, or take a trolley or sump'm?

Enter **Beatrice** *with coffee.*

Rodolpho   Oh, no, the machine, the machine is necessary. A man comes into a great hotel and says, I am a messenger. Who is this man? He disappears walking, there is no noise, nothing. Maybe he will never come back, maybe he will never deliver the message. But a man who rides up on a great machine, this man is responsible, this man exists. He will be given messages. (*He helps* **Beatrice** *set out the coffee things.*) I am also a singer, though.

Eddie   You mean a regular—?

Rodolpho   Oh, yes. One night last year Andreola got sick. Baritone. And I took his place in the garden of the hotel. Three arias I sang without a mistake! Thousand-lire notes they threw from the tables, money was falling like a storm in the treasury. It was magnificent. We lived six months on that night, eh, Marco?

Marco *nods doubtfully.*

Marco   Two months.

Eddie *laughs.*

Beatrice   Can't you get a job in that place?

Rodolpho   Andreola got better. He's a baritone, very strong.

Beatrice *laughs.*

Marco (*regretfully, to* **Beatrice**)   He sang too loud.

Rodolpho   Why too loud?

Marco   Too loud. The guests in that hotel are all Englishmen. They don't like too loud.

Rodolpho (*to* **Catherine**)   Nobody ever said it was too loud!

Marco   I say. It was too loud. (*To* **Beatrice**:) I knew it as soon as he started to sing. Too loud.

Rodolpho   Then why did they throw so much money?

Marco   They paid for your courage. The English like courage. But once is enough.

Rodolpho (*to all but* **Marco**)   I never heard anybody say it was too loud.

Catherine   Did you ever hear of jazz?

Rodolpho   Oh, sure! I *sing* jazz.

Catherine (*rises*)   You could sing jazz?

Rodolpho   Oh, I sing Napolidan, jazz, bel canto—I sing "Paper Doll," you like "Paper Doll"?

Catherine   Oh, sure, I'm crazy for "Paper Doll." Go ahead, sing it.

Rodolpho (*takes his stance after getting a nod of permission from* **Marco**, *and with a high tenor voice begins singing*)

I'll tell you boys it's tough to be alone,
And it's tough to love a doll that's not your own.
I'm through with all of them,
I'll never fall again,
Hey, boy, what you gonna do?
I'm gonna buy a paper doll that I can call my own,
A doll that other fellows cannot steal.

Eddie *rises and moves upstage.*

And then those flirty, flirty guys
With their flirty, flirty eyes
Will have to flirt with dollies that are real—

Eddie   Hey, kid—hey, wait a minute—

Catherine (*enthralled*)   Leave him finish, it's beautiful! (*To* **Beatrice**:) He's terrific! It's terrific, Rodolpho.

Eddie   Look, kid; you don't want to be picked up, do ya?

Marco   No—no! (*He rises.*)

Eddie (*indicating the rest of the building*)   Because we never had no singers here . . . and all of a sudden there's a singer in the house, y'know what I mean?

Marco   Yes, yes. You'll be quiet, Rodolpho.

Eddie (*he is flushed*)   They got guys all over the place, Marco. I mean.

Marco   Yes. He'll be quiet. (*To* **Rodolpho**:) You'll be quiet.

Rodolpho *nods.*

Eddie *has risen, with iron control, even a smile. He moves to* **Catherine**.

Eddie   What's the high heels for, Garbo?

Catherine   I figured for tonight—

Eddie   Do me a favor, will you? Go ahead.

Embarrassed now, angered, **Catherine** *goes out into the bedroom.* **Beatrice** *watches her go and gets up; in passing, she gives* **Eddie** *a cold look, restrained only by the strangers, and goes to the table to pour coffee.*

Eddie (*striving to laugh, and to* **Marco**, *but directed as much to* **Beatrice**)   All actresses they want to be around here.

Rodolpho (*happy about it*)   In Italy too! All the girls.

Catherine *emerges from the bedroom in low-heel shoes, comes to the table.* **Rodolpho** *is lifting a cup.*

Eddie (*he is sizing up* **Rodolpho**, *and there is a concealed suspicion*)   Yeah, heh?

Rodolpho   Yes! (*Laughs, indicating* **Catherine**:) Especially when they are so beautiful!

Catherine   You like sugar?

Rodolpho   Sugar? Yes! I like sugar very much!

Eddie *is downstage, watching as she pours a spoonful of sugar into his cup, his face puffed with trouble, and the room dies.*

Lights rise on **Alfieri**.

Alfieri   Who can ever know what will be discovered? Eddie Carbone had never expected to have a destiny. A man works, raises his family, goes bowling, eats, gets old, and then be dies. Now, as the weeks passed, there was a future, there was a trouble that would not go away.

The lights fade on **Alfieri**, *then rise on* **Eddie** *standing at the doorway of the house.* **Beatrice** *enters on the street. She sees* **Eddie**, *smiles at him. He looks away.*

She starts to enter the house when **Eddie** *speaks.*

Eddie   It's after eight.

Beatrice   Well, it's a long show at the Paramount.

Eddie   They must've seen every picture in Brooklyn by now. He's supposed to stay in the house when he ain't working. He ain't supposed to go advertising himself.

Beatrice   Well that's his trouble, what do you care? If they pick him up they pick him up, that's all. Come in the house.

Eddie   What happened to the stenography? I don't see her practice no more.

Beatrice   She'll get back to it. She's excited, Eddie.

Eddie   She tell you anything?

Beatrice (*comes to him, now the subject is opened*)   What's the matter with you? He's a nice kid, what do you want from him?

Eddie   That's a nice kid? He gives me the heeby-jeebies.

Beatrice (*smiling*)   Ah, go on, you're just jealous.

Eddie   Of *him*? Boy, you don't think much of me.

Beatrice   I don't understand you. What's so terrible about him?

Eddie   You mean it's all right with you? That's gonna be her husband?

Beatrice   Why? He's a nice fella, hard workin', he's a good-lookin' fella.

Eddie   He sings on the ships, didja know that?

Beatrice   What do you mean, he sings?

Eddie   Just what I said, he sings. Right on the deck, all of a sudden, a whole song comes out of his mouth—with motions. You know what they're callin' him now? Paper Doll they're callin' him, Canary. He's like a weird. He comes out on the pier, one-two-three, it's a regular free show.

Beatrice   Well, he's a kid; he don't know how to behave himself yet.

Eddie   And with that wacky hair; he's like a chorus girl or sump'm.

Beatrice   So he's blond, so—

Eddie   I just hope that's his regular hair, that's all I hope.

Beatrice   You crazy or sump'm? (*She tries to turn him to her.*)

Eddie (*he keeps his head turned away*)   What's so crazy? I don't like his whole way.

Beatrice   Listen, you never seen a blond guy in your life? What about Whitey Balso?

Eddie (*turning to her victoriously*)   Sure, but Whitey don't sing; he don't do like that on the ships.

Beatrice   Well, maybe that's the way they do in Italy.

Eddie   Then why don't his brother sing? Marco goes around like a man; nobody kids Marco. (*He moves from her, halts. She realizes there is a campaign solidified in him.*) I tell you the truth I'm surprised I have to tell you all this. I mean I'm surprised, B.

Beatrice (*she goes to him with purpose now*)   Listen, you ain't gonna start nothin' here.

Eddie   I ain't startin' nothin', but I ain't gonna stand around lookin' at that. For that character I didn't bring her up. I swear, B., I'm surprised at you; I sit there waitin' for you to wake up but everything is great with you.

Beatrice   No, everything ain't great with me.

Eddie   No?

Beatrice   No. But I got other worries.

Eddie   Yeah. (*He is already weakening.*)

Beatrice   Yeah, you want me to tell you?

Eddie (*in retreat*)   Why? What worries you got?

Beatrice   When am I gonna be a wife again, Eddie?

Eddie   I ain't been feelin' good. They bother me since they came.

Beatrice   It's almost three months you don't feel good; they're only here a couple of weeks. It's three months, Eddie.

Eddie   I don't know, B. I don't want to talk about it.

Beatrice   What's the matter, Eddie, you don't like me, heh?

Eddie   What do you mean, I don't like you? I said I don't feel good, that's all.

Beatrice   Well, tell me, am I doing something wrong? Talk to me.

Eddie (*Pause. He can't speak, then*)   I can't. I can't talk about it.

Beatrice   Well tell me what—

Eddie   I got nothin' to say about it!

She stands for a moment; he is looking off; she turns to go into the house.

Eddie   I'll be all right, B.; just lay off me, will ya? I'm worried about her.

Beatrice   The girl is gonna be eighteen years old, it's time already.

Eddie   B., he's taking her for a ride!

Beatrice   All right, that's her ride. What're you gonna stand over her till she's forty? Eddie, I want you to cut it out now, you hear me? I don't like it! Now come in the house.

Eddie   I want to take a walk, I'll be in right away.

Beatrice   They ain't goin' to come any quicker if you stand in the street. It ain't nice, Eddie.

Eddie   I'll be in right away. Go ahead. (*He walks off.*)

She goes into the house. **Eddie** *glances up the street, sees* **Louis** *and* **Mike** *coming, and sits on an iron railing.* **Louis** *and* **Mike** *enter.*

Louis   Wanna go bowlin' tonight?

Eddie   I'm too tired. Goin' to sleep.

Louis   How's your two submarines?

Eddie   They're okay.

Louis   I see they're gettin' work allatime.

Eddie   Oh yeah, they're doin' all right.

Mike   That's what we oughta do. We oughta leave the country and come in under the water. Then we get work.

Eddie   You ain't kiddin'.

Louis   Well, what the hell. Y'know?

Eddie   Sure.

Louis (*sits on railing beside* **Eddie**)   Believe me, Eddie, you got a lotta credit comin' to you.

Eddie   Aah, they don't bother me, don't cost me nutt'n.

Mike   That older one, boy, he's a regular bull. I seen him the other day liftin' coffee bags over the Matson Line. They leave him alone he woulda load the whole ship by himself.

Eddie   Yeah, he's a strong guy, that guy. Their father was a regular giant, supposed to be.

Louis   Yeah, you could see. He's a regular slave.

Mike (*grinning*)   That blond one, though—(**Eddie** *looks at him.*) He's got a sense of humor. (**Louis** *snickers.*)

Eddie (*searchingly*)   Yeah. He's funny—

Mike (*starting to laugh*)   Well, he ain't exackly funny, but he's always like makin' remarks like, y'know? He comes around, everybody's laughin'. (**Louis** *laughs.*)

Eddie (*uncomfortably, grinning*)   Yeah, well . . . he's got a sense of humor.

Mike (*laughing*)   Yeah, I mean, he's always makin' like remarks, like, y'know?

Eddie   Yeah, I know. But he's a kid yet, y'know? He—he's just a kid, that's all.

Mike (*getting hysterical with* **Louis**)   I know. You take one look at him—everybody's happy. (**Louis** *laughs.*) I worked one day with him last week over the Moore-MacCormack Line, I'm tellin' you they was all hysterical. (**Louis** *and he explode in laughter.*)

Eddie   Why? What'd he do?

Mike   I don't know . . . he was just humorous. You never can remember what he says, y'know? But it's the way he says it. I mean he gives you a look sometimes and you start laughin'!

Eddie   Yeah. (*Troubled:*) He's got a sense of humor.

Mike (*gasping*)   Yeah.

Louis (*rising*)   Well, we see ya, Eddie.

Eddie   Take it easy.

Louis   Yeah. See ya.

Mike   If you wanna come bowlin' later we're goin' Flatbush Avenue.

Laughing, they move to exit, meeting **Rodolpho** *and* **Catherine** *entering on the street. Their laughter rises as they see* **Rodolpho**, *who does not understand but joins in.* **Eddie** *moves to enter the house as* **Louis** *and* **Mike** *exit.* **Catherine** *stops him at the door.*

Catherine   Hey, Eddie—what a picture we saw! Did we laugh!

Eddie (*he can't help smiling at sight of her*)   Where'd you go?

Catherine   Paramount. It was with those two guys, y'know? That—

Eddie   Brooklyn Paramount?

Catherine (*with an edge of anger, embarrassed before*
Rodolpho)   Sure, the Brooklyn Paramount. I told you we wasn't goin'
to New York.

Eddie (*retreating before the threat of her anger*)   All right, I only asked
you. (*To* **Rodolpho***:*) I just don't want her hangin' around Times Square,
see? It's full of tramps over there.

Rodolpho   I would like to go to Broadway once, Eddie. I would like to
walk with her once where the theaters are and the opera. Since I was a
boy I see pictures of those lights.

Eddie (*his little patience waning*)   I want to talk to her a minute,
Rodolpho. Go inside, will you?

Rodolpho   Eddie, we only walk together in the streets. She teaches me.

Catherine   You know what he can't get over? That there's no fountains
in Brooklyn!

Eddie (*smiling unwillingly*)   Fountains? (**Rodolpho** *smiles at his own
naïveté.*)

Catherine   In Italy he says, every town's got fountains, and they meet
there. And you know what? They got oranges on the trees where he
comes from, and lemons. Imagine—on the trees? I mean it's interesting.
But he's crazy for New York.

Rodolpho (*attempting familiarity*)   Eddie, why can't we go once to
Broadway—?

Eddie   Look, I gotta tell her something—

Rodolpho   Maybe you can come too. I want to see all those lights. (*He
sees no response in* **Eddie***'s face. He glances at* **Catherine***.*) I'll walk by
the river before I go to sleep. (*He walks off down the street.*)

Catherine   Why don't you talk to him, Eddie? He blesses you, and you
don't talk to him hardly.

Eddie (*enveloping her with his eyes*)   I bless you and you don't talk to
me. (*He tries to smile.*)

Catherine   *I* don't talk to you? (*She hits his arm.*) What do you mean?

Eddie   I don't see you no more. I come home you're runnin' around someplace—

Catherine   Well, he wants to see everything, that's all, so we go . . . You mad at me?

Eddie   No. (*He moves from her, smiling sadly.*) It's just I used to come home, you was always there. Now, I turn around, you're a big girl. I don't know how to talk to you.

Catherine   Why?

Eddie   I don't know, you're runnin', you're runnin', Katie. I don't think you listening any more to me.

Catherine (*going to him*)   Ah, Eddie, sure I am. What's the matter? You don't like him?

Slight pause.

Eddie (*turns to her*)   *You* like him, Katie?

Catherine (*with a blush but holding her ground*)   Yeah. I like him.

Eddie (*his smile goes*)   You like him.

Catherine (*looking down*)   Yeah. (*Now she looks at him for the consequences, smiling but tense. He looks at her like a lost boy.*) What're you got against him? I don't understand. He only blesses you.

Eddie (*turns away*)   He don't bless me, Katie.

Catherine   He does! You're like a father to him!

Eddie (*turns to her*)   Katie.

Catherine   What, Eddie?

Eddie   You gonna marry him?

Catherine   I don't know. We just been . . . goin' around, that's all. (*Turns to him.*) What're you got against him, Eddie? Please, tell me. What?

Eddie   He don't respect you.

Catherine   Why?

Eddie   Katie . . . if you wasn't an orphan, wouldn't he ask your father's permission before he run around with you like this?

Catherine   Oh, well, he didn't think you'd mind.

Eddie   He knows I mind, but it don't bother him if I mind, don't you see that?

Catherine   No, Eddie, he's got all kinds of respect for me. And you too! We walk across the street he takes my arm—he almost bows to me! You got him all wrong, Eddie; I mean it, you—

Eddie   Katie, he's only bowin' to his passport.

Catherine   His passport!

Eddie   That's right. He marries you he's got the right to be an American citizen. That's what's goin' on here. (*She is puzzled and surprised.*) You understand what I'm tellin' you? The guy is lookin' for his break, that's all he's lookin' for.

Catherine (*pained*)   Oh, no, Eddie, I don't think so.

Eddie   You don't think so! Katie, you're gonna make me cry here. Is that a workin' man? What does he do with his first money? A snappy new jacket he buys, records, a pointy pair new shoes and his brother's kids are starvin' over there with tuberculosis? That's a hit-and-run guy, baby; he's got bright lights in his head, Broadway. Them guys don't think of nobody but theirself! You marry him and the next time you see him it'll be for divorce!

Catherine (*steps toward him*)   Eddie, he never said a word about his papers or—

Eddie   You mean he's supposed to tell you that?

Catherine   I don't think he's even thinking about it.

Eddie   What's better for him to think about! He could be picked up any day here and he's back pushin' taxis up the hill!

Catherine   No, I don't believe it.

Eddie   Katie, don't break my heart, listen to me.

Catherine   I don't want to hear it.

Eddie   Katie, listen . . .

Catherine   He loves me!

Eddie (*with deep alarm*)   Don't say that, for God's sake! This is the oldest racket in the country—

Catherine (*desperately, as though he had made his imprint*)   I don't believe it! (*She rushes to the house.*)

Eddie (*following her*)   They been pullin' this since the Immigration Law was put in! They grab a green kid that don't know nothin' and they—

Catherine (*sobbing*)   I don't believe it and I wish to hell you'd stop it!

Eddie   Katie!

They enter the apartment. The lights in the living room have risen and **Beatrice** *is there. She looks past the sobbing* **Catherine** *at* **Eddie**, *who in the presence of his wife makes an awkward gesture of eroded command, indicating* **Catherine**.

Eddie   Why don't you straighten her out?

Beatrice (*inwardly angered at his flowing emotion, which in itself alarms her*)   When are you going to leave her alone?

Eddie   B., the guy is no good!

Beatrice (*suddenly, with open fright and fury*)   You going to leave her alone? Or you gonna drive me crazy? (*He turns, striving to retain his dignity, but nevertheless in guilt walks out of the house, into the street and away.* **Catherine** *starts into a bedroom.*) Listen, Catherine. (**Catherine** *halts, turns to her sheepishly.*) What are you going to do with yourself?

Catherine   I don't know.

Beatrice   Don't tell me you don't know; you're not a baby any more, what are you going to do with yourself?

Catherine   He won't listen to me.

Beatrice   I don't understand this. He's not your father, Catherine. I don't understand what's going on here.

Catherine (*as one who herself is trying to rationalize a buried impulse*)   What am I going to do, just kick him in the face with it?

Beatrice   Look, honey, you wanna get married, or don't you wanna get married? What are you worried about, Katie?

Catherine (*quietly, trembling*)   I don't know B. It just seems wrong if he's against it so much.

Beatrice (*never losing her aroused alarm*)   Sit down, honey, I want to tell you something. Here, sit down. Was there ever any fella he liked for you? There wasn't, was there?

Catherine   But he says Rodolpho's just after his papers.

Beatrice   Look, he'll say anything. What does he care what he says? If it was a prince came here for you it would be no different. You know that, don't you?

Catherine   Yeah, I guess.

Beatrice   So what does that mean?

Catherine (*slowly turns her head to* **Beatrice**)   What?

Beatrice   It means you gotta be your own self more. You still think you're a little girl, honey. But nobody else can make up your mind for you any more, you understand? You gotta give him to understand that he can't give you orders no more.

Catherine   Yeah, but how am I going to do that? He thinks I'm a baby.

Beatrice   Because *you* think you're a baby. I told you fifty times already, you can't act the way you act. You still walk around in front of him in your slip—

Catherine   Well, I forgot.

Beatrice   Well, you can't do it. Or like you sit on the edge of the bathtub talkin' to him when he's shavin' in his underwear.

Catherine   When'd I do that?

Beatrice   I seen you in there this morning!

Catherine   Oh . . . well, I wanted to tell him something and I—

Beatrice   I know, honey. But if you act like a baby and he be treatin' you like a baby. Like when he comes home sometimes you throw yourself at him like when you was twelve years old.

Catherine   Well, I like to see him and I'm happy so I—

Beatrice   Look, I'm not tellin' you what to do, honey, but—

Catherine   No, you could tell me, B.! Gee, I'm all mixed up. See, I—He looks so sad now and it hurts me . . .

Beatrice   Well, look, Katie, if it's goin' to hurt you so much you're gonna end up an old maid here.

Catherine   No!

Beatrice   I'm tellin' you, I'm not makin' a joke. I tried to tell you a couple of times in the last year or so. That's why I was so happy you were going to go out and get work, you wouldn't be here so much, you'd be a little more independent. I mean it. It's wonderful for a whole family to love each other, but you're a grown woman and you're in the same house with a grown man. So you'll act different now, heh?

Catherine   Yeah, I will. I'll remember.

Beatrice   Because it ain't only up to him, Katie, you understand? I told him the same thing already.

Catherine (*quickly*)   What?

Beatrice   That he should let you go. But, you see, if only I tell him, he thinks I'm just bawlin' him out, or maybe I'm jealous or somethin', you know?

Catherine (*astonished*)   He said you was jealous?

Beatrice   No, I'm just sayin' maybe that's what he thinks. (*She reaches over to* **Catherine**'s *hand; with a strained smile:*) You think I'm jealous of you, honey?

Catherine   No! It's the first I thought of it.

Beatrice (*with a quiet sad laugh*)   Well, you should have thought of it before . . . but I'm not. We'll be all right. Just give him to understand; you don't have to fight, you're just—You're a woman, that's all, and you got a nice boy, and now the time came when you said good-by. All right?

Catherine (*strangely moved at the prospect*)   All right . . . If I can.

Beatrice   Honey . . . you gotta.

Catherine, *sensing now an imperious demand, turns with some fear, with a discovery, to* **Beatrice**. *She is at the edge of tears, as though a familiar world had shattered.*

Catherine   Okay.

Lights out on them and up on **Alfieri**, *seated behind his desk.*

Alfieri   It was at this time that he first came to me. I had represented his father in an accident case some years before, and I was acquainted with the family in a casual way. I remember him now as he walked through my doorway—

Enter **Eddie** *down right ramp.*

His eyes were like tunnels; my first thought was that he had committed a crime,

Eddie *sits besides the desk, cap in hand, looking out.*

but soon I saw it was only a passion that had moved into his body, like a stranger. (**Alfieri** *pauses, looks down at his desk, then to* **Eddie** *as though he were continuing a conversation with him.*) I don't quite understand what I can do for you. Is there a question of law somewhere?

Eddie   That's what I want to ask you.

Alfieri   Because there's nothing illegal about a girl falling in love with an immigrant.

Eddie   Yeah, but what about it if the only reason for it is to get his papers?

Alfieri   First of all you don't know that.

Eddie   I see it in his eyes; he's laughin' at her and he's laughin' at me.

Alfieri   Eddie, I'm a lawyer. I can only deal in what's provable. You understand that, don't you? Can you prove that?

Eddie   I know what's in his mind, Mr. Alfieri!

Alfieri   Eddie, even if you could prove that—

Eddie   Listen . . . will you listen to me a minute? My father always said you was a smart man. I want you to listen to me.

Alfieri   I'm only a lawyer, Eddie.

Eddie   Will you listen a minute? I'm talkin' about the law. Lemme just bring out what I mean. A man, which he comes into the country illegal, don't it stand to reason he's gonna take every penny and put it in the sock? Because they don't know from one day to another, right?

Alfieri   All right.

Eddie   He's spendin'. Records he buys now. Shoes. Jackets. Y'understand me? This guy ain't worried. This guy is *here.* So it must be that he's got it all laid out in his mind already—he's stayin'. Right?

Alfieri   Well? What about it?

Eddie   All right. (*He glances at* **Alfieri***, then down to the floor.*) I'm talking to you confidential, ain't I?

Alfieri   Certainly.

Eddie   I mean it don't go no place but here. Because I don't like to say this about anybody. Even my wife I didn't exactly say this.

Alfieri   What is it?

Eddie (*takes a breath and glances briefly over each shoulder*)   The guy ain't right, Mr. Alfieri.

Alfieri   What do you mean?

Eddie   I mean he ain't right.

Alfieri   I don't get you.

Eddie (*shifts to another position in the chair*)   Dja ever get a look at him?

Alfieri   Not that I know of, no.

Eddie   He's a blond guy. Like . . . platinum. You know what I mean?

Alfieri   No.

Eddie   I mean if you close the paper fast—you could blow him over.

Alfieri   Well, that doesn't mean—

Eddie   Wait a minute, I'm tellin' you sump'm. He sings, see. Which is—I mean it's all right, but sometimes he hits a note, see. I turn around. I mean—high. You know what I mean?

Alfieri   Well, that's a tenor.

Eddie   I know a tenor, Mr. Alfieri. This ain't no tenor. I mean if you came in the house and you didn't know who was singin', you wouldn't be lookin' for him you be lookin' for her.

Alfieri   Yes, but that's not—

Eddie   I'm tellin' you sump'm, wait a minute. Please, Mr. Alfieri. I'm tryin' to bring out my thoughts here. Couple of nights ago my niece brings out a dress which it's too small for her, because she shot up like a light this last year. He takes the dress, lays it on the table, he cuts it up; one-two-three, he makes a new dress. I mean he looked so sweet there, like an angel—you could kiss him he was so sweet.

Alfieri   Now look, Eddie—

Eddie   Mr. Alfieri, they're laughin' at him on the piers. I'm ashamed. Paper Doll they call him. Blondie now. His brother thinks it's because he's got a sense of humor, see—which he's got—but that ain't what they're laughin'. Which they're not goin' to come out with it because they know he's my relative, which they have to see me if they make a crack, y'know? But I know what they're laughin' at, and when I think of that guy layin' his hands on her I could—I mean it's eatin' me out, Mr. Alfieri, because I struggled for that girl. And now he comes in my house and—

Alfieri   Eddie, look—I have my own children. I understand you. But the law is very specific. The law does not . . .

Eddie (*with a fuller flow of indignation*)   You mean to tell me that there's no law that a guy which he ain't right can go to work and marry a girl and—?

Alfieri   You have no recourse in the law, Eddie.

Eddie   Yeah, but if he ain't right, Mr. Alfieri, you mean to tell me—

Alfieri   There is nothing you can do, Eddie, believe me.

Eddie   Nothin'.

Alfieri   Nothing at all. There's only one legal question here.

Eddie   What?

Alfieri   The manner in which they entered the country. But I don't think you want to do anything about that, do you?

Eddie   You mean—?

Alfieri   Well, they entered illegally.

Eddie   Oh, Jesus, no, I wouldn't do nothin' about that, I mean—

Alfieri   All right, then, let me talk now, eh?

Eddie   Mr. Alfieri, I can't believe what you tell me. I mean there must be some kinda law which—

Alfieri   Eddie, I want you to listen to me. (*Pause.*) You know, sometimes God mixes up the people. We all love somebody, the wife, the kids—every man's got somebody that he loves, heh? But sometimes . . . there's too much. You know? There's too much, and it goes where it mustn't. A man works hard, he brings up a child, sometimes it's a niece, sometimes even a daughter, and he never realizes it, but through the years—there is too much love for the daughter, there is too much love for the niece. Do you understand what I'm saying to you?

Eddie (*sardonically*)   What do you mean, I shouldn't look out for her good?

Alfieri Yes, but these things have to end, Eddie, that's all. The child has to grow up and go away, and the man has to learn to forget. Because after all, Eddie—what other way can it end? (*Pause.*) Let her go. That's my advice. You did your job, now it's her life; wish her luck, and let her go. (*Pause.*) Will you do that? Because there's no law, Eddie; make up your mind to it; the law is not interested in this.

Eddie You mean to tell me, even if he's a punk? If he's—

Alfieri There's nothing you can do.

Eddie *stands.*

Eddie Well, all right, thanks. Thanks very much.

Alfieri What are you going to do?

Eddie (*with a helpless but ironic gesture*) What can I do? I'm a patsy, what can a patsy do? I worked like a dog twenty years so a punk could have her, so that's what I done. I mean, in the worst times, in the worst, when there wasn't a ship comin' in the harbor, I didn't stand around lookin' for relief—I hustled. When there was empty piers in Brooklyn I went to Hoboken, Staten Island, the West Side, Jersey, all over—because I made a promise. I took out of my own mouth to give to her. I took out of my wife's mouth. I walked hungry plenty days in this city! (*It begins to break through.*) And now I gotta sit in my own house and look at a son-of-a-bitch punk like that—which he came out of nowhere! I give him my house to sleep! I take the blankets off my bed for him, and he takes and puts his dirty filthy hands on her like a goddam thief!

Alfieri (*rising*) But, Eddie, she's a woman now.

Eddie He's stealing from me!

Alfieri She wants to get married, Eddie. She can't marry you, can she?

Eddie (*furiously*) What're you talkin' about, marry me! I don't know what the hell you're talkin' about!

Pause.

Alfieri I gave you my advice, Eddie. That's it.

Eddie *gathers himself. A pause.*

Eddie Well, thanks. Thanks very much. It just—it's breakin' my heart, y'know. I—

Alfieri I understand. Put it out of your mind. Can you do that?

Eddie   I'm—(*He feels the threat of sobs, and with a helpless wave.*) I'll see you around. (*He goes out up the right ramp.*)

Alfieri (*sits on desk*)   There are times when you want to spread an alarm, but nothing has happened. I knew, I knew then and there—I could have finished the whole story that afternoon. It wasn't as though there was a mystery to unravel. I could see every step coming, step after step, like a dark figure walking down a hall toward a certain door. I knew where he was heading for, I knew where he was going to end. And I sat here many afternoons asking myself why, being an intelligent man, I was so powerless to stop it. I even went to a certain old lady in the neighborhood, a very wise old woman, and I told her, and she only nodded, and said, "Pray for him . . ." And so I—waited here.

As lights go out on **Alfieri**, *they rise in the apartment where all are finishing dinner.* **Beatrice** *and* **Catherine** *are clearing the table.*

Catherine   You know where they went?

Beatrice   Where?

Catherine   They went to Africa once. On a fishing boat. (**Eddie** *glances at her.*) It's true, Eddie.

Beatrice *exits into the kitchen with dishes.*

Eddie   I didn't say nothin'. (*He goes to his rocker, picks up a newspaper.*)

Catherine   And I was never even in Staten Island.

Eddie (*sitting with the paper*)   You didn't miss nothin'. (*Pause.* **Catherine** *takes dishes out.*) How long that take you, Marco—to get to Africa?

Marco (*rising*)   Oh . . . two days. We go all over.

Rodolpho (*rising*)   Once we went to Yugoslavia.

Eddie (*to* **Marco**)   They pay all right on them boats?

Beatrice *enters. She and* **Rodolpho** *stack the remaining dishes.*

Marco   If they catch fish they pay all right. (*Sits on a stool.*)

Rodolpho   They're family boats, though. And nobody in our family owned one. So we only worked when one of the families was sick.

Beatrice   Y'know, Marco, what I don't understand—there's an ocean full of fish and yiz are all starvin'.

Eddie   They gotta have boats, nets, you need money.

Catherine *enters.*

Beatrice   Yeah, but couldn't they like fish from the beach? You see them down Coney Island—

Marco   Sardines.

Eddie   Sure. (*Laughing:*) How you gonna catch sardines on a hook?

Beatrice   Oh, I didn't know they're sardines. (*To* **Catherine***:*) They're sardines!

Catherine   Yeah, they follow them all over the ocean, Africa, Yugoslavia . . . (*She sits and begins to look through a movie magazine.* **Rodolpho** *joins her.*)

Beatrice (*to* **Eddie**)   It's funny, y'know. You never think of it, that sardines are swimming in the ocean! (*She exits to kitchen with dishes.*)

Catherine   I know. It's like oranges and lemons on a tree. (*To* **Eddie***:*) I mean you ever think of oranges and lemons on a tree?

Eddie   Yeah, I know. It's funny. (*To* **Marco***:*) I heard that they paint the oranges to make them look orange.

Beatrice *enters.*

Marco (*he has been reading a letter*)   Paint?

Eddie   Yeah, I heard that they grow like green.

Marco   No, in Italy the oranges are orange.

Rodolpho   Lemons are green.

Eddie (*resenting his instruction*)   I know lemons are green, for Christ's sake, you see them in the store they're green sometimes. I said oranges they paint, I didn't say nothin' about lemons.

Beatrice (*sitting; diverting their attention*)   Your wife is gettin' the money all right, Marco?

Marco   Oh, yes. She bought medicine for my boy.

Beatrice   That's wonderful. You feel better, heh?

Marco   Oh, yes! But I'm lonesome.

Beatrice   I just hope you ain't gonna do like some of them around here. They're here twenty-five years, some men, and they didn't get enough together to go back twice.

Marco   Oh, I know. We have many families in our town, the children never saw the father. But I will go home. Three, four years, I think.

Beatrice   Maybe you should keep more here. Because maybe she thinks it comes so easy you'll never get ahead of yourself.

Marco   Oh, no, she saves. I send everything. My wife is very lonesome. (*He smiles shyly.*)

Beatrice   She must be nice. She pretty? I bet, heh?

Marco (*blushing*)   No, but she understand everything.

Rodolpho   Oh, he's got a clever wife!

Eddie   I betcha there's plenty surprises sometimes when those guys get back there, heh?

Marco   Surprises?

Eddie (*laughing*)   I mean, you know—they count the kids and there's a couple extra than when they left?

Marco   No—no . . . The women wait, Eddie. Most. Most. Very few surprises.

Rodolpho   It's more strict in our town. (**Eddie** *looks at him now.*) It's not so free.

Eddie (*rises, paces up and down*)   It ain't so free here either, Rodolpho, like you think. I seen greenhorns sometimes get in trouble that way— they think just because a girl don't go around with a shawl over her head that she ain't strict, y'know? Girl don't have to wear black dress to be strict. Know what I mean?

Rodolpho   Well, I always have respect—

Eddie   I know, but in your town you wouldn't just drag off some girl without permission, I mean. (*He turns.*) You know what I mean, Marco? It ain't that much different here.

Marco (*cautiously*)   Yes.

Beatrice   Well, he didn't exactly drag her off though, Eddie.

Eddie   I know, but I seen some of them get the wrong idea sometimes. (*To* **Rodolpho***:*) I mean it might be a little more free here but it's just as strict.

Rodolpho   I have respect for her, Eddie. I do anything wrong?

Eddie   Look, kid, I ain't her father, I'm only her uncle—

Beatrice   Well, then, be an uncle then. (**Eddie** *looks at her, aware of her criticizing force.*) I *mean.*

Marco   No, Beatrice, if he does wrong you must tell him. (*To* **Eddie***:*) What does he do wrong?

Eddie   Well, Marco, till he came here she was never out on the street twelve o'clock at night.

Marco (*to* **Rodolpho**)   You come home early now.

Beatrice (*to* **Catherine**)   Well, you said the movie ended late, didn't you?

Catherine   Yeah.

Beatrice   Well, tell him, honey. (*To* **Eddie***:*) The movie ended late.

Eddie   Look, B., I'm just sayin'—he thinks she always stayed out like that.

Marco   You come home early now, Rodolpho.

Rodolpho (*embarrassed*)   All right, sure. But I can't stay in the house all the time, Eddie.

Eddie   Look, kid, I'm not only talkin' about her. The more you run around like that the more chance you're takin'. (*To* **Beatrice***:*) I mean suppose he gets hit by a car or something. (*To* **Marco***:*) Where's his papers, who is he? Know what I mean?

Beatrice   Yeah, but who is he in the daytime, though? It's the same chance in the daytime.

Eddie (*holding back a voice full of anger*)   Yeah, but he don't have to go lookin' for it, Beatrice. If he's here to work, then he should work; if he's here for a good time then he could fool around! (*To* **Marco***:*) But I understood, Marco, that you was both comin' to make a livin' for your family. You understand me, don't you, Marco? (*He goes to his rocker.*)

Marco   I beg your pardon, Eddie.

Eddie   I mean, that's what I understood in the first place, see.

Marco   Yes. That's why we came.

Eddie (*sits on his rocker*)   Well, that's all I'm askin'.

Eddie *reads his paper. There is a pause, an awkwardness. Now* **Catherine** *gets up and puts a record on the phonograph—"Paper Doll."*

Catherine (*flushed with revolt*)   You wanna dance, Rodolpho?

Eddie *freezes.*

Rodolpho (*in deference to* **Eddie**)   No, I—I'm tired.

Beatrice   Go ahead, dance, Rodolpho.

Catherine   Ah, come on. They got a beautiful quartet, these guys. Come.

She has taken his hand and he stiffly rises, feeling **Eddie**'s *eyes on his back, and they dance.*

Eddie (*to* **Catherine**)   What's that, a new record?

Catherine   It's the same one. We bought it the other day.

Beatrice (*to* **Eddie**)   They only bought three records. (*She watches them dance;* **Eddie** *turns his head away.* **Marco** *just sits there, waiting. Now* **Beatrice** *turns to* **Eddie**.) Must be nice to go all over in one of them fishin' boats. I would like that myself. See all them other countries?

Eddie   Yeah.

Beatrice (*to* **Marco**)   But the women don't go along, I bet.

Marco   No, not on the boats. Hard work.

Beatrice   What're you got, a regular kitchen and everything?

Marco   Yes, we eat very good on the boats—especially when Rodolpho comes along; everybody gets fat.

Beatrice   Oh, he cooks?

Marco   Sure, very good cook. Rice, pasta, fish, everything.

Eddie *lowers his paper.*

Eddie   He's a cook, too! (*Looking at* **Rodolpho**.) He sings, he cooks . . .

Rodolpho *smiles thankfully.*

Beatrice   Well, it's good, he could always make a living.

Eddie   It's wonderful. He sings, he cooks, he could make dresses . . .

Catherine   They get some high pay, them guys. The head chefs in all the big hotels are men. You read about them.

Eddie   That's what I'm sayin'.

Catherine *and* **Rodolpho** *continue dancing.*

Catherine   Yeah, well, I mean.

Eddie (*to* **Beatrice**)   He's lucky, believe me. (*Slight pause. He looks away, then back to* **Beatrice**.) That's why the water front is no place for him. (*They stop dancing.* **Rodolpho** *turns off phonograph.*)

I mean like me—I can't cook, I can't sing, I can't make dresses, so I'm on the water front. But if I could cook, if I could sing, if I could make dresses, I wouldn't be on the water front. (*He has been unconsciously twisting the newspaper into a tight roll. They are all regarding him now; he senses he is exposing the issue and he is driven on.*) I would be someplace else. I would be like in a dress store. (*He has bent the rolled paper and it suddenly tears in two. He suddenly gets up and pulls his pants up over his belly and goes to* **Marco**.) What do you, say, Marco, we go to the bouts next Saturday night. You never seen a fight, did you?

Marco (*uneasily*)   Only in the moving pictures.

Eddie (*going to* **Rodolpho**)   I'll treat yiz. What do you say, Danish? You wanna come along? I'll buy the tickets.

Rodolpho   Sure. I like to go.

Catherine (*goes to* **Eddie**; *nervously happy now*)   I'll make some coffee, all right?

Eddie   Go ahead, make some! Make it nice and strong. (*Mystified, she smiles and exits to kitchen. He is weirdly elated, rubbing his fists into his palms. He strides to* **Marco**.) You wait, Marco, you see some real fights here. You ever do any boxing?

Marco   No, I never.

Eddie (*to* **Rodolpho**)   Betcha you have done some, heh?

Rodolpho   No.

Eddie   Well, come on, I'll teach you.

Beatrice   What's he got to learn that for?

Eddie   Ya can't tell, one a these days somebody's liable to step on his foot or sump'm. Come on, Rodolpho, I show you a couple a passes. (*He stands below table.*)

Beatrice   Go ahead, Rodolpho. He's a good boxer, he could teach you.

Rodolpho (*embarrassed*)   Well, I don't know how to—(*He moves down to* **Eddie**.)

Eddie   Just put your hands up. Like this, see? That's right. That's very good, keep your left up, because you lead with the left, see, like this. (*He gently moves his left into* **Rodolpho**'s *face*.) See? Now what you gotta do is you gotta block me, so when I come in like that you—(**Rodolpho** *parries his left*.) Hey, that's very good! (**Rodolpho** *laughs*.) All right, now come into me. Come on.

Rodolpho   I don't want to hit you, Eddie.

Eddie   Don't pity me, come on. Throw it, I'll show you how to block it. (**Rodolpho** *jabs at him, laughing. The others join*.) 'At's it. Come on again. For the jaw right here. (**Rodolpho** *jabs with more assurance*.) Very good!

Beatrice (*to* **Marco**)   He's very good!

Eddie *crosses directly upstage of* **Rodolpho**.

Eddie   Sure, he's great! Come on, kid, put sump'm behind it, you can't hurt me. (**Rodolpho**, *more seriously, jabs at* **Eddie**'s *jaw and grazes it*.) Attaboy.

Catherine *comes from the kitchen, watches*.

Eddie   Now I'm gonna hit you, so block me, see?

Catherine (*with beginning alarm*)   What are they doin'?

They are lightly boxing now.

Beatrice (*she senses only the comradeship in it now*)   He's teachin' him; he's very good!

Eddie   Sure, he's terrific! Look at him go! (**Rodolpho** *lands a blow*.) 'At's it! Now, watch out, here I come, Danish! (*He feints with his left hand and lands with his right. It mildly staggers* **Rodolpho**. **Marco** *rises*.)

Catherine (*rushing to* **Rodolpho**)   Eddie!

Eddie   Why? I didn't hurt him. Did I hurt you, kid? (*He rubs the back of his hand across his mouth*.)

Rodolpho   No, no, he didn't hurt me. (*To* **Eddie** *with a certain gleam and a smile*:) I was only surprised.

Beatrice (*pulling* **Eddie** *down into the rocker*)   That's enough, Eddie; he did pretty good though.

Eddie   Yeah. (*Rubbing his fists together:*) He could be very good, Marco. I'll teach him again.

Marco *nods at him dubiously.*

Rodolpho   Dance, Catherine. Come. (*He takes her hand; they go to phonograph and start it. It plays "Paper Doll."*)

Rodolpho *takes her in his arms. They dance.* **Eddie** *in thought sits in his chair, and* **Marco** *takes a chair, places it in front of* **Eddie***, and looks down at it.* **Beatrice** *and* **Eddie** *watch him.*

Marco   Can you lift this chair?

Eddie   What do you mean?

Marco   From here. (*He gets on one knee with one hand behind his back, and grasps the bottom of one of the chair legs but does not raise it.*)

Eddie   Sure, why not? (*He comes to the chair, kneels, grasps the leg, raises the chair one inch, but it leans over to the floor.*) Gee, that's hard, I never knew that. (*He tries again, and again fails.*) It's on an angle, that's why, heh?

Marco   Here. (*He kneels, grasps, and with strain slowly raises the chair higher and higher, getting to his feet now.* **Rodolpho** *and* **Catherine** *have stopped dancing as* **Marco** *raises the chair over his head.*)

Marco *is face to face with* **Eddie***, a strained tension gripping his eyes and jaw, his neck stiff, the chair raised like a weapon over* **Eddie***'s head—and he transforms what might appear like a glare of warning into a smile of triumph, and* **Eddie***'s grin vanishes as he absorbs his look.*

Curtain.

Act Two

Light rises on **Alfieri** *at his desk.*

Alfieri   On the twenty-third of that December a case of Scotch whisky slipped from a net while being unloaded—as a case of Scotch whisky is inclined to do on the twenty-third of December on Pier Forty-one. There was no snow, but it was cold, his wife was out shopping. Marco was still at work. The boy had not been hired that day; Catherine told me later that this was the first time they had been alone together in the house.

Light is rising on **Catherine** *in the apartment.* **Rodolpho** *is watching as she arranges a paper pattern on cloth spread on the table.*

Catherine   You hungry?

Rodolpho   Not for anything to eat. (*Pause.*) I have nearly three hundred dollars. Catherine?

Catherine   I heard you.

Rodolpho   You don't like to talk about it any more?

Catherine   Sure, I don't mind talkin' about it.

Rodolpho   What worries you, Catherine?

Catherine   I been wantin' to ask you about something. Could I?

Rodolpho   All the answers are in my eyes, Catherine. But you don't look in my eyes lately. You're full of secrets. (*She looks at him. She seems withdrawn.*) What is the question?

Catherine   Suppose I wanted to live in Italy.

Rodolpho (*smiling at the incongruity*)   You going to marry somebody rich?

Catherine   No, I mean live there—you and me.

Rodolpho (*his smile vanishing*)   When?

Catherine   Well . . . when we get married.

Rodolpho (*astonished*)   You want to be an Italian?

Catherine   No, but I could live there without being Italian. Americans live there.

Rodolpho   Forever?

Catherine   Yeah.

Rodolpho (*crosses to rocker*)   You're fooling.

Catherine   No, I mean it.

Rodolpho   Where do you get such an idea?

Catherine   Well, you're always saying it's so beautiful there, with the mountains and the ocean and all the—

Rodolpho   You're fooling me.

Catherine   I mean it.

Rodolpho (*goes to her slowly*)   Catherine, if I ever brought you home with no money, no business, nothing, they would call the priest and the doctor and they would say Rodolpho is crazy.

Catherine   I know, but I think we would be happier there.

Rodolpho   Happier! What would you eat? You can't cook the view!

Catherine   Maybe you could be a singer, like in Rome or—

Rodolpho   Rome! Rome is full of singers.

Catherine   Well, I could work then.

Rodolpho   Where?

Catherine   God, there must be jobs somewhere!

Rodolpho   There's nothing! Nothing, nothing, nothing. Now tell me what you're talking about. How can I bring you from a rich country to suffer in a poor country? What are you talking about? (*She searches for words.*) I would be a criminal stealing your face. In two years you would have an old, hungry face. When my brother's babies cry they give them water, water that boiled a bone. Don't you believe that?

Catherine (*quietly*)   I'm afraid of Eddie here.

Slight pause.

Rodolpho (*steps closer to her*)   We wouldn't live here. Once I am a citizen I could work anywhere and I would find better jobs and we would have a house, Catherine. If I were not afraid to be arrested I would start to be something wonderful here!

Catherine (*steeling herself*)   Tell me something. I mean just tell me, Rodolpho—would you still want to do it if it turned out we had to go live in Italy? I mean just if it turned out that way.

Rodolpho   This is your question or his question?

Catherine   I would like to know, Rodolpho. I mean it.

Rodolpho   To go there with nothing.

Catherine   Yeah.

Rodolpho   No. (*She looks at him wide-eyed.*) No.

Catherine   You wouldn't?

Rodolpho   No; I will not marry you to live in Italy. I want you to be my wife, and I want to be a citizen. Tell him that, or I will. Yes. (*He moves about angrily.*) And tell him also, and tell yourself, please, that I am not a beggar, and you are not a horse, a gift, a favor for a poor immigrant.

Catherine   Well, don't get mad!

Rodolpho   I am furious! (*Goes to her.*) Do you think I am so desperate? My brother is desperate, not me. You think I would carry on my back the rest of my life a woman I didn't love just to be an American? It's so wonderful? You think we have no tall buildings in Italy? Electric lights? No wide streets? No flags? No automobiles? Only work we don't have. I want to be an American so I can work, that is the only wonder here— work! How can you insult me, Catherine?

Catherine   I didn't mean that—

Rodolpho   My heart dies to look at you. Why are you so afraid of him?

Catherine (*near tears*)   I don't know!

Rodolpho   Do you trust me, Catherine? You?

Catherine   It's only that I—He was good to me, Rodolpho. You don't know him; he was always the sweetest guy to me. Good. He razzes me all the time but he don't mean it. I know. I would—just feel ashamed if I made him sad. 'Cause I always dreamt that when I got married he would be happy at the wedding, and laughin'—and now he's—mad all the time and nasty—(*She is weeping.*) Tell him you'd live in Italy—just tell him, and maybe he would start to trust you a little, see? Because I want him to be happy; I mean—I like him, Rodolpho—and I can't stand it!

Rodolpho   Oh, Catherine—oh, little girl.

Catherine   I love you, Rodolpho, I love you.

Rodolpho   Then why are you afraid? That he'll spank you?

Catherine   Don't, don't laugh at me! I've been here all my life . . . Every day I saw him when he left in the morning and when he came home at night. You think it's so easy to turn around and say to a man he's nothin' to you no more?

Rodolpho   I know, but—

Catherine   You don't know; nobody knows! I'm not a baby, I know a lot more than people think I know. Beatrice says to be a woman, but—

Rodolpho   Yes.

Catherine   Then why don't she be a woman? If I was a wife I would make a man happy instead of goin' at him all the time. I can tell a block away when he's blue in his mind and just wants to talk to somebody quiet and nice . . . I can tell when he's hungry or wants a beer before he even says anything. I know when his feet hurt him, I mean I *know* him and now I'm supposed to turn around and make a stranger out of him? I don't know why I have to do that, I mean.

Rodolpho   Catherine. If I take in my hands a little bird. And she grows and wishes to fly. But I will not let her out of my hands because I love her so much, is that right for me to do? I don't say you must hate him; but anyway you must go, mustn't you? Catherine?

Catherine (*softly*)   Hold me.

Rodolpho (*clasping her to him*)   Oh, my little girl.

Catherine   Teach me. (*She is weeping.*) I don't know anything, teach me, Rodolpho, hold me.

Rodolpho   There's nobody here now. Come inside. Come. (*He is leading her toward the bedrooms.*) And don't cry any more.

Light rises on the street. In a moment **Eddie** *appears. He is unsteady, drunk. He mounts the stairs. He enters the apartment, looks around, takes out a bottle from one pocket, puts it on the table. Then another bottle from another pocket, and a third from an inside pocket. He sees the pattern and cloth, goes over to it and touches it, and turns toward upstage.*

Eddie   Beatrice? (*He goes to the open kitchen door and looks in.*) Beatrice? Beatrice?

Catherine *enters from bedroom; under his gaze she adjusts her dress.*

Catherine   You got home early.

Eddie   Knocked off for Christmas early. (*Indicating the pattern:*) Rodolpho makin' you a dress?

Catherine   No. I'm makin' a blouse.

Rodolpho *appears in the bedroom doorway.* **Eddie** *sees him and his arm jerks slightly in shock.* **Rodolpho** *nods to him testingly.*

Rodolpho   Beatrice went to buy presents for her mother.

Pause.

Eddie   Pack it up. Go ahead. Get your stuff and get outa here. (**Catherine** *instantly turns and walks toward the bedroom, and* **Eddie** *grabs her arm.*) Where you goin'?

Catherine (*trembling with fright*)   I think I have to get out of here, Eddie.

Eddie   No, you ain't goin' nowheres, he's the one.

Catherine   I think I can't stay here no more. (*She frees her arm, steps back toward the bedroom.*) I'm sorry, Eddie. (*She sees the tears in his eyes.*) Well, don't cry. I'll be around the neighborhood; I'll see you. I just can't stay here no more. You know I can't. (*Her sobs of pity and love for him break her composure.*) Don't you know I can't? You know that, don't you? (*She goes to him.*) Wish me luck. (*She clasps her hands prayerfully.*) Oh, Eddie, don't be like that!

Eddie   You ain't goin' nowheres.

Catherine   Eddie, I'm not gonna be a baby any more! You—

He reaches out suddenly, draws her to him, and as she strives to free herself he kisses her on the mouth.

Rodolpho   Don't! (*He pulls on* **Eddie's** *arm.*) Stop that! Have respect for her!

Eddie (*spun round by* **Rodolpho**)   You want something?

Rodolpho   Yes! She'll be my wife. That is what I want. My wife!

Eddie   But what're you gonna be?

Rodolpho   I show you what I be!

Catherine   Wait outside; don't argue with him!

Eddie   Come on, show me! What're you gonna be? Show me!

Rodolpho (*with tears of rage*)   Don't say that to me!

Rodolpho *flies at him in attack.* **Eddie** *pins his arms, laughing, and suddenly kisses him.*

Catherine   Eddie! Let go, ya hear me! I'll kill you! Leggo of him!

She tears at **Eddie***'s face and* **Eddie** *releases* **Rodolpho***.* **Eddie** *stands there with tears rolling down his face as he laughs mockingly at* **Rodolpho***. She is staring at him in horror.* **Rodolpho** *is rigid. They are like animals that have torn at one another and broken up without a decision, each waiting for the other's mood.*

Eddie (*to* **Catherine**)   You see? (*To* **Rodolpho***:*) I give you till tomorrow, kid. Get outa here. Alone. You hear me? Alone.

Catherine   I'm going with him, Eddie. (*She starts toward* **Rodolpho***.*)

Eddie (*indicating* **Rodolpho** *with his head*)   Not with that. (*She halts, frightened. He sits, still panting for breath, and they watch him helplessly as he leans toward them over the table.*) Don't make me do nuttin', Catherine. Watch your step, submarine. By rights they oughta throw you back in the water. But I got pity for you. (*He moves unsteadily toward the door, always facing* **Rodolpho***.*) Just get outa here and don't lay another hand on her unless you wanna go out feet first. (*He goes out of the apartment.*)

The lights go down, as they rise on **Alfieri***.*

Alfieri   On December twenty-seventh I saw him next. I normally go home well before six, but that day I sat around looking out my window at the bay, and when I saw him walking through my doorway, I knew why I had waited. And if I seem to tell this like a dream, it was that way. Several moments arrived in the course of the two talks we had when it occurred to me how—almost transfixed I had come to feel. I had lost my strength somewhere. (**Eddie** *enters, removing his cap, sits in the chair, looks thoughtfully out.*) I looked in his eyes more than I listened—in fact, I can hardly remember the conversation. But I will never forget how dark the room became when he looked at me; his eyes were like tunnels. I kept wanting to call the police, but nothing had happened. Nothing at all had really happened. (*He breaks off and looks down at the desk. Then he turns to* **Eddie***.*) So in other words, he won't leave?

Eddie   My wife is talkin' about renting a room upstairs for them. An old lady on the top floor is got an empty room.

Alfieri   What does Marco say?

Eddie   He just sits there. Marco don't say much.

Alfieri   I guess they didn't tell him, heh? What happened?

Eddie   I don't know; Marco don't say much.

Alfieri   What does your wife say?

Eddie (*unwilling to pursue this*)   Nobody's talkin' much in the house. So what about that?

Alfieri   But you didn't prove anything about him. It sounds like he just wasn't strong enough to break your grip.

Eddie   I'm tellin' you I know—he ain't right. Somebody that don't want it can break it. Even a mouse, if you catch a teeny mouse and you hold it in your hand, that mouse can give you the right kind of fight. He didn't give me the right kind of fight, I know it, Mr. Alfieri, the guy ain't right.

Alfieri   What did you do that for, Eddie?

Eddie   To show her what he is! So she would see, once and for all! Her mother'll turn over in the grave! (*He gathers himself almost peremptorily.*) So what do I gotta do now? Tell me what to do.

Alfieri   She actually said she's marrying him?

Eddie   She told me, yeah. So what do I do?

Slight pause.

Alfieri   This is my last word, Eddie, take it or not, that's your business. Morally and legally you have no rights, you cannot stop it; she is a free agent.

Eddie (*angering*)   Didn't you hear what I told you?

Alfieri (*with a tougher tone*)   I heard what you told me, and I'm telling you what the answer is. I'm not only telling you now, I'm warning you—the law is nature. The law is only a word for what has a right to happen. When the law is wrong it's because it's unnatural, but in this case it is natural and a river will drown you if you buck it now. Let her go. And bless her. (*A phone booth begins to glow on the opposite side of the stage; a faint, lonely blue.* **Eddie** *stands up, jaws clenched.*) Somebody had to come for her, Eddie, sooner or later. (**Eddie** *starts turning to go and* **Alfieri** *rises with new anxiety.*) You won't have a friend in the world, Eddie! Even those who understand will turn against you, even the ones who feel the same will despise you! (**Eddie** *moves off.*) Put it out of your mind! Eddie! (*He follows into the darkness, calling desperately.*)

Eddie *is gone. The phone is glowing in light now. Light is out on* **Alfieri**. **Eddie** *has at the same time appeared beside the phone.*

Eddie   Give me the number of the Immigration Bureau. Thanks. (*He dials.*) I want to report something. Illegal immigrants. Two of them. That's right. Four-forty-one Saxon Street, Brooklyn, yeah. Ground floor. Heh? (*With greater difficulty:*) I'm just around the neighborhood, that's all. Heh?

Evidently he is being questioned further, and he slowly hangs up. He leaves the phone just as **Louis** *and* **Mike** *come down the street.*

Louis   Go bowlin', Eddie?

Eddie   No, I'm due home.

Louis   Well, take it easy.

Eddie   I'll see yiz.

They leave him, exiting right, and he watches them go. He glances about, then goes up into the house. The lights go on in the apartment. **Beatrice** *is taking down Christmas decorations and packing them in a box.*

Eddie   Where is everybody? (**Beatrice** *does not answer.*) I says where is everybody?

Beatrice (*looking up at him, wearied with it, and concealing a fear of him*)   I decided to move them upstairs with Mrs. Dondero.

Eddie   Oh, they're all moved up there already?

Beatrice   Yeah.

Eddie   Where's Catherine? She up there?

Beatrice   Only to bring pillow cases.

Eddie   She ain't movin' in with them.

Beatrice   Look, I'm sick and tired of it. I'm sick and tired of it!

Eddie   All right, all right, take it easy.

Beatrice   I don't wanna hear no more about it, you understand? Nothin'!

Eddie   What're you blowin' off about? Who brought them in here?

Beatrice   All right, I'm sorry; I wish I'd a drop dead before I told them to come. In the ground I wish I was.

Eddie   Don't drop dead, just keep in mind who brought them in here, that's all. (*He moves about restlessly.*) I mean I got a couple of rights here. (*He moves, wanting to beat down her evident disapproval of him.*) This is my house here not their house.

Beatrice   What do you want from me? They're moved out; what do you want now?

Eddie   I want my respect!

Beatrice   So I moved them out, what more do you want? You got your house now, you got your respect.

Eddie (*he moves about biting his lip*)   I don't like the way you talk to me, Beatrice.

Beatrice   I'm just tellin' you I done what you want!

Eddie   I don't like it! The way you talk to me and the way you look at me. This is my house. And she is my niece and I'm responsible for her.

Beatrice   So that's why you done that to him?

Eddie   I done what to him?

Beatrice   What you done to him in front of her; you know what I'm talkin' about. She goes around shakin' all the time, she can't go to sleep! That's what you call responsible for her?

Eddie (*quietly*)   The guy ain't right, Beatrice. (*She is silent.*) Did you hear what I said?

Beatrice   Look, I'm finished with it. That's all. (*She resumes her work.*)

Eddie (*helping her to pack the tinsel*)   I'm gonna have it out with you one of these days, Beatrice.

Beatrice   Nothin' to have out with me, it's all settled. Now we gonna be like it never happened, that's all.

Eddie   I want my respect, Beatrice, and you know what I'm talkin' about.

Beatrice   What?

Pause.

Eddie (*finally his resolution hardens*)   What I feel like doin' in the bed and what I don't feel like doin'. I don't want no—

Beatrice   When'd I say anything about that?

Eddie   You said, you said, I ain't deaf. I don't want no more conversations about that, Beatrice. I do what I feel like doin' or what I don't feel like doin'.

Beatrice   Okay.

Pause.

Eddie   You used to be different, Beatrice. You had a whole different way.

Beatrice   *I'm* no different.

Eddie   You didn't used to jump me all the time about everything. The last year or two I come in the house I don't know what's gonna hit me. It's a shootin' gallery in here and I'm the pigeon.

Beatrice   Okay, okay.

Eddie   Don't tell me okay, okay, I'm tellin' you the truth. A wife is supposed to believe the husband. If I tell you that guy ain't right don't tell me he is right.

Beatrice   But how do you know?

Eddie   Because I know. I don't go around makin' accusations. He give me the heeby-jeebies the first minute I seen him. And I don't like you sayin' I don't want her marryin' anybody. I broke my back payin' her stenography lessons so she could go out and meet a better class of people. Would I do that if I didn't want her to get married? Sometimes you talk like I was a crazy man or sump'm.

Beatrice   But she likes him.

Eddie   Beatrice, she's a baby, how is she gonna know what she likes?

Beatrice   Well, you kept her a baby, you wouldn't let her go out. I told you a hundred times.

Pause.

Eddie   All right. Let her go out, then.

Beatrice   She don't wanna go out now. It's too late, Eddie.

Pause.

Eddie   Suppose I told her to go out. Suppose I—

Beatrice   They're going to get married next week, Eddie.

Eddie (*his head jerks around to her*)   She said that?

Beatrice   Eddie, if you want my advice, go to her and tell her good luck. I think maybe now that you had it out you learned better.

Eddie   What's the hurry next week?

Beatrice   Well, she's been worried about him bein' picked up; this way he could start to be a citizen. She loves him, Eddie. (*He gets up, moves about uneasily, restlessly.*) Why don't you give her a good word? Because I still think she would like you to be a friend, y'know? (*He is standing, looking at the floor.*) I mean like if you told her you'd go to the wedding.

Eddie   She asked you that?

Beatrice   I know she would like it. I'd like to make a party here for her. I mean there oughta be some kinda send-off. Heh? I mean she'll have trouble enough in her life, let's start it off happy. What do you say? Cause in her heart she still loves you, Eddie. I know it. (*He presses his fingers against his eyes.*) What're you, cryin'? (*She goes to him, holds his face.*) Go . . . whyn't you go tell her you're sorry? (**Catherine** *is seen on the upper landing of the stairway, and they hear her descending.*) There . . . she's comin' down. Come on, shake hands with her.

Eddie (*moving with suppressed suddenness*)   No, I can't, I can't talk to her.

Beatrice   Eddie, give her a break; a wedding should be happy!

Eddie   I'm goin', I'm goin' for a walk.

He goes upstage for his jacket. **Catherine** *enters and starts for the bedroom door.*

Beatrice   Katie? . . . Eddie, don't go, wait a minute. (*She embraces* **Eddie's** *arm with warmth.*) Ask him, Katie. Come on, honey.

Eddie   It's all right, I'm—(*He starts to go and she holds him.*)

Beatrice   No, she wants to ask you. Come on, Katie, ask him. We'll have a party! What're we gonna do, hate each other? Come on!

Catherine   I'm gonna get married, Eddie. So if you wanna come, the wedding be on Saturday.

Pause.

Eddie   Okay. I only wanted the best for you, Katie. I hope you know that.

Catherine   Okay. (*She starts out again.*)

Eddie   Catherine? (*She turns to him.*) I was just tellin' Beatrice . . . if you wanna go out, like . . . I mean I realize maybe I kept you home too much. Because he's the first guy you ever knew, y'know? I mean now that you got a job, you might meet some fellas, and you get a different idea, y'know? I mean you could always come back to him, you're still only kids, the both of yiz. What's the hurry? Maybe you'll get around a little bit, you grow up a little more, maybe you'll see different in a couple of months. I mean you be surprised, it don't have to be him.

Catherine   No, we made it up already.

Eddie (*with increasing anxiety*)   Katie, wait a minute.

Catherine   No, I made up my mind.

Eddie   But you never knew no other fella, Katie! How could you make up your mind?

Catherine   'Cause I did. I don't want nobody else.

Eddie   But, Katie, suppose he gets picked up.

Catherine   That's why we gonna do it right away. Soon as we finish the wedding he's goin' right over and start to be a citizen. I made up my mind, Eddie. I'm sorry. (*To* **Beatrice***:*) Could I take two more pillow cases for the other guys?

Beatrice   Sure, go ahead. Only don't let her forget where they came from.

Catherine *goes into a bedroom.*

Eddie   She's got other boarders up there?

Beatrice   Yeah, there's two guys that just came over.

Eddie   What do you mean, came over?

Beatrice   From Italy. Lipari the butcher—his nephew. They come from Bari, they just got here yesterday. I didn't even know till Marco and Rodolpho moved up there before. (**Catherine** *enters, going toward exit with two pillow cases.*) It'll be nice, they could all talk together.

Eddie   Catherine! (*She halts near the exit door. He takes in* **Beatrice** *too.*) What're you, got no brains? You put them up there with two other submarines?

Catherine   Why?

Eddie (*in a driving fright and anger*)   Why! How do you know they're not trackin' these guys? They'll come up for them and find Marco and Rodolpho! Get them out of the house!

Beatrice   But they been here so long already—

Eddie   How do you know what enemies Lipari's got? Which they'd love to stab him in the back?

Catherine   Well, what'll I do with them?

Eddie   The neighborhood is full of rooms. Can't you stand to live a couple of blocks away from him? Get them out of the house!

Catherine   Well, maybe tomorrow night I'll—

Eddie   Not tomorrow, do it now. Catherine, you never mix yourself with somebody else's family! These guys get picked up, Lipari's liable to blame you or me and we got his whole family on our head. They got a temper, that family.

Two men in overcoats appear outside, start into the house.

Catherine   How'm I gonna find a place tonight?

Eddie   Will you stop arguin' with me and get them out! You think I'm always tryin' to fool you or sump'm? What's the matter with you, don't you believe I could think of your good? Did I ever ask sump'm for myself? You think I got no feelin's? I never told you nothin' in my life that wasn't for your good. Nothin'! And look at the way you talk to me! Like I was an enemy! Like I—(*A knock on the door. His head swerves. They all stand motionless. Another knock.* **Eddie**, *in a whisper, pointing upstage.*) Go up the fire escape, get them out over the back fence.

Catherine *stands motionless, uncomprehending.*

First Officer (*in the hall*)   Immigration! Open up in there!

Eddie   Go, go. Hurry up! (*She stands a moment staring at him in a realized horror.*) Well, what're you lookin' at!

First Officer   Open up!

Eddie (*calling toward door*)   Who's that there?

First Officer   Immigration, open up.

Eddie *turns, looks at* **Beatrice**. *She sits. Then he looks at* **Catherine**. *With a sob of fury* **Catherine** *streaks into a bedroom.*

Knock is repeated.

Eddie   All right, take it easy, take it easy. (*He goes and opens the door. The* **Officer** *steps inside.*) What's all this?

First Officer   Where are they?

Second Officer *sweeps past and, glancing about, goes into the kitchen.*

Eddie   Where's who?

First Officer   Come on, come on, where are they? (*He hurries into the bedrooms.*)

Eddie   Who? We got nobody here. (*He looks at* **Beatrice**, *who turns her head away. Pugnaciously, furious, he steps toward* **Beatrice**.) What's the matter with *you*?

First Officer *enters from the bedroom, calls to the kitchen.*

First Officer   Dominick?

Enter **Second Officer** *from kitchen.*

Second Officer   Maybe it's a different apartment.

First Officer   There's only two more floors up there. I'll take the front, you go up the fire escape. I'll let you in. Watch your step up there.

Second Officer   Okay, right, Charley. (**First Officer** *goes out apartment door and runs up the stairs.*) This is Four-forty-one, isn't it?

Eddie   That's right.

Second Officer *goes out into the kitchen.*

Eddie *turns to* **Beatrice**. *She looks at him now and sees his terror.*

Beatrice (*weakened with fear*)   Oh, Jesus, Eddie.

Eddie   What's the matter with *you*?

Beatrice (*pressing her palms against her face*)   Oh, my God, my God.

Eddie   What're you, accusin' me?

Beatrice (*final thrust is to turn toward him instead of running from him*)   My God, what did you do?

Many steps on the outer stair draw his attention. We see the **First Officer** *descending, with* **Marco**, *behind him* **Rodolpho**, *and* **Catherine** *and the two strange immigrants, followed by* **Second Officer**. **Beatrice** *hurries to door.*

Catherine (*backing down stairs, fighting with* **First Officer**; *as they appear on the stairs*)   What do yiz want from them? They work, that's all. They're boarders upstairs, they work on the piers.

Beatrice (*to* **First Officer**)   Ah, Mister, what do you want from them, who do they hurt?

Catherine (*pointing to* **Rodolpho**)   They ain't no submarines, he was born in Philadelphia.

First Officer   Step aside, lady.

Catherine   What do you mean? You can't just come in a house and—

First Officer   All right, take it easy. (*To* **Rodolpho**:) What street were you born in Philadelphia?

Catherine   What do you mean, what street? Could you tell me what street you were born?

First Officer   Sure. Four blocks away, One-eleven Union Street. Let's go, fellas.

Catherine (*fending him off* **Rodolpho**)   No, you can't! Now, get outa here!

First Officer   Look, girlie, if they're all right they'll be out tomorrow. If they're illegal they go back where they came from. If you want, get yourself a lawyer, although I'm tellin' you now you're wasting your money. Let's get them in the car, Dom. (*To the men:*) *Andiamo, andiamo,* let's go.

The men start, but **Marco** *hangs back.*

Beatrice (*from doorway*)   Who're they hurtin', for God's sake, what do you want from them? They're starvin' over there, what do you want! Marco!

Marco *suddenly breaks from the group and dashes into the room and faces* **Eddie**; **Beatrice** *and* **First Officer** *rush in as* **Marco** *spits into* **Eddie**'*s face.*

Catherine *runs into hallway and throws herself into* **Rodolpho**'*s arms.* **Eddie**, *with an enraged cry, lunges for* **Marco**.

Eddie   Oh, you mother's—!

First Officer *quickly intercedes and pushes* **Eddie** *from* **Marco**, *who stands there accusingly.*

First Officer (*between them, pushing* **Eddie** *from* **Marco**)   Cut it out!

Eddie (*over the* **First Officer**'*s shoulder, to* **Marco**)   I'll kill you for that, you son of a bitch!

First Officer   Hey! (*Shakes him.*) Stay in here now, don't come out, don't bother him. You hear me? Don't come out, fella.

For an instant there is silence. Then **First Officer** *turns and takes*
Marco'*s arm and then gives a last, informative look at* **Eddie**. *As he and*
Marco *are going out into the hall,* **Eddie** *erupts.*

Eddie   I don't forget that, Marco! You hear what I'm sayin'?

Out in the hall, **First Officer** *and* **Marco** *go down the stairs. Now, in the*
street, **Louis**, **Mike**, *and several neighbors including the butcher,*
Lipari—*a stout, intense, middle-aged man*—*are gathering around the*
stoop.

Lipari, *the butcher, walks over to the two strange men and kisses them.*
His wife, keening, goes and kisses their hands. **Eddie** *is emerging from*
the house shouting after **Marco**. **Beatrice** *is trying to restrain him.*

Eddie   That's the thanks I get? Which I took the blankets off my bed for
yiz? You gonna apologize to me, Marco! *Marco!*

First Officer (*in the doorway with* **Marco**)   All right, lady, let them go.
Get in the car, fellas, it's right over there.

Rodolpho *is almost carrying the sobbing* **Catherine** *off up the street, left.*

Catherine   He was born in Philadelphia! What do you want from him?

First Officer   Step aside, lady, come on now . . .

The **Second Officer** *has moved off with the two strange men.* **Marco**,
taking advantage of the **First Officer**'*s being occupied with* **Catherine**,
suddenly frees himself and points back at **Eddie**.

Marco   That one! I accuse that one!

Eddie *brushes* **Beatrice** *aside and rushes out to the stoop.*

First Officer (*grabbing him and moving him quickly off up the left*
street)   Come on!

Marco (*as he is taken off, pointing back at* **Eddie**)   That one! He killed
my children! That one stole the food from my children!

Marco *is gone. The crowd has turned to* **Eddie**.

Eddie (*to* **Lipari** *and wife*)   He's crazy! I give them the blankets off my
bed. Six months I kept them like my own brothers!

Lipari, *the butcher, turns and starts up left with his arm around his wife.*

Eddie   Lipari! (*He follows* **Lipari** *up left.*) For Christ's sake, I kept
them, I give them the blankets off my bed!

Lipari *and wife exit.* **Eddie** *turns and starts crossing down right to* **Louis** *and* **Mike**.

Eddie   Louis! *Louis!*

Louis *barely turns, then walks off and exits down right with* **Mike**. *Only* **Beatrice** *is left on the stoop.* **Catherine** *now returns, blank-eyed, from offstage and the car.* **Eddie** *calls after* **Louis** *and* **Mike**.

Eddie   He's gonna take that back. He's gonna take that back or I'll kill him! You hear me? I'll kill him! I'll kill him! (*He exits up street calling.*)

There is a pause of darkness before the lights rise, on the reception room of a prison. **Marco** *is seated;* **Alfieri**, **Catherine**, *and* **Rodolpho** *standing.*

Alfieri   I'm waiting, Marco, what do you say?

Rodolpho   Marco never hurt anybody.

Alfieri   I can bail you out until your hearing comes up. But I'm not going to do it, you understand me? Unless I have your promise. You're an honorable man, I will believe your promise. Now what do you say?

Marco   In my country he would be dead now. He would not live this long.

Alfieri   All right, Rodolpho—you come with me now.

Rodolpho   No! Please, Mister. Marco—promise the man. Please, I want you to watch the wedding. How can I be married and you're in here? Please, you're not going to do anything; you know you're not.

Marco *is silent.*

Catherine (*kneeling left of* **Marco**)   Marco, don't you understand? He can't bail you out if you're gonna do something bad. To hell with Eddie. Nobody is gonna talk to him again if he lives to a hundred. Everybody knows you spit in his face, that's enough, isn't it? Give me the satisfaction—I want you at the wedding. You got a wife and kids, Marco. You could be workin' till the hearing comes up, instead of layin' around here.

Marco (*to* **Alfieri**)   I have no chance?

Alfieri (*crosses to behind* **Marco**)   No, Marco. You're going back. The hearing is a formality, that's all.

Marco   But him? There is a chance, eh?

Alfieri   When she marries him he can start to become an American. They permit that, if the wife is born here.

Marco (*looking at* **Rodolpho**)   Well—we did something. (*He lays a palm on* **Rodolpho's** *arm and* **Rodolpho** *covers it.*)

Rodolpho   Marco, tell the man.

Marco (*pulling his hand away*)   What will I tell him? He knows such a promise is dishonorable.

Alfieri   To promise not to kill is not dishonorable.

Marco (*looking at* **Alfieri**)   No?

Alfieri   No.

Marco (*gesturing with his head—this is a new idea*)   Then what is done with such a man?

Alfieri   Nothing. If he obeys the law, he lives. That's all.

Marco (*rises, turns to* **Alfieri**)   The law? All the law is not in a book.

Alfieri   Yes. In a book. There is no other law.

Marco (*his anger rising*)   He degraded my brother. My blood. He robbed my children, he mocks my work. I work to come here, mister!

Alfieri   I know, Marco—

Marco   There is no law for that? Where is the law for that?

Alfieri   There is none.

Marco (*shaking his head, sitting*)   I don't understand this country.

Alfieri   Well? What is your answer? You have five or six weeks you could work. Or else you sit here. What do you say to me?

Marco (*lowers his eyes. It almost seems he is ashamed*)   All right.

Alfieri   You won't touch him. This is your promise.

Slight pause.

Marco   Maybe he wants to apologize to me.

Marco *is staring away.* **Alfieri** *takes one of his hands.*

Alfieri   This is not God, Marco. You hear? Only God makes justice.

Marco   All right.

Alfieri (*nodding, not with assurance*)   Good! Catherine, Rodolpho, Marco, let us go.

Catherine kisses **Rodolpho** and **Marco**, *then kisses* **Alfieri**'s *hand.*

Catherine   I'll get Beatrice and meet you at the church. (*She leaves quickly.*)

Marco rises. **Rodolpho** *suddenly embraces him.* **Marco** *pats him on the back and* **Rodolpho** *exits after* **Catherine**. **Marco** *faces* **Alfieri**.

Alfieri   Only God, Marco.

Marco *turns and walks out.* **Alfieri** *with a certain processional tread leaves the stage. The lights dim out.*

The lights rise in the apartment. **Eddie** *is alone in the rocker, rocking back and forth in little surges. Pause. Now* **Beatrice** *emerges from a bedroom. She is in her best clothes, wearing a hat.*

Beatrice (*with fear, going to* **Eddie**)   I'll be back in about an hour, Eddie. All right?

Eddie (*quietly, almost inaudibly, as though drained*)   What, have I been talkin' to myself?

Beatrice   Eddie, for God's sake, it's her wedding.

Eddie   Didn't you hear what I told you? You walk out that door to that wedding you ain't comin' back here, Beatrice.

Beatrice   Why! What do you want?

Eddie   I want my respect. Didn't you ever hear of that? From my wife?

Catherine *enters from bedroom.*

Catherine   It's after three; we're supposed to be there already, Beatrice. The priest won't wait.

Beatrice   Eddie. It's her wedding. There'll be nobody there from her family. For my sister let me go. I'm goin' for my sister.

Eddie (*as though hurt*)   Look, I been arguin' with you all day already, Beatrice, and I said what I'm gonna say. He's gonna come here and apologize to me or nobody from this house is goin' into that church today. Now if that's more to you than I am, then go. But don't come back. You be on my side or on their side, that's all.

Catherine (*suddenly*)   Who the hell do you think you are?

Beatrice   Sssh!

Catherine   You got no more right to tell nobody nothin'! Nobody! The rest of your life, nobody!

Beatrice   Shut up, Katie! (*She turns* **Catherine** *around.*)

Catherine   You're gonna come with me!

Beatrice   I can't Katie, I can't . . .

Catherine   How can you listen to him? This rat!

Beatrice (*shaking* **Catherine**)   Don't you call him that!

Catherine (*clearing from* **Beatrice**)   What're you scared of? He's a rat! He belongs in the sewer!

Beatrice   Stop it!

Catherine (*weeping*)   He bites people when they sleep! He comes when nobody's lookin' and poisons decent people. In the garbage he belongs!

Eddie *seems about to pick up the table and fling it at her.*

Beatrice   No, Eddie! Eddie! (*To* **Catherine***:*) Then we all belong in the garbage. You, and me too. Don't say that. Whatever happened we all done it, and don't you ever forget it, Catherine. (*She goes to* **Catherine**.) Now go, go to your wedding, Katie, I'll stay home. Go. God bless you, God bless your children.

Enter **Rodolpho**.

Rodolpho   Eddie?

Eddie   Who said you could come in here? Get outa here!

Rodolpho   Marco is coming, Eddie. (*Pause.* **Beatrice** *raises her hands in terror.*) He's praying in the church. You understand? (*Pause.* **Rodolpho** *advances into the room.*) Catherine, I think it is better we go. Come with me.

Catherine   Eddie, go away please.

Beatrice (*quietly*)   Eddie. Let's go someplace. Come. You and me. (*He has not moved.*) I don't want you to be here when he comes. I'll get your coat.

Eddie   Where? Where am I goin'? This is my house.

Beatrice (*crying out*)   What's the use of it! He's crazy now, you know the way they get, what good is it! You got nothin' against Marco, you always liked Marco!

Eddie   I got nothin' against Marco? Which he called me a rat in front of the whole neighborhood? Which he said I killed his children! Where you been?

Rodolpho (*quite suddenly, stepping up to* **Eddie**)   It is my fault, Eddie. Everything. I wish to apologize. It was wrong that I do not ask your permission. I kiss your hand. (*He reaches for* **Eddie**'*s hand, but* **Eddie** *snaps it away from him.*)

Beatrice   Eddie, he's apologizing!

Rodolpho   I have made all our troubles. But you have insult me too. Maybe God understand why you did that to me. Maybe you did not mean to insult me at all—

Beatrice   Listen to him! Eddie, listen what he's tellin' you!

Rodolpho   I think, maybe when Marco comes, if we can tell him we are comrades now, and we have no more argument between us. Then maybe Marco will not—

Eddie   Now, listen—

Catherine   Eddie, give him a chance!

Beatrice   What do you want! Eddie, what do you want!

Eddie   I want my name! He didn't take my name; he's only a punk. Marco's got my name—(*To* **Rodolpho**:) and you can run tell him, kid, that he's gonna give it back to me in front of this neighborhood, or we have it out. (*Hoisting up his pants:*) Come on, where is he? Take me to him.

Beatrice   Eddie, listen—

Eddie   I heard enough! Come on, let's go!

Beatrice   Only blood is good? He kissed your hand!

Eddie   What he does don't mean nothin' to nobody! (*To* **Rodolpho**:) Come on!

Beatrice (*barring his way to the stairs*)   What's gonna mean somethin'? Eddie, listen to me. Who could give you your name? Listen to me, I love you, I'm talkin' to you, I love you; if Marco'll kiss your hand outside, if he goes on his knees, what is he got to give you? That's not what you want.

Eddie   Don't bother me!

Beatrice   You want somethin' else, Eddie, and you can never have her!

Catherine (*in horror*)   B.!

Eddie (*shocked, horrified, his fists clenching*)   Beatrice!

Marco *appears outside, walking toward the door from a distant point.*

Beatrice (*crying out, weeping*)   The truth is not as bad as blood, Eddie! I'm tellin' you the truth—tell her good-by forever!

Eddie (*crying out in agony*)   That's what you think of me—that I would have such a thoughts? (*His fists clench his head as though it will burst.*)

Marco (*calling near the door outside*)   Eddie Carbone!

Eddie *swerves about; all stand transfixed for an instant. People appear outside.*

Eddie (*as though flinging his challenge*)   Yeah, Marco! Eddie Carbone. Eddie Carbone. Eddie Carbone. (*He goes up the stairs and emerges from the apartment.* **Rodolpho** *streaks up and out past him and runs to* **Marco**.)

Rodolpho   No, Marco, please! Eddie, please, he has children! You will kill a family!

Beatrice   Go in the house! Eddie, go in the house!

Eddie (*he gradually comes to address the people*)   Maybe he come to apologize to me. Heh, Marco? For what you said about me in front of the neighborhood? (*He is incensing himself and little bits of laughter even escape him as his eyes are murderous and he cracks his knuckles in his hands with a strange sort of relaxation.*) He knows that ain't right. To do like that? To a man? Which I put my roof over their head and my food in their mouth? Like in the Bible? Strangers I never seen in my whole life? To come out of the water and grab a girl for a passport? To go and take from your own family like from the stable—and never a word to me? And now accusations in the bargain! (*Directly to* **Marco***:*) Wipin' the neighborhood with my name like a dirty rag! I want my name, Marco. (*He is moving now, carefully, toward* **Marco**.) Now gimme my name and we go together to the wedding.

Beatrice and Catherine (*keening*)   Eddie! Eddie, don't! Eddie!

Eddie   No, Marco knows what's right from wrong. Tell the people, Marco, tell them what a liar you are! (*He has his arms spread and* **Marco** *is spreading his.*) Come on, liar, you know what you done! (*He lunges for* **Marco** *as a great hushed shout goes up from the people.*)

Marco *strikes* **Eddie** *beside the neck.*

Marco   Animal! You go on your knees to me!

Eddie *goes down with the blow and* **Marco** *starts to raise a foot to stomp him when* **Eddie** *springs a knife into his hand and* **Marco** *steps back.* **Louis** *rushes in toward* **Eddie**.

Louis   Eddie, for Christ's sake!

Eddie *raises the knife and* **Louis** *halts and steps back.*

Eddie   You lied about me, Marco. Now say it. Come on now, say it!

Marco   Anima-a-a-l!

Eddie *lunges with the knife.* **Marco** *grabs his arm, turning the blade inward and pressing it home as the women and* **Louis** *and* **Mike** *rush in and separate them, and* **Eddie**, *the knife still in his hand, falls to his knees before* **Marco**. *The two women support him for a moment, calling his name again and again.*

Catherine   Eddie, I never meant to do nothing bad to you.

Eddie   Then why—Oh, B.!

Beatrice   Yes, yes!

Eddie   My B.!

He dies in her arms, and **Beatrice** *covers him with her body.* **Alfieri**, *who is in the crowd, turns out to the audience. The lights have gone down, leaving him in a glow, while behind him the dull prayers of the people and the keening of the women continue.*

Alfieri   Most of the time now we settle for half and I like it better. But the truth is holy, and even as I know how wrong he was, and his death useless, I tremble, for I confess that something perversely pure calls to me from his memory—not purely good, but himself purely, for he allowed himself to be wholly known and for that I think I will love him more than all my sensible clients. And yet, it is better to settle for half, it must be! And so I mourn him—I admit it—with a certain . . . alarm.

Curtain.